C0-BJH-073

Explorer
Florence
& Tuscany

Tim Jepson

AA Publishing

Front cover: (a) *Tuscan landscape*
(b) *Replica of Michelangelo's David*
(c) *The Palio in Sienna*
Spine: *Detail of the Neptune fountain*
Back cover: *The Duomo*
Page 2: *Outside the Uffizi*
Page 3: *Villa Torreguinigi, near Lucca*
Page 4 (top): *Pitigliano, Tuscany*
Page 5 (top): *Ponte Vecchio detail, Florence*
Page 5 (bottom): *Countryside near San Gimignano*
Page 6–7 (top): *Olive Grove near San Gimignano*
Page 6 (bottom): *Il Porcellino, Mercato Nuovo, Florence*
Page 7 (bottom): *balconies on the main square in Siena*
Page 8: *Palazzo Vecchio detail*
Page 9: *Neptune, Piazzale della Signoria*
Page 27: *Cappelle Medicee detail*
Page 49: *local priest*
Page 189: *Palazzo del Commune, Pistoia*
Page 251: *Roman road arch, Saturnia*
Page 273: *eating out in Florence*

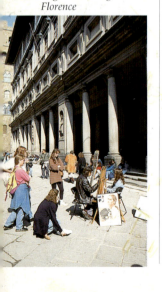

Written by Tim Jepson
Verified by Tim Jepson
Original photography by Clive Sawyer
Cover design by Carroll Associates
Edited, designed and produced by AA Publishing
Maps © The Automobile Association 1998, 2000

Revised fourth edition 2000
Reprinted with new cover 1999
Revised second edition 1998
First published 1995

Distributed in the United Kingdom by AA Publishing, Norfolk House, Priestley Road, Basingstoke, Hampshire, RG24 4NY.

The contents of this publication are believed correct at the time of printing. Nevertheless, the publishers cannot be held responsible for any errors or omissions or for changes in the details given in this guide or for the consequences of any reliance on the information provided by the same. Assessments of attractions, hotels, restaurants and so forth are based upon the author's own personal experience and, therefore, descriptions given in this guide necessarily contain an element of subjective opinion which may not reflect the publishers' opinion or dictate a reader's own experiences on another occasion. We have tried to ensure accuracy in this guide, but things do change and we would be grateful if readers would advise us of any inaccuracies they may encounter.

© The Automobile Association 1995, 1998, 1999, 2000

All rights reserved. No part of this publication may be reproduced, stored in a retrieval system, or transmitted in any form or by any means – electronic, photocopying, recording, or otherwise – unless the written permission of the publishers has been obtained. This book may not be lent, resold, hired out or otherwise disposed of by way of trade in any form of binding or cover other than that which it is published, without the prior consent of the publishers.

A CIP catalogue record for this book is available from the British Library.

ISBN 0 7495 2280 1

Published by AA Publishing (a trading name of Automobile Association Developments Limited, whose registered office is Norfolk House, Priestley Road, Basingstoke, Hampshire RG24 4NY. Registered number 1878835).

Colour separation by LC Repro
Printed and bound in Italy by Printer Trento srl, Turin

AA World Travel Guides publish nearly 300 guidebooks to a full range of cities, countries and regions across the world. Find out more about AA Publishing and the wide range of services the AA provides by visiting our Web site at www.theaa.co.uk

How to use this book

ORGANISATION

Florence Is
Discusses aspects of life and living today, from tourism and restoration to café life.

Florence Was
Places the city in its historical context and explores those past events whose influences are felt to this day.

A–Z
Breaks down into two chapters, covering Florence and Tuscany, and describing places to visit, including walks and drives. Within this section fall the Focus On articles, which consider a variety of topics in greater detail.

Travel Facts
Has the strictly practical information vital for a successful trip.

Hotels and Restaurants
Lists recommended establishments in Florence and Tuscany, giving a brief summary of what they offer.

ABOUT THE RATINGS
Most places described in this book have been given a separate rating. These are as follows:

▶▶▶　**Do not miss**

▶▶　**Highly recommended**

▶　**Worth seeing**

MAPS
To make the location of a particular place easier to find, every main entry in this book is given its own map reference, such as 176B3. The first number (176) indicates the page on which the map can be found, the letter (B) and the second number (3) pinpoint the square in which the main entry is located. The maps on the inside front cover and inside back cover are referred to as IFC and IBC respectively.

Contents

My Tuscany

Tim Jepson acquired his love for travel when he journeyed through Europe as a street performer. Since then, his wanderlust has taken him from the Umbrian hills to the Yukon's windswept tundra. Hopelessly in love with Italy – like many a romantic Englishman before him – he has lived in Rome, Venice, and Tuscany. He is also the author of the AA *Explorer* guides to *Italy* and *Canada*.

Tuscany for me is the Tuscany of popular cliché. I can think of nowhere else in the world where landscape, art, food, wine and culture come together to create a region that is so close to perfection. Florence, the region's capital, may perhaps be less than perfect as a city, but as a place where so many great works of art are gathered together, it is indeed incomparable. I first came to Tuscany 20 years ago, and have been returning every year since then. Never in all that time have I tired of the paintings, the churches or the cypress-dotted hills. Never have I thought 'enough of frescoes'; never felt the silver grey of olive trees, or the verdant green of vines, was anything other than the most sublimely beautiful.

There are landscapes in Tuscany in which I could live forever: this is true of those of Sienna, for example, but not of Florence, although I could happily return to many paintings time and again and find myself endlessly captivated (Fra Angelico's *Annunciation* in the Museo di San Marco is the one I'd take away with me if I could).

But Florence and Tuscany are not simply about art and landscape. Several years ago I lived near Montalcino, a tiny Tuscan hilltown. Over several drowsy summer months my beautiful pastoral surroundings gradually became nothing more than a backdrop to an idyllic way of life. I visited Pienza, Montepulciano and other of the region's gem-like hilltowns. I explored Romanesque churches and crumbling medieval monasteries. But as time went by, the obvious attractions of art and country-side drifted into the background. Instead I found that my idea of Tuscany began to revolve around more subtle and sedentary pleasures: food – simple and enjoyable; wine – an essential part of the daily routine; coffee – the world's best *cappuccini*; cafés – just watching the world go by; nightlife – a quiet Campari and the flickering of a thousand fire-flies. The list went on...

Landscape, art and all the things that make for civilised good living: this is my idea of Florence and Tuscany. The perfect region, the near-perfect city: add in love and a little work, and you'd have the recipe for a perfect life.
Tim Jepson

Florence Is

Florence is a city-sized shrine to the Renaissance. Its churches, museums, and galleries catalogue an epoch that shaped history and produced some of the world's greatest works of art. But if you come here only for art you will have missed the heart of a living city.

MUSEUM CITY You go to Rome to look at Rome, to Venice to look at Venice, but to Florence to look at paintings or so it might sometimes seem. As a city to see for its own sake, Tuscany's capital has always ranked below its big Italian rivals. It has no ruins (unlike Rome) and no fairy-tale settings (unlike Venice). Florence, one is told, lacks romance, lacks an atmosphere to call its own. This city has no lost lagoons, no crumbling layers of history. It is neither timeless like Venice, nor eternal like Rome. This is the received wisdom, and being wisdom it contains a

A detail of Pietro Tacca's fountain in Piazza Santissima Annunziata

truth of sorts. If approached in the wrong way Florence *can* seem an indoor city: its sights, for the most part, are concealed within churches and museums. Its streets can, at times, seem gloomy. Its architecture is often stolid and forbidding. Seen from a different angle, however, the picture looks very different.

ANOTHER SIDE Florence's appeal goes way beyond the world of sculptures and gallery Madonnas. It has a river to give it heart, markets to give it life. Its citizens are proud and stylish, its streets part of a living city. Old-world artisans flourish, and designers – Gucci and Ferragamo the most famous – dress it in a fashion to match Milan. Its cuisine – rustic but refined – is superb, its cafés stylish and sedate.

Cultural life abounds: the Maggio Musicale is one of Italy's finest arts festivals. The Giardino di Boboli is Italy's most visited garden, giving the lie to the idea of Florence as an indoor city. And this is without the art, without one of Europe's greatest galleries (the Uffizi), without Michelangelo's *David* or the world's finest Renaissance sculptures (in the Bargello).

ROMANCE Florence is also a city with its share of romance – the Ponte Vecchio, for example, glimpsed across the Arno on a summer's evening; a late-night drink sipped in Piazza della Signoria; the flower-hung streets of the Oltrarno explored on a warm afternoon; or the majestic cityscapes to be enjoyed from San Miniato or Giotto's lofty Campanile. It is also a city to fire the historical imagination. Picture, for example, Dante, Machiavelli, Boccaccio, and

Galileo wandering its streets. Or Lorenzo the Magnificent in the Duomo fleeing his would-be assassins; or Michelangelo striding the city's defences in preparation for the siege of the city by the combined armies of the emperor and the pope; or Savonarola's huge Bonfire of Vanities crackling fiercely in Piazza della Signoria.

SEEING IT ALL At first glance, it might seem that you can see all of Florence within a few days. It is small, and all the sights are close together. Don't be fooled. Every gallery, however modest, is essential; every church a treasure-house of art – some sights require two or more visits to do them justice. A week's stay here is only going to scratch the surface. And that is without the Uffizi, the Bargello, or the churches of Santa Croce and Santa Maria

Novella – each worth a whole morning on its own.

Still, you should avoid trying to see more than is pleasurable. Nothing is worse than the misery of museum fatigue. Accept your limitations and pick out the highlights. Plan ahead, don't tackle too much, and avoid the streets in the heat of the afternoon. Head-on confrontation with the city, however energetically you join battle, will always leave you the dispirited loser. Allow time for lounging in gardens, an hour in a sun-drenched café, a quiet meal under a starry sky, or an ice cream from possibly Italy's best gelateria (Vivoli). And then, of course, when you have exhausted the city, you have the rest of Tuscany – Italy's most beautiful region – waiting to be explored.

Make time to relax in Florence's beautiful Boboli gardens

11

Florentines, like any group of Italians, are a breed apart, riddled with their own particular faults and foibles, vices and virtues. Stereotypes are invidious things, but no one meeting a Roman or a Neapolitan, for example, could confuse them with a Florentine.

FOREIGNERS IN THEIR OWN COUNTRY Italians are never simply Italians. Centuries of divisive history have left them fiercely provincial, bound by that force known neatly as *campanilismo* – the idea that all that matters is what takes place within the sound of your own church bells, and that everything else belongs to a foreign country. Tuscans are never Italians, therefore – except perhaps when the national soccer team is playing. Nor, however, are they simply

Art, architecture – and daily life

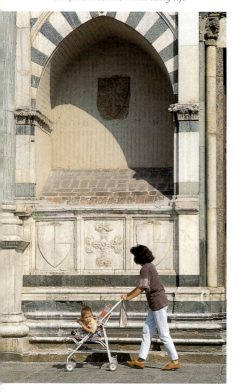

Tuscans. Someone from Siena is Sienese, and proud of the fact; someone from Pisa is Pisan, and woe betide anyone who calls them otherwise.

> ❏ 'Beyond all others, a treacherous and mercenary race'. Walter Savage Landor (1775–1864) ❏

FLORENTINES ON FLORENTINES Michelangelo, who grew up in Florence, said 'I never had to do with a more ungrateful and arrogant people than the Florentines.' Dante, a native of the city, described his fellow citizens as *'gente avara, invidiosa e superba'* (mean, envious, and proud people). A Renaissance proverb described them as perpetual moaners – possessed of 'sharp eyes and bad tongues'.
  Leaving aside personal agendas – Michelangelo was habitually bad-tempered and Dante was exiled by his fellow Florentines – the assessments, if deliberately overpitched for rhetorical purposes, mention qualities that are still seen today as distinctively Florentine: pride and haughtiness.

> ❏ 'Prodigal of cry and gesture when the world goes right'. Elizabeth Barrett Browning (1806–61) ❏

FLORENTINE PRIDE The proverbial Florentine pride is an affront to many Italians, who wonder what it is, exactly, that makes Florentines regard themselves so highly. The Renaissance, it seems, is one answer,

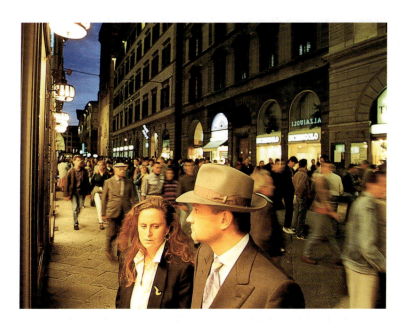

Enjoying the bright lights of Via dei Calzaiuoli

13

a golden age that merely reflects qualities – hard work, genius, flair, ambition, verve, civic pride – that are still possessed by the average Florentine. Certainly there are other reasons – poets, painters and sculptors, scientists and political theorists; Dante and Boccaccio; Botticelli and Michelangelo; Galileo and Machiavelli; Europe's first public library; the western world's first chair of Greek; the creation of a literary language; the rediscovery of perspective; the foundation of capitalism; the invention of opera, eyeglasses, the piano – the list is long.

Somehow the past still reflects well on modern Florentines. And yet their pride is no retrospective reaching after past glories. Nor does constant confrontation with their past produce an incipient inferiority complex. Rather, the past provides the Florentines with a powerful sense of their own identity, a sense of self-

❏ 'The Florentines… invented the Renaissance, which is the same as saying they invented the modern world – not, of course, an unmitigated good'. Mary McCarthy (1912–89) ❏

confidence borne of the knowledge that Florence – through good times and bad – has prospered for more than 2,000 years. And the reason it has prospered, of course, as any Florentine will tell you, is the Florentines themselves.

CULTURE AND CIVILISATION Italians, albeit grudgingly, concede almost without exception that the Florentines are some of the most cultured and civilised people in Italy. Florentines are hard working and well-spoken. Their dialect is said to be the finest. They are also active and enterprising – witness the city's army of artisans – and, unlike the people of much of modern Italy, they still have a healthy respect for those who work the land (Tuscan farmers have long been considered the most intelligent of Italy's farmers).

Yet for all their supposed pride, Florentines are also decorous and dignified people. And though individual in the extreme, they never cultivate the cult of the individual. Urbane, busy, cultured, and quietly self-satisfied – these are the Florentine watchwords.

Florence's wealth was founded on textiles and its artistic reputation on the sublimities of its Renaissance painters. No wonder, then, that cloth and the cult of the beautiful, together with the work of designers and craftspeople, continue to make Florence one of Italy's capitals of fashion and style.

GOOD TASTE AND HIGH QUALITY

You have to look a long way in Italy to find a scruffy Italian. You have to look even farther in Florence, where old and young alike parade the city streets dressed as if preening on some vast outdoor catwalk. Nowhere, with the exception of Milan, is the art of the *bella figura*, of creating a good impression, more keenly practiced.

Cool and intellectual, the Florentines look to subtle and sober-minded clothes, mixing tweedy English classicism with dashes of Renaissance opulence. On the business side, the city's textile barons favour quality. Artisans and upscale couturiers cohabit quite happily, weaving their magic from the most luxurious cloth, or conjuring up the jewellery and leatherware, for which the city is famous, from the most exclusive of materials.

GOODBYE GUCCI?

Three big names roll off the tongue when talk in Florence turns to fashion. Biggest of all, though perhaps not the most fashionable, is Gucci, still based at Via de' Tornabuoni 73r where the firm was founded three generations ago. The company has been through some difficult times, though the problems of widely available fakes and the excessive range of products that threatened to sink the firm have been fought off. New management and a new advertising campaign has begun to turn things around. Where it

Emilio Pucci: high priest of Florentine fashion

counts, however, in the shop window, the company's leather goods – made from fine-quality, honey-cured hide – continue to appeal to those who covet the panache of the famous 'double G'.

EMILIO PUCCI

With his aristocratic bearing and ambassadorial aplomb, Il Marchese Emilio Pucci is the doyen of Florentine fashion, a popular society figure who often entertains visiting royalty and heads of state. He launched his fashion career in the 1950s with dramatically dyed silks – still fashionable today, when his company's design credentials extend to cars, perfume, and objets d'art. Pucci even dresses Florence's local traffic police (the *vigili urbani*). In

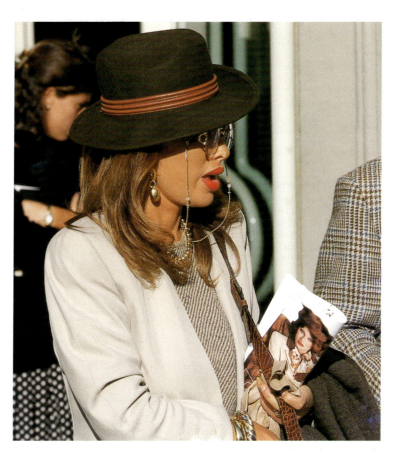

Stepping out in style: hat, handbag, and all the trimmings

❏ Machiavelli is known to have complained that the main preoccupations of the Florentines were 'to appear splendid in apparel and obtain a crafty shrewdness in discourse'. ❏

1957, he launched his famous lingerie range – made from scraps of discarded silk. Unashamedly romantic, Pucci can also be refreshingly down to earth, once describing his fashion empire as a 'modest endeavour in the rag trade'.

SALVATORE FERRAGAMO Born in Naples, Ferragamo emigrated to the United States when he was 15. He made his fortune in Hollywood, crafting shoes for the likes of Greta Garbo, Vivien Leigh, Gloria Swanson, and the gladiators in Cecil B de Mille costume epics. His spiritual home was really Florence, however, where his family still administers a fashion empire that now produces accessories and clothes to accompany the trademark shoes.

❏ The average Florentine spends well over a million lire annually on clothes. Some 10 per cent of Florence's income is generated by its fashion industry, whose main showcase is the famous trade fair, Pitti Moda, held in the Fortezza da Basso. ❏

Sober and hardworking they may be, but Tuscans happily let the mask slip when it comes to celebration. Florence and Siena have the big set-piece festivals – Calcio in Costume, Maggio Musicale, and the Palio – but not even the smallest village lets the year go by without at least one excuse for celebration.

MUSIC AND THE ARTS Tuscans, and Florentines in particular, pride themselves on their culture. Colourful medieval memories may be evoked in their most famous pageants, but it is past glories of a cultural kind that they seek to celebrate in their more highbrow arts festivals.

Performances of music, dance, and drama are held throughout the

16

Poster for a Saracen joust

❑ Art and music festivals in Tuscany include the following:
Arezzo Choral music (late August)
Barga Opera and theatre (late July)
Fiesole Estate Fiesolana – music, film, ballet, and drama (June–August)
Florence Maggio Musicale – orchestral concerts, ballet, movies, and fringe events (April–June)
Lucca Sacred music (April–June)
Montepulciano Cantiere Internazionale – music and arts (end July/beginning August)
Siena Settimana Musicale – concerts by pupils and staff of the Accademia Musicale Chigiana (August)
Torre del Lago Puccini operas performed outdoors (August) ❑

region, often in magnificent medieval settings or, as in the case of Fiesole, in outdoor theatres of Roman vintage. Concert series fill Florentine churches, and they are also presented in green secluded corners (as in Barga's famous opera festival). Some festivals, such as San Gimignano's, are provincial affairs confined to the town square. Others, such as Florence's Maggio Musicale (see page 183), are among Italy's most popular and prestigious arts events. Visit any Tuscan tourist office for details of current festivals.

FOOD AND WINE It need not be much – an obscure saint, the humble potato – anything will do as long as it provides an excuse for a party. Small *feste* or *sagre* erupt across Tuscany throughout the year. Most take place in the summer, when long balmy evenings provide the perfect background for a night of festivities. Autumn will do just as well, for then the grapes are brought in (the *vendemmia*), and what better reason for celebration than a good harvest? Most village festivals begin with a special Mass, followed by much dancing, overindulgence (of food rather than drink) and a rousing fire-works finale. Brass bands provide a musical accompaniment (often of excruciating quality but quite remarkable enthusiasm). You should stumble across many such festivals by accident. If not, they are widely advertised on street posters and in local newspapers.

MEDIEVAL ECHOES Italians love nothing more than spectacle and sen-suality. Siena's famous Palio (see pages 240–1), therefore, like many similar pageants, may seem to be lit-tle more than an excuse to dress up and indulge in days of rampant (but motiveless) merrymaking. To the cynical, such festivities can also appear like attempts to woo the wealthy tourist. Nothing, however, could be further from the truth. Many such events recall ancient but still passionately felt enmities (Siena's Palio, with its inter district rivalries, is a perfect example). Most are means of expressing fiercely felt civic pride. Some, like Florence's Scoppio del Carro (see page 75), wear a spurious religious mantle – often no more than a mask for an event whose origins have pagan roots.

The majority revel in competition, usually between neighbouring dis-tricts. Encounters can range from the ferocious – as in Siena's horse-race – to the faintly ridiculous, as in Montepulciano's comical barrel-

❑ Among the more entertaining traditional festivals are:
Arezzo Giostro del Saracino (September)
Florence Scoppio del Carro (Easter Sunday); Festa di San Giovanni (June); Calcio in Costume (June); Festa del Grillo (15 August); Festa del Rificolone (7 September)
Lucca San Paolino (July); Luminara (13 September); Santa Croce (14 September)
Montepulciano Bravio delle Botti (August)
Pisa Luminara & Regatta di San Ranieri (June); Gioco del Ponte (June)
Pistoia Giostro dell'Orso (July)
Prato Festa degli Omaggi (September)
Siena Palio (2 July and 16 August)

rolling contest, the Bravio delle Botti (see page 215). Ludicrous or not, the stakes are always high, the battles furiously contested. For example, Florence's Calcio in Costume – a mass game of soccer in medieval dress – involves bruising passages of play and a medley of viciously underhanded tactics.

The Campo in Siena during the Palio, Italy's most famous pageant

17

Old traditions of craft and artistic endeavour die hard. Florence's modern artisans, worthy successors to their Renaissance forebears, are still part of the city's mythology, whether carving furniture in dusty workshops or crafting jewellery in the venerable environs of the Ponte Vecchio.

CRAFT ON EVERY CORNER Few modern cities would find a place in their hard-pressed hearts for a breed straight out of the Middle Ages. In Florence, however, artisans (*artigiani*) are very much a part of life. Although rising rents have driven craftsmen out of some central districts, other areas buzz with skilled activity. On Via della Porcellana, for example, near Ognissanti, almost every doorway is a tumult of chair legs and dismembered tables, every interior a vignette of wood shavings and leather-aproned carpenters. A similar scene greets you around Santa Croce, where the smell of wood glue fills your nostrils and the clank of wrought iron rends the air. The picture is repeated (though in a different guise) on the Ponte Vecchio, where you can look over the shoulders of latter-day portrait painters as they flatter their eager clients. Around

them, as likely as not, will be the wares of less subtle deceivers – the fake bags and watches of less reputable artisans, tucked away in more discreet workshops. Shops on the bridge itself are packed with glittering jewellery, the work of skilled successors to Renaissance goldsmiths such as Ghiberti and Benvenuto Cellini. Nowhere is the lack of distinction between artist and artisan more apparent than in Florence.

Continue beyond the bridge into the Oltrarno and you enter another artisans' heartland. While fine antique shops front the thoroughfares, small ateliers jam the back-streets, home to leather workshops (that of Santo Spirito the most famous) and some of the city's longest-established cabinetmakers. If their wares prove too expensive,

Artisans are still an integral and important feature of the city

visit the market around San Lorenzo for a huge choice of leather and clothing. If not, broaden your scope by visiting the stores on Via de' Tornabuoni, a shop window for the city's finest craftsmanship (see Shopping, pages 178–81, for details).

TRADITION Artisans provide a living reminder of the past in a city whose history otherwise seems confined to museums and galleries. Not only in their workshops (whose appearance has probably changed little in five centuries) but also in the crafts they carry out, these workers continue to provide a glimpse of a lost world. They may not produce paintings of Renaissance calibre, but in virtually all other areas their skills are as sharply honed as ever. The variety of craftspeople, too, is as broad as ever: from frame makers, ceramicists, stonecutters, and jewellers, to furniture makers, silversmiths, weavers and textile designers.

PRESSED INTO SERVICE At no time was the strength of the city's craft tradition more dramatically revealed, nor more desperately needed, than in the aftermath of the 1966 flood. Dozens of skills old and new had to be found to deal with the deluge of damaged artifacts. Many ancient crafts had to be revived (notably the art of illuminating manuscripts); others were virtually unknown (such as the restoration of paper). For the most part, however, the city was able to draw on talent still latent in its thriving artistic subculture.

The Opificio delle Pietre Dure provides an excellent example of tradition merging with modern tech-

In the shadow of the Uffizi gallery, local artists look for work

niques in the service of art. Founded in 1588, the institute started life making mosaics from *pietre dure* (literally 'hard stone') – usually semi-precious stones like agate and amethyst. The epitome of its work is found in the Medici Chapels' Cappella dei Principi (see pages 64–5). Its teaching departments and modern laboratories are world leaders in restoration of all kinds, drawing from the craftspeople of Florence for *pietre dure* specialists, and for experts in furniture, painting, stone, marble, bronze and textiles.

Good food is as much a part of the pleasure of a holiday in Florence and Tuscany as visiting the region's museums and art galleries. Eating out in a wayside trattoria or a downtown restaurant should provide a medley of memories every bit as satisfying as a Donatello nude or a Masaccio fresco.

FLORENCE AND FRENCH CUISINE

Florentines never tire of telling visitors how they invented French cuisine. In 1533, so the story goes, Caterina de' Medici, aged just 14, married Henri de Valois, later to become Henri II of France. Loath (like any good Italian) to leave the joys of home cooking, and appalled by the prospect of foreign food and French table manners, the young Caterina ensured that a train of chefs and an encyclopedia of recipes followed her to Paris. Hence, supposedly, the range of classic

Mushrooms are a speciality of the region in the autumn

Gallic dishes with more than a hint of Tuscan seasoning: *dolce forte* (from *lepre dolce e forte*); canard à l'orange (Tuscany's *papero alla melarancia*); and *vol au vents* (sold in Florentine pasticcerie as *turbanate di sfoglia*). Caterina is also supposed to have introduced the French to that most vital piece of table equipment, the fork.

RICH REPASTS

Whatever the truth of the story, medieval Tuscan meals, at least on big occasions, were far richer than the simple dishes that make up today's regional cuisine. The banquets of Pope Leo X, the Medici pope, for example, featured delicacies such as peacocks' tongues, and spectacles such as nightingales flying out of pies and children springing naked from puddings. At the other extreme, poor Florentines might sup on little more than dried figs and oak-bark bread. The average family, by contrast, would settle down to something resembling a modern meal – wine, pasta, ravioli, sausage and grilled meat, and fruit or cheese to finish.

Medieval flavourings, however, would raise eyebrows in a modern kitchen. Their soups, for example, might have been seasoned with cloves, cinnamon, and ginger, and garnished with sugar, cheese, and almonds. Pies overflowed with oil, orange and lemon juice, cloves, nutmeg, parsley, saffron, dates, raisins, bay leaves, and marjoram. One sauce, *savore sanguino*, boasted cinnamon, raisins, sandalwood, and sumac, the last now used only for tanning leather.

TODAY'S TEMPTATIONS

You would be hard pressed to find anything as

exotic in today's restaurants. Quite the contrary: Florentines – wrongly – are now known for their culinary parsimony, and are labelled by other Italians as mere *mangiafagioli* (bean eaters). Beans, in many forms, certainly feature in many Florentine dishes, but they are symbols rather than staples of the city's healthily robust cuisine.

There is much else to appeal, from warming Tuscan vegetable soups like *ribollita* and *acquacotta*, to that mother of all steaks, the hearty *bistecca alla fiorentina*. Fruit and vegetables, locally grown and market-bought, are superb, and in season there are such delights as black truffles and porcini mushrooms to tempt the taste buds.

As in Rome, which loves its brains and offal dishes, Florence can also taunt the palate with specialities that some might consider a little beyond

the culinary pale. Tripe (*trippa*) and pigs' intestines (*lampredotto*) are two classic dishes, as are the combs, livers, hearts and testicles of freshly killed roosters. You may wish to pass over such delicacies, but do try to move beyond dull staples like spaghetti and tomato sauce.

❑ Downtown restaurants run the gamut, from expensive post-modern to tatty *trattorie*. The areas around Santo Spirito (in Oltrarno) and Santa Croce are rewarding, with many small, interesting restaurants. Cheap pizzerias and lively *osterie* cluster around the station and Santa Maria Novella. ❑

21

A tempting sight – take your pick of the city's trattorie

Trattoria

No one pretends that Florentines revel in the dolce vita to the extent of their Roman counterparts. With a café on every corner, however, and a summer sun overhead, opportunities for the dolce far niente – the sweet doing of nothing – are as rich in Florence as almost anywhere in Italy.

TIME OUT The simple pleasures of a quiet *cappuccino*, or a calming *aperitivo*, are as much a part of enjoying Italy as trudging around museums and galleries (and this is as true for a native as it is for a foreigner). No self-respecting Italian city, therefore, can do without its bars and cafés. And while Florence's streets and piazzas may seem less welcoming than some in Italy, they still provide a colourful and more than adequate stage for lazy self-indulgence. They also provide the venue for that other passive pastime – people-watching.

Cafés are there to be used – and not merely as pit stops for a gulp of coffee before another round of Giotto and Michelangelo. After hours of paintings and sculpture, of churches dutifully seen, treat yourself to at least an hour of

> ❏ Florence's best-known cafés are the 'Big Four' on Piazza della Repubblica: **Donnini** (excellent coffee and cakes), **Paszkowski** (literary associations, music on the terrace summer evenings), **Giubbe Rosse** (peruse the daily papers with your coffee), and (best of them all, one-time haunt of the intelligentsia) the *belle-époque* **Gilli**. ❏

more wholehearted self-indulgence. Such simple delights may be denied you on your return to daily routines.

A CHOICE OF STYLES There is a bar on almost every Florentine street corner – functional, stand-up places designed for a kick-start *espresso*, a breakfast *cornetto* (a horn-shaped, custard-filled croissant), or a hurried lunchtime snack. All human life is here, together with all it needs to keep body and soul together. Bars are shops, pubs, phone booths, and social meeting places rolled into one. Cafés are a little different. You can still stand and fight for service, but more often than not they provide oases of leisurely and sun-drenched contemplation. Relaxation, not to mention waiter service, comes at a price (you pay extra to sit down), but even the most humble purchase buys the right to read, daydream, or simply get your bearings for as long as you wish.

A slightly different

Service with a smile

22

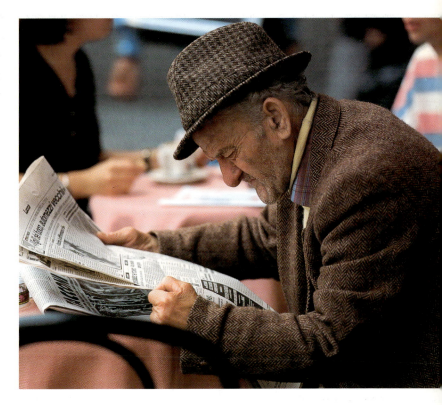

Taking time, with a cup of coffee, to catch up on the news

experience awaits in the city's wine cellars, old-fashioned institutions that parade under a variety of names – *enoteche, vinaio, fiaschetteria, mescita*. Some, like the *Cantinetta Antinori* (in Piazza Antinori), are stylish, rather upscale affairs. Others, like the hole-in-the-wall *Vini del Chianti* (Via dei Cimatori), are more modest neighbourhood joints. Most of them offer places to meet for a bite to eat and a glass of wine.

PEOPLE-WATCHING There comes a time – when the postcards are written and you are dead on your feet – when the world has to come to you. Then is the moment to forget the galleries, ignore the churches, and sit back, drink in hand, to watch the Italians and your fellow travellers at play. People-watching in Italy is a rare delight. No time is better to indulge in it than during the social ritual known as the *passeggiata*, a stylised evening parade when the object is to dress up and then to see

and be seen (in Florence its ebb and flow centres on Piazza della Signoria and the streets around Via dei Calzaiuoli). Traffic and narrow streets preclude ranks of Parisian-style boulevard cafés, premium spots for the amateur voyeur: in Florence, the most famous cafés crowd Piazza della Signoria or the more dour margins of Piazza della Repubblica. Many equally picturesque spots – with a more 'local' feel – await discovery in the quieter corners of the Oltrarno and Sant'Ambrogio.

❏ The expensive but essential Rivoire on Piazza della Signoria is one of Florence's most famous cafés, perfect for admiring the clothes-conscious Italians indulging in their evening *passeggiata*. ❏

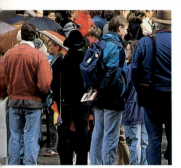

Tourism in any great city is invariably a double-edged blessing. On the one hand it offers revenue and employment, on the other it encourages the less scrupulous and adds to the wear and tear on the very monuments visitors come to see. Restoration, as a result, is a constant Florentine preoccupation. Today more than ever, the city is struggling to maintain a balance between protecting the legacy of its illustrious past and carving for itself a realistic and economically sound future.

24

TOO MANY TOURISTS Estimates vary as to how many people visit Florence every year. The evidence of one's own eyes suggests it is too many. It is as well, therefore, to come expecting to share the city's attractions with a great many other people: prepared for the crowds forever clustered around the Uffizi's Botticellis, and for the numbers of young visitors of many countries sprawled around the Duomo and the Ponte Vecchio.

Overcrowding is a problem that touches the Florentine at least as much as the harassed tourist. Those who live in Florence are the ones who bear the intolerable strain visitors place on the city's infrastructure – though they are also, of course, the ones who reap tourism's financial benefits. Visitors can only be partly blamed for the city's traffic, a daily threat to life and limb (quite apart from the effects of vehicle-induced pollution on the health of statues and stonework). Here locals are their own worst enemies: there are, on average, 2.7 cars for every Florentine family. And cars – with food, family, and soccer – are the things closest to an Italian's heart. Getting rid of them has been an uphill battle: downtown restrictions were introduced only in 1988, but only after considerable argument.

FLORENCE FOSSILISED? Florentines are currently faced with a difficult choice: whether to go for broke (perhaps literally as well as metaphorically) and retain Florence as a living city, or whether to turn it over entirely to the demands of tourism. If they tend toward the latter, Florence may be in danger of becoming a historical fossil, a moribund city dressed up as a Renaissance theme park. Death by tourism can be brought on by a variety of causes. They include slow strangulation by traffic, paralysis by depopulation, food shops replaced by souvenir stands, workshops replaced by boutiques, neighbourhood *trattorie* sacrificed to the gods of fast food.

The problem echoes that of Venice, whose population has dropped to 67,000 today from 180,000 in 1945. Florentine figures show a similar trend, down from 400,000 before the 1966 flood to an estimated 150,000 today. But for Florence, such discouraging statistics are generally tempered by glimmers of optimism.

FIRENZE NUOVA One much-heralded way forward for Florence is the new town on the city's north-western outskirts, around the airport. Firenze Nuova, so the theory goes, will encourage urban decentralisation and create the focus for a broad-based industrial and municipal metropolis, its economy increasingly intertwined with that of its booming neighbour, Prato. Florence itself, the planners hope, will increasingly be freed to develop as a culture and service-oriented city. Critics (of which, as ever in Italy, there are many) complain that the scheme could have the opposite effect, creating a desiccated downtown on the one hand, and a steel and glass wasteland on the other. So far, the critics appear to have been confounded: many of the traditional businesses, such as banking, publishing, architecture, and legal services, seem likely to remain in central Florence. Many Florentine professionals perhaps prefer the more stimulating environment of the city itself, with its Renaissance palaces and statues, and have no intention of surrendering Florence to tourism.

CRIME Whatever the impression given by the city's urbane citizens and benign-looking streets, all is not well below the surface. Florentines talk of *Firenze snaturata* (Florence corrupted), a phrase used to describe both the threat of the city's surrender to tourists and its growing catalogue of crime. Prostitution and drug dealing are mainstays of the Florentine underworld, just as in many cities in the 1990s. The drug deals on Via de' Neri and the Piazza Santissima Annunziata are all too obvious, as is the late-night lowlife around the station and the Cascine park. There is more to the city than statues and sweet-faced gallery Madonnas. However, this is not to say that

The volume of visitors (top, Uffizi and below, Piazza SS Annunziata) increases wear on the monuments

Making friends with the Porcellino near the Mercato Nuovo. Rubbing its snout brings good luck!

Florence is particularly dangerous, nor is it plagued with the petty crime of, say, Rome or Naples. Pickpockets aside, the city's criminal element is unlikely to affect most reasonably vigilant visitors.

POLLUTION AND RESTORATION Still on the down side, but again in common with cities the world over, air pollution is an increasing worry in Florence. It is true that the city has some way to go before it faces the pollution problems of Rome or Milan. Nonetheless, the danger signs are already there, and are of special concern in a city that has more than its share of outdoor art treasures. The begrimed Battistero is a prominent victim, its bronze doors now removed from their proximity to belching exhausts and replaced by copies. Gone, too, are most of Orsanmichele's exterior statues, removed – like the Campanile's corroded reliefs and Michelangelo's *David* – to the pollution-free sanctuary of museums and galleries.

The unending task of restoring works of art damaged by time and pollution is one thing; repairing the damage done in a mere few hours by the 1966 flood is quite another. The deluge created one of the greatest artistic (and human) disasters in Italy's recent history (see pages 130–1). Some of the thousands of damaged artworks were lost forever and many are still waiting to see the light of day. Most, however, were almost miraculously restored – testament to the dedication and technical skills of Florence's restorers.

The sheer size of Italy's artistic heritage means that funds for restoration are constantly at a premium. After the 1966 flood, however, huge additional sums of money were donated to Florence. Much of the money is still being put to good use in a massive restoration project that is destined to last another 20 years.

Not all the city's restoration projects have been without incident. Piazza della Signoria provided the worst recent upheaval: excavations turned the square into a construction site, then the original medieval paving stones were mysteriously 'lost'. The traffic restriction scheme in the centre (known as the *Zona Blu*) has also been a mixed success. It is, however, typical of the projects increasingly needed by a city struggling to reconcile two disparate sets of demands – the requirements of visitors seeking its Renaissance past and the needs of citizens looking to its 21st-century future.

❏ Now more than 30 years after the 1966 flood, some 80 full-time staff are still restoring books and manuscripts in the National Library, where more than a million volumes were ruined. About 2,000 of the 3,000 paintings and sculptures dredged from the mud left by the flood have so far been returned to public view. ❏

Florence Was

Florence was a late arrival on the historical stage – only six decades before the birth of Christ – but its beginnings have become entangled in a mix of myth and countermyth. Even the origins of its name are obscured by an opaque combination of fact and fantasy.

THE ETRUSCANS Florence was probably first inhabited by Italic tribes from latter-day Emilia-Romagna around the end of the 10th century BC. The attraction of the site was simple: it provided a crossing point over the Arno, one of the region's more formidable natural barriers (the ford was close to the site of the present-day Ponte Vecchio).

When the Etruscans drifted into the area five centuries later, however (see pages 246–7), they ignored the river in favour of a more easily defended position in the hills to the north. In time their fortress became Fiesole (see pages 82–3), a colony that developed into a leading member of the Etruscans' 12-city federation. At the same time, the Etruscans probably kept a small market on the Arno, and a breakaway group from Fiesole may also have established a community near the river in the 4th century BC.

THE END OF FIESOLE By this time, Rome was encroaching on the Etruscan dominions. Fiesole was first defeated in 283 BC, but it continued, like many Etruscan cities, to enjoy a relationship of benevolent neutrality with the ever more powerful city of Rome. Fiesole's end, according to legend, came around 60 BC, when Rome sent an expedition to hunt down Catiline, a fugitive from Roman justice. Catiline, it seems, had fled to Fiesole and assumed control of the city, to the delight of its inhabitants. Fiorino, commander of the Roman forces, realising Fiesole was powerfully defended, decided to build a camp on the Arno and take the city by siege. Fiorino was killed in a surprise raid, however, and his plans came to nothing, but his successor, Julius Caesar, consolidated the riverside camp and eventually defeated Fiesole. As for Catiline, he escaped, only to be hunted down and killed near Pistoia.

FACT AND FICTION Most of this colourful account is pure fiction – and with it the notion that Florence took its name and owed its existence to the slain

Etruscan art: (top) black figure vase and (left) funerary urn from Chiusi

28

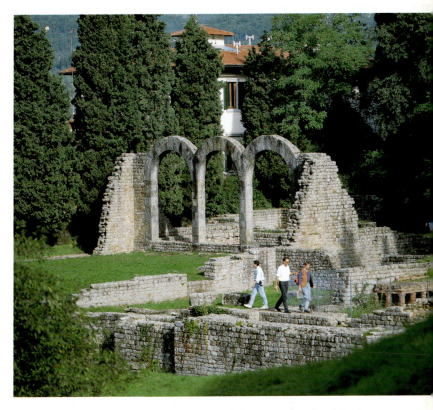

commander, Fiorino. Catiline *was* a historical figure, *was* in Fiesole, and was defeated at Pistoia in 62 BC. Fiorino, however, seems to be an entirely literary invention. Julius Caesar probably never fought in Tuscany; nor did he found Roman Florentia (though he is often described as doing so). His role in the city's birth was passive. It was his agrarian law of 59 BC that – by making provision for land to be granted to retired army veterans – actually created the conditions for Florence's establishment and early growth.

THE NAME OF FLORENCE How Florence came by its romantic name is a mystery. Many would still like to believe it was named after Fiorino and his fictitious camp (and, though history is silent on the subject, there may well have been such a general in Caesar's army). Others think it derives from *fluentia*, after the fact that the Arno 'flows' through the city

Wandering among the ruins of Fiesole, Florence's Etruscan predecessor in the hills above the Arno

(though plenty of rivers flow through cities). Another theory, along similar lines, suggests that *fluentia* refers to the 'confluence' of the Arno and Mugnone, the river that joins the Arno about 2km west of the city.

Popular tradition, however, favours more poetic semantic possibilities – centring on Florence as a 'city of flowers' (*fiori*). Roman Florentia, for example, might have taken its name from the wildflowers that dot the city's hills and plains. Or it may have derived from the Ludi Floreales, the spring games held to honour the goddess Flora. The city's cathedral is still known as Santa Maria del Fiore, after the *giaggiolo*, or *Iris florentia*, the violet-scented iris of the Florentine hills. The purple flower (shaped like a fleur-de-lis) is the city's emblem and the symbol of the Virgin Mary.

Under Roman domination, Florence enjoyed a period of quiet prosperity. After Rome's fall the city took the barbarian invasions more or less in its stride. Lombard and Carolingian rule then laid the foundations of an independent city, and with it the prospect of Florence's medieval power and prosperity.

A ROMAN CITY Florence's Roman stalwarts established a walled *castrum*, a camp whose grid outline is still clearly imprinted on the city's present-day streets. Its northern and southern limits, for example, are marked by Via de' Cerretani and Via Porta Rossa, its eastern and western boundaries by Via del Proconsolo and Via de' Tornabuoni. Piazza della Repubblica was the old Forum, Via degli Strozzi its main street (the *Decumanus Maximus*). The old theatre lay behind the Palazzo Vecchio, the amphitheatre within the curve of Via Torta and Piazza dei Peruzzi (near Santa Croce).

Today, only a few columns remain as direct memorials of the colony of Florentia. Some are in the church of San Miniato al Monte, others form part of the Battistero, site of the Roman *praetorium* or guardhouse (and possibly the Roman governor's residence). Otherwise, monuments amount to no more than historical echoes, vague memories recalled by street names such as Via delle Terme (Street of the Baths) or Via del Campidoglio (Street of the Capitol).

DECLINE AND FALL Florence's main role under the Romans was strategic. Florentia not only provided a route over the Arno, but also controlled the passes across the Apennines into Emilia-Romagna. Although the settlement's first walls took no account of the Arno, it was the river – navigable to this point – that provided a conduit for trade and generated the colony's early prosperity. Consular roads, too, made the camp their focus, notably the Via Cassia, a link between Rome and its big colonies at Bononia (Bologna) and Mediolanum (Milan). The Via Aurelia, the Via Clodia, and the Via Flaminia – built

Top: The façade on the Roman villa at Poggio a Chiano. Below: the great Roman theatre at Fiesole

30

before Florentia's rise – also crisscrossed the region, further emphasising the new colony's strategic importance.

Although Florentia was never a major player in the Roman world, by around the 3rd century AD (after expansion during the Augustan period) the city's population had probably reached about 10,000.

THE BARBARIANS After Rome's decline in the 5th century, Florence suffered repeated attacks from Goth and Byzantine invaders. Ultimately, however, it was the Lombards, a Germanic people from the north, who dominated the city during the Dark Ages.

After taking Tuscany in AD 570, they brought two centuries of relative peace to the troubled region, which they administered from Pavia and Lucca. Their reign was cut short by the Franks (another northern race), first under Pepin the Short, and then under his more famous son, Charlemagne, who probably visited the city on a couple of occasions. Tuscany became part of the Franks' Carolingian Empire (later the Holy Roman Empire), ruled on behalf of its northern emperors by a series of Lucca-based princes who were known as the Margraves.

THE RULE OF THE MARGRAVES The Carolingian empire's hold over the Margraves grew progressively weaker. As it waned, the Margraves were becoming increasingly fond of Florence. Willa, widow of the Margrave Uberto, for example, founded the Badia Fiorentina, the city's first abbey (see page 55), in 978. By 1001 Willa's son, the Margrave

Rome continued to influence the art of Tuscany long after the fall of the empire

Ugo, transferred the region's capital from Lucca to Florence. Thereafter, Margrave allegiance to northern-based emperors slackened still further. By 1077 the pious Margrave Matilda (1046–1115), founder of many churches and one of the era's most successful rulers, had transferred her loyalties to the pope (by now already involved in virulent disputes with the emperor – see pages 36–7). She arranged that after her death her titles were bequeathed to Pope Gregory VII – all, that is, except Lucca, Florence, and Siena, all three of which found themselves on the verge of independence and self-determination.

Florence's medieval prosperity was based on Europe's greatest woollen and textiles industry. This enterprise in turn nurtured a banking system whose success laid the foundations of modern capitalism and made the Florentines bankers to much of the world.

EARLY SUCCESS At its peak, the textiles industry in Florence employed an estimated 30,000 people – about one third of the city's population. During the 12th century, barely 100 years after the trade began, some 300 textile workshops were scattered across the city. Even by the end of the 13th century, when production had dropped by 90 per cent, Florence still provided the Western world with at least one tenth of its textiles.

There were several reasons for Florence's success. One was water, fundamental to the woollen industry (both sorted wool and finished cloth, for example, had to be washed and rinsed). In the Arno, therefore, the city had a primary resource. Another was the availability of expertise and cheap labour. The expertise was provided by the Umiliati, a group of monks introduced to the city from Lombardy. Their riverside workshops made Ognissanti (see page 109) one of the industry's main centres. They helped train the city's teeming ranks of carders, combers, weavers, shearers, spinners, and other specialised artisans. Money, too, was of prime importance, and here

Top: detail, Villa Medicea Poggio a Caiano. Below: an eagle, symbol of the Arte di Calimala, crowns San Miniato al Monte

Florence's bankers came into their own, providing the industry with capital investment and extended lines of credit.

Florence was also renowned for the quality of its cloth. Its reputation for dyeing, in particular, was second to none. Exotic dyestuffs came from every corner of the Orient and the Mediterranean basin, Florentine reds becoming particularly prized (many of the dyers' secrets, incidentally, are now lost – one of history's more tantalising mysteries). All Florence lacked was wool. This problem was solved by the city's enterprising merchants who – 'in the name of God and profit' – travelled to England, Portugal, Spain, Flanders, and the Barbary Coast to buy raw materials to feed their flourishing businesses.

EUROPE'S BANKERS Florentine bankers championed the use of bills of exchange, and invented cheques, credit, life insurance, double-entry bookkeeping, and Europe's first single currency, the gold florin. On their own these might seem dry achievements. In the context of what a banker might do with his profits, however, they provided the financial wherewithal for

Top and above: details, the Palazzo dell'Arte della Lana

many of the greatest buildings and works of art of the Renaissance.

The best known of the bankers were the Medici, whose bank, in its day, was Europe's wealthiest business. A 15th-century phenomenon, the family were latecomers to an industry that by 1250 already dominated the world of European commerce. The Bardi and the Peruzzi, for example, were chief bankers to the kings of England and France; the Acciaiuoli dealt with the Angevin monarchs of Naples and Sicily; while the Pazzi, the Alberti (and the Medici) handled the highly lucrative papal account. Lesser financiers from among Florence's 24 banking dynasties – involved with Holy Roman emperors, German potentates, and Burgundian princes – are remembered today in the palace and street names – Alberti, Albizzi, Antinori, Capponi, Cerchi, Davanzati, Guardi, Mozzi, Portinari, Ricci, Strozzi and Tornabuoni.

THE FLORIN One of the bankers' key achievements was the *fiorino d'oro* (gold florin), a coin which was adopted across Europe after its introduction in 1252, and which remained in use until the middle of the 15th century. Florentines had previously used the *mark*, minted in Pisa, while the only internationally accepted coin had been the Byzantine *hyperper*. The English florin, whose name survived in British coinage until recently, took its name from the *fiorino*. Purity was vital to the coin's stability, and standards at the Zecca (Mint), alongside the Palazzo Vecchio, were rigorously applied. By 1422, 2 million *fiorini* were in circulation. One side bore a likeness of John the Baptist, Florence's patron saint; the other was inscribed with the city's Latin name, Florentia, and its floral emblem.

❑ In the 1430s, a family could live comfortably on 150 florins a year; a *palazzo* could be bought for 1,000, a Botticelli painting for 100, a slave for 50, and a servant for 10. The Medici accounts for the years 1433–71 showed 663,755 florins spent over 38 years on 'buildings, charities and taxes'. ❑

Florence's great mercantile endeavours were organised into Arti (Guilds). Their leading lights were invariably to be found either running the city as officeholders in the official machinery of government, or manipulating affairs more subtly through their position at the head of its supposedly independent institutions.

A SOCIETY OF MERCHANTS As early as the 11th century, Florentine merchants organised themselves into a *societas mercatorum*. Ranged against them was the *societas militium*, a grouping of nobles and leading Florentine families. The former provided the backbone of the *Comune*, the independent city-state, run by a 100-strong assembly and established in Florence after Margrave Matilda's death in 1115. In time, the *societas* was replaced by the first of the guilds, the Arte di Calimala, an umbrella organisation devoted to most mercantile vocations. By the end of the 12th century, however, splinter groups had broken away to form seven major guilds, the Arti Maggiori.

THE ARTI MAGGIORI The most prestigious of the guilds, though not the wealthiest, was the lawyers' Arte dei Giudici e Notai. Next came the wool, silk, and cloth merchants – the Arte della Lana, the Arte di Por Santa Maria, and the refashioned Arte di Calimala. Lower down came the Arte del Cambio, or bankers' guild (bankers preferred the term 'money-changers,' usury being a sin in the eyes of the Church). The Arte dei Vaccai e Pellicciai looked after the furriers. The Arte dei Medici, Speziali e Merciai embraced a hodgepodge of doctors, apothecaries, and spice- and dye-merchants (as well as the occasional poet, painter, and craftsman).

THE ARTI MINORI While the Arti Maggiori embraced wealthy merchants, the 14 minor guilds (founded in 1289) catered more to middle-ranking tradesmen. These included anyone from butchers, bakers, and armourers to carpenters, masons, and innkeepers (not to mention vintners, tanners, cooks, locksmiths and leather workers). Ordinary workers, the so-called *Popolo Minuto*, had no representation at all – despite making up 75 per cent of the population. Those employed in the wool, silk,and cloth industries, moreover, were prevented by law from forming guilds.

THE POWER OF THE MERCHANT CLASS Merchants, known as the *Popolo Grasso* (literally the 'fat' or prosperous people), controlled Florence during much of the 13th and 14th centuries. Sometimes the control was covert, at other times plain to see, as in the so-called Primo Popolo (1248), a quasi-democratic regime dominated by mercantile elements (whose 10-year rule, according to Dante, was the only period of civic peace in Florence's history). During the Secondo Popolo (1284), the Arti Maggiori introduced the *Ordinamenti della Giustizia* (1293), a written constitution that, while theoretically the blueprint for republican rule, in fact entrenched mercantile power further.

GOVERNMENT BY GUILDS Florence's much-vaunted republicanism worked well in theory. The names of selected guild members (and only guild members) were placed in eight leather bags (*borse*) kept in Santa Croce. Names were then drawn at random in public. Those selected were known as *Priori*, the government they formed the *Signoria*. There were usually nine *Priori*, six chosen from the Arti Maggiori, two from the Arti Minori, and one standard-bearer, the

Gonfaloniere. The *Priori* served a maximum term of office of two months – a deliberately short period, in order to reduce the chances of corruption or favouritism. In times of crisis a *Parlemento*, or assembly, was summoned, consisting of all male citizens over the age of 14. When a two-thirds quorum was reached, the *Parlemento* was asked to approve a *balia*, a committee delegated to deal with the crisis as it saw fit.

Florence's republican system looked good on paper. In practice it was far from democratic. The lowliest workers, the *Popolo Minuto*, were totally excluded, as were the *grandi*, or nobles. Despite the random selec-

tion process, merchant cliques easily ensured that only the names of likely supporters found the cliques' way into the *borse*. If things did not go their way, it was easy enough to summon a *Parlemento* and form a *balia* whose first act would be to replace the offending *Priori* with more pliable candidates. It was thus, through the long decades of Medici rule, that the family retained the reins of power while only rarely holding formal office.

Top: sails, the symbol of the Rucellai family, S Maria Novella. Below: patron saints of the major guilds decorate Orsanmichele's exterior

Florence was torn by disputes throughout the medieval period. Matters came to a head during the 13th century with the so-called Guelph–Ghibelline conflicts. Ostensibly these were encounters between papal and imperial supporters; often they were often simply labels for any number of different feuds and factions.

ENDLESS ENMITY There has hardly been a time in Florence's 2,000-year history when the city was not divided into two or more rival camps. Dante compared its constant political struggles to a sick man forever tossing and turning in bed. So unending was the discord that contemporaries believed two different races had settled Florence: the nobles, descended from Roman soldiers, and the commoners, descendants of Fiesole's ancient Etruscans. Trying to

Emperor Barbarossa – 'Red Beard' – and (top) his court at Mayence

follow the city's litany of feuds is pointless – and makes monotonous reading. All one can do is trace the main divisions, and remember that, for all the apparent conflict, Florence went from strength to strength.

POPE VERSUS EMPEROR The Guelphs and the Ghibellines took their names from 'Welf' – the family name of Otto IV and the dukes of Bavaria – and 'Waiblingen' – the name of a castle belonging to their rivals, the imperial family of Hohenstaufen. The Guelphs, broadly speaking, were supporters of the pope, the Ghibellines supporters of the Holy Roman Emperor. Disputes between emperor and pope dated back to the investiture of Charlemagne, who in the 8th century had given lands conquered in Italy to the papacy (the beginnings of the Papal States). In return he had been anointed and crowned Holy Roman Emperor. This was the root of irreconcilable differences: the popes claimed the right to crown emperors; the emperors claimed the right to sanction popes. Even more importantly, both parties claimed the right to rule the lands that made up the ancient Roman empire: the pope argued that Constantine the Great had bequeathed the empire to the Church, while the emperor cited lineal descent from the Roman and Byzantine emperors.

The dispute first came to a head in 1079 when Emperor Henry IV rejected Pope Gregory VII's proposals for radical reform, aimed at securing exclusive papal powers to control the selection and investiture of bishops. Gregory responded by excommunicating the emperor, in theory thereby

36

freeing his subjects from imperial allegiance. While diplomacy eventually settled this dispute (in the Concordat of Worms), subsequent disagreements were to involve violent confrontations in northern and central Italy, the most notorious of which was Emperor Barbarossa's 12th-century rampage to restore imperial authority.

FLAGS OF CONVENIENCE Conflicts within Italy's city-states, including Florence, rarely divided along simple Guelph–Ghibelline lines. By the time the words entered the language (in the 12th century) they were little more than convenient labels for a variety of feuding factions. Cities used alliances with pope or emperor, for example, as means to their own ends, the terms 'Guelph' and 'Ghibelline' serving as mere window dressing for squabbles between cities, or feuds between families within cities. If your sympathies were broadly Guelph (like those of Florence), the chances are your neighbour (and enemy) would be nominally Ghibelline (like Siena).

FLORENCE DIVIDED The main division among the citizens of Florence was between the old nobility, who had Ghibelline sympathies, and the new class of mercantile entrepreneurs, who were Guelphs. By 1193, the infighting was so disruptive that the *Comune* introduced political refinements such as the post of

The Bargello's courtyard, scene of countless executions during the Guelph and Ghibelline conflicts

Podestà (a chief magistrate) to help defuse the situation (see pages 56 and 57). In 1216, street battles were triggered by the murder of a Buondelmonti, stabbed for reneging on a promise to marry a member of the Amidei family. This was said to be the spark of Florence's Guelph–Ghibelline conflicts. Although Ghibelline regimes reigned briefly (in both 1237 and 1260), Florence was predominantly a Guelph (mercantile) city – though, in keeping with the divisive spirit of the times, the Guelphs managed to quarrel and split into two factions – the Whites and the Blacks (see page 71).

Civil chaos in most cities of the period invariably had the same outcome – the emergence of a single man or family with the wealth and power to cut through the tangle of feuding and factionalism. It was only a matter of time before just such a family emerged in Florence.

> ❏ 'Nearly every form of government was tried … in Florence, 'but Florentines were 'too articulate, politically, for government to be possible at all.' Mary McCarthy (1912–89) ❏

Few families' names are more associated with a city than that of the Medici with Florence. The phenomenal wealth of their banking business sustained them as the city's virtual rulers for 350 years. During this period, Medici patronage produced some of the greatest buildings and works of art ever seen.

Giovanni di Bicci de' Medici (1360–1429), founder of the Medici banking business in the late 14th century, could scarcely have predicted that his descendants would rule Florence until 1737, that they would include popes and cardinals, and that they would marry into the noble families of Spain and Austria, providing spouses for illustrious names such as Charles I of England, Philip II and Philip IV of Spain, Henri II and Henri IV of France, Emperor Ferdinand II, the Elector Palatine and Mary Queen of Scots.

THE FAMILY SYMBOL You come across the Medici emblem time and again in Florence. It is a cluster of red balls on a gold background. Yet its origins are a complete mystery. Legend claims the family were descended from Averardo, a Carolingian knight who, passing through the Mugello (northeast of Florence), had fought and killed a giant in battle. During the encounter his shield received six massive blows from the giant's mace. Charlemagne, as a reward for his bravery, allowed Averardo to represent the dents as red balls on his coat of arms. Others say the balls (*palle*) had less exalted origins: that they were pawnbrokers' coins, or medicinal pills (or cupping glasses) that recalled the family's origins as doctors (*medici*) or apothecaries. Others say they are *bezants*, Byzantine coins, inspired by the arms of the Arte del Cambio (the bankers' guild, to which the Medici belonged).

> ❏ Whatever the origin of the Medici family emblem, it is interesting to note that the number of *palle* (balls) depicted in it varied. Originally there were 12; in Cosimo de' Medici's time it was seven; the ceiling of San Lorenzo's Sagrestia Vecchia has eight; Cosimo I's tomb in the Cappelle Medicee has five; and Ferdinand's coat of arms in the Forte di Belvedere six. ❏

COSIMO DE' MEDICI (1389–1464)
From humble origins (two wool workshops), Giovanni di Bicci had engineered a business that put the Medici in the first rank of Florentine

VIVET·DVX·ALEXANDER
MED·SECVLA·PER·OMNIA·

The Medici family crest – object of much historical speculation

38

society. His son, Cosimo, was to prove the greatest of the Medici. A patron of the arts, he increased his fortune tenfold and established the family's political credentials.

Cosimo (later to be known as 'Il Vecchio' – 'the old man', enabling posterity to distinguish him from later Medici also called Cosimo) took on and defeated the ruling Albizzi family after briefly leading the opposition party and being exiled for his pains in 1434. By 1458, Pope Pius II could describe him as 'master of the country … Political questions are settled at his house. The man he chooses holds office … He it is who decides peace and war and controls the laws … He is King in everything but name.'

LORENZO THE MAGNIFICENT

(1449–92) Cosimo's son Piero (1416–69) was cursed by ill health, outliving his father by only five years. Lorenzo, Cosimo's grandson, carried on where his grandfather had left off. His 23-year reign, a period of relative peace in the city (and in Italy), was to be looked back on as a golden age. A scholar and accomplished poet, known as Il Magnifico, Lorenzo was perfectly at one with this period at the height of

the Renaissance. He enjoyed country villas, and sponsored a host of humanist thinkers and writers (though he commissioned surprisingly few paintings and buildings). He was a skilled diplomat, despite occasional disagreements with the papacy (and the trauma of the Pazzi Conspiracy – see pages 74–5). Only in business, where it mattered, did he lack the family touch (both Medici fortunes and the Florentine economy were in decline during his period of ascendancy). His death marked the close of an era. 'The peace of Italy is at an end', remarked Pope Innocent VIII on hearing of his demise.

❏ 'Do not appear to give advice,' Giovanni di Bicci de' Medici told his son Cosimo, 'but put your views forward discreetly in conversation … never display any pride should you receive a lot of votes … Avoid litigation and political controversy, and always keep out of the public eye.' ❏

39

Top: medieval Florence. Below: Botticelli's Adoration of the Magi *contains portraits of Cosimo, Piero, Giovanni, and Lorenzo de' Medici*

Few periods in Florence's history have been as bizarre as the reign of Savonarola, a charismatic but fanatical Dominican monk whose dazzling sermons fired the city to moral and literal revolt before papal ire and mob rule brought his downfall and eventual execution.

EARLY LIFE On his deathbed, Lorenzo the Magnificent had sent for two clerics – Fra Mariano and a 40-year-old firebrand named Girolamo Savonarola. Few who had known the young Girolamo would have prophesied such an honour. Born in 1452, the son of a Paduan physician, he was a man unpromising in looks – hook-nosed and thick-lipped – and of uncompromising personal habits. He slept on straw or on wooden boards, ate little, drank no liquor, and rarely addressed women (except when

Fra Bartolomeo's portrait of the fiery Girolamo Savonarola

preaching). His youth passed in the study of scripture, or in the composition of religious poetry. Only his eyes suggested passion – green orbs that sometimes (according to one source) gave forth red flashes. At 23 he ran away to a Dominican monastery in Bologna, later moving to Florence's San Marco convent. The pope appointed him Vicar General of the Order in 1493.

A STIRRING PREACHER In his first sermons, to quote a chronicler, Savonarola scarcely knew 'how to move a hen'. By 1491, despite his continuing awkwardness, the content and apocalyptic passion of his preaching were drawing large audiences: 10,000 people came to the Duomo to hear his Lenten sermon that year. In old age Michelangelo claimed he could still hear the friar's speeches ringing in his ears. Savonarola's sermons, however, were not mere harangues. He believed them to be divinely inspired: 'It is not I who preach,' he said, 'but God who speaks through me.' Florence, he thundered, had condemned itself to perdition by its idolatries. Its painters made the Virgin 'look like a harlot'; its prostitutes were 'pieces of meat with eyes'; its sodomites were to be burned alive. 'Repent, O Florence, while there is still time','he warned, conjuring visions of plague, war, and foreign invaders 'armed with gigantic razors', should Florence reject the 'white garments of purification'.

SAVONAROLA IN POWER When Charles VIII of France entered Italy in 1494 (pressing a claim to the Neapolitan throne), Savonarola saw him as a vehicle of divine retribution:

'Behold! the sword has descended; the scourge has fallen; the prophecies are being fulfilled.' Lorenzo's son and successor, the ineffectual Piero, fled Charles's military advance. Savonarola, who held the terrified populace in his palm, filled the power vacuum to become, in effect, the city's ruler. Decrees and invocations flowed from San Marco: there was to be continual fasting; treasures were to be removed from churches; 'blessed bands' of children were to spy on their parents. Most famous of all, a vast 'Bonfire of Vanities' was built in Piazza della Signoria, stacked with books and board games, clothing, wigs and false beards, paintings, mirrors, and pots of rouge.

DOWNFALL AND DEATH Charles, meanwhile, had won Naples and retreated to France. Every two of his soldiers, it is said, were accompanied by a mule burdened with treasure pilfered from the peninsula. Savonarola, for his part, declined to involve Florence in the Holy League convened against the French king (an alliance of the papacy, Milan, Venice, Ferdinand of Aragon, and the

The execution of Savonarola in Piazza della Signoria: the scene depicts three separate episodes

Emperor Maximilian). Furthermore, he denounced Alexander VI, the corrupt Borgia pope, as an agent of Satan. Alexander summoned him to Rome to explain his conduct. Savonarola refused. Alexander pleaded, even offering him a cardinal's hat. Eventually, in July 1497, Savonarola suffered the inevitable fate: he was excommunicated.

By now the tide of Savonarola's popularity had turned. He always had enemies, the so-called *arrabbiati* ('the angry ones'), mobsters who derided his followers as *piagnoni* ('snivelers'). Poor harvests, plague, and war with Pisa now strengthened their hand (while excommunication chastened the Florentines). In 1498, when Savonarola ducked a trial by fire (a Franciscan idea), the mob, robbed of its spectacle, dragged the friar from San Marco. He was found guilty of heresy and burned in Piazza della Signoria. The place of execution is still marked by a commemorative plaque.

The Medici heyday lasted just over 100 years (see page 44), from the birth of Cosimo in 1389 to the death of Lorenzo in 1492. The rule of their descendants kept Florence in thrall for much longer – from the rise of Cosimo I in 1537 to the dynasty's extinction in 1737.

42

TROUBLED TIMES Republican rule returned briefly to Florence after Savonarola's execution. However, a decade of peace under Piero Soderini, assisted by Machiavelli, proved to be the calm before the storm. In 1512, Florence found itself France's only Italian ally against the combined papal and Spanish armies. Defeat was swift, and was followed by the return of Giuliano de' Medici – Lorenzo's vicious son – and the syphilitic Lorenzo, Duke of Urbino – a grandson of Lorenzo the Magnificent. Real control of the city, however, now lay with Lorenzo the Magnificent's second son, Giovanni, better known as Pope Leo X.

MEDICI POPES The papal account had long been the mainstay of Medici fortunes. What better way to secure it, therefore, than by creating a Medici pope? Plans for just such an eventuality had preoccupied the Medici for years. In the 1470s, for example, bribery and diplomacy had seen the eight-year-old Giovanni ordained. Similar tactics five years later had bought him a cardinal's hat (at 13 he was the youngest cardinal in history). Given his route to success, it was heartening to find that Giovanni, for all his jollity and love of pleasure, was not entirely without papal merit. On assuming office in 1513, following the death of Julius II, he launched his pontificate with the cry 'God has

given us the papacy. Let us enjoy it!' He proved as good as his word. He patronised the arts, threw lavish feasts, and generally ran papal (and Medici) finances into the ground. He 'could no more save a thousand ducats', wrote a friend of Machiavelli, 'than a stone could fly through the air'. While free-spending, he was also shrewd. Into a Curia packed with Medici supporters – 31 new cardinals were created – he launched Giulio de' Medici (previously Archbishop of Florence), the illegitimate son of Lorenzo the Magnificent's brother, Giuliano (murdered in the Pazzi Conspiracy – see pages 74–5).

In 1523, after the brief rule of Adrian VI (1522–3), Giulio duly

Top: grotto in the gardens of Cosimo I's Palazzo Pitti.
Right: Giovanni de' Medici, Pope Leo X

became Pope Clement VII, reigning until his death in 1534. Like Leo before him, Clement VII ruled Florence from Rome, and two thoroughly unattractive Medici bastards were used as stooges – Ippolito and Alessandro (the latter probably Clement's son). The sack of Rome by Charles V's imperial army in 1527, however, destroyed Medici papal ambitions at a stroke. With Clement powerless and humiliated, Florence rid itself of the Medici – only for them to return when Charles and Clement made peace in 1529. Alessandro, created the first Duke of Florence, was married to Charles's bastard daughter, Margaret of Parma. The marriage, an obviously political affair, proved a prelude to Florence's subsequent role as a minor supporting actor to the main players, Austria and Spain.

COSIMO I After Alessandro was murdered by a distant cousin in 1537, the city elders and their imperial puppeteers fished around for a suitably pliable replacement. No directly descended Medici figurehead being available, they chose Cosimo, descended from Cosimo de' Medici's brother via an obscure branch of the family tree. In the event, Cosimo I, as he was known, turned out to be more than they bargained for, proving

determined to remain his own man. More than 30 years of autocratic and conceited rule under the thumbs of foreign powers saw him take the title of Grand Duke of Tuscany in 1570.

THE BEGINNING OF THE END
Cosimo I was succeeded by two sons, Francesco I and Ferdinando I, both more or less capable and honourable rulers. They were also, in the family tradition, inveterate collectors and patrons. Under them, universities were founded and the port of Livorno was created; they sponsored the work of Galileo and promoted the exploratory voyages of Amerigo Vespucci into the New World. Sadly, their successors began the dynasty's steady decline: the sickly Cosimo II and the cultured but ineffectual Ferdinando II presided over a period of failing trade and dwindling prestige. The eccentric and foolish Cosimo III was succeeded in 1723 by Gian Gastone – the decadent and debauched last male member of a once-great dynasty. He died without an heir in 1737. Fortunately for the future of Florence, his sister Anna Maria Luisa bequeathed the entire Medici estate to the city in perpetuity.

The city of Florence as it appeared on a map of 1830

43

FIRENZE

1 Porta S. Gallo
2 P.ta Pinti
3 P.ta alla Croce
4 P.ta S. Niccolo'
5 Forte di Belvedere
6 P.ta Romana
7 P.ta S. Frediano
8 Porticciola
9 P.ta al Prato
10 Fortezza da Basso
11 Piazza S. Marco
12 P.za S. Maria Novella
13 P.za del Duomo
14 P.za S. Croce
15 P.za del Gran Duca
16 Ponte alla Carraja
17 P.ta S. Trinita
18 P.te Vecchio
19 P.te alle Grazie
20 Piazza dei Pitti
21 Arno Fiume

1 Porta Nuova
2 P.ta Lucchese
3 P.ta alle Piagge
4 P.ta Fiorentina
5 P.ta Mare
6 Piazza del Duomo
7 P.za de' Cavalieri
8 P.za S. Caterina
9 Il Bagno
10 Ponte a Mare
11 P.te di Mezzo
12 P.ta alla Fortezza
13 Piazza S. Silvestro
14 P.za S. Martino
15 Fortezza
16 Arno Fiume

Giovanni di Bicci (1360–1429)

Cosimo (il Vecchio) (1389–1464)

Lorenzo (1395–1440)

Piero (il Gottoso) (1416–69)

Pierfrancesco (1431–77)

Lorenzo Il Magnifico (1449–92)

Giuliano (1453–1478)

Lorenzo (1463–1503)

Giovanni (1467–1514)

Giulio (Pope Clement VII) (1478–1534)

Pier Francesco (1487–1525)

Giovanni delle Bande Nere (1498–1527)

Piero (1471–1503)

Giovanni (Pope Leo X) (1475–1521)

Giuliano Duke of Nemours (1478–1516)

Lorenzaccio (1514–47)

Cosimo I (1519–74)

Lorenzo Duke of Urbino (1492–1519)

Francesco I (1541–87)

Ferdinando I (1549–1609)

Caterina (1519–89) m. Henry II of France

Alessandro (1510–37)

Maria (1573–1642) m. Henry IV of France

Cosimo II (1590–1621)

Louis XIII of France (1601–43)

Henrietta Maria (1609–69) m Charles I of England

Ferdinando II (1610–70)

Leopoldo (1617–75)

Cosimo III (1642–1723)

Gian Gastone (1671–1737)

Anna Maria Luisa (1667–1743)

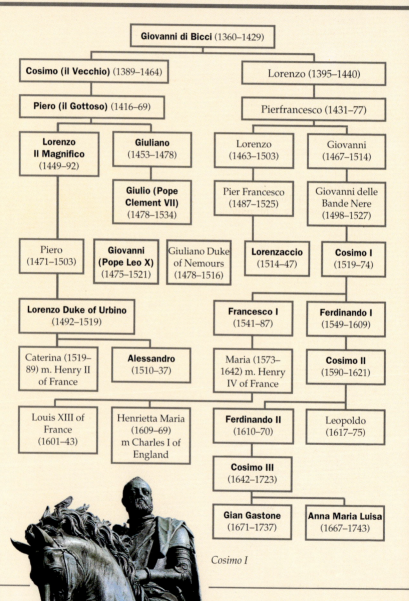

Cosimo I

After almost 350 years of direct and indirect Medici rule, Florence passed first to Austria (by treaty) and then to France (under Napoleon). Its days of glory past, the city became a favoured haunt of foreign writers, artists and poets.

AUSTRIA In the end, Florence's independence, so often at issue, was extinguished with barely a whimper. Two years before Gian Gastone's death, when it was clear no Medici heir was to be forthcoming, Gastone's sister, Anna Maria Luisa, signed a treaty handing the Tuscan Grand Duchy to Francis Stephen, the Duke of Lorraine (later to marry the Empress Maria Theresa and become Emperor Francis I of Austria). The new incumbent positively shone by comparison with his predecessors. Under his enlightened rule, and that of his successor, Pietro Leopoldo (1765–90), Tuscany enjoyed the brisk benefits of Teutonic reform. Its administration was modernised, its religious houses were reorganised, and agricultural improvements were made (notably the draining of areas in the Maremma and Valdichiana).

FRANCE AND AUSTRIA Austria's defeat by France in 1799 brought Napoleon into Italy. His troops occupied Tuscany – though to little lasting effect – for some 15 years. Renamed the Kingdom of Etruria (1801–2), the region was placed under the control of the Infante Louis of Bourbon. In 1809, it was conferred on Napoleon's sister, Elisa Bonaparte Baciocchi. Napoleon's fall in 1814 saw the return of the exiled House of Lorraine. The 1815 Congress of Vienna ceded Elba, Piombino, and the Argentario to Tuscany. (Lucca, then still a separate duchy, was absorbed in 1847.)

Ferdinand II and then Leopold II (1824–59) continued their predecessors' reforms. The march toward Italian independence, however, was by now well under way, and the nationalist uprisings of 1848 saw

Leopold briefly exiled. In 1859, as the Risorgimento reached its climax, he stepped aside for good. A year later, Tuscany voted in favour of annexation to a united Italy.

Napoleon ruled Tuscany for 15 years until 1814

Florence's centuries-long struggle for self-determination finally came to an end in 1861 with the birth of the Italian state. Florence became its temporary capital. The city was then destined to share Italy's fate in two world wars, its artistic heritage emerging safely from the second only to be devastated by the tumultuous flood of 1966.

46

MOMENT OF GLORY Proclaiming the Italian state was one thing. Creating it was another, for Rome, its natural capital, was still in the hands of the papacy, defended by a garrison of French troops. In 1865, therefore, Florence became the country's provisional capital. King Vittorio Emanuele (1869–1947) moved into the Palazzo Pitti, and the Italian Parliament was installed in the Palazzo Vecchio together with the country's Foreign Ministry. The honour was to be short-lived. When France was defeated in the Franco-Prussian war of 1870, its Rome-based troops were withdrawn from papal sentry duty. Italian troops made a ceremonial entry into Rome and within a few months the city had taken over from Florence as capital.

TWO WORLD WARS World War I had a devastating effect on Italy. War memorials are poignant features of even the smallest Tuscan villages. After the war, when economic and political turmoil ushered in Mussolini and Fascism, Florence appeared to rediscover the enmities of old. Florentine Fascists, it seems, were some of the country's most

The Ponte Vecchio – a landmark that has survived floods, wars, and seven centuries of political turmoil

vociferous. Yet, at the same time, Florence proved an intellectual centre of anti-Fascism, and when the chance came to fight, Tuscany's hilltowns provided some of the country's strongest partisan bands.

As World War II unravelled, the battle for Italy became one of grinding attrition, and step-by-step advance in the face of a determined and well-organised German retreat. In its wake the country's artistic heritage came under severe threat. The great abbey of Monte Cassino (between Rome and Naples) had already been destroyed. Rome, however, had been saved, thanks to its status as an 'open' or demilitarised city. Hopes that the same could be achieved in Florence proved to be in vain. The Arno in general, and Florence in particular, were simply too important as strategic redoubts to be surrendered without a fight.

The American 5th Army took Rome in June 1944. As it marched on Florence, the Nazis made plans to remove as many works of art as possible to Germany (they failed only because of a shortage of trucks). Ludwig Heydenreich, director of the Kunsthistorisches Institut (the body overseeing the city's treasures), still had to fight bravely to keep works from falling into the hands of Goering and Himmler's SS. Parachutists under Adolf Fuchs were charged to slow the Allied advance

Some of the thousands of catalogues and manuscripts damaged by the 1966 flood

by mining the Arno's bridges and their main approaches. All were dynamited on 4 August except the Ponte Vecchio – spared, it appears, on Hitler's direct orders.

TO THE PRESENT DAY The flood of 1966 (see pages 130–1) inflicted more damage in a day than had been suffered during four years of war. Florentines, backed by a massive international effort, rallied magnificently in a valiant attempt to repair the city and its works of art. It was perhaps the first time this century that Florence had been obliged to take stock of its future. Recently, though, Florence has been forced to look to its laurels with increasing frequency. Measures to combat pollution and congestion, for example, were introduced in 1988, though not without considerable procrastination. Still more soul-searching now seems certain in the light of the city's overdependence on tourism (see pages 24–5). Florentines must also cast a wry eye over the turmoil that periodically convulses Italy's body politic. The death of a political system, after all, is something the Florentines have lived through – and survived – time and again during their city's troubled but ultimately triumphant history.

Florence

OPENING TIMES
Of all Florence's potential problems, juggling opening times will cause you the most headaches. To avoid disappointment, double-check all the opening times before starting a day's sightseeing. Visit the tourist office at Via Cavour 1r (a minute from the Duomo) to obtain a copy of the *Orario di Apertura dei Principali Musei e Monumenti*, a list of current hours and prices. Most museums close on Sunday afternoon and all day Monday. To confuse matters, however, some close on Tuesday or Wednesday instead. (See pages 268–9.)

The tower of the Palazzo Vecchio

Florence orientation

Its compact size and dense concentration of 'sights' means there is no obviously useful way to compartmentalise Florence into manageable chunks for the visitor. The city has few 'old quarters' such as might be found in Rome or Venice. Even in the Middle Ages Florence was only roughly divided into four districts (known as *rioni*). It is the Arno that really defines the city, a watery divide that separates the **centro storico** (historic centre) on the north bank from the hillier **Oltrarno** ('Over the Arno') district to the south. This makes sightseeing somewhat arbitrary. What you see, and when, is often determined by opening times (see panel), and by which sights happen to be in the same area. Other itineraries are possible of course – Brunelleschi's churches, say, or the Florence of Dante and Michelangelo – but they require considerable planning and much legwork.

OLD BOUNDARIES Although the city has few Roman remains, Florence's tight-knit city centre still conforms to the gridiron plan of the first Roman colony (see page 30). The successive walls built by the Byzantines, the Carolingians, and by the Countess Matilda mostly followed those of the Romans, except where they paralleled the Arno along Borgo Santi Apostoli. The city's first major expansion came in 1173, when a new set of walls more than doubled Florence's metropolitan area. In the west they ran up Via del Moro and Via del Giglio, enclosed San Lorenzo (then the city's northernmost point), and continued east and south along Via dei Pucci, Via Giuseppe Verdi, and Via de' Benci. Succeeding centuries saw the building of new walls as the city grew, but today only fragments of these survive, since they were demolished in the 19th century to create the broad *viali* (boulevards) that divide the centre from the suburbs.

TACKLING THE 'SIGHTS' Since there are no convenient downtown divisions to guide your sightseeing, the best way to approach Florence is to break the city's sights into clusters within manageable areas – although the areas may have little geographical distinction. Before you begin, however, do walk around the centre to get the feel of the city. Diving into the Duomo on your first morning is too intimidating a start to any vacation. See page 250 of this book for some suggested itineraries to help you plan your sightseeing.

PIAZZA DEL DUOMO Once you are acclimatised, Piazza del Duomo makes the most obvious place to start a visit. The **Battistero** (Baptistery), the **Campanile di Giotto** (Giotto's Campanile), and the **Duomo** (Cathedral) form Florence's finest religious ensemble. Nearby lies the **Museo dell' Opera del Duomo** (Cathedral

Works Museum), home to works of art removed from these three world-famous religious buildings over the centuries. The city's second-ranking sculpture gallery, the Museo dell'Opera del Duomo, could well be combined with the **Bargello**, housing Italy's greatest collection of Renaissance sculpture (and more). A monastery church, the **Badia Fiorentina**, is easily seen at the same time.

PIAZZA DELLA SIGNORIA After Florence's religious heart, it makes sense to see the piazza that has been the city's civic centre for centuries. Enjoy its people-watching possibilities, perhaps from the famous **Rivoire** café, then take in its statues, particularly the masterpieces of Cellini and Giambologna in the **Loggia dei Lanzi**. Then visit the **Palazzo Vecchio**, home to sculptures by Michelangelo and Donatello, as well as frescoes by Ghirlandaio and several Mannerist masters. More paintings await next door in the **Uffizi**, Italy's greatest art gallery.

Also within easy reach of Piazza della Signoria are the distinctive church of **Orsanmichele** and the **Museo della Casa Fiorentina Antica** (Museum of the Old Florentine House), a lovely Renaissance house complete with period furniture. Spare time, too, for the little-visited **Museo di Storia della Scienza** (Museum of the History of Science) tucked away just behind the Uffizi.

EAST, WEST, AND NORTH Florence's greatest church, **Santa Croce**, is the starting point for visits in the eastern part of the city – to the **Casa Buonarroti** (Michelangelo's House), the Sant'Ambrogio market, the Museo della Fondazione Horne and, just across the Arno, the **Museo Bardini** (Horne and Bardini museums).

Another fine church, **Santa Maria Novella**, is the focus of more dispersed sights in the west, namely the Palazzo Strozzi and nearby Palazzo Rucellai, and the churches of Ognissanti and **Santa Trinita**.

In the north, wander through the San Lorenzo market to the Mercato Centrale, the city's covered food market, then see the church of **San Lorenzo** and the **Cappelle Medicee** (Medici Chapels) with their Michelangelo sculptures. Moving on, try and drop into the **Palazzo Medici–Riccardi** (for frescoes by Benozzo Gozzoli) and Sant'Apollonia (for Andrea del Castagno's fresco of the *Last Supper*). You can then enjoy the **Museo di San Marco** (frescoes by Fra Angelico), the church of Santissima Annunziata and its attractive piazza, and Michelangelo's majestic *David* in the **Accademia**.

OLTRARNO The shop-lined **Ponte Vecchio** leads to the Oltrarno, a quieter part of the city and one of the nicest areas to explore for its own sake. Two days at least are needed here, with at least a morning devoted to the **Palazzo Pitti's** several museums (notably the paintings of the Galleria Palatina). Close by, the macabre medical waxworks of the Museo Zoologico – La Specola (Zoological Museum) make essential, if eccentric, viewing. Among the churches, Santa Maria del Carmine stands out for the famous fresco cycle in the adjacent **Cappella Brancacci** (Brancacci Chapel), while **San Miniato al Monte**, away on its hilltop, is among Tuscany's most beautiful Romanesque buildings.

Giambologna's Rape of the Sabines; *one of several statues competing for attention with Michelangelo's* David *in the Accademia*

FOUR SLAVES

Michelangelo's unfinished *Slaves* (or *Prisoners*) – the Accademia's other highlight – illustrate the sculptor's maxim that sculpture was the liberation of a form already within the stone. Originally intended for the tomb of Pope Julius II and sculpted between about 1521 and 1523, they were presented to the Medici in 1564 and installed in the Boboli gardens. The figures may have been intended to represent the liberal arts, left 'enslaved' by Julius's death. The Accademia also houses Michelangelo's *St Matthew* (1504–1508), intended as one of 12 figures commissioned for the Duomo, but the only one that the sculptor actually started.

THE PAINTINGS OF THE ACCADEMIA

Most of the Accademia's rooms are filled with paintings, but many are by minor or unknown artists. The exceptions are Botticelli's *Madonna and Child* and *Madonna of the Sea*, and works by Perugino and Filippino Lippi (downstairs); the canvases of Pontormo (*Venus and Cupid*) and Bronzino (in the tribune); and (upstairs) the 14th-century and early 15th-century paintings, notably Lorenzo Monaco's *Christ in Pietà*.

52

▶▶▶ Accademia, Galleria dell'   *IFCE5*

Via Ricasoli 60
Open: Tue–Sat 8.30–6.50, Sun 8.30–1.50. Closed Mon.
Admission charge

Europe's first artistic academy (founded in 1563) is today visited by most people almost solely for Michelangelo's *David*. Viewing the world's most famous sculpture, however, can be anything but an unmitigated pleasure. Long lines form outside the gallery, tripping over sheets spread with fake Chanel and Louis Vuitton accessories, laid out for sale by hopeful street vendors. Then visitors are herded through battered railings into a cramped atrium desperately in need of a coat of paint. Here, finally, one of the city's highest admission charges admits you into the company of *David*, five other Michelangelo sculptures, and a collection of only intermittently interesting Gothic and Renaissance paintings.

David is not the first thing in the gallery, but it is the beacon to which most people gravitate. The image's familiarity does little to dull the statue's impact: in the chill, marble flesh its sheer size still comes as some surprise. Commissioned by the Opera del Duomo in 1501 (when Michelangelo was just 26), the work (David defeating the tyrant Goliath) was deliberately designed to symbolise the virtues of Republican Florence and its freedom from foreign and papal domination (and perhaps also its recent liberation from Savonarola and the Medici). More recently, it has come to represent the ultimate symbol of the artistic and intellectual ambitions of the Renaissance.

The 15m high block of marble that Michelangelo used, known as *Il Gigante* (the Giant), had been quarried in Carrara 40 years earlier. Not only was it thin and riddled with cracks – adding a technical challenge which Michelangelo relished – it had also been partly spoiled by earlier sculptors (including Agostino di Duccio) and offered to other artists such as Andrea Sansovino and Leonardo da Vinci. Once in Michelangelo's hands, however, the crude stone was transformed, in just three years, into a work which, with the Rome *Pietà* of six years earlier, was to establish Michelangelo's reputation as the foremost sculptor of his day.

Its masterpiece completed, Florence was left with the problem of how and where it might be displayed it. Thirty leading artists were asked to select a site, among them Leonardo, Botticelli, Filippino Lippi, Perugino, Sansovino, and Andrea della Robbia. Leonardo and Botticelli favoured the Loggia dei Lanzi (see page 86); others suggested a plinth in front of the Duomo. In the end the statue was finally placed in Piazza della Signoria (see panel). Here it remained until 1873, when it was removed to the specially built tribune in the Accademia where it is now displayed. Before its initial installation, the statue remained under wraps while a skirt of copper leaves was prepared, to spare citizens' blushes. This is now long gone, along with the gilding of the hair and of the band across the chest, which has been worn away by sun and rain during the centuries the work spent outside.

David, a statue of great strength and poise, was always intended as a piece of outdoor public sculpture rather than for indoor display. This perhaps explains the over-large head and hands, which emphasise its monumental effect. Just by discouraging the admiration of beauty for its own effect, Michelangelo succeeds in focusing more attention on David's character – 'on heroic conception of the human will.' The statue's lack of identifying props may have served the same purpose – compare the obvious sling and severed head of Donatello's *David* in the **Bargello** (see page 58).

MOVING *DAVID*
'The marble giant was taken out of the Opera del Duomo ... at 8 pm ... they had to break down the wall above the door to allow it through. During the night stones were thrown at the giant [by supporters of the Medici], therefore it was necessary to keep watch ... It was moved along by 40 men ... bound in an erect position, and suspended so that it did not touch the ground ... Beneath it were 14 greased beams, which were changed from hand to hand ... it took four days to reach the piazza, arriving on the 18th June ...They then laboured until 8th July to place it on the ringhier'. Luca Landucci, *Diario Fiorentino* (1504)

53

The 'heroic conception of the human will': Michelangelo's David

Map

Stazione Centrale di
Santa Maria Novella

PIAZZA DELLA STAZIONE

VIA SANTA CATERINA

VIA DELLA SCALA

Chiostri di
Santa Maria
Novella

Santa Maria
Novella

PIAZZA SANTA MARIA NOVELLA

VIA FAENZA

PIAZZA DELL' UNITA ITALIANA

VIA DEL GIGLIO

VIA DEI PANZANI

Mercato
Centrale

San
Lorenzo

Cappelle
Medicee

PIAZZA MADONNA DEGLI ALDOBRANDINI

Palazzo
Medici-
Riccardi

VIA CAVOUR

VIA RICASOLI

VIA DEI PUCCI

VIA DE' MARTELLI

Biblioteca
Laurenziana

VIA DE' CERRETANI

Museo dell'
Opera del
Duomo

VIA PALAZZUOLO

BORGO OGNISSANTI

Ognissanti

PIAZZA OGNISSANTI

VIA DELLA PORCELLANA

VIA DE' FOSSI

VIA DELLA SPADA

San
Pancrazio

Palazzo
Rucellai

Palazzo
Larderel

VIA DELLA VIGNA NUOVA

VIA DEL PURGATORIO

VIA DEL PARIONE

VIA DEL MORO

Palazzo
Corsini

PIAZZA C. GOLDONI

VIA DE' BANCHI

VIA DEI RONDINELLI

VIA DE' TORNABUONI

VIA DELLE BELLE DONNE

Palazzo
Strozzi

VIA DEGLI STROZZI

VIA DE' PECORI

Battistero

Duomo

Campanile

PIAZZA DEL DUOMO

SAN GIOVANNI

Loggia del
Bigallo

PIAZZA DELLA REPUBBLICA

Poste

PIAZZA DAVANZATI

VIA PORTA ROSSA

Santa
Trinita

PIAZZA SANTA TRINITA

Museo
della Casa
Fiorentina
Antica

Palazzo
di Parte
Guelfa

VIA VACCHERECCIA

VIA DI SANTO SPIRITO

Arno

LUNGARNO CORSINI

PONTE ALLA CARRAIA

Palazzo
Spini
Ferroni

PONTE S. TRINITA

LUNGARNO ACCIAIUOLI

Santi
Apostoli

VIA PORT S. MARIA

LUNGARNO GUICCIARDINI

Ponte
Vecchio

Santo
Stefano

Galleria degli
Uffizi

PIAZZALE DEGLI UFFIZI

Palazzo
Vecchio

PIAZZA DELLA SIGNORIA

Mercato
Nuovo

Loggia
dei Lanzi

Orsanmichele

San Martino
del Vescovo

Casa
di Dante

Badia
Fiorentina

San Firenze

VIA DEL PROCONSOLO

VIA DEL CORSO

Santa
Margherita
de' Cerchi

Palazzo
Salviati

VIA DEL CALZAIUOLI

VIA DEI SPEZIALI

CALIMALA

VIA CALIMARUZZA

VIA DELLA CONDOTTA

VIA VECCHIETTI

VIA DE' SASSETTI

100   200 m
100   200 yards

Walk

The heart of the city

A good introduction to the city's main streets and piazzas, taking in several of the smaller churches and palaces, quiet lanes of artisans' workshops, and the great church of Santa Maria Novella (2km; allow 1 hour).

Start at Piazza del Duomo, one of Florence's three main piazzas and the city's religious heart. The **Duomo**▶▶ (pages 76–81) and the **Battistero**▶▶▶ (pages 60–2) are among some of Italy's most familiar landmarks. Walk south on the pedestrianised Via dei Calzaiuoli, passing the distinctive church of **Orsanmichele**▶▶ (pages 110–11) to reach **Piazza della Signoria**▶▶▶ (pages 126–7), the second of the big piazzas and the city's civic forum since medieval times. Leave the

square on Via Vacchereccia and turn right, then left onto Via Porta Rossa. From here you can glimpse Piazza della Repubblica, third of the piazzas, a dour 19th-century creation carved out over the heart of the old Roman city. On Via Porta Rossa stands the Palazzo Davanzati, now home to the **Museo della Casa Fiorentina Antica**▶▶ (pages 90–1), an excellent introduction to medieval Florence. A short distance beyond it is the church of **Santa Trinita**▶▶ (page 154). Take Via del Parione, to the right of Santa Trinita, then the first or second alley on the right to emerge on Via del Purgatorio, turning left onto Via della Vigna Nuova. The elegant façade of the **Palazzo Rucellai**▶ (pages 120–1) faces you at the end of Via del Purgatorio. Cross Piazza Goldoni, beside the Arno, and walk up Borgo Ognissanti to see the church after which the street is named, **Ognissanti**▶ (page 109). Walk up Via della Porcellana, a street of artisans' workshops, and turn right at the end to emerge in the huge piazza fronting the Gothic **Santa Maria Novella**▶▶▶ (pages 148–53).

▶ Badia Fiorentina
IFCE3

Via del Proconsolo – Piazza San Firenze
Open: Mon–Sat 5–7pm, Sun 7.30–11am. Admission free

Restorations in the Badia, Florence's oldest monastery, mean you may have to make do with a view of its façade and beautiful campanile, one of the city skyline's most distinctive landmarks. The Benedictine abbey was founded in 978 by Willa, the widow of Umberto, Margrave of Tuscany, in memory of her husband, and later re-endowed by their son, Ugo (see panel). The abbey was the city's focal point for centuries, its bell tolled the divisions of the Florentine day and its cells housed one of Florence's earliest hospitals, established in 1031. In 1285, it was rebuilt along Cistercian Gothic lines, probably under the eye of Arnolfo di Cambio, architect of the Duomo and the Palazzo Vecchio. The hexagonal campanile was completed between 1310 and 1330, its base Romanesque, its delicate upper registers more Gothic.

Inside, the church is something of a disappointment, the result of a baroque remodelling inflicted during the 17th century. Two outstanding works of art survive, however – Filippino Lippi's *The Madonna Appearing to St Bernard* (1485), left of the entrance (currently on Via del Proconsolo), and the tomb of Count Ugo (1481) by Mino da Fiesole, close to Lippi's *Madonna* on the transept's left wall. The figure of Ugo, who died in 1001, lies above his tomb, hands calmly folded, the edge of his cloak hanging casually over the edge of his marble plinth.

Also well worth seeing is the **Chiostro degli Aranci**, a two-storey cloister entered by way of a staircase through a door off the right-hand side of the choir (as you face the choir). It contains a lovely series of frescoes on the life of St Benedict, painted by an unknown hand around 1440.

THE BADIA AND DANTE
The Badia is one of only three Florentine churches mentioned by Dante. He alludes to the Badia's bell and remembers gazing on Beatrice here. Boccaccio also used the church to deliver celebrated lectures on the *Divine Comedy*.

VISIONARY WARNING
Ugo's generosity to the Badia was not entirely philanthropic. The story goes that he experienced a vision of 'black and deformed men ... tormenting others with fire and hammer ... damned souls all'. He was told that his own soul was condemned to similar pains 'by reason of his worldly life, unless he should repent'. Ugo took the hint, sold his family lands in Germany, and endowed the Badia and six other Tuscan monasteries.

The Badia (to the left) and the Bargello

55

Florence

56

A TOUGH JOB
The post of *Podestà* was created in 1193 to bring an unbiased governing magistrate to arbitrate in the violent internal feuds then threatening to tear Florence apart. Elected for just one year, the incumbent was always a 'foreigner' and supposedly above local political machinations. He had to hail from a town at least 80km from the city.

▶▶▶ Bargello, Museo Nazionale del   *IFCE3*

Via del Proconsolo 4
Open: Tue–Sun 8.30–1.50, plus same hours 1st, 3rd and 5th Mon, and 2nd and 4th Sun of the month. Admission charge

Behind its fortress-like walls, the Bargello shields Italy's greatest collection of Renaissance sculpture. This museum is second only to the Uffizi in its importance – an essential morning's viewing on any Florentine itinerary. Sculpture aside, it also devotes a surprising amount of space to the decorative arts, its collection ranging from enamels, majolica, and ivories to carpets, tapestries, silverware, glassware and paintings.

The museum building – all bristling towers and battlements – was Florence's earliest public palace (1255–1350), and the first seat of the city's government. Its tower and airy courtyard were a model for the **Palazzo Vecchio** (see pages 122–3). Initially home to the *Capitano del Popolo*, a post created just before the palace was built (see panel opposite), the building was given over to the *Podestà* (chief magistrate) in 1261, when it also became the city's main law court. When the Medici abolished the post of *Podestà* (in 1574), the palace passed to the chief of police, and served as a prison, torture chamber, and place of execution. It continued as a prison until 1859, though torture and execution were abolished in 1786. The Bargello became a museum in 1865.

The first floor The Bargello spreads over three floors and its ground plan is rather confusing at first glance. In fact, the key sculptures reside in just two rooms (on the first and second floors), and in a delightful courtyard – a fine spot to escape the crowds clustered around the first-floor masterpieces. To join the fray, turn right from the ticket hall into the main hall, a room whose open-plan scheme and generously spaced exhibits make a pleasant change from some of the city's dustier and more claustrophobic museums. The modern setting dates from the 1966 flood, when the whole floor was covered in 4m of water.

Room 1 concentrates on the late-Renaissance works of Michelangelo, Giambologna, and Benvenuto Cellini and their followers. The works are arranged almost at random, encouraging pleasantly casual inspection. Most people head for Michelangelo's sculptures – three dramatically contrasting works whose variety vividly illustrates the sculptor's versatility. Most delicate is the *Madonna and Child* tondo (1503–5), half-finished except for a slight polish to the Virgin's cheeks and forehead. It represents a fine example of *sciacciato*, or low relief, a technique in which subtlety of line is more important than the depth of a sculpture. Notice the more rounded but less effective treatment of the same subject by Rustici, whose tondo is placed behind Michelangelo's to provide a telling contrast. The drunken

A stained-glass stemma (coat of arms) from the Bargello

The Bargello's airy court-yard has been a showcase for numerous statues since it became a national museum in 1865

SLAUGHTER OUTSIDE THE BARGELLO

The Bargello has seen many dark deeds. Augustus Hare, a biographer and travel writer (1792–1834), described the events of 1 August, 1343. 'The Duke of Athens had taken refuge in the fortress, and the members of the noble Florentine families … who had suffered from his tyranny were besieging him. They demanded, as the price of his life, that the Conservatore Guglielmo d'Assisi and his son, a boy of 18, who had been the instruments of his cruelty, should be given up to them. Forced by hunger, he caused them to be pushed out of the half-closed door to the populace, who tore them limb from limb, hacking the boy to pieces first before his father's eyes, and then parading the bloody fragments on their lances through the streets.' *Florence* (1834)

Bacchus (ca1497), loutish and soft-bellied, was Michelangelo's first large free-standing statue, a character piece carved in Rome. The tipsy tilt of the head and the lurching shoulders are as convincing a portrayal of drunkenness as you could find. Still more impressive is the powerful *Brutus* (1539–40), a much later work and Michelangelo's only known portrait bust. Perhaps intended as a celebration of republicanism, it was carved after the assassination of the tyrannical Alessandro de' Medici.

Other highlights of the room include Giambologna's famous *Mercury* (1564), a sublime study in speed, from pointed finger to discreetly winged feet. Lithe, slim, and full of athletic grace, the figure has been copied for centuries as the definitive interpretation of the subject. The same sculptor's *Victory of Florence over Pisa* (1570), by contrast, is heavy in the extreme. Cellini's many works include several small statuettes; a model for the infamous *Perseus* (see page 86); and a bust of Cosimo I, his first work in bronze (on the entrance wall).

Also eye-catching, if only for their scale, are Bandinelli's statues of Adam and Eve, deemed unsuitable for the Duomo, for which they were designed; two statues by Ammannati – one standing, one reclining – designed for the Nari tomb in Santissima Annunziata (but never installed because of Bandinelli's jealous opposition); and Ammannati's erotic *Leda and the Swan*, inspired by a picture of the subject that was painted by Michelangelo but later destroyed.

From the exit, enter the sunny courtyard, once site of the Bargello's gallows but now crammed with sculptural fragments and the coats of arms (*stemmi*) of the palace's successive *Podestà*. Cross over to the small **Room 2**, whose

THE PEOPLE'S CHOICE

The *Capitano del Popolo* – a post created in 1250 – performed a similar role to the Podestà. Also elected for a year from a distant city, he had the dual task of safeguarding middle-class interests against the aristocracy, and of commanding the local militia, an often unruly body raised predominantly from the city's working population. He was helped by two councils, one of 90 men, the other of 300.

A ROGUES' GALLERY

Paintings of executed criminals were commissioned to decorate the Bargello's tower and courtyard walls. Cosimo de' Medici commissioned Andrea del Castagno to paint the Albizzi, a family hanged for subversion. According to Vasari, the artist showed them 'in the strangest attitudes … infinitely varied and exceedingly fine'. The works – 'a perfect wonder' – earned Andrea the nickname *Andrea degli Impiccati* (Andrea of the Hanged Men). Botticelli painted the Pazzi conspirators (at a rate of 40 florins a corpse), as did Leonardo da Vinci, who drew Bernardo Baroncelli, one of the plotters, noting the cadaver's 'turquoise blue jacket' and 'black satin vest' as it swayed from a Bargello window.

PALAZZO PAZZI-QUARATESI

Based on designs by Brunelleschi, this palace lies north of the Bargello at Via del Proconsolo 10. It was built in 1462–72 for Jacopo Pazzi, who was executed after its completion for his part in the Pazzi Conspiracy (see pages 74–5). Note the dolphins on the capitals of the inner courtyard's columns, taken from the Pazzi coat of arms, and the vases, symbols of the Pazzi's right to take a flame from the high altar on Easter Sunday. The privilege was awarded to Pazzino de' Pazzi, who in 1101, during the First Crusade, was the first to scale Jerusalem's walls and plant a Christian flag in the Holy City.

cruder collection of exterior 14th-century sculpture contrasts with the more delicate exhibits of Room 1. The most impressive works are Paolo di Giovanni's vast *Madonna and Child* (on the end wall) and the figures of St Peter and St Paul, removed from the city's Porta Romana. **Room 3** is used for temporary exhibitions.

The second floor Climb the courtyard's grand staircase to the *verone*, a lovely arched loggia which provides the setting for some charming and eccentric bronze novelties by Giambologna. Created for the **Villa Medicea di Castello** (see page 170), they include a menagerie of cockerel, peacock, and vividly detailed turkey.

Now turn right to enter the immense Salone del Consiglio Generale, a glorious vaulted hall (the former courtroom) now filled with masterpieces of early-Renaissance sculpture. Here, too, the room's arrangement encourages random wandering, though the works of Donatello, star of the room, invite attention almost immediately. Pride of place goes to his *St George* (centre of the far wall), carved for the Armaiuoli (armourers' guild) in 1416 and brought here from Orsanmichele. The figure epitomises fresh-faced Christian chivalry and 'the beauty of youth, courage, and valour of arms' (in Vasari's words). In front and to its left stands Donatello's debonair *David* (*c*1430–40), the first freestanding nude since antiquity. Famously androgynous, the figure sports only a dipped, dandified hat and long boots, one of which rests on Goliath's bloodied head. Mary McCarthy described the statue as 'a transvestite's and fetishist's dream of alluring ambiguity' (*The Stones of Florence*, 1959).

Other works by Donatello include a smaller marble *David* (1408); the *Atys-Amorino* (1440), a bronze putto of unknown mythological significance (perhaps Cupid); the shallow bas-relief *St George Slaying the Dragon* (*c*1430–40, alongside the Orsanmichele St George); and the stone *Marzocco*, Florence's heraldic lion symbol (1420; see the panel on page 127). Two easily missed panels, reliefs of the sacrifice of Isaac, by Ghiberti and Brunelleschi, sit on the right wall. Both were entries in the 1401 competition to choose an artist to design the second set of doors for the **Battistero** (see page 61). Numerous other sculptures (all well labelled) decorate the walls, dominated by the blue-and-white glazed terracottas of Luca della Robbia.

The gallery's remaining 10 rooms (on the second and third floors) are explored clockwise from the rear of the Salone. Starting with **Room 7** – dimly lit and full of rugs, carpets, and tapestries – all the rooms are beautifully appointed and packed with artifacts running the gamut of the decorative arts. It would be easy to spend at least as much time here as in the four rooms of sculpture. Worthy of special attention are **Room 9**, the **Cappella di Santa Maria Maddalena** (see panel), the **Sala delle Maioliche** (**Room 12**), and (on the third floor) the **Salone del Camino** (**Room 16**), the most important collection of small bronzes in Italy. It includes works by Giambologna, Bandinelli and Benvenuto Cellini.

SANTA MARIA MADDALENA

This chapel's frescoes, once attributed to Giotto, were discovered in 1841 during its conversion from a prison cell. Among the scenes of Heaven and Hell on the end wall is a portrait of Dante (in maroon in the right-hand group, fifth from the right). The fine wooden pulpit, lectern, and stalls (1498) all came from the church of San Miniato al Monte (see pages 136–7). The striking triptych is by Giovanni di Francesco and dates from the mid-15th century. Entry to the chapel is by steps leading from the blue-and-gold vaulted Room 8.

59

SCULPTORS OF LESS RENOWN

Desiderio da Settignano (1428–64) specialised in portrait busts and low reliefs, using techniques pioneered by Donatello. Several of his busts are in the Bargello. Other works in Florence include a fine tomb in Santa Croce and a tabernacle in San Lorenzo. Benedetto da Maiano (1442–97) also concentrated on portrait busts, examples of which can be seen in the Bargello. He worked as well on bas-reliefs, the best of which adorn Santa Croce's pulpit.

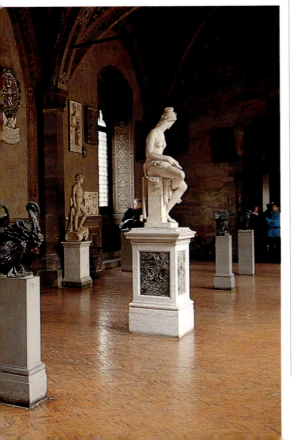

A resplendent setting for one of Italy's most important collections of sculpture

Aerial view: the Battistero from the Campanile di Giotto

BAPTISMS
In the early Middle Ages, all the children born in Florence in each year were brought to the Battistero for a communal baptism on March 21, which was New Year's Day in the old Florentine calendar. When a child was born, a bean was dropped into an urn in the Battistero, a black bean for a boy, a white one for a girl. By this means, the average annual birth rate during the 14th century was estimated at 6,000, out of a total city population of 90,000.

▶▶▶ Battistero (Baptistery)   IFCD4

Piazza San Giovanni
Open: Mon–Sat 1.30–6.30, Sun 8.30–1.30. Admission charge
Mystery surrounds the origins of Florence's Baptistery, one of the oldest and most appealing of the city's buildings. During the Renaissance it was thought to be a Roman temple to Mars, built to celebrate the defeat of Fiesole and the founding of Florence. Pavement fragments confirm the existence of a Roman building – probably part of a 1st-century AD palace – but most scholars now date the core of the building to the 6th or 7th century (the 4th at the earliest). It is first documented in 897, when it is recorded as the city's cathedral.

The exterior The octagon's largely Romanesque appearance dates from a period of remodelling (1059–1128) initiated by the Arte di Calimala, the most powerful of the city's guilds and the body responsible for most of the building's subsequent embellishments. Clad in white and green marble, the classically inspired exterior decoration – friezes, cornices, triangular window heads and grooved pilasters – was stunningly innovative in its day. The geometrical design in coloured marble was to inspire generations of Florentine architects and provide the model for countless Tuscan churches.

The interior The Baptistery's rather disappointing first impression of being bare and sparsely decorated evaporates in the light of the breathtaking ceiling mosaics. In early Christian basilicas, mosaics were arranged along the naves, or in the straightforward domes of churches such as San Marco in Venice. Here, however, where they are forced into an awkward octagonal space, their narrative scheme is difficult to decipher. It was precisely these early churches, nonetheless, that the Calimala wished to emulate, particularly those of Rome and Venice, then in the process of being restored. Venetian craftsmen, at the time Europe's most accomplished mosaicists, were drafted in to start the panels, instructing the local artists in their Byzantine intricacies.

The earliest mosaics (c1225), above the square apse (*scarsella*), depict the Virgin and John the Baptist, to whom the Battistero is dedicated. The Baptist is also the patron saint of Florence. Above them stands a complicated wheel of prophets circling the Lamb of God. Immediately over the *scarsella*, in the main vaults, is the unmistakable figure of Christ, flanked by three bands depicting the Last Supper. Detail and narrative in the rest of the ceiling's four bands are almost impossible to follow. From the inner ring outward they depict the story of Genesis, the life of Joseph, the life of Christ, and the life of John the Baptist. Parts of the last band are believed to be the work of Cimabue.

The mosaic's splendor is mirrored in the pavement, a tessellated patchwork of multicoloured marble. The site of the original font is still obvious, clearly marked in the pavement's centre by a large octagonal inlay.

Floor and ceiling aside, the interior seems to boast few artistic afterthoughts. Closer inspection, though, reveals a lower ring of granite columns (probably removed from the city's Roman Capitol); a fine mosiac frieze; a beautiful upper gallery; and – to the right of the *scarsella* – the distinctive tomb of the antipope, John XXIII (see panel).

The south doors (1328–36) Just as the Calimala had looked elsewhere for its mosaics, so they cast an envious eye to Pisa when it came to decorating the Battistero exterior. Not only was Pisa's cathedral famous for its 12th-century bronze doors, but Pisan craftsmen had recently cast similar doors for the cathedral of Monreale in Sicily. It was decided that Andrea Pisano was the man to do the same for Florence. Commissioned in 1328, the Pisan artist completed working wax models of the proposed doors within three months. Over the next eight years these were cast by Venetian bell makers, then Europe's most accomplished bronzesmiths. The result, 28 simple and uncluttered reliefs, describe the life of John the Baptist and the theological and cardinal virtues.

The north doors (1403–24) Sixty years of plague and political upheaval ensued before another set of doors could be comfortably considered. A famous competition was arranged to award the commission in 1401, a date widely considered as the 'start' of the Florentine Renaissance. The doors were to be a votive offering to spare the city a repeat of the 1348 plague. Lorenzo Ghiberti was left to do the work alone after the haughty Brunelleschi, with whom he had jointly won the competition, refused to share the task. Ghiberti proceeded to emulate Pisano's 28-panel plan – though not its speedy execution. Another 20 years passed before the reliefs were finished, a period during which Ghiberti's style inevitably matured. Something of this maturing process reveals itself in the doors, from the simple narrative of their early reliefs to the crowded, perspective-filled schemes of later panels. The scenes described are the life of Christ (upper five registers) and the Evangelists and Doctors of the Church (lower two registers).

PAPAL FAVOUR
The controversial antipope John XXIII (deposed in 1415) was lucky to be given a memorial of any sort, let alone the only one in Florence's Holy of Holies. However, the tomb of John XXIII, carved by Donatello and Michelozzo in 1427 as a reward for services rendered, is one of the city's earliest Renaissance tombs. It was through the Pope's patronage that Giovanni di Bicci de' Medici, who commissioned the tomb, became chief banker to the Papal Curia and thus laid the foundations of the Medici fortunes (half of the Medici income came from just two branches of the bank in Rome).

61

FLORENCE'S OWN MIRACLE
A column north of the Battistero commemorates a miracle that occurred as the body of St Zenobius, Florence's first bishop, was being moved from San Lorenzo to Santa Reparata. One writer tells the story as follows:
'… take notice of a little round pillar … with the figure of a tree in iron nayled to it, and old words engraven upon it importing, that in this very place stood anciently an Elmtree, which being touched by the hearse of St Zenobious … budded forth with green leaves of sweet odour though in the month of January.'Richard Lassels', *The Voyage of Italy* (1603)

62

A PISAN GIFT

Two pitted maroon columns flank the east doors of the Battistero. In 1117, the Pisans set off to conquer Mallorca. Fearful of attack from Lucca in their absence, they begged Florence to watch over Pisa. In gratitude, on their return, they offered Florence two reputedly magic porphyry columns plundered from Mallorca – whose polished surface foretold acts of treason against the state. Before making the gift, however, the Pisans are said to have ruined the pillars by baking them in embers. In any event, they proved too weak to be used structurally inside the Battistero and have remained outside.

The east doors (1425–52) Such was the success of Ghiberti's doors that he was immediately commissioned to produce another set. This second labour – when he strove 'to imitate nature to the utmost' – was to occupy him 'with the greatest diligence and greatest love' for almost 27 years. The result was the finest of the Battistero's three pairs of doors, sometimes known as 'The Gates of Paradise'.

All the panels, however, have now been replaced with copies and the originals are being restored. Several of the renovated originals are already on show in the Museo dell'Opera del Duomo (see pages 96–7). Even the copies, however, suggest Ghiberti's virtuosity. More like paintings than sculpture, the 10 rectangular panels depict their Old Testament episodes with extraordinary clarity, often weaving several narrative episodes into a single frame (see below).

Although the original panels have been replaced by copies, Ghiberti's 'Gates of Paradise' still attract the crowds

THE EAST DOOR PANELS

Moving from the top left (and then across and down) the panels depict:

1. Creation, original sin, the expulsion from Paradise
2. Cain and Abel, Cain slays Abel, the wrath of God
3. Noah's Ark, Noah plants the vine, Noah's drunkenness
4. Three angels visit Abraham, Sarah at the tent
5. Esau sells his birthright, Rebecca talks with God and advises Jacob
6. Joseph pulled from the pit and sold to merchants, Joseph explains the Pharoah's dreams
7. Moses receives the Tablets
8. Crossing the Jordan, Joshua at the Battle of Jericho
9. David beheads Goliath, Battle with the Philistines
10. The Queen of Sheba visits King Solomon.

▶▶▶ Campanile di Giotto   *IFCE4*
Piazza del Duomo
Open: daily, Apr–Oct 9–6.50, Nov–Mar 9–4.20.
Admission charge

Next to the **Duomo** (see pages 76–81) stands the 85m-high, multicoloured Campanile – 'the Duomo's fit ally', in the words of poet Robert Browning. One of the most beautiful bell towers in Italy, Longfellow described it as 'the Lily of Florence blossoming in stone'. Ruskin thought it 'the model and mirror of perfect architecture,' adding that an hour's study of its decorative reliefs would 'give you strength for all your life'.

The tower was begun by Giotto in 1334 during his reign as city architect and *capomaestro* (head of works) of the Duomo. Only the base, however – the first of its five present levels – had been completed at his death in 1337. Andrea Pisano, fresh from work on the south doors of the **Battistero** (see page 61), took over the third storey (1337–42). When he moved on, Francesco Talenti rounded things off (1348–59). Before Giotto died, he drew up detailed plans for the tower's decoration, but he seems to have given rather less thought to its 12m base, whose walls Pisano and Talenti were forced to double in thickness to prevent their collapse. Two sets of reliefs decorate the second storey, the lower tier set in hexagonal frames, the upper in diamonds. Both cycles are copies; the originals are now in the **Museo dell'Opera del Duomo** (see pages 96–7). The hexagonal panels, some designed by Giotto but all executed by Pisano and his pupils, depict Creation, the Seven Planets, the Seven Sacraments, and the Seven Virtues: the Five Liberal Arts on the north face are by Luca della Robbia (Grammar, Philosophy, Music, Arithmetic, and Astrology). The upper reliefs are also by Pisano. The niches of the third storey contain copies of the *Prophets* and the *Sibyls* by Donatello and others (originals in the Museo dell'Opera del Duomo).

Decorative detail

CLIMBING THE CAMPANILE
Though it may not offer the structural insights to be enjoyed in the cathedral dome, the Campanile has an outstanding view of the city. Notice, on the way up, the pulleys and central stays used to keep the bell ropes in place. Be warned, though, that it is a stiff 414-step climb: not for nothing is there a first-aid post at the top.
Open: daily, 9–7.30; winter 9–4.30.
Admission charge.

AN ASTONISHED AUTHOR
'Giotto's tower, with its delicate pinkish marble, its delicate windows with twisted columns, and its tall lightness … is a thing not easily to be forgotten … This evening we have been mounting to the top – a very sublime getting-upstairs indeed – and our muscles are much astonished at the unusual exercise.' George Eliot, *Letter* (1861)

DYNASTIC DECAY

Forty-nine Medici coffins were opened in 1857: 'some had been broken into and robbed, some were the hiding place of rats and every kind of vermin. In many nothing remained but bones and a handful of dust … some were in a dreadful state of putrefaction. Ghastly and grinning skulls were there, adorned with crowns of gold. Dark and parchment-dried faces were seen, with thin golden hair, rich as ever, and twisted with gems and pearls and golden nets. The cardinals still wore their mitres and red cloaks … the dried bones of Vittoria della Rovere were draped in black silk trimmed with lace, with a golden medal on her breast, and the portrait of her as she was in life lying on one side … while all that remained of herself was few bones … Anna Luisa, almost a skeleton, robed in rich violet velvet, with the electoral crown surmounting a black, ghastly face of parchment … Francesco, her uncle, lay beside her, a mass of putrid robes and rags.'
William Wetmore Story (an American sculptor, writing in 1857)

MICHELANGELO'S LORENZO

No other work 'that ever came from a sculptor's hand' was like Michelangelo's *Lorenzo*, said the poet Longfellow. 'No such grandeur and majesty have elsewhere been put into human shape. It is all a miracle: the deep repose, and deep life within.'
Outre-mer: A Pilgrimage Beyond the Sea (1833–4)

▶▶▶ Cappelle Medicee (Medici Chapels) *IFCD4*

Piazza Madonna degli Aldobrandini
Open: Tue–Sat 8.30–1.50, plus same hours 1st, 3rd and 5th
Mon and 2nd and 4th Sun of the month. Admission charge

The Medici Chapels consist of three distinct areas: the Crypt, a mausoleum for minor members of the Medici family; the Cappella dei Principi, a gaudily opulent chapel for six of the Medici grand dukes; and (what most people come to see) the Sagrestia Nuova, last resting place of four family members, two of whom are commemorated with tombs sculpted by Michelangelo. Although the chapels are part of **San Lorenzo** (see pages 132–5), their entrance is located separately in the piazza to the rear of the church.

The Crypt This dimly lit, low-vaulted space is dotted with the brass-railed tombs of many lesser Medici. Today, everything in the crypt seems suitably decorous, a far cry from 1791, when Ferdinand III piled the family corpses 'together pell-mell in the subterranean vaults … caring scarcely to distinguish one from another'. This rather unseemly arrangement lasted until 1857, when, after much procrastination, the bodies were exhumed and given a more dignified burial. The operation was enjoyed and recorded in fine detail by an American eyewitness (see panel).

The Cappella dei Principi Steps at the rear of the crypt lead up to the Cappella dei Principi, an enormous space whose extraordinarily opulent decoration has aroused much comment over the years – most of it derogatory. Lord Byron called it 'fine frippery in great slabs of various expensive stones, to commemorate fifty rotten and forgotten carcases'. Conceived by Cosimo I as a family mausoleum and begun in 1604, this was to be the most expensive project ever commissioned by the Medici. It was still draining dynastic coffers when the family died out in 1743, and finishing touches were still being added as recently as 1927.

Plans for the chapel suggest the extent of the Medici family's conceit. Its octagonal blueprint, for example, was based on the Battistero, while its interior was designed to accommodate the Holy Sepulchre, which was to be stolen from Jerusalem. This plan was abandoned only when the expedition to the Holy Land failed to accomplish the burglary. Instead, colossal slabs of porphyry and fine Roman marbles were carted to Florence, captured Turkish slaves being ordered to hack the pilfered stone into pieces of manageable size.

Everything in the chapel except the frescoed ceiling is smothered in these marbles, or with swathes of magnificently worked semi-precious stones (*pietre dure*): *verde antica*, jasper, oriental agate, alabaster, mother-of-pearl, red coral, chalcedony, and many more. The Medici's six-ball symbol is omnipresent.

The chapel's best feature is the 16 coats of arms, a series of white-backed mosaics that are ranged at head height around the walls. Each represents a different Tuscan town. Otherwise, all there remains to marvel at before leaving is the vulgarity of it all: the gloomy, mismatched colours and the bombastic, almost Fascistic, lines of the grand dukes' huge tombs. Looking around this monument to a dynasty's decadent decline, it is hard to remember that earlier members of the same family were actually responsible for commissioning some of Europe's most sublime art.

The Sagrestia Nuova A corridor leads left off the chapel to Michelangelo's New Sacristy, whose medley of calm whites and airy greys was designed as a riposte to Brunelleschi's Sagrestia Vecchia (Old Sacristy) in **San Lorenzo** (see page 134). The space contains three groups of sculpture (1520–34), two wholly and one partly by Michelangelo. On the left, as you stand with your back to the entrance, is the tomb of Lorenzo, Duke of Urbino (grandson of Lorenzo the Magnificent). Lorenzo, head in hand, is intended as a symbol of the contemplative life (see panel opposite). The figures at his feet are *Dawn* and *Dusk*.

On the chapel's right-hand side stands the tomb of Giuliano, Duke of Nemours (third son of Lorenzo the Magnificent), intended to symbolise the man of action, with the figures *Day* and *Night* below. Both dukes were minor to the point of insignificance, making it ironic that the tombs of the chapel's real stars were never completed – those of Lorenzo the Magnificent and his brother Giuliano (murdered in the Pazzi Conspiracy, see pages 74–5). Only the unfinished *Madonna and Child* of the third sculptural group was ever started. The illustrious pair are now buried in a simple tomb close to the *Madonna*.

MICHELANGELO'S GRAFFITI

Some of the faint drawings on the Sagrestia Nuova's altar walls and in a side room are by Michelangelo. He reputedly made them while hiding from the Medici in 1530 under the protection of San Lorenzo's prior. They can be seen on occasional guided tours. Inquire at ticket desk for details.

POSSESSED

' … I am become the slave of a demon. I sit gazing, day after day, on that terrible phantom, the Duke of Urbino … You can just discern the likeness of human features; but whether alive or dead, whether a face or a skull, that of a mortal man or a Spirit from heaven or hell, you cannot say.' Samuel Rogers, *Italy* (1836)

The Sagrestia Nuova

Michelangelo, poet, painter, sculptor and architect, was a consummate genius. His prodigious energy and virtuoso technique overcame the political and artistic vicissitudes of almost a century to produce some of the greatest sculpture of his – or indeed any – age.

DEFINITIONS
'By sculpture,' said Michelangelo, 'I understand an art that takes away superfluous material; by painting, one that attains its result by laying on'.

INGESTED GENIUS
Michelangelo claimed that his sculptural prowess came from marble dust in the milk of his wet nurse, a woman from Carrara in the quarry- and marble-streaked mountains of Tuscany's Alpi Apuane.

BEAUTY OR BUST
'Michelangelo detested to imitate the living person unless it were one of the most incomparable beauty'. Vasari, *Lives of the Artists* (1550)

ARCHITECTURE
'There is no question', wrote Michelangelo, 'that architectural members reflect the members of Man and that those who do not know the human body cannot be good architect'. His own architectural career began in Florence, with San Lorenzo's Sagrestia Nuova and Biblioteca Laurenziana. Here, and in his later projects in Rome – Piazza del Campidoglio and the dome of St Peter's – he laid the foundations of Mannerist architecture, by deliberately subverting classical ideals in favour of dynamism, expressiveness and originality.

Michelangelo (1475–1564) was born in the small and remote village of Caprese, in the mountains about 90km east of Florence. His father, of impoverished noble stock, was an administrator in the village. The family returned to Florence soon after their son's birth and settled there permanently.

Artistic beginnings Michelangelo's father, it seems, may have objected to an artistic career (then something of a social come down) for his son. This was perhaps the reason for Michelangelo's late apprenticeship, taken up when he was around 13. 'Why, this boy knows more than I do', remarked his teacher, Ghirlandaio, then one of the city's leading painters. Michelangelo left his studies within a year, partly because he had nothing to learn, and partly because he was showing a marked preference for sculpture (a bias that remained with him all his life).

Michelangelo quickly found himself in a charmed circle, working with a group of artists sponsored by Lorenzo the Magnificent. It was his first brush with patronage, a system whose constant demands – those of the popes in Rome, those of the Medici in Florence – were to prove a source of lifelong frustration. Many of his works remained unfinished because of it.

A flawed genius At the same time, Michelangelo could be his own worst enemy. His personal habits were 'repulsive': he never washed (on his father's advice), and when working he would only eat crusts of bread. He was consumed by worry, and desperate to accumulate property. He was also jealous of other artists: 'they want to ruin me', he once wrote, and (referring to Raphael) 'all he had in art he had of me.' Overambition also proved to be a fatal flaw. 'No particular work could satisfy the magnitude of his ambition', wrote Mary McCarthy in *The Stones of Florence* (1959).

Florence and Rome Fate, however, was no kinder, political turmoil frequently intervening to disrupt his work. One such upheaval, the Medici's exile in 1494, saw him leave Florence for Bologna. A little later he was in Rome, where he produced the Bargello *Bacchus* (see pages 56–7), his earliest surviving large-scale sculpture (c1497). A year later, still in Rome, came the work which secured his reputation: the *Pietà* (1498), now in Rome's St Peter's.

The Accademia's *David*, sculpted on his return to Florence in 1501, consolidated his position. This Florentine interlude also produced the Uffizi's Doni Tondo, one of his rare excursions into easel painting.

In 1504, he started work on murals in the Palazzo Vecchio (of which only copies survive) and also began a set of 12 Apostles for the Duomo (of which only the Accademia's *St Matthew* was ever started). Both projects were abandoned in favour of the tomb of Pope Julius II in Rome – a proposed 40-figure sculpture that distracted him intermittently for almost 50 years. Soon after he began that project came his most famous commission, the painting of the Sistine Chapel (1508–12).

By 1516 he was back in Florence, dispatched by Leo X (a Medici pope) to work under the pope's cousin, Cardinal de' Medici (later Pope Clement VII). During this period, though turning increasingly to architecture (see panel opposite), he embarked on San Lorenzo's Medici tombs (1523–33), yet another unfinished work. Chastened by the Republic's overthrow, he also helped to design the city defences before the siege of Charles V.

Poetry and architecture Michelangelo finally left Florence in 1534, spending the rest of his days in Rome. During this period he wrote the best of his 300-odd poems. He also painted the Sistine Chapel's *Last Judgment* (1534-41), its tone more sombre than that of his earlier work in the vaults.

Architecture again dominated as old age encroached: Piazza del Campidoglio and the dome of St Peter's were the two great works of his later years. Two tortured sculptures also materialised, one of which – the *Pietà* in the Museo dell'Opera del Duomo – was intended for his tomb. He died at the age of 88 and was buried in Florence's Santa Croce.

Opposite: one of four unfinished Slaves, *commissioned by Pope Julius II for his tomb*

MICHELANGELO IN FLORENCE
Sculpture: *Madonna della Scala, Battle of the Centaurs, Torso* (Casa Buonarroti); *Bacchus, Madonna and Child* tondo, *Brutus* (Bargello); *David, St Matthew, Four Slaves* (Accademia); *Lorenzo, Dawn* and *Dusk, Giuliano, Day* and *Night, Madonna and Child* (Cappelle Medicee); *Pietà* (Museo dell'Opera del Duomo).
Architecture: Sagrestia Nuova (Cappelle Medicee); Biblioteca Laurenziana (San Lorenzo).
Paintings and drawings: Doni Tondo (Uffizi); drawings (Casa Buonarroti); graffiti and wall drawings (attributed to Michelangelo; Sagrestia Nuova, Cappelle Medicee).

67

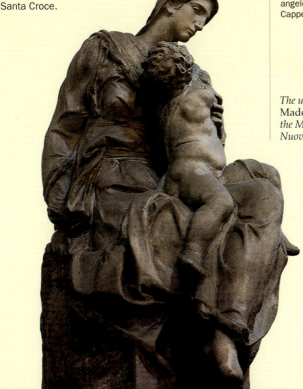

The unfinished Madonna and Child *in the Medici's Sagrestia Nuova*

*Man of action:
Michelangelo's*
Giuliano de' Medici

MORE MICHELANGELO
Among the Casa
Buonarroti's decorated
salons, the cases of
bozzetti (models) in Room
IX contain smaller works
that are attributed to
Michelangelo: a torso of a
hermaphrodite; a
fragment of a female fig-
ure (perhaps intended as
part of Giuliano's tomb in
the Cappelle Medicee); a
tiny wooden Crucifix (possibly the model for a work
the sculptor intended to
execute in his old age);
and a terracotta study for
statues of Hercules and
Cacus which, if they had
been realised, would have
partnered the famous
David outside the
Palazzo Vecchio.

► **Casa Buonarroti**   *IFCF3*

Via Ghibellina 70
Open: Mon, Wed–Sun 9.30–1.30. Admission charge
Michelangelo's house is something of a fraud, for,
although he bought the property in 1508, he never lived
here. The present house, its decoration, and its collection
of Michelangelo memorabilia were arranged by his
nephew Leonardo (his sole descendant), and subsequently by Leonardo's son, Michelangelo the Younger.
The admission charge is exorbitant, given that the collection contains only four minor works and a handful of
drawings by the master. And while the small maze of
decorated rooms is pleasant enough – full of furniture,
objets d'art, and frescoed ceilings – the house is impersonal, and does not impart the *frisson* it might have
induced had Michelangelo ever lived here.

This said, the museum is beautifully presented, its sleek
appearance the result of restoration precipitated by the
1966 flood. Climb the stairs and turn left (at the case of
swords) for the sculptural highlights. The first, the
Madonna della Scala (c1491), is a delicate, shallow relief
showing the influence of Donatello. Carved when
Michelangelo was 15 or 16, it is the sculptor's earliest surviving work. The second, the *Battle of the Centaurs* (c1492),
was executed during his period at the court of Lorenzo
the Magnificent. A more complex and tangled carving, it
already suggests the sense of the heroic and *sfinito* (unfinished) effects that are characteristic of his subsequent
work.

In the adjoining room (on the left) is a wooden model
of Michelangelo's plan for the façade of San Lorenzo,
which was never implemented Alongside sprawls an age-
darkened wood-and-wax model of a torso, part of a huge
river god, perhaps intended for the **Cappelle Medicee**
(see pages 64–5). It is the only such model by the sculptor
in existence.

Return to the swords at the top of the stairs: the room
straight ahead contains a selection of Michelangelo drawings. To the right is a room with a slender, poplar-wood
Crucifix. Found in 1963, this long-documented work was
previously believed lost.

▶ Casa di Dante

IFCE4

Via Dante Alighieri–Via Santa Margherita 1r
Open Mon, Wed–Sun, summer 9–6; winter 10–4; closed Tue.
Admission charge

Dante's supposed birthplace has old stonework, wooden eaves, and wrought ironwork that conspire to produce one of the city's most convincing-looking medieval houses. Sadly, the whole thing is a 19th-century pastiche: Dante probably never set foot in the place (though he was almost certainly born nearby, doubtless on the street that now bears his name). Before turning into the house, now a modest museum, look at the small plaque on the wall opposite, etched with buildings pertinent to episodes in Dante's life (see page 72).

The museum entrance is not under the prominent porch, but a little way down Via Santa Margherita on the left. Little of the material inside is original, or relates directly to the poet's life. Nonetheless, the modest offerings are worth a few minutes, particularly the collection of antique editions of the *Divine Comedy*. The best of these are a poster produced by a demented Milanese printer, presenting the entire work in miniature, and copies of Botticelli's line illustrations for the epic.

Outside the museum, just down Via Santa Margherita, stands the small church of **Santa Margherita de' Cerchi** (*Open* Mon–Sat 9–12 and 3–6.30, Sun, 9–12). Dante's Beatrice attended Mass here with her father, Folco Portinari, and some claim the church witnessed Dante's marriage to Gemma Donati (see page 70). In fact, the nuptials probably took place in the parish church of the Donati and Alighieri families, **San Martino del Vescovo** (see panel), positioned immediately across from the Casa di Dante on Piazza San Martino (*Open* Mon–Sat 10–12 and 3–5. *Closed* Sun).

DANTE'S SPYHOLE

At the northern end of Via Santa Margherita, at Via del Corso 6, stands the Palazzo Salviati, which is located on the site of the house owned by Beatrice's father, Folco Portinari. Its courtyard harbours the so-called Nicchia di Dante (Dante's Niche), from which Dante is supposed to have watched his beloved.

DANTE'S CHURCH

69

San Martino del Vescovo was founded in 986 but the church as Dante knew it was rebuilt in 1479, when it became the head-quarters of a charitable body, the Compagnia dei Buonomini. They commissioned the church's frescoes – *The Life of San Martino and Works of Charity* (by the school of Ghirlandaio), delightful vignettes of daily life in 15th-century Florence. The church also has two renowned paintings of the Madonna, one attributed to Perugino.

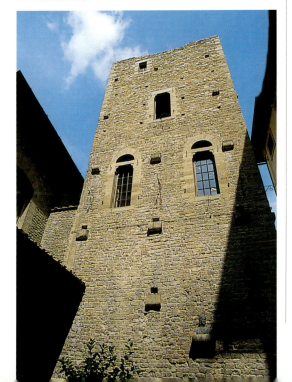

Medieval pretensions: the largely 19th-century 'Casa di Dante'

Dante (1265–1321) signed himself 'Dante Alighieri, a Florentine by birth but not by character' – an ironic allusion to the city he served as a politician but which later cast him into exile and which was to inspire some of the most bitter passages in his great epic poem, the Divine Comedy.

FIRST LOVE

Dante, at the age of nine, records his feelings on first seeing Beatrice (aged eight). 'Love ruled my soul ... and began to hold such sway over me ... that it was necessary for me to do completely all his pleasure. He commanded me often that I should endeavour to see this so youthful angel, and I saw in her such noble and praiseworthy deportment that truly of her might be said these words of the poet Homer – *She appeared to be born not of mortal man but of God.*' *La Vita Nuova* (1293)

Top: Dante mural in the Duomo. Right: a belated honour: Dante in Piazza Santa Croce

Dante was born in 1265, a member of a minor and genteelly impoverished noble family. He was educated at Bologna, one of Europe's leading universities at the time, and later at Padua, where he studied philosophy and astronomy.

Dante and Beatrice Learning was one thing; love was to be another. Dante first glimpsed Beatrice, the daughter of Florentine nobleman Folco Portinari, when he was nine years old. She was to be his lifelong muse, and the inspiration for one of Europe's greatest works of literature (the dramatic *coup de foudre* of their first meeting was described by both Boccaccio and Dante himself – see panel). Sadly for Dante, however, Beatrice was never to be his lover: when she was eight, her family had arranged for her to marry Simone de' Bardi. Such marriages, designed to cement alliances between families, were nothing new. Beatrice's began in 1283 (when Dante was 18), only to end seven years later with Beatrice's death.

Marriage and politics Dante, for his part, had also been coaxed into a pragmatic marriage, to Gemma Donati, arranged when he was 12. The ceremony – tellingly, perhaps – did not take place until he was almost 30. Once married, Dante completed *La Vita Nuova*, his first major work, and then he moved into a political career. He signed up to the Apothecaries' Guild as a 'poet', and operated on a variety of minor city councils. In 1300, he was sent from Florence to San Gimignano, charged with winning the town over to an alliance against Pope Boniface VIII. Boniface, who had designs on Tuscany, was among the most violent and vice-ridden of popes. (One of his tricks was to have the tongues of heretics nailed to doors.) Dante was later to pay a heavy price for provoking such a powerful enemy.

In 1300, the poet joined the Priorate (see pages 34–5). As one of the city's *Priori* he continued his campaign against Boniface, attempting at the same time to heal the rifts between the Black (anti-imperial) and White (more conciliatory) factions of Florence's ruling Guelph party. The division had its origins in money. Members of the White faction included prominent bankers to the imperial powers such as the Cerchi, Mozzi, Davanzati, and Frescobaldi. The Blacks, by contrast, included a roll call of the most powerful papal bankers, notably the Pazzi, Bardi, and Donati. Boniface, as was to be expected, sided with the Blacks, who eventually emerged triumphant.

Poetry and exile Dante's White sympathies and anti-papal stance were his undoing. In 1302, following spurious charges of corruption, he was sentenced – with other important Whites – to two years' exile. Most of the exiles were later able to return, but Dante rejected his city of 'self-made men and fast-got gain', wandering far and wide for several years before settling in Ravenna, where he probably wrote most of the *Divine Comedy*, which he completed just before his death.

Dante's epic of history, philosophy, science and theology, in which he seeks to bring about his own and humanity's redemption, begins on Holy Thursday in 1300. The poet finds himself in a dark wood, a symbol of his moral and lovelorn darkness since the death of Beatrice. Grace, however, in the person of the poet Virgil, appears to point the way to his salvation, guiding him through *Inferno* and *Purgatorio* (thronged with a cast of historical and contemporary characters) before finally delivering him to *Paradiso*.

Dante's exile perhaps makes it fitting that his body was never returned to Florence (though Santa Croce has a commemorative monument). Every year, however, on 14 September, the anniversary of his death, the city sends a gift of Florentine oil to Ravenna to light the votive lamps on Dante's tomb.

In a fanciful 19th-century interpretation, a wedding party emerges from the Church of Santa Margherita de' Cerchi, where Dante is supposed to have been married – but not to Beatrice

FATEFUL ENCOUNTER
Boccaccio describes the meeting of Dante and Beatrice at a party thrown by the girl's father: 'Beatrice [had] habits and language more serious and modest than her age warranted; and besides this with features so delicate and so beautifully formed, and full, beside mere beauty, of so much candid loveliness that many thought her almost an angel…Dante…though still a child, received her image into his heart with so much affection that from that day forth, as long as he lived, it never again departed from him'. *Life of Dante* (1321)

Walk

Dante's Florence

A short walk through Dante's district and the eastern part of the city to Santa Croce (1km; 30 minutes).

Start at the **Battistero**▶▶▶ (pages 60–2), Dante's *bel San Giovanni*, one of only three churches in the city mentioned by the poet. Dante was baptised here but in his day the building still lacked most of its marble veneer. The Campanile did not yet exist and work on the Duomo had only just started. To the south of the Duomo, hunt out the so-called **Sasso di Dante** (Dante's Stone), set into the wall between Via dello Studio and Via del Proconsolo. Dante is supposed to have sat here and watched the building of the cathedral.

Walk down Via dello Studio to the junction with Via dei Corso where, at No 6, the site of Beatrice's home, the

Palazzo Salviati's courtyard still boasts the **Nicchia di Dante** (see the panel on page 69). Go down Via Santa

Margherita to reach the **Casa di Dante**▶ (see page 69) and the churches of **Santa Margherita de' Cerchi** and **San Martino del Vescovo** (see page 69). Nearby, on Via del Proconsolo, pass the **Badia Fiorentina**▶ (page 55), where Dante often saw Beatrice. During the poet's lifetime the **Bargello**▶▶▶, opposite, was still being built (pages 56–9). Streets dotted with artisans' workshops lead to **Santa Croce**▶▶▶ (pages 138–43) where a monument in Dante's honour was raised in 1829 – over 500 years after his death.

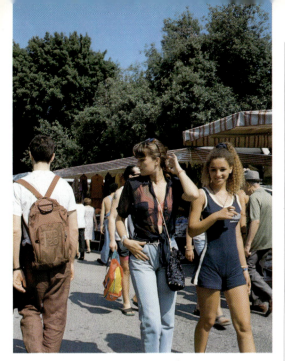

Florence's only large public park, and once a fashionable meeting place for the city's élite, the Cascine is nowadays especially popular for its Tuesday market

Cascine, Le   IFCA5

Ponte della Vittoria–Piazza Vittorio Veneto
Bus: 17c from the Duomo or the train station

Florence is not blessed with generous expanses of green space, making it unfortunate that the Cascine, its one big public park, is shabby around the edges and a long way from the centre of Florence (30 minutes' walk). It also has a well-deserved reputation as a place to avoid after dark. If you want readily available peace and quiet, therefore, make for the more bucolic pleasures of the **Giardino di Boboli** (see page 84).

This said, the park is not all bad. Mothers bring their children here, and on a summer's afternoon there are worse places to escape the traffic and enjoy a break from sightseeing. If you do decide to come here, try a Tuesday morning, when thousands of people flood in for the city's largest general **market** (see page 114).

The park is barely 100m wide in places, but stretches along the Arno for almost 3km, petering out at the river's confluence with the Mugnone. Originally a tract of wilderness known as the *isola* (island), the area that is now the park later became a Medici-owned dairy farm (*cascina*), later serving as one of the family's favourite hunting estates. Napoleon's sister, Elisa Baciocchi Bonaparte, laid it out as a public park in 1811.

Over the next 100 years the Cascine emerged as the most fashionable meeting place for Florence's social élite. Charles Lever, a visitor in 1856, observed the great jam of carriages 'side by side like great liners', noting that 'the Cascine is to the world of society what the Bourse is to the world of trade'. He also added, 'Scandal holds here its festival', a sentiment echoed by several commentators on the more salacious undercurrents of the Cascine's social intercourse (see panel).

SHELLEY AND THE CASCINE

'Yellow and black and pale and hectic red, pestilence-stricken multitudes' – Shelley's description of the Cascine's autumn leaves. The park occupies a small place in the annals of literary history, for it was here, 'on a day when the tempestuous wind … was collecting the vapours that pour down the autumnal rains', that the poet wrote his famous 'Ode to the West Wind'.

73

OUTDOOR OVERTURES

Elizabeth Barrett Browning, who came to live in Florence in 1847, hints at the Cascine's potential for sexual dalliance, talking of 'carriages alive with Florentine beauties,/ Who lean and melt to music as the band plays,/ To smile and chat with some one … afoot … in observance of male duties'. Alexandre Dumas also analysed these 'male duties': 'everyone makes or receives visitors. It goes without saying the visitors are men. The women remain in their carriages, the men go from one to another and, some on foot, some on horseback and some, more familiar, standing on the pavement, converse at the carriage doors … glances are exchanged … meetings fixed'. *Une Année à Florence* (1851)

In its execution and aftermath, the attempted assassination of Lorenzo and Giuliano de' Medici in 1478 – the Pazzi Conspiracy – was perhaps the most bloodthirsty and compelling of all Florence's murkier acts of treachery. Had it succeeded, Florentine history might have been very different.

JACOPO DE' PAZZI

Jacopo escaped Florence after the conspiracy but was recaptured, tortured, stripped naked, and hanged from the Palazzo Vecchio. After his burial in Santa Croce, his corpse was dug up by the mob (who blamed his evil spirit for heavy rains), tossed in a ditch, and then dragged through the streets.

GIULIANO'S DEATH

'Baroncelli, crying out "Take that, traitor" … brought down his dagger in a ferocious blow that almost split [Giuliano's] skull in two. Francesco de' Pazzi thereupon stabbed him with such frenzy, plunging the blade time and again into the unresisting body, that he even drove the point of the dagger through his own thigh. Giuliano fell to his knees while his assailant continued to rain savage blows upon him, slashing and stabbing until the corpse was rent by nineteen wounds'. Quoted in Christopher Hibbert's, *Rise and Fall of the House of Medici* (1974)

Pope versus Medici When Sixtus IV was elected pope in 1471, he began to distribute money and favours with a largesse remarkable even by medieval papal standards. One nephew in particular, Girolamo Riario (widely believed to be the pope's son), received special attention. Having decided to buy Imola, a town near Bologna, as a present for the youth, Sixtus petitioned his banker, Lorenzo the Magnificent, for the necessary loan. Lorenzo refused, despite the importance of the papal account, viewing Imola as too important to be handed over to papal control. Angered by the snub, Sixtus looked to the Pazzi, the Medici's leading rivals as Florentine bankers in Rome.

Further friction arose when Lorenzo refused to recognise Francesco Salviati as Archbishop of Pisa. Sixtus had ignored an agreement by which such appointments in the Republic – of which Pisa was a part – could only be made by mutual agreement. Thus, by 1477, three men (as well as the pope) were ready to challenge Lorenzo: Riario, who was now in possession of Imola but desperate for greater spoils; Salviati, outraged at Lorenzo's veto and keen to be Archbishop of Florence; and Francesco de' Pazzi, head of the Pazzi's Rome operation, and eager to usurp Medici power in Florence.

The plot Any conspiracy worthy of the name required military muscle. The man chosen to provide it – a bluff mercenary known as Montesecco – proved wary of the whole business: 'beware of what you do,' he counselled, 'Florence is a big affair.' Eventually he was won over by the promise of papal backing for the project. When the plotters met with Sixtus, approval was quickly forthcoming. 'Go, and do what you wish,' he told them, adding the disingenuous caveat 'provided there be no killing.'

It then remained to win over Jacopo de' Pazzi, the head of the family, a grizzled godfather who proved 'colder than ice' when informed of the proposed coup. He was on relatively good terms with the Medici, despite the bulwark they formed against his family's ambitions. His nephew, moreover, was married to one of Lorenzo's sisters. Like Montesecco, however, he was quickly won over by the pope's mealymouthed support.

Murder in the cathedral Lorenzo and his brother Giuliano were to be murdered while they attended Mass in the Duomo. The day of destiny was to be Sunday, April 26, 1478. The reluctant Montesecco, however, now refused to add sacrilege to murder in a place where 'God would see him.' Lorenzo's murder, therefore, was handed over

Pope Sixtus IV (opposite page) and the assassins' targets: Giuliano (left) and (below) Lorenzo de' Medici

A PAPAL HYPOCRITE
Pope Sixtus – though desiring Lorenzo's death – made sure to distance himself from the Pazzi conspirators: 'I do not wish the death of anyone', he lied, 'since it does not accord with our office to consent to such a thing. Though Lorenzo is a villain, and behaves ill towards us, yet we do not on any account desire his death, but only a change of government.' Quoted in Christopher Hibbert's, *Rise and Fall of the House of Medici* (1974)

to two embittered priests, Maffei and Bagnone. Giuliano was to be dispatched by Francesco de' Pazzi and Bernardo Baroncelli, the latter a violent Pazzi acolyte deeply in debt to the family. Salviati, meanwhile, accompanied by a band of armed men, would seize the members of the Signoria.

It all went wrong. Giuliano was killed, but the bungling priests were only able to wound Lorenzo, who took refuge in the Duomo's Sagrestia Nuova. Across the city, Salviati, separated from his troop, was arrested by the Gonfaloniere, Cesare Petrucci. An angry mob – most of them Medici supporters – was then summoned to Piazza della Signoria by the Palazzo Vecchio's famous bell. On discovering the plot, they dispensed summary justice to several of the conspirators, and then, despite entreaties from Lorenzo, indulged in a five-day rampage through the city in which 80 people were killed.

The day of reckoning After the plot's failure, Salviati's armed troop were massacred in the Palazzo Vecchio. Francesco de' Pazzi was dragged from hiding, stripped naked, and hanged alongside Salviati. The humanist Poliziano recorded that 'as the Archbishop rolled and struggled at the end of his rope, his eyes goggling in his head, he fixed his teeth into Francesco de' Pazzi's naked body'. Maffei and Bagnone were castrated and hanged. Montesecco was tortured, but given a soldier's execution in the Bargello. Baroncelli escaped to Constantinople, but was extradited and executed.

SCOPPIO DEL CARRO
Reviled by posterity for their conspiracy against the Medici, the Pazzi ironically inspired one of the city's most popular festivals. During the Crusades, Pazzino de' Pazzi brought back three flints from Jerusalem's Holy Sepulcher. At Easter these flints are used, in celebration of Christ's Resurrection, to relight lamps that were extinguished on Good Friday. On Easter Sunday they are used to ignite a dove-shaped rocket that is suspended on a wire above the Duomo's high altar. This is then sent whizzing down the wire to the piazza outside, where it sets off a cart (*carro*) full of fireworks. The size and splendour of the resulting bang and conflagration is taken as an omen, predicting the likely outcome of the year's harvest.

THE CRYPT

The Duomo was rebuilt on top of the remains of Santa Reparata, its predecessor on the site, which was demolished but not completely destroyed. Remains of the old church can be seen in the crypt (see the plan on page 79). The ruins, however, are confusing, and it is not worth paying to see more than can be glimpsed from the bottom of the crypt's steps. The most interesting feature, moreover, can be seen for free: the tomb of Brunelleschi, located to the left of the steps. Such a burial place was a singular honour for the architect of the cathedral dome.

▶▶▶ Duomo (Santa Maria del Fiore)   IFCE4

Piazza del Duomo
Open: Mon–Sat 10–5 except first Sat of month 10–3.30; Sun, 1–5. Crypt Mon–Sat 10–5. Closed Sun. Admission: Duomo free; crypt and dome admission charge

Rising above close-packed streets and houses, the Duomo's colourful exterior and orange-tiled dome form not only Florence's heart, but also a landmark that has become the city's virtual emblem. Europe's fourth-largest church, it is surpassed only by St Peter's in Rome and the cathedrals of Milan and London; big enough, in Leon Battista Alberti's estimation, 'to cover with its shadow all the Tuscan people' (*De re aedificatoria*, 1452). Something tawdry, however, hangs around its square, the result of too many people, too much traffic, and too little space. The mood is hardly lightened by the begrimed Battistero, nor by the tacky souvenir stands.

Santa Reparata The first church here was founded in the 7th century (possibly earlier) and dedicated to Santa Reparata, a somewhat obscure Syrian or Palestinian martyr. Remains of this church were rediscovered in 1965 (see panel). By the 13th century, when Florence had become a burgeoning commercial capital, the priorate deemed the old building too 'crudely built and too small for such a city'. In its place was needed something to rival the cathedrals of Pisa and Siena, something, as an edict of 1294 put it, of 'the most exalted and most prodigal magnificence, in order that the industry and power of men may never create or undertake anything whatsoever more vast and more beautiful'. The building was to be 'so magnificent in its height and beauty that it shall surpass anything … produced in the times of their greatest power by the Greeks and Romans'.

Building the Duomo The job of creating this architectural *nonpareil* was given to Arnolfo di Cambio, architect of the Palazzo Vecchio, who in 1296 proposed a vaulted basilica, polygonal apse, and magnificently domed octagon. How the dome – the largest since ancient times – was to be built, he neglected to say. Some 10 per cent of the building's cost was raised by a property tax levied on all citizens. As late as 1800 a tax of two *soldi* was still being deducted from every Florentine will and diverted to the Duomo. All fines for drunk and disorderly behaviour were also turned over to the building.

After a hiatus caused by Arnolfo's death in 1302, work restarted on the project in 1331 under the auspices of the Arte della Lana (Wool Merchants' Guild). Giotto was appointed master of the works in 1334, but spent most of his time preoccupied with the **Campanile** (see page 63). Francesco Talenti (1357–64) and a string of lesser architects then nursed the nave to completion (1380). The tribunes (apses) and drum of the dome were finished by 1418, but the problem of how to build the dome remained unresolved (see pages 80–1).

The exterior Some may find it hard to dislike the Duomo's decorative impact, with its rainbow of coloured marbles (green from Prato, white from Carrara and red from the Maremma), but the exterior has been criticised. 'A huge architectural zebra … a gigantic harlequin', said James Johnson in 1831, who abhorred the whole 'gothic and tasteless idea'. 'Like Victorian wallpaper,' and 'a cathedral wearing pyjamas' have been two more recent derogatory comments.

However, the façade was added as recently as 1887. Arnolfo di Cambio's projected frontage, only a quarter finished by 1420, was demolished in 1587 on the orders of Ferdinand I. A few statues saved are now in the **Museo dell'Opera del Duomo** (see pages 96–7.) A competition then drew five new façade designs (the models are in the same museum), but none was deemed worthy. Nothing happened for three centuries and then, between 1861 and 1868, a total of 92 plans were considered, that of Emilio de Fabris emerging triumphant. Its adoption has been generally regretted ever since.

The interior The simple austerity of the interior comes as a shock after the exterior's decorative exuberance. Its size, though, is overwhelming, the crowds that mill about in the vast open space dwarfed by doughty pillars and lofty

Detail from the Duomo doors

CARPING CRITICISM
Not every visitor has found the Duomo or its piazza to their liking. 'A temple to damp the spirit, dead or alive, by the immense impression of stony bareness, of drab vacuity,' wrote the American novelist WD Howells in 1891. 'A vast pile that has been sapping the purses of her citizens for five hundred years,' commented Mark Twain in 1869. A 'hackney coach stand and omnibus station', complained John Ruskin, full of the 'smell of variously mixed horse manure … cigars, spitting, and harlot-planned fineries …'

THE MISERICORDIA
Established in the 13th century, this hospital charity, in the manner of the Red Cross, has its headquarters to the south of the Duomo, in a building usually surrounded by ambulances. Today, the organisation has 6,000 volunteers, each of whom devotes an hour's service a week for life. During services, the members traditionally wear black hoods, so that their identities are kept secret.

MARKING TIME

Paolo Uccello's clock of 1443 uses the so-called *hora italica*, whereby the 24th hour of the day ended at sunset. This system of telling the time remained common in Italy until the 18th century.

THE SAGRESTIA NUOVA

Lined with exquisite intarsia work of the mid-15th century, this is one of the Duomo's most fascinating corners (it is also known as the North Sacristy). It was here in 1478 that Lorenzo the Magnificent took refuge during the Pazzi Conspiracy after the murder of his brother Giuliano (see pages 74–5). Above the entrance to the Sagrestia Nuova is another lunette by Luca della Robbia, the *Resurrection* (1442), his first important work in the enamelled terracotta for which he was to become famous. The sacristy doors (1446–67), easily overlooked, are also by Luca della Robbia (his only work in bronze), assisted by Michelozzo. Above them stood della Robbia's exquisite choir loft, now on display in the Museo dell'Opera del Duomo (see page 97).

DANTE AND THE DUOMO

Domenico di Michelino's painting, *Dante with the Divine Comedy*, was commissioned to celebrate the bicentenary of the poet's birth. Notice the drum of the cathedral dome, painted before it received its marble cladding. Dante stands outside the city walls, a symbol of his exile.

A rainbow of Tuscan marbles on the cathedral's exterior

78

arches. Unlike the piazza outside, where people seem to clutter the surroundings, the constant throng inside the Duomo itself only emphasises the building's epic scale. The Duomo is capable of accommodating up to 10,000 people: its most dramatic moments came during the Pazzi Conspiracy, when men were hacked down in the apse (see pages 74–5), and when huge congregations crammed the nave to hear the sermons of Savonarola (see pages 40–1).

These days there appears little to see inside at first glance, as if the exterior had taken the lion's share of the decoration. On closer inspection, however, you will see that there are several fine works of art, as well as two interesting smaller excursions, into the crypt and up into the dome. The principal features of interest are identified on the plan on page 79.

1. Tomb of Antonio d'Orso, Bishop of Florence, by Tino da Camaino (1323).

2. Mosaic *The Coronation of the Virgin* (*c*1300), attributed to Gaddo Gaddi (*c*1260–1332).

3. Clock, decorated by Paolo Uccello (see panel opposite).

4. Bust of Brunelleschi (in a tondo) by his pupil and adopted son, Andrea Cavalcanti (1447).

5. Gothic water stoup (*c*1380). The angel and basin are copies.

6. *St Blaise* by Jacopo Franchi (1408).

7. Two frescoed cenotaphs, to Cardinal Pietro Corsini and Fra Luigi Marsili, by Bicci di Lorenzo (1422–39).

8. Stained-glass windows depicting six saints, designed by Agnolo Gaddi (1394–95).

9. Bust of Marsilio Ficino, philosopher friend of Cosimo de' Medici, holding a copy of Plato's works.

10. The three apses are divided into five chapels; each has two levels of stained glass. Most of these 30 windows were designed by Lorenzo Ghiberti.

11. Fresco fragment, the Madonna del Popolo, attributed to Giotto. Heavily restored frescoes lie below the stained-glass windows in all the chapels.

12. Sagrestia Vecchia (Old, or South, Sacristy). A large terracotta lunette of the Ascension by Luca della Robbia (1446–51) is situated above the entrance. Above this originally stood Donatello's great choir loft, now reassembled in the Museo dell'Opera del Duomo.

13. Two kneeling angels holding candles, by Luca della Robbia, and a superb bronze reliquary (1432–42) by Lorenzo Ghiberti. This contains the relics of St Zenobius, Florence's first bishop (see the panel on page 61). Note: this third chapel of the central apse is often roped off for prayer and confessions.

14. Sagrestia Nuova (New, or North, Sacristy – see panel opposite).

15. Vasari's dome frescoes (1572–9), long-covered for restoration, depict the Last Judgment. Over the years many have felt them to be unworthy of the dome, and debate rages over whether they should be removed elsewhere.

16. Entrance to the dome (see panel on page 81).

17. *Dante with the Divine Comedy* (1465), a painting by Domenico di Michelino. (See panel opposite.)

18. *St Cosmos and St Damian*, the Medici's patron saints, by Bicci di Lorenzo (1429). (See panel on page 134.)

19. Large frescoed equestrian cenotaph by Paolo Uccello (1436) of Sir John Hawkwood, an English mercenary who headed the Florentine army between 1377 and his death in 1394.

20. Frescoed equestrian cenotaph of Niccolò da Tolentino, another mercenary hero, by Andrea del Castagno (1456).

21. Entrance to the crypt. (See panel on page 76.)

The largest and highest dome of its day, the crowning glory of Florence's cathedral is not only a miracle of Renaissance engineering, but also symbolises the unbounded aspirations and achievements of its era.

STRANGE SOLUTIONS

The problem of building a dome drew several eccentric proposals. One was to build it entirely from pumice stone. Another was to support it, during its construction, on a vast mound of earth, liberally seeded with small coins (*quattrini*). Once the dome was finished, the people of Florence were to be invited to dig away the earth, spurred on by the prospect of carrying away a small fortune.

MICHELANGELO'S PRAISE

Richard Lassels, in *The Voyage of Italy* (1670), comments that Michelangelo, coming now and then to Florence while he was planning the cupola of St Peter's in Rome, reputedly viewed Florence's cupola attentively and said of it: 'Come te non voglio, meglio di te non posso' (Similar to you I will not; better than you I cannot).

A miracle of medieval engineering: Brunelleschi's dome

By 1418, the cathedral – its shell complete – possessed a yawning gap (45m wide) patiently awaiting its long-projected dome. Domes were nothing new. The cathedrals of Pisa and Siena already had them, and Rome's Pantheon had stood unbowed for over 1,000 years. None, though, approached the scale of Florence's endeavour, destined to be grander than anything attempted since antiquity.

The problem of how to build it had preoccupied the committee of the Opera del Duomo for years. The members bickered constantly over the final design (signs of collapse in the Battistero further focused their minds on the project's potential pitfalls). In August 1418, in desperation, they threw the scheme open to competition.

Brunelleschi and Ghiberti Brunelleschi had been appointed engineering consultant to the Opera del Duomo in 1404, two years after being chosen as joint winner, with Lorenzo Ghiberti, in the competition to design the doors of the Battistero. The fiery Brunelleschi, who thought he should have won outright, refused to work with Ghiberti, leaving the plodding former goldsmith to create the doors alone. Revenge of sorts came Brunelleschi's way in 1418, when he defeated Ghiberti in the competition to build the dome. Ghiberti, however, proved an equally poor loser and, as a part-time consultant, joined the chorus of doomsayers who poured scorn on Brunelleschi's plans. Brunelleschi, in an attempt to counter his critics, built a scale model on the banks of the Arno. The interfering Ghiberti, however, continued to dog him. In the end, as an excuse for abandoning the dome, Brunelleschi feigned illness. His ploy had almost immediate success: Ghiberti, left to his own architectural devices, soon found the project beyond his abilities. By 1423, Brunelleschi had been formally recognised as the dome's sole 'inventor and chief director'.

The problem and Brunelleschi's solution Domes were conventionally built using a wooden scaffold, the stone shell being supported on a temporary wooden dome until the last brick was in place and the mortar had hardened fully. In Florence, however, the cost of such an undertaking was deemed to be prohibitive. It was also unclear where the sheer quantity of wood required for such a frame would be found. Worse still, the cathedral's masons were unable to calculate the dimensions and the stresses generated by such a structure. The impasse generated many suggestions, several of them remarkably far-fetched (see panel opposite).

Brunelleschi's solution consisted of two shells; a light outer covering around 1m thick, and a concentric inner shell about 4m thick. Leon Battista, a contemporary, described the engineering as being of a kind that 'not even the ancients knew or understood'. Indeed, many of its finer points are still not understood today. At its most basic, the plan copied the octagonal vaults of the Battistero, the dome being arranged around eight principal and 16 lesser ribs, bound together with horizontal brick rings designed to absorb some 25,000 tonnes of lateral thrust. No additional buttressing was required.

The main key to the scheme's success, however, was the herringbone patterning of the inner shell's brickwork, arranged in cantilevered rings, a technique that allowed the dome to support itself as it rose. Innovative tools, lightweight materials, and quick-drying mortar were also devised, some now on show in the **Museo dell'Opera del Duomo** (see pages 96–7).

Finishing touches The dome took 16 years to complete, a period during which Brunelleschi was also busy on San Lorenzo and the Ospedale degli Innocenti (see page 112). Despite these distractions, however, no detail was too small for the architect, whether it was providing the labourers with meal-kitchens in the dome (to save time), or creating a labyrinth of corridors – still in use today – to speed up movement around the shells. He even thought to provide scaffolding hooks for cleaning and repairs.

Despite such diligence, and notwithstanding the dome's successful completion, Brunelleschi endured another competition to convince the authorities that he was the right person to complete the dome's lantern. His design prevailed, but was realised only in 1461, 15 years after his death. The external gallery around the dome's base – not Brunelleschi's design – was abandoned half-built in 1515, leaving raw brickwork on seven sides (reputedly because the design was ridiculed by Michelangelo).

Take the climb to the top for a look at the dome's construction, as well as fine views

THE WAY TO THE TOP
The reasonably able-bodied (except those who suffer from claustrophobia or vertigo) should climb the 463 steps that lead up the dome. The entrance is at the eastern end of the nave's north aisle. On the way up, enjoy the views and the engineering insights offered by the corridors between the dome's two shells. Midway, an internal balcony provides close-up views of Vasari's dome frescoes and of the seven stained-glass windows designed by Uccello, Donatello, Castagno, and Ghiberti. *Open*: daily, 10–5. *Closed* Sun. *Admission charge*

EGGHEAD
At a meeting of the Opera del Duomo, called to quiz him on his plans, Brunelleschi produced an egg, saying that he alone knew how to make it stand on end. When other committee members admitted defeat he cracked its end and left it – broken, but standing. 'But we could all have done that,' they argued. 'Yes,' Brunelleschi replied, 'and you would say the same thing if I told you how I intend to build the dome.'

A detail of the exquisitely decorative inlaid marble façade of the Badia Fiesolana. The 9th-century church was Fiesole's cathedral until 1028

PRACTICALITIES
The best way to reach Fiesole is to take ATAF bus No 7 from Florence's train station, Piazza San Marco or Via Martelli, near the Duomo. Buses run every 15 minutes and take about 25 minutes to reach Fiesole. Buses drop you in Piazza Mino, where you will find the tourist office (No 37).

►► Fiesole   IBCD5

The hill town of Fiesole, to the Florentines' chagrin, is centuries older than its neighbour, Florence. Dante complained of 'that ungrateful and malignant people of old who came down from Fiesole'. Settled around 800 BC, it became an Etruscan town about 600 BC, emerging as a leading member of the Etruscans' 12-city federation. As Faesulae under Roman occupation it became capital of Etruria but, despite its relatively secure strategic position, it fell to Florence in 1125. Since then, Fiesole's attractive site and its reputedly healthy climate have made the town a favoured rural retreat, patronised by everyone from the *Decameron's* fictional storytellers, who came here to escape the plague, to the army of British expatriates who swarmed through its villas and gardens in the 19th century.

Today, reached by an easy bus ride, with promising cooling breezes and wonderful views, Fiesole is promoted as the perfect antidote to the sweltering heat and constant crowds of central Florence, only 6km to the southwest. In reality, while Fiesole's green surroundings may make it appear cooler, temperatures here on a hot August day are barely a degree lower than those of the city below. As for the crowds, Fiesole has its fair share of worthwhile sights, and is now so well established as the day-trip from Florence that it tends to be as cluttered as the city itself. This said, the streets retain something of the atmosphere of a small village, and tracts of rolling Tuscan countryside lie close by if you are prepared for some modest walking. In high summer, Fiesole is the focus for one of Tuscany's major arts festivals, the Estate Fiesolana, when concerts are held in the Badia Fiesolana and the Teatro Romano (see page 183).

Fiesole

A walk around Fiesole and surroundings (2km; allow a morning).

Start in Piazza Mino, Fiesole's central square and site of the Roman forum. The dull, 19th-century exterior of the **Duomo** conceals a more appealing interior. The Cappella Salutati has two fine works by Mino da Fiesole: the tomb of Bishop Salutati and an altar frontal of the Madonna and Child.

The 3,000-seat, 1st-century BC **Teatro Romano▶▶** and the **Museo Archeologico** lie off Via Marini. The other ruins – two Etruscan temples, baths, and defensive walls – are set amid olive groves with pleasant shady spots. *Open* same hours as Museo Bandini. The **Museo Bandini▶** (Via Dupre 1; *Open* Apr–Sep, daily 9–7; Nov–Feb, 9.30–5; Mar and Oct, 9.30–6. *Closed* first Tue of the month.

Admission charge; combined ticket with Museo Archeologico) contains a collection of terracottas, ivories and Florentine paintings.

Go up the steep Via San Francesco to visit two churches. **Sant' Alessandro▶** was built in the 6th century over Etruscan and Roman temples. Inside, its ancient *cipollino* (onion-ring) columns help make it one of Fiesole's loveliest buildings. **San Francesco▶▶** occupies the site of the ancient acropolis and contains an important 15th-century painting, *The Immaculate Conception* by Piero di Cosimo. It also has cloisters, good views of Florence, and a museum.

Either retrace your steps or take the wooded path from San Francesco back to Piazza Mino. Walk down Via Vecchia Fiesolana, past the **Villa Medici**, built by Michelozzo in 1458 and one of the earliest Renaissance villas (not open). **San Domenico▶**, once home to Fra Angelico, contains his *Madonna and Angels* (*c*1430).

Walk down Via della Badia dei Roccettini. The Romanesque façade of the **Badia Fiesolana▶** is a jewel of coloured marble incorporated into a larger 15th-century frontage.

The Fontana del Bacco

FORTE DI BELVEDERE
The fort above the Giardino di Boboli was built for Ferdinand I by Buontalenti (1590–95) to defend the city and remind errant citizens of Medici muscle. It is crowned by a three-storey *palazzina*, built in the style of the Medici villas and now used for exhibitions. Views over Florence from here are some of the best in the city. Access is from Via di Belvedere and the Costa di San Giorgio (see page 156). *Open* daily 9–8 or dusk, if earlier. *Admission free* except during exhibitions.

GROTTA GRANDE
This cave is the most bizarre of the Boboli's Mannerist monuments (constructed 1583–8). A pebble-mosaic menagerie of limestone animals struggles to escape from the cave's carved stone and fake stalactites. Copies of Michelangelo's *Slaves* (see page 52) occupy its four corners, along with statues of Pan, *Paris Abducting Helen of Troy*, and Giambologna's *Venus Emerging from her Bath*.

▶▶ Giardino di Boboli   *IFCC2*

Entrance via the Palazzo Pitti
Open: Tue–Sun: Mar and Oct 9–5.30; Apr, May and Sep 9–6.30; Jun–Aug 9–7.30; Nov–Feb 9–4.30. Closed Mon. Admission charge

Five million people annually used to visit the Giardino di Boboli, making them Italy's most visited gardens. Among the visitors were thousands of mothers and children, for whom this magnificent open space in the Oltrarno was the only green retreat in a hot and dusty city. Imagine, then, the fury when the Rome-based Ministry of Culture insisted (in 1992) that the city should start charging for admission to what had previously been a free public park. Florentines took to the streets, demonstrating in Piazza della Signoria, and with right on their side: after all, Anna Maria Luisa, sister of the last Medici grand duke, had bequeathed the entire Medici estate – palaces, paintings, parks, and all – to the people of Florence in perpetuity. It was not for Rome to dictate to them what they should do with their own property. Since then a compromise has been reached: Florentines now have special access to the gardens, while the rest of us have to pay for each visit. One only hopes (but probably in vain) that the authorities might one day be shamed into reversing a decision that does it no credit.

Initiated in 1549, when the Medici took over the Palazzo Pitti, the gardens were completed in the 17th century and first opened to the public in 1766. Today, sightseeing possibilities include dozens of Mannerist and antique statues and fountains, beautiful views, and all manner of charming incidental details. Bring a picnic, or find a shady nook for an hour's siesta.

The main path leads from the entrance, in the Palazzo Pitti's courtyard, to the Amphitheatre, at the rear of the Palazzo Pitti. This was laid out for Medici entertainments

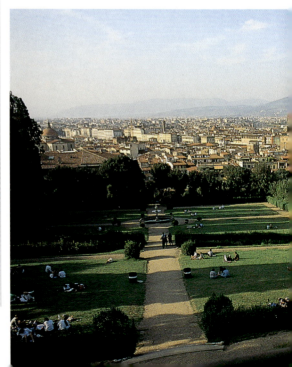

in the manner of a Roman *circo* over the quarry used to provide the Palazzo's building stone. The basin at the centre is from Rome's Terme di Caracalla; the obelisk comes from Luxor and dates from 1500 BC.

The best views are from the terrace beside the rococo *Kaffeehaus* (which serves as a bar in summer) or from the secluded and unkempt Giardino del Cavaliere perched on a bastion created by Michelangelo. Further afield, stroll the Viottolone, a statue-lined cypress avenue aimed at the Isolotto, a moated island dominated by a copy of Giambologna's famous *Oceanus* fountain.

As you leave the gardens, look for the famous statue of Cosimo I's favourite dwarf, depicted riding on a turtle, on the Fontana del Bacco (Bacchus Fountain) to the right. About 50m before it lies the extraordinary Grotta Grande, probably the work of Buontalenti (see panel).

▶ Giardino dei Semplici   IFCE5

Via Micheli 3
Open: Mon, Wed 9–12, 2.30–5, Fri–Sat 9–12.
Admission free

Open space, however modest, is to be treasured in Florence, where it is a rare commodity. The Semplici gardens provide a convenient bucolic escape after the sight-seeing rigors of the Accademia, the Museo di San Marco, or Santissima Annunziata.

Founded in 1545 by Cosimo I, the Giardino dei Semplici was created – like much else in Florence – to keep up with rival cities, in this case Pisa and Genoa, both of which possessed botanical gardens. Cosimo's creation embraced – and still embraces – a wide range of medicinal plants and Tuscan shrubs, trees, and miscellaneous flora (as well as greenhouse exhibits). Be sure also to spend some time in the less scholarly and more relaxing surroundings of the garden's original lawns and avenues.

UNIVERSITY MUSEUMS

A visit to the Giardino dei Semplici could easily be combined with a look at three of the city's smaller museums, all at present entered from a courtyard cluttered with temporary huts, cycles, and student mopeds at Via Giorgio La Pira 4, but destined to move eventually to a new site on Via Circondaria.

The **Museo Botanico** is Italy's foremost botanical collection. Its 4 million exhibits include some beautiful wax and plaster models, and plants collected by Charles Darwin on his first major voyage. The museum also contains one of the world's oldest herbariums. *(Closed temporarily.)*

Pride of place in the dowdy **Museo di Mineralogia** goes to a Brazilian topaz weighing 150kg or 755,000 carats, a monster that dwarfs Tuscany's endemic minerals (mainly from Elba) and the Medici's worked-stone trinkets – vases, snuff boxes, and the like. (tel: 216 939; *Open* Mon–Fri 9–1. Sat by appointment only. *Closed* Sun. *Admission free.*)

The **Museo di Paleontologia** contains one of Italy's best fossil collections, but is probably not for the casual visitor – unless you want to see prehistoric elephant skeletons dredged up from the Arno Valley. (*Open* Tue, Wed, Thu and Sat, 9–1; Mon 2–6. *Admission free.*)

85

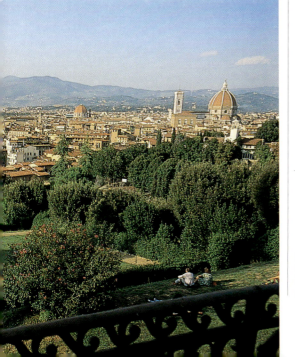

Forget the city hubbub in the green retreat of the Boboli gardens, Florence's most famous park

Cellini's **Perseus** *holds aloft the head of Medusa*

PERSEUS

A passage in Cellini's swashbuckling *Autobiography* (1558–62) describes the casting of Perseus (a feat many thought impossible). On the appointed day, Cellini stoked the furnaces so high he caught a fever. Retiring to bed, he left an assistant in charge. Not only did the bronze begin to cool too soon, but the foundry (in Cellini's house) caught fire. Resurfacing as the inferno raged, Cellini hurled all available metal into the furnace (including his cutlery and the family pewter). Two days later, when the bronze had cooled, the figure was revealed, complete except for three toes on the right foot which were added later.

LOGGIA LOUNGING

In the 15th century Alberti wrote of the 'Portico under which the old men may spend the heat of the day', adding that 'the presence of the fathers may deter and restrain the youth, who are sporting and diverting themselves in the other part of the place, from the mischievousness and folly natural to their age'.

In 1896, Augustus Hare wrote that 'hundreds of men stand here for hours, as if they had nothing else to do, talking cease-lessly in deep Tuscan tones [and] wrapped in long cloaks thrown over the shoulder'.

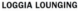

▶▶ ▶ **Loggia dei Lanzi**   *IFCE3*
Piazza della Signoria

The area occupied by this triple-arched loggia was long used as Florence's *arringhiera*, a platform from which officials harangued the city's hapless *Parlemento* (see page 35). Florence began to consider the comfort of its politicians only in 1376, a year in which numerous public ceremonies were washed out by heavy rain (San Gimignano's worthies, by contrast, had been protected from the weather by a loggia since 1338). Masons were transferred from the Duomo to work on the new loggia – hence the similarities between its arched vaulting and the cathedral's nave. The artist Orcagna may have drawn up its plans, for in its early days the Loggia della Signoria, as it was later called, was known as the Loggia dell'Orcagna. The present name dates from the 16th century, when the Swiss lancers (Lanzichenecchi) of Cosimo I's personal bodyguard were garrisoned in nearby Via Lambertesca.

For the past 200 years, a collection of statues has enjoyed the protection of the loggia. Along the back wall are six antique pieces, said to be the figures of Roman empresses. In the centre row, from left to right, are Pio Fedi's *Rape of Polyxena* (1866); *Ajax and Patroclus*, a Greek work; and Giambologna's *Hercules and the Centaur* (1599). To the left of the lions flanking the stairs stands Cellini's *Perseus* (1545), one of the supreme masterpieces of the Renaissance, made for Cosimo I. (Note that there is a possibility the restored original statue will be replaced by a copy: the original will probably reside in the Uffizi.) A bravura piece of casting (see panel), it shows Perseus (son of Zeus and Danae) standing over Medusa and clutching her snake-covered head (a glance from which turned men to stone). To the right is Giambologna's *Rape of the Sabines* (1583), carved from one of the largest pieces of marble ever brought to Florence. In extracting three powerful figures, in violent spiral motion, out of its awkward shape, Giambologna created one of Mannerism's masterpieces. The artist had no ambition other than to carve figures representing an old man, a young man, and a young woman – the statue's present name was coined later.

▶ Museo Archeologico

IFCF5

Palazzo della Crocetta, Via della Colonna 38
Open: Tue–Sat 9–2, plus 2nd and 4th Sun of the month 9–1.
Also open Mon following closing on 1st, 3rd, 5th Sun of the
month. Admission charge

Even non-specialists, such as Oscar Wilde, who spent
'two delightful hours' here in 1874, should find much to
admire in Florence's archeological museum, still the best
of its kind in northern Italy despite appalling damage
inflicted during the 1966 flood. The Etruscan collection is
especially good – a perfect introduction to Tuscany's
Etruscan sites – while the Greek and Roman sections provide a graphic illustration of the wells from which
Renaissance art drew much of its inspiration. Although
some rooms remain closed, and various works are still
unrestored, most of the museum's real highlights are usually on display.

The **first floor** is devoted to Greek and Etruscan art. The
star of the first room is the François Vase, a huge Attic
krater made in Athens around 570 BC and used to mix
water and wine. Its 638 pieces were painstakingly stuck
together after being dropped by a hapless custodian in
1900. Room II contains examples of Etruscan tomb sculpture recovered from around Chiusi and Chianciano in
southern Tuscany.

The Egyptian displays fill eight rooms on the **second
floor**. Though some consider this to be one of the
museum's less captivating areas, it contains some unique
exhibits such as 3,000-year-old hats, baby clothes, and other
everyday items. There is even a 14th-century BC wooden
chariot – the only one known in the world.

More Greek, Roman, and Etruscan pieces follow, notably
the Hellenic *Horse's Head* (Room XIII), removed from the
courtyard of the Palazzo Medici-Riccardi, where it was
studied by Verrocchio and Donatello in anticipation of their
own equestrian statues in Venice and Padua.

The same room boasts the
famous *Idolino*, a young
athlete in bronze, which is
probably a Roman copy of
a 5th-century BC Greek
original. The Long
Gallery (Room XIV)
displays some equally
accomplished Etru-
scan bronzes, notably
the *Chimera* (see panel)
and the toga-wearing
Arringatore (Orator),
whose naturalism had
a great influence on
Renaissance sculptors.
The **third floor** is often
closed – not usually a
cause for disappoint-
ment, as the rooms
here are given over to
an endless succession
of dusty Greek and
Etruscan urns.

THE *CHIMERA*
This mythical beast with
its three heads (lion, ram,
and snake) was an
ancient religious icon that
symbolised the three
seasons of the
Mediterranean's agricul-
tural year. When it was
found in 1555, however,
Cosimo I imbued it with
fresh meaning, declaring it
a symbol of the state's
enemies and the peace
he brought to Florence.
This interpretation suited
his favourite political
claim: that in assuming
power over Tuscany he
was reuniting a region
(Etruria) that had existed
in the Etruscan age.

*Left: Head of a coffin lid
in the Egyptian rooms*

87

88

STEFANO BARDINI (1836–1922)

Bardini was one of Italy's most successful 19th-century art dealers. He scoured Italy and Europe for more general 15th- and 16th-century Italian artifacts at a time when Renaissance art was unfashionable and could be bought very cheaply. Bardini had an instinct for knowing when churches and palaces were about to be demolished and he would always be there, buying up precious bits and pieces to furnish his clients' needs. The second-floor windows of the Museo Bardini, for example, are framed by altarpieces from a church in Pistoia. He provided the cornerstone of many famous collections and sold countless paintings to museums in both Europe and the United States. He left his own private collection to Florence in 1922.

▶▶ Museo Bardini   *IFCE2*

Piazza de' Mozzi 1
Open: Mon, Tue, Thu–Sat 9–2, Sun 8–1. Closed Wed.
Admission charge. Biglietto Cumulativo *(combined ticket)*
available, also covering the Palazzo Vecchio, the Museo di
Firenze com'era, and the Museo di Santa Maria Novella.

One of Florence's unsung museums, the Museo Bardini remains unknown to many visitors. It is still not fully cat-alogued, and receives little or no publicity, but its wide-ranging collection is fascinating, and more enjoy-able than the similar Museo della Fondazione Horne across the river (see page 93). Walk here on Via de' Bordi and pop into the tiny church of Santa Lucia dei Magnoli.

Like the Horne, this museum was created by a 19th-century private collector, Stefano Bardini (see panel), who – by occasionally dubious means – acquired hundreds of historic architectural details and miscellaneous artifacts. When the collection became too extensive for his home, parts of it were incorporated into the made-to-measure medieval *palazzo* that Bardini had built for himself. A 13th-century church that stood on the site was simply pulled down. For all its modernity (it was built just a hundred years ago in 1883), the *palazzo* still feels thoroughly medieval – not least because its doors, ceilings, and fireplaces lend it the requisite authenticity (some of them salvaged from medieval buildings that were demolished in order to create Piazza della Repubblica in the 1860s).

The first floor The museum as described may sound com-plicated, but in practice you should have few problems in finding your way around. All the rooms are numbered, and the more valuable exhibits have been labelled. Fragments of stone frieze and other architectural carvings in the vestibule immediately set the tone for what is to come. More of the same follows in Rooms 1 and 2 (to the right of the vestibule in the open-plan arrangement). In Room 2, look for the large decorative fresco, made to appear as a curtain tapestry, especially with the woman painted peeping from its left-hand corner. (Rooms 3–5 are closed.)

Room 8, straight on from the vestibule, is dominated by a worn wellhead of red Veronese marble, and opens out into Room 7, formerly an open courtyard. This contains several beautiful objects, notably the stone emblems on the wall on the right and the Romanesque pulpit (inlaid with glass and precious stones) on the wall opposite. The tiny (labelled) head in the centre of the right wall is attributed to Nicola Pisano (*c*1220–84). The room's finest piece is also one of the museum's highlights – a Gothic *aedicule* (frame) and statue of Charity by Tino da Camaino, on the rear wall. The aedicule, incidentally, is a pastiche, cobbled together from disparate reliefs and statuettes.

Room 9 lies to the left of the vestibule and is entered through a worn but beautifully carved doorway. It contains two impressive fireplaces and a monumental porphyry basin from the reign of Diocletian (AD 284–305). Climb the stairs to the first landing to reach Room 10. The exhibits in this room include an enamelled terracotta altarpiece by Andrea della Robbia as well as pavement tombs that have been gathered together from as far afield as Venice.

The second floor Rooms 11–13, to the left at the top of the stairs, bulge with all manner of death-dealing medieval weaponry – pikes, pistols, crude mortars, crossbows, daggers, and a rather effete-looking collection of swords and rapiers. Room 14 (straight ahead at the top of the stairs) boasts two of the museum's most precious treasures: a polychrome terracotta of the *Madonna and Child* by Donatello (on the right-hand wall) and the same artist's extraordinary *Madonna dei Cordai*, an almost modern-looking collage of glass, stucco, and mosaic.

Room 16 offers a vast, anonymous *Crucifix*, chests, furniture, and several Florentine paintings of the Madonna and Child – an image of which Bardini seems to have been inordinately fond. The bright orange-tiled floor of Room 15 (which follows 16) sets off half a dozen magnificent carpets. The remaining five rooms are crammed with a miscellany of reliefs, furniture, majolica, and paintings, among which Antonio Pollaiuolo's St *Michael* in Room 18 stands out. Room 20 (steps down from 18) contains one of the city's most sumptuous wooden ceilings, as well as two exquisitely inlaid choir stalls.

A roomful of statues and sculptures – just part of Stefano Bardini's eclectic collection

Opposite page:
Adoration of the Christ Child with the Young St John the Baptist, *attributed to Pier Francesco Fiorentino (fl. 1475–1500). The Madonna and Child was a favourite image of Bardini's*

A FAÇADE FOR ALL PURPOSES

Barely hinting at the luxury within, the dour façade of the Palazzo Davanzati is topped by a sixth-storey loggia, a replacement for battlements removed in the 16th century. The medley of metalwork on the lower façade served for tying up animals, suspending birdcages, supporting festive banners, or hanging out wool and washing to dry. The vaulted entrance hall (now the ticket office) was once a loggia, used to close off the house in times of danger. Later it was used as a site for family parties, while later still it became a mall of medieval wool shops.

A FAMILY HOME

The Palazzo Davanzati was built around 1330 for the Davizzi, a family of wealthy wool merchants. In 1578 it was sold to the Davanzati, with whom it remained until 1838, when the clan's last member committed suicide by jumping from an upper window. After being divided into apartments, the palace was restored (1904) to its 14th-century appearance by Elia Volpi, a painter and antiquarian, who furnished the rooms with artifacts appropriate to the period. Opened as a museum in 1910, the palace was bought by the State in 1951.

►►► Museo della Casa Fiorentina Antica (Museum of the Old Florentine House)   IFCD3

Palazzo Davanzati, Piazza Davanzati, Via Porta Rossa 13
Currently closed for long-term restoration.

You should perhaps see this beautiful medieval house before visiting almost anything else in Florence. In offering an insight into how the city's artists, merchants, and noble families might once have lived, it both makes up for the medievalism missing from the streets of today and provides a welcome context for the paintings and sculptures that can sometimes seem rather lifelessly displayed in the museums and galleries. Few Florentine museums are as captivating.

The courtyard Amid the courtyard's redoubtable stone-work only the modern lighting strikes a false note: this perfect medieval vignette might be the stage set for some swashbuckling B-movie epic. The private well served the whole house, operating by means of a complex system of pulleys – something of a luxury at a time when most people drew their water from public fountains. Storerooms to the rear were replenished directly from side and back alleys, and were stocked with up to a year's supply of oil and grain to insure against the threat of siege, famine, or runaway inflation.

Notice the courtyard's rear right-hand pillar, carved with heads thought to be portraits of the Davizzi family (see panel). The glorious wood and stone staircase is the only one of its kind left in Florence.

The second floor Turn right at the top of the stairs into the Sala Madornale, originally used for family gatherings, when the wall hooks would have supported decorative drapes. In less happy times the floor's four wood-covered holes were used to bombard attackers in the entrance hall below. The ceiling, like most in the house, is magnificent, but smaller details – such as the powerful set of bellows – are equally captivating.

Two small rooms to the right have been set aside for displays of lace and embroidery. More beguiling, however, is the Sala dei Pappagalli to the left, which was named after the tiny parrots (*pappagalli*) that decorate its wall frescoes (whose *trompe-l'oeil* folds and tucks have been artfully made to resemble textile hangings). Such wall paintings were once common in contemporary houses: these are now some of the last surviving examples in the city. The leaded windows were originally covered with turpentine-soaked rags, that were stretched across the frames in order to repel water, even though they admitted only a tiny amount of light.

A small passage leads to the plain-walled Sala Piccola (small room), probably a child's bedroom, with another fine ceiling, a fantastically elaborate safe, and four parts of a painted wedding chest (*cassone nuziale*). The house's most covetable room, however, is the neighbouring Sala Pavoni or Camera Nuziale (Wedding Room). Under a beautiful ceiling runs a frescoed frieze of trees, peacocks (*pavoni*), and exotic birds, interwoven with the coats of arms of all the families related to the Davizzi. The two-winged tabernacle has an *Angel and Saints* by Neri di Bicci, while the linen bedspread is a rare piece of 14th-century Sicilian work decorated with the story of Tristan. Only the adjoining bathroom strikes a disconcertingly rudimentary note (see panel opposite).

The third floor The layout of this floor is the same as that of the second, and all its rooms are similarly filled with furniture, tapestries, ceramics, paintings, and decorated wedding chests.

Notice the shoe-shaped hand warmers and the Davanzati family tree in the main *salone*, the dining room's intricate salt cellars, and the bedroom's faded frescoes, their narrative lifted from a medieval French romance.

The fourth floor This is given over to the kitchen, a room that was often situated at the top of medieval *palazzi* to minimise damage in the event of fire. The house's cosiest corner, this was where the women would spend most of their time, using the sorts of kitchen utensils that are displayed around the room. Many of these look like medieval instruments of torture.

Notice, in particular, the *girapolenta*, a polenta stirrer, and the *impastatori*, which was used for mixing the dough for bread or pasta.

BARE NECESSITIES

In the 14th century Palazzo Davanzati's lavatories were the best that money could buy. Drains were a recent innovation, a law of 1325 having forbidden the disposal of sewage into the streets. An earlier statute had required three loud warning cries to be given before a chamber pot was emptied. Florence may have had public latrines (San Gimignano certainly had them), but for most people the arrangement was as described in Boccaccio's *Decameron* – two planks of wood perched over a small pit.

Pots and pans in the Palazzo Davanzati's medieval kitchen

One of van Utens' lunettes of the Medici villas

SANTA MARIA MADDALENA DEI PAZZI

This church, at Borgo Pinti 58, is only a few minutes from the Museo di Firenze com'era. It is well worth a visit to see its chapter house, home to a beautiful three-part *Crucifixion* (1496) by Perugino, one of the painter's masterpieces. The church, built in 1257 (but with a baroque interior), was reputedly named after a 'mad' (*pazzo*) Florentine nun who habitually covered herself in boiling wax as a mark of devotion. Now run by French Augustinians, the church is a favourite of Florence's French community. *Open* daily 9–12 and 5–7, but times liable to change without notice. *Admission by donation.*

▶ **Museo di Firenze com'era (Museum of Florence as it was)**   IFCE4

Via dell'Oriuolo 4

Open: Mon–Wed, Fri–Sat 9–2, Sun 8–1. Closed Thu. Admission charge. Biglietto Cumulativo *(combined ticket) available, also covering the Palazzo Vecchio, the Museo di Santa Maria Novella, and the Museo Bardini.*

One sad aspect of Florence today is the lack of public parks and grassy squares, something easily overlooked until – with some surprise – you stumble across somewhere like the Museo di Firenze com'era, whose small garden of lawns and mature trees reminds you how more of the city must once have looked. It is a fitting introduction to a museum which, with engravings and topographical paintings, documents the Florence of days gone by. Unashamedly modest, it is nonetheless a charming and – to its benefit – a relatively undervisited spot.

Turning right at the entrance into the first room you are confronted with the museum's prize piece – the *Pianta della Catena* – a bewitching medieval view of Florence stretched across an entire wall. Painted in 1887 from a 1470 original (now in Berlin), it offers a fascinating panorama of the city walls, towers, and buildings. It was painted by an unknown artist, perhaps the red-cloaked figure in the right-hand foreground. The Arno, a lovely blue, is particularly vivid, and is depicted complete with swimmers, fishermen, and a puntlike ferry. Many of the churches shown still lack their present façades; the Uffizi and the Cappelle Medicee have yet to be built; and the Medici and Pitti palaces are still only a fraction of their later size.

The room to the right contains lunettes (circular murals) of the Medici villas (1599) by the Flemish painter van Utens, reproductions of which are on sale all over the city in the form of cards and posters. The originals – 12 aerial views of neatly arranged woods, houses, and gardens – are among the loveliest things in this museum. More maps, pictures, and engravings follow, the highlights being a painting of Savonarola's execution and the engravings of Telemaco Signorini (1874).

Return to the entrance; the vaulted room to the left is filled with covetable engravings of the city's major buildings, the most interesting of which are the exploded diagrams (dated 1755) of the Duomo, the Battistero, and the Campanile on the right-hand wall.

▶ Museo della Fondazione Horne

IFCE3

Palazzo Corsi-Alberti, Via de' Benci 6
Open: Mon–Sat 9–1, plus Tue 8.30pm–11pm in summer.
Closed Sun. Admission charge

Like the nearby Museo Bardini (see pages 88–9), the Museo Horne was founded by a private collector, in this case the Englishman Herbert Percy Horne (1864–1916), known in his day for a pioneering biography of Botticelli. The collection is more modest than Bardini's (Horne was not a wealthy man), but also a touch more intimate and discerning than its rival. It is worth seeing the two museums in conjunction.

Exhibits are numbered rather than labelled, but a catalogue is generally available at the ticket desk. The first floor has just one room, whose highlight is Jacopo Sansovino's *Madonna and Child*, its protagonists' haloes delicately picked out in gold against the coarser carved stone. Andrea Sansovino's workshop was responsible for the capitals of the courtyard's two central pillars, which are among the finest in the city.

The second floor contains the core of the collection's paintings and furniture. Room I's highlights are a faded *Crucifix* by Filippino Lippi (between the second and third windows); a tiny, bowed panel by Masaccio depicting St Julian (on the far wall); a group of *Saints* by Pietro Lorenzetti (centre of the far wall); and the adjoining wall's age-darkened *Deposition* by Benozzo Gozzoli. Room II contains the museum's biggest attraction, Giotto's *Santo Stefano*, part of a polyptych (centre of the right-hand wall), and the face and upper torso of a *Redeemer* by Luca Signorelli. Room III offers Beccafumi's important tondo of the *Holy Family*, a lovely frame enclosing a group of tousle-haired, redheaded children.

The third floor follows the same three-room plan. The main room boasts a tiny *Pietà* by Filippo Lippi (behind glass on the left of the end wall) and Filippino Lippi's almost infantile *Esther*, part of a marriage chest, its simple background no more than a scratch of paint. The two book-size panels in the centre of the room are attributed to Simone Martini.

PALAZZO CORSI-ALBERTI

The palace housing the Museo della Fondazione Horne was built in 1489 for the Corsi, a family of cloth manufacturers attracted to the area around Santa Croce, then the heart of Florence's textile industry. A typical house of the period, it included a large cellar for dyeing vats and an open-air upper gallery in the courtyard for drying skeins of wool.

One man's collection: part of the Museo Horne's display of paintings, decorative arts, and furniture

Walk

The north of the city – Michelangelo and Fra Angelico

A walk taking in Florence's main market area and the most important churches and galleries in the north of the city (3km; start early and allow a full morning, remembering that most sights close by 2pm).

Start in Piazza Madonna degli Aldobrandini by visiting the **Cappelle Medicee (Medici chapels)▶▶▶**, the remarkable last resting place of many of the Medici family (see pages 64–5). The church of **San Lorenzo▶▶** itself (entered from Piazza San Lorenzo) is a masterpiece of Renaissance church design. The interior boasts bronze pulpits and other works by Donatello. Do not miss Brunelleschi's Sagrestia Vecchia or Michelangelo's Biblioteca Laurenziana (see pages 132–5).

Explore the market north of San Lorenzo (see pages 114–15), cut through the lively covered Mercato Centrale, and return to Piazza San Lorenzo. On the north side of the square is the **Palazzo Medici-Riccardi▶▶**, worth a visit to see Benozzo Gozzoli's frescoes depicting the journey of the Magi (see page 113). Follow Via Cavour, Via degli Alfani, Via San Reparata, and Via XXVII Aprile to reach the former convent of **Sant'Apollonia▶**, whose large fresco of the Last Supper is by Andrea del Castagno (see panel on page 100).

Walk east to Piazza San Marco, pausing to view Michelangelo's David in the **Galleria dell' Accademia▶▶▶** (see pages 52–3). The ex-convent on the north side of the square houses the **Museo di San Marco▶▶▶**, devoted to the frescoes and paintings of Fra Angelico (see pages 100–2).

Continue eastward to Piazza della Santissima Annunziata, one of the city's most distinctive squares. Its church, **Santissima Annunziata▶▶**, is known for its frescoes by Andrea del Sarto and others (see page 155). Across the square is the **Ospedale degli Innocenti▶** (see page 112). If time permits, go inside to see the modest museum and the two Brunelleschi cloisters.

▶ Museo Nazionale di Antropologia ed Etnologia (National Museum of Anthropology and Ethnology)

IFCE4

Palazzo Nonfinito, Via del Proconsolo 12
Open: Mon–Thu 8.30–1.30, 2–6; Fri 8.30–1.30. Closed
Sat–Sun. Admission charge

Few museums could be as out of place in a Florentine setting as the Museum of Anthropology and Ethnology. Founded in 1869, it was the first such museum in Italy, and is still the best of its kind in the country. In Florence, however, it suffers badly by comparison with its illustrious and better-known neighbours, and is little visited, both for that reason and because would-be visitors are frustrated by its very restricted opening times (see above). Nevertheless, it is centrally placed, and is worth a quick visit in passing – perhaps if you are on the way from the Duomo to the Bargello.

The collection is housed in the 35 rooms of a palace (1593) which was left unfinished (*nonfinito* – hence its name) after the death of its architect, Buontalenti. The museum includes a range of artifacts and folk art from as far afield as Japan, Peru, and Tibet. The Peruvian mummies and endless rows of desiccated skulls are ghoulishly fascinating, but of most anthropological interest is the collection relating to the Kafiri tribe of Pakistan (amassed between 1955 and 1960).

Of more general appeal are the many musical instruments and the Pacific Basin exhibits collected by Captain Cook during his last voyage in 1776–9.

95

In a city devoted to fine art, the Anthropological Museum has something a little different for the visitor to see

The entrance to the Museo dell'Opera del Duomo: within it, many of the city's sculptural treasures are given protection from the elements

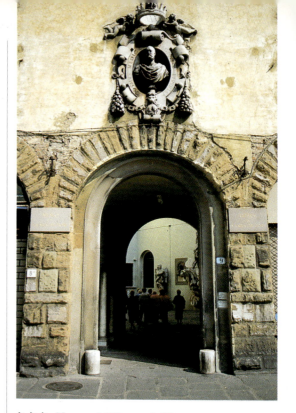

MICHELANGELO'S PIETÀ

A late work begun around 1550, this sculpture was intended for Michelangelo's tomb. According to Vasari, the head of Nicodemus was a self-portrait. The sculptor became so disenchanted with the marble, however, and with his own poor craftsmanship, that he took a hammer to Christ's left arm and leg. The resulting damage is still clearly visible. A pupil, Tiberio Calcagni, repaired the limbs and finished the (clearly inferior) figure of Mary Magdalene after Michelangelo's death.

HOLY RELICS

Florence has relics that other cities would covet, but rather than parade them in her churches, prefers to hide them away in the Opera del Duomo museum. The museum's saintly fragments include nails from the True Cross, a finger of John the Baptist, the jaw of St Jerome, St Philip's arm, and one of the arrows used in the attempted martyrdom of St Sebastian.

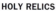

▶▶▶ Museo dell'Opera del Duomo (Cathedral Works Museum)   IFCE4

Opera di Santa Maria del Fiore, Piazza del Duomo 9
Open: Apr–Oct, Mon–Sat 9–6.50, Nov–Mar, Mon–Sat 9–6.20. Closed Sun. Admission charge

The Opera del Duomo ('Work of the Cathedral') was created in 1296 to look after the Duomo. In 1331, it was placed under the care of the Arte della Lana (Wool weavers' Guild). Its present home, built alongside Ghiberti's workshop, was established in the 15th century. Since 1891, it has housed works of art removed for safe keeping from the Duomo, the Battistero, and the Campanile – usually those endangered by pollution.

The first floor Michelangelo's *David* was carved in the *cortile* (courtyard) of the Opera del Duomo, a fitting prelude to a museum whose sculpture collection is second only to that of the Bargello (see pages 56–9). Now stacked with Roman sarcophagi and lesser sculpture, the *cortile* provides one or two artistic 'appetisers' before the gallery proper. On the left after the entrance is a room full of ropes, winding gear, giant pincers, and other instruments used by Brunelleschi during construction of the Duomo. Another small room to the left contains Brunelleschi's grinning death mask, plus a lopsided and woodworm-damaged model of the dome (possibly made for the 1418 competition to settle the dome's design).

Room I contains a multitude of statues, most of them 14th-century works salvaged from Arnolfo di Cambio's quarter-finished Duomo façade before it was demolished by Ferdinand I in 1587. *Santa Reparata*, one of Florence's patron saints, sits on the left, together with a stiff-backed *Boniface VIII*, one of the most vicious of popes (distinguished here by stumplike hands and a comically elongated hat). Straight ahead the heavily jowled *Madonna of the Glass Eyes* fixes her famously unsettling gaze (note the lovely pink marble and gold-backed mosaic to the rear). Donatello carved the figure of St John, one of the room's four stone Evangelists.

Room II presents a distinct contrast to Room I's stony austerity. Darker and warmer in tone, its prize exhibits are four wooden models entered in a 1588 competition to design the Duomo's new façade. Alongside stand several huge *codici*, some of the 58 sumptuously illustrated books of choral music used in the cathedral until as recently as 1930. All have been immaculately restored after being damaged in the 1966 flood. The modern octagonal chapel contains precious reliquaries and a lovely altarpiece of the Madonna and Saints Catherine and Zenobius (1334) attributed to Bernardo Daddi. A corridor of sculptural fragments leads to stairs and Michelangelo's *Pietà* (see panel opposite).

The second floor Room I contains a pair of exquisitely carved *cantorie* (choir lofts), both masterpieces of the Renaissance. They languished in storage for almost two centuries, all but forgotten after their removal from the Duomo in the 17th century. Luca della Robbia's beautifully lyrical piece on the left (1431–38) was his first major commission. It bursts with life as deliriously happy children dance and sing in line with Psalm 33's instruction: 'Praise the Lord with harp and sing unto Him...' (the psalm is inscribed in the choir's frame). The loft opposite is by Donatello (1433–39), a far more turbulent and free-spirited character. These qualities are reflected in the wild abandon of its figures – 'A rowdy lot of winged street urchins', in the words of one critic.

Below the loft stands Donatello's *Mary Magdalene* (removed from the Battistero), a hollow-eyed wooden figure of extraordinary intensity. Of the 16 figures ranged around the room (all removed from Giotto's Campanile), the most eye-catching is Donatello's bald and madly staring *Abacuc* (the Old Testament prophet Habbakuk), to which the artist himself gave the nickname *lo zuccone* (the marrow). Room II, to the left, is studded with bas-reliefs removed from the Campanile, most of them the work of Andrea Pisano. Although worn and age-blackened, their stories and allegorical content remain eminently intelligible (see also page 63).

Room III has as its centrepiece a case containing four panels from Ghiberti's Baptistery doors (see panel), now displayed here following painstaking restoration (the others will follow in due course). Do not miss the tiny Byzantine mosaic on the right wall as you enter, so finely detailed as to resemble the pages of an illuminated manuscript. Giovanni del Biondo's triptych on the long left wall depicts perhaps the most heavily arrowed St Sebastian in the canon of Italian art. The vast altar is a miracle of 14th-century Florentine goldwork, decorated in infinitesimal detail, as is the silver cross (1459) on top, crafted principally by Antonio Pollaiuolo.

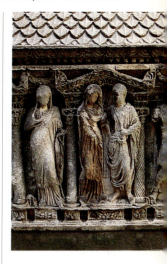

Detail from a Roman sarcophagus in the courtyard of the Museo dell'Opera del Duomo

97

BAPTISTERY DOORS
All 10 panels from Ghiberti's east doors will eventually be displayed in the Museo dell'Opera del Duomo. The first four to be displayed are:
1. The creation of Adam and Eve, original sin, and the expulsion from Paradise
2. Cain the shepherd, Abel the tiller of the land, Cain slays Abel, and the wrath of God
3. Joseph pulled from a pit and sold, Joseph explains the Pharaoh's dreams
4. Saul and David, the battle with the Philistines, David kills Goliath.

From the 14th century onwards, the most important type of wall painting in Italy was known as fresco (because the artist painted onto wet – or fresh – plaster). Frescoes are such a familiar feature of churches and galleries in Florence and elsewhere that it is easy to forget the artistic and technical difficulties that accompanied their creation.

Top: frescoes in the Palazzo Vecchio, Sala di Gigli

ESSENTIAL FRESCOES IN FLORENCE
Museo di San Marco (pages 100–2): Fra Angelico; Ghirlandaio (Refettorio).
Ognissanti (page 109): Ghirlandaio (Convento).
Palazzo Medici-Riccardi (page 113): Gozzoli.
Sant'Apollonia (panel, page 100): Andrea del Castagno.
Santa Croce (pages 138–43): Giotto.
Santa Maria del Carmine (pages 145–7): Masolino, Lippi, Masaccio (Cappella Brancacci).
Santa Maria Novella (pages 148–53): Masaccio, Ghirlandaio, Filippino Lippi; Andrea da Firenze (Cappellone degli Spagnoli); Uccello (Chiostro Verde).
Santa Trinita (page 154): Ghirlandaio.
Santissima Annunziata (page 155): Andrea del Sarto (Chiostrino dei Voti).

The chemistry At the heart of fresco technique is a chemical reaction, aided by the drying and fixing qualities of plaster (a mixture of lime, water, and fine sand). As plaster dries, carbon dioxide is absorbed from the air, converting the lime (calcium hydroxide) to calcium carbonate. This crystallises around the sand particles, binding them to the wall. If powdered pigments (usually mineral clays and silicates) are mixed with water and applied to the wet plaster, then the carbonisation process also fixes the particles of pigment. In this way a durable surface is created in which the pigment is permanently fixed and becomes resistant to further action by water. Only the subsequent crumbling of the plaster, or chemical deterioration of the pigment itself, can then affect a fresco's colours.

The preparation Layers of plaster, or 'ground', were applied to a bare wall in several stages. The first was a thick base coat known as the *arrichio* (one part lime to three parts sand). Onto this the artist incised lines to indicate the scene's main outlines. He then drew a sketch of the whole composition in red ochre. This sketch is known as the *sinopia,* named after the red pigment used in the drawings (many Florentine churches contain such preliminary sketches).

A daily limit Wet plaster was the key to fresco, so each day an artist could only work on an area of a painting small enough to be completed in that day, before the plaster dried. Paintings were therefore divided into sections called *giornate* (days). Each morning the artist or his assistant added a thin coat of fine white finishing plaster, or *intonaco,* to the chosen portion of *arrichio.* This obscured part of the *sinopia,* which was redrawn in *verdaccio,* a mixture of lime and black pigment. Only then was the surface ready for painting.

A race against time Artists had to work quickly, and know exactly the final effect they desired. Once the plaster had dried there was no room for correction or improvisation. Mistakes could be altered only by cutting away the day's *intonaco* and starting again. Changes of colour also proved a constant headache. The range of pigments available, for example, was initially limited, and only natural pigments were considered suitable. These tended to lighten, or lose subtleties of tone, as they dried. Surface crystals also gave an added lustre to the dry plaster. The blending of colours was also difficult, making depth of tone difficult to achieve.

Final effects were therefore accomplished with hatching, or the deft use of base coats. Parts of a fresco that were to represent flesh, for example, were given an undercoat of *terra verde*, a green earth pigment, while the skin tone itself was achieved using *cinabrese*, a red pigment composed of *sinopia* and lime-white.

Shortcuts Although great advances were made in fresco technique during the 15th century, artists always remained in thrall to the tyranny of wet plaster. Many innovations, in any case, came too late for Florence's most famous frescoes. However, certain pigments that were introduced could not be applied wet, and were painted instead onto dry plaster using *tempera* (where egg yolk is used to fix the pigment). Leonardo da Vinci, for example, frustrated by fresco's limitations, painted the whole of his famous but badly deteriorated *Last Supper* in Milan on dry plaster, using many new pigments of his own invention – with disastrous results. Colours added in this way were much less durable and easily flaked off the surface if subjected to external moisture. Vasari, with some justification, considered such processes 'a vile practice'.

CARTOONS
These were used as detailed aids to composition as frescoes became more complicated. The design was transferred to the walls by a variety of methods. The outlines were either scratched onto wet plaster, or enlarged from a small drawing onto a wall squared up for the purpose. Alternatively, small holes were made on a full-sized cartoon along the lines of the drawing and charcoal or chalk dusted through them onto the wall behind.

Andrea del Sarto's **Assumption of the Virgin,** *in the Chiostrino dei Voti of Santissima Annunziata*

99

SAN MARCO

If the church next to the museum is open, go in to see Fra Bartolomeo's *Madonna and Saints* (1509; second altar on the right) and the *Madonna in Prayer* (third altar on the right), a superb 8th-century mosaic which had to be cut in half during its journey from Constantinople. The join across the Virgin's midriff is still obvious. *Open*: daily, 7–12.30 and 4–8.

SANT'APOLLONIA

Quite close to San Marco, this former convent on Via XXVII Aprile is worth seeing. Little survives of the old building save a vestibule with paintings by Paolo Schiavo and Neri di Bicci, but one entire wall of the room beyond, the former monastic refectory, is covered by a fresco of the *Last Supper* (1450), the unsettling masterpiece of Andrea del Castagno. Above are much-ruined murals of the Crucifixion, Deposition, and Resurrection. The sinopie underlying these frescoes (see pages 98–9) were discovered during restoration and are displayed at the opposite end of the room. *Open*: same hours as Museo di San Marco (see above). *Admission free.*

▶▶▶ Museo di San Marco   IFCE5

Piazza San Marco

Open: Tue–Sat 8.30–1.50, plus same hours 1st, 3rd, and 5th Mon and 2nd and 4th Sun of the month. Admission charge

Busy with traffic roaring to and from the centre, and usually thronged by students from the nearby university buildings, Piazza San Marco is a long way from anyone's idea of monastic calm. On its north side, however, stands the baroque-fronted church of San Marco (see panel) and its erstwhile convent, which is now well known as a museum devoted almost entirely to the paintings of Fra Angelico. Owned first by Vallombrosan and then by Sylvestrine monks, the convent was given to the Dominicans in 1436 after a word to Pope Eugenius IV from Cosimo de' Medici.

The monks moved from their previous home in Fiesole, and the following year Cosimo assumed financial responsibility for the convent, deciding, in the words of Vasari, that it should be 'rebuilt on a larger and more magnificent scale … with all the conveniences which the friars could desire'. Cosimo's largesse was partly to assuage the guilt stirred by his banking successes (usury was still a sin in the eyes of the Church). 'Never', he announced to the monks, unnerved by his generosity, 'shall I be able to give God enough to set him down as my debtor'.

The Medici's pet architect, Michelozzo, was commissioned to design the building, described by Vasari as 'the best appointed, finest, and most convenient convent in Italy'. It was consecrated in 1444, with theologian Antonino Pierozzi (1389–1459) as its founding Dominican prior (he was later to become Archbishop of Florence). Subsequent priors were to include Fra Angelico and, even more famously, Savonarola (1491), who was eventually besieged and captured in the convent before being tried and executed in Piazza della Signoria (see pages 40–1).

The first floor After buying your ticket you enter the **Chiostro di Sant'Antonino** (Cloister of Sant'Antonino), designed by Michelozzo and named after the convent's first prior. Most of the faded frescoes here, panels on the life of Sant'Antonino, date from the 16th century. Fra Angelico's contribution consists of four small frescoes in the four corners of the cloister.

Turn right in the cloister and immediately on your right you enter the **Ospizio dei Pellegrini**, the spot where visiting pilgrims were offered hospitality. Now it is home to most of the museum's freestanding paintings, most of them brought from elsewhere when the convent was suppressed and turned into a museum. Its two most famous works occupy the opposing end walls. On your right as you enter stands Fra Angelico's *Deposition* (c1440), an altarpiece removed from Santa Trinita. It was originally commissioned by the Strozzi family from Lorenzo Monaco, who completed only the top three triangular pinnacles before his death.

On the opposite end wall hangs the *Madonna dei Linaiuoli*, commissioned by the *linaiuoli*, or flax workers' guild, for their headquarters. Angelico came to painting comparatively late in life, and this tabernacle, painted in 1433 (when he was 33), among his earliest major commissions. The magnificent frame was designed by Lorenzo Ghiberti.

Other masterpieces to look for include panels from the *Life of Christ*, originally used as cupboard doors in Santissima Annunziata, and an altarpiece of the *Last Judgment* (1431) in which the saved are shown in their finery, and the damned stripped bare in readiness for the tortures of hell.

Located off the far right-hand corner of the cloister, the small **lavatorium** contains two works by Uccello and three by Fra Angelico. Off to the right is the **Refettorio Maggiore** (Great Refectory), which is dominated by an eye-catching *Last Supper* (but otherwise filled with insignificant paintings). Off to the left are two smaller rooms, the first with seven winsome 'portraits' by Fra Bartolomeo and a large sepia fresco around the walls, the second graced by a narrow panel by Benozzo Gozzoli, who was a pupil of Fra Angelico.

Back out in the courtyard, the entrance to the *Sala Capitolare* (Chapter House) lies to the right of the huge convent bell. The single vaulted room contains a large but rather over-restored *Crucifixion and Saints* (1442) by Fra Angelico. The convent bell also marks the entrance to the museum's shop and the first floor. Before taking the stairs up to the Dormitory Cells, however, turn left into the **Refettorio**, home to a large *Last Supper* (*Cenacolo*) by Domenico Ghirlandaio (an almost exact facsimile of his similar work in Ognissanti – see page 109). Beyond lies the **Foresteria** (Guest Rooms), reached along a gloomy corridor of unintelligible stone fragments, worth visiting

THE ANNUNCIATION
This was a favourite theme with Florentine painters, partly because, according to the Florentine calendar, New Year's Day fell on 25 March, the Feast of the Annunciation. The city dated the start of its year *ab incarnazione* – from the conception or incarnation of Christ (nine months before Christmas). Parallels with pagan spring fertility rituals, and with the Roman New Year, which started with the spring equinox (21 March) are inescapable. The Florentine calendar survived until 1750, when the reforming dukes of Lorraine, inheriting Florence from the Medici, adopted the papal calendar.

101

mainly for the lovely views it offers of the (closed) Chiustro di San Domenico.

The second floor One of the loveliest masterpieces of the Renaissance stops you in your tracks at the top of the stairs – Fra Angelico's simple but sublimely beautiful *Annunciation* (see panel). Notice the inscription, a

Fra Angelico's Annunciation, *whose subject was a favourite of Florentine painters*

Florence

Visitors admire the paintings in the Museo di San Marco

THE CHIOSTRO DELLO SCALZO

Knock on the door for admission to this small cloister (which is a minute from San Marco at Via Cavour 69) containing 16 skillful monochrome frescoes of the Cardinal Virtues and scenes from the life of John the Baptist, both early works by Andrea del Sarto. The cloister is all that remains of a convent once owned by the Brotherhood of St John, an order whose monks walked around *scalzo* (barefoot). *Open*: Mon and Thu 9–1, plus Sat by ringing cloister bell. *Closed* Aug, and Sat in July. *Admission free.*

reminder to monks to say a Hail Mary as they pass the painting. Beyond, under a huge-beamed roof, the rest of the first floor is taken up by the *Dormitory Cells*, 44 small monastic cells, most of them frescoed by Fra Angelico and his assistants between 1439 and 1445. The cells on the left side of the corridor ahead of you (Nos 1–11) contain the frescoes most confidently attributed to Fra Angelico (notice cells 17 and 22, whose floors conceal 'secret', recently discovered medieval frescoes). The expressive *Madonna and Saints* on the corridor's right-hand wall is by Fra Angelico.

Turn right at the end of the corridor, and at the far end of the next (south) corridor are three cells once occupied by Savonarola (Nos 12–14). His erstwhile presence is commemorated by an unexceptional memorial and two powerful portraits (the bloodied head in one of the portraits is an allusion to Peter the Martyr, an eminent Dominican martyred by having a cleaver sunk in his skull). Also here is a copy of a painting depicting Savonarola's execution, and fragments of the stake to which he was tied when the bonfire was lit.

Turn right at the *Annunciation* to pass Europe's first public library, instigated by Cosimo de' Medici in 1441 (and designed by Michelozzo). A short way beyond are two cells (Nos 38 and 39) used by Cosimo personally, both significantly larger than the others, and each decorated with two frescoes, as opposed to the one allocated to each of the monks.

▶ Museo Stibbert   IFCE6

Via Federico Stibbert 26
Open: winter, Mon–Fri 10–2, Sat–Sun 10–6; summer, Mon–Wed, Fri–Sat 10–1, 3–6, Sun 10–1, 3–6. Closed Thu. Guided tours only (hourly, on the hour). Admission charge
Were it not so far from the heart of Florence, the Museo Stibbert would doubtless have achieved cult status long

PRACTICALITIES
The Museo Stibbert is
around 2km north of San
Marco. Buses 1, 7, or 33
run from the train station.

STIBBERT'S PARK
Stibbert created a small
park alongside his house
that is open to visitors
daily, 9–dusk.

103

ago. As it is, few people make the trek into Florence's
northern suburbs to sample its bizarre collection.
Remarkable for its 50,000 exhibits – which range from
buttons to bronzes – it is almost as alluring for the eccentric decoration of its 64-room labyrinth (part of a 14th-century mansion).

Half-Scottish, half-Italian, Frederick Stibbert (1838–1906) was born in Florence, distinguishing himself in
Garibaldi's army before inheriting a fortune and becoming an artist, traveller, intimate of Queen Victoria, and
inveterate collector. After being left the house as part of
his inheritance, he bought an adjoining *palazzo* and
adapted the two to serve as a joint home and museum.
Alterations made after his death are now being removed,
returning the rooms to the wonderfully gloomy Gothic
state in which Stibbert left them.

Stibbert's passion was militaria, and the museum
contains what many consider one of the world's greatest
collections of armour, much of it arranged on a phalanx of
mannequins, magnificently drawn up as if ready for battle, in the mansion's Great Hall. Etruscan, Roman,
oriental, and medieval pieces are all here, as well as novelties such as the costume worn by Napoleon when he
was crowned King of Italy (in Room 50, the *Sala Impero*).

Even if armour fails to appeal, you will find something
to captivate, be it tapestries, gilded candelabra, malachite
fireplaces, snuffboxes, Murano glass chandeliers, flags
from the Sienese Palio, pre-Raphaelite paintings (some by
Stibbert himself), stained glass, small bronzes, French furniture, oriental porcelain, bronze washbasins, family
photographs, and even Stibbert's dress kilt – altogether an
eclectic assemblage, representing the fruits of Stibbert's
many magpielike obsessions.

The museum's best paintings are those by Carlo Crivelli
and Botticelli (attributed) in the *Sala delle Bandiere* (Room
32), and Pietro Lorenzetti's *Crucifixion* in Room 36.

Detail of Fra Angelico's
Deposition, *in the*
Museo di San Marco

THE ACCADEMIA DEL CIMENTO

The world's first academy for scientific experiment was founded in 1657 by two former pupils of Galileo, Grand Duke Ferdinand II and his brother Prince (later Cardinal) Leopold. *Cimento* means 'trial' or 'experiment'. The Academy's motto was 'Try and try again', testimony to Galileo's empirical methods of inquiry, deduction, and proof by experiment. First housed in the Palazzo Pitti – where the kiln in the Giardino di Boboli was used to produce scientific glass-ware – the *Cimento* now has its home in the museum's Palazzo dei Castellani, previously home to the Accademia della Crusca, which was founded in 1582 to study the Italian language.

Galileo's telescope

▶▶ Museo di Storia della Scienza (Museum of the History of Science) *IFCE3*

Piazza dei Giudici 1
Open: Mon–Sat, 9.30–1; Mon, Wed, and Fri also 2–5. Closed Sun. Admission charge

Although Florence's artistic star waned in the 16th and 17th centuries, the achievements of men like Galileo, working under the patronage of sympathetic rulers such as Ferdinand II and Cosimo II, ensured that the city remained at the forefront of science and learning. Something of the flavour of the times is captured in this fascinating museum which, as befits a gallery given over to science and rational thought, is one of the most carefully presented in the city. Although it is devoted to science (each room deals with a different scientific theme), it would be a mistake to think its appeal is for specialists only. As well as revealing a different historical side to the city (distinct from art and architecture), its old instruments and miscellaneous exhibits are endlessly fascinating and often extremely beautiful.

The second floor Rooms 1–3 display cases full of astronomical, mathematical, and navigational instruments. Like many of the museum's displays, these require close scrutiny for a full appreciation of their intricate beauty. In Room 1, the left-hand case on the right-hand wall contains compasses that belonged to Michelangelo. In Room 2, look for the quadrant (No 42), studded with beautiful enamel vignettes, and Sir Samuel Morland's early calculating machine. In Room 3, the large Tuscan astrolabe (No 27) and coloured polyhedrons command most attention. Room 4 is devoted to Galileo's instruments, notably a large inclined wooden plane used to demonstrate the acceleration of bodies.

Slightly less prosaic are the bones of the middle finger of Galileo's left hand, kept on the top shelf of a case on the room's left. They were removed when his body was transferred to the church of Santa Croce. Also here is the lens used by Galileo to discover the moons of Jupiter. The scientist deliberately cracked the lens before he presented it to Ferdinand II.

Room 5 contains telescopes, including two belonging to Galileo (in a case on the left). Many are covered in leather or marbled paper, graphic illustrations of the Florentines' ability to turn even utilitarian objects into works of art. Highlights in Room 6 are some amusing optical games, though you are quickly tempted to Room 7, whose vivid displays of maps and globes make it perhaps the museum's most impressive room.

Notice, in particular, the detailed but hopelessly impractical map on the left wall, which shows the known world radiating from the Holy Land. Take in, too, the eccentric coffee table, also on the left, etched with a marble map (1694) depicting the course of the Danube. Microscopes in Room 9 lead into a room devoted to the Accademia del Cimento (see panel), the body that, along with the Medici, amassed most of the museum's exhibits. A menagerie of barometers and telescopes follows (Room 11), looking for all the world like a battery of medieval cannons.

The third floor The lovely timepieces in Room 12 probe the mysteries of the mechanical clock, investigating the finer points of escapement, mainspring, pendulum, and striking mechanism. Room 13 records the advances made in mathematical instruments in the 18th and 19th centuries, a theme continued in Room 14, where the accelerating pace of scientific discovery is reflected in the increasing variety of magnetic, electrostatic, and electromagnetic instruments. Succeeding rooms of pneumatic and hydrostatic exhibits are less arresting, though Room 18 brings you up short with some alarming surgical instruments and a collection of horrifying anatomical models made of wax. Expectant mothers should pass these up, for they deal mainly with obstetric complications, breech births, and all manner of less than straightforward passages into the world. As a literal account of where babies come from, few exhibits could be as graphic or as compelling.

Things calm down again in Room 19, which analyses the role of the alchemist and medieval pharmacist. Notice the jars and vases that advertise such unlikely medicines as *Coca Boliviana* (Bolivian cocaine), *Sangue del Drago* (dragon's blood) and *Confetti di Seme Santo* (confections made of blessed seed).

PRACTICALITIES
The science museum is arranged over two floors, each room being devoted to a particular branch of science or technology. On each floor be sure to pick up the excellent free guides, available in four languages, which not only describe each room's contents, but also explain the exhibits' historical and scientific background.

The History of Science Museum will fascinate all visitors, scientists and non-scientists alike

105

Physicist, astronomer and mathematician, Galileo Galilei was the first modern scientist. He revolutionised the study of astronomy and mechanics, insisting on an empirical approach to all scientific inquiry. Unfortunately for him, his objectivity was not welcomed by the Church, and his beliefs could easily have seen him executed by the Inquisition as a heretic.

Galileo Galilei

Galileo was born in Pisa in 1564, the son of a musician. He moved, with his family, to Florence in 1574. After a period with the monks of Vallombrosa, his education involved a short spell at the University of Pisa, where lack of funds prevented him from completing his degree (in medicine). An iconoclast from the outset, he dissented from even basic orthodoxies, refusing, for example, to wear the university's toga outside the classroom. After returning to Florence, he published a paper describing the hydrostatic balance, an invention that made his name throughout Italy. He then moved to a university post in Pisa, where – famously – he is said to have dropped weights from the Leaning Tower to disprove Aristotle's assertion that bodies of different masses fall at different speeds. In 1592, he secured the chair of mathematics at Padua, a post he was to hold for 18 years.

THE MOONS OF JUPITER
'I have discovered four planets, neither known nor observed by any one of the astronomers before my time, which have their orbits around a certain bright star, one of those previously known, like Venus and Mercury round the sun, and are sometimes in front of it, sometimes behind it, though they never depart beyond certain limits. All which facts were discovered and observed a few days ago by the help of the telescope devised by me, through God's grace first enlightening my mind'. *The Starry Messenger* (1610)

Galileo's discoveries Dutch glassmakers, not Galileo, invented the telescope (in 1608), but within a year Galileo had taken the Dutch original and produced a model 10 times as powerful, which was soon in demand all over Europe. Equipped with this new tool Galileo made a series of astronomical discoveries, expounded in a groundbreaking paper of 1610, *Sidereus Nuncis* (*The Starry Messenger*). The first to observe the moon's surface, he was also the first to realise that the Milky Way consisted of stars. He discovered Jupiter's four principal moons, which he named the Sidera Medicea (Medicean Stars), after his former pupil and future patron, Grand Duke Cosimo II. He went on to make observations of the moons of Saturn, the phases of Venus, and sunspots travelling across the sun's surface, suggesting the sun was not a perfect sphere, as traditional philosophy had always maintained.

Science and religion In the summer of 1610, Galileo left Padua to become 'first philosopher and mathematician' to Grand Duke Cosimo II. Freed by the move to spend more time on research, he confirmed, in his own mind at least, the Copernican heliocentric view of the heavens –

that the Earth and other planets orbited the sun. This was contrary to the Ptolemaic assertion, long supported by the Church, that the Earth was at the centre of the universe. Seeing its vested interests threatened, the Church rose against him, the Jesuits asserting he would do more damage in the fight against Protestantism 'than Luther and Calvin put together'.

The crunch came in 1616 with the Inquisition's decree declaring Copernicus 'false and erroneous'. Galileo was told he could neither 'hold nor defend' the doctrine. In private, however, Cardinal Bellarmine, the pope's chief theologian, told Galileo his ideas could be discussed as 'mathematical supposition'. In doing so he tacitly acknowledged Galileo's genius, underlining at the same time the gulf that was to separate religious faith and scientific 'truth'.

Papal support Galileo then lay low at his house in Bellosguardo for seven years. A paper he published during this time contained the famous assertion that the 'Book of Nature ... is written in mathematical characters'. A virtuoso treatise of 1632 reopened old wounds, and this time the Jesuits were determined to bring the scientist down. Galileo's supporters, however, included Pope Urban VIII, who (as Maffeo Barberini) had been his life-long friend and protector. Though he could not prevent a trial, the pope was able to ensure Galileo was tried on lesser charges, which, if upheld, would at least not lead to the scientist's execution. In June 1633, the Inquisition forced Galileo to kneel in the church of Santa Maria sopra Minerva in Rome and agree that he 'abjured, cursed, and detested' his errors. Imprisonment was waived on condition that he remained in Florence under the protection of Ferdinand II. Overcoming house arrest and the onset of blindness, Galileo continued with scientific work until his death in 1642.

LAWS OF MOTION
Galileo's work on the movement of bodies was as important as his more famous astronomical discoveries. In establishing mechanics as a science, he paved the way for the theories of the English physicist and mathematician Isaac Newton, born in the year of Galileo's death. He defined the laws governing pendulum motion, and in 1640 wrote a treatise on which the Dutch scientist, Huygens, based his own invention of the first mechanical pendulum clock. He formulated the laws of parabolic motion (the curving path followed by a ball thrown in the air as it falls to the ground). He also studied the natural acceleration of bodies in free fall; discovered the nature of percussive force; devised a rudimentary thermometer; patented a device to raise water; and discovered the brachistochrone (the shortest path taken by any object describing a curve as it moves).

Galileo Galilei's tomb in Santa Croce

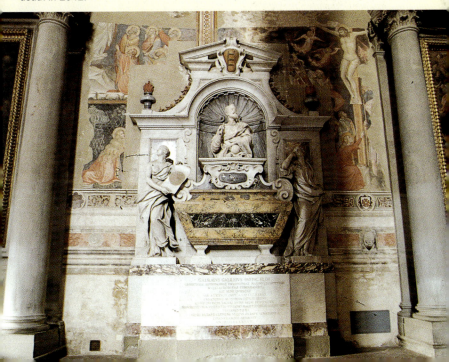

Florence

►► Museo Zoologico, La Specola (Zoological Museum)

IFCC2

Via Romana 17
Open: Waxworks: Tue and Sat 9–12; Museum: Mon, Tue and Thu–Sun 9–1. Admission charge

Most people come to the zoological museum not for its stuffed animals but to revel in Florence's strangest museum collection, the Cere Anatomiche, a wonderfully stomach-turning assemblage of anatomical waxworks. Finding this little house of horrors, however, is something of a battle, for it is not signposted either from the street or within the dour palazzo at Via Romana 17 (formerly an astronomical observatory, 'La Specola'). To reach it, walk straight on at the threshold, keeping the courtyard parking lot on your right, and at the statue of Torricelli climb the stairs to the fourth floor.

The ghoulish show opens with hundreds of identical glass cases, filled with some 1,400 lovingly constructed models of arms, legs, and internal organs. It culminates in several splayed and dissected wax corpses, each sinew, nerve fibre, and blood vessel sculpted in the most careful detail. All around, the museum's worn, rather lurid red

THE PLAGUE
The poet Longfellow, musing on the character of Zumbo, creator of the plague tableau, wrote: 'a man of the most gloomy and saturnine imagination, and more akin to the worm ... thus to have revelled night and day in the hideous mysteries of death, corruption, and the charnel-house. It is strange how this representation haunts one ... with its loathsome corpses, with 'the blackening, the swelling, the bursting of the trunk – the worm, the rat, and the tarantula at work. You breathe more freely as you step out into the open air ... the bright sunshine ... the crowded busy streets.' *Outre-mer: A Pilgrimage Beyond the Sea* (1833–4)

108

One of the hundreds of anatomical waxworks on view in Florence's most macabre museum

tiles serve to heighten the charnel-house atmosphere, which is emphasised still more by the sickly yellow hue pervading many of the aging models. Created as a teaching aid, the collection dates from 1775 to 1814.

There are, however, several more highlights (if they can be called that), notably the chastening obstetrics section and a famous four-piece tableau of Florence during the plague. The latter – not for the squeamish – is tucked away in a small room on the left side of the museum (through the rooms devoted to dissected animals). Made by a Sicilian cleric, it comprises four three-dimensional vignettes worthy of Dante's *Inferno*. All are very obviously the product of a disturbed imagination (see panel opposite). The corpses of men, women, and children are shown piled high, each in various stages of colourful putrescence. Smaller details, though, prove even more bloodcurdling – such as the rats gnawing at curled intestines, and the tiny clumps of mushrooms growing from the mulch of human and animal detritus.

▶ Ognissanti IFCC4

Piazza d'Ognissanti

Florence's early mercantile dynamism owed much to the Umiliati, a skilled Benedictine order brought from Lombardy in the 13th century to help foster the city's nascent woolen industry. On land leased by the *Comune* in 1239, much of it near the Arno, they built workshops and the church (completed in 1259) that was to become Ognissanti (All Saints). Under their sway the area became a focus of the city's carding, weaving, and dyeing industries. Some idea of the order's stature can be gained from the fact that it commissioned the great Giotto to paint an altarpiece for its church – the stupendous *Maestà* that now forms a majestic introduction to the Uffizi.

In 1561, the church passed to the Franciscans, who instigated two centuries' worth of 'improvements'. These spared the old campanile but produced a baroque façade (one of the city's earliest) that outraged Florentines by flouting what they considered to be Tuscany's architectural traditions.

Inside, amid the gloom of murky baroque décor and grey stone altars, lie several works of artistic and historical interest. The second altar on the right contains two early works by brothers Davide and Domenico Ghirlandaio. In the lower, *The Madonna of Mercy*, the Virgin's cloak protects the Vespucci, a merchant family who hailed from the surrounding area. Between the Virgin and the dark-cloaked man is the young boy who was to give his name to a continent – Amerigo Vespucci (1451–1512) – an agent for the Medici based in Seville, Spain. The woman beneath her left hand is Simonetta Vespucci, mistress to Giuliano de' Medici and reputedly the most beautiful woman of her age. Legend has it that she was the model for Botticelli's famous *Venus*, in the Uffizi.

The claim may not be too far-fetched, for Botticelli also came from the parish of Ognissanti. It was he who painted the fresco between Ognissanti's third and fourth altars, *St Augustine's Vision of St Jerome*, mirrored by Ghirlandaio's *St Jerome* on the opposite side of the nave. Moreover, Botticelli is buried in the church, beneath a round pavement tomb in the south transept.

THE LAST SUPPER
Ognissanti's convent refectory, entered through a cloister to the left of the church, contains a superb fresco of the Last Supper (1480) by Ghirlandaio, a variation on his similar painting in the Museo di San Marco (see pages 100–2). It is thought to have inspired Leonardo da Vinci's famous *Last Supper* in Milan.
Open: Mon, Tue and Sat 9–noon; *Closed* Wed. *Admission charge.*

PONTE ALLA CARRAIA
To the south of Ognissanti stood the city's second oldest bridge after the Ponte Vecchio. The original, built around 1218, was entrusted to Ognissanti's Umiliati, who built a new bridge in 1269. That bridge collapsed in 1304, buckled by the weight of spectators who had gathered to watch the Calendimaggio (Maytime) celebrations. Today's Ponte alla Carraia is a modern copy of the bridge's 16th-century replacement. Its name derives from the *carri* (carts) used at one time to carry raw and finished wool across the Arno between the cloth-making districts of Ognissanti and San Frediano.

MIRACULOUS MADONNA
'The sick were healed, the lame walked again, and the possessed were liberated', wrote Giovanni Villani about Orsanmichele's miraculous image of the Madonna. '...people came there on pilgrimage from all over Tuscany...' *Cronache Fiorentine* (1300)

ANDREA ORCAGNA
Although few works survive, Orcagna (1308–68) was the most important Florentine painter, sculptor, and architect after Giotto's death. Orsanmichele's tabernacle is his best Florentine work.

110

PALAZZO DELL'ARTE DELLA LANA
This lovely building opposite Orsanmichele is decorated with a tabernacle, exterior fresco, and fine wooden eaves. But the decoration is ersatz 19th-century medievalism. A covered passage on the first floor gives access to Orsanmichele's medieval upper stories and small museum. *Open*: daily only at 9, 9.45, 10.30 and 11.30. *Closed* 1st and last Mon of the month. *Admission free.*

STATUES
Starting on Via dei Calzaiuoli and working left to right , Orsanmichele's surviving statues and copies are: 1. *John the Baptist*, Ghiberti; 2. *Quattro Coronati*, Nanni di Banco (for the Masons' and Carpenters' Guild – notice the workmen in the lower relief); 3. *St George*, Donatello (original in the Bargello); 4. *St Matthew*, Ghiberti; 5. *St Stephen*, Ghiberti; 6. *St Eligius*, Nanni di Banco; 7. *St Mark*, Donatello; 8. *Madonna and Child*, Lamberti; 9. *St John*, Baccio di Montelupo.

▶ ▶ Orsanmichele

IFCD3

Via dei Calzaiuoli
Open: daily 9–12 and 4–6. Closed first and last Mon of the month. Admission free

Few churches are as calm and beguiling as Orsanmichele, whose deceptively gaunt bulk punctuates the walk between the Duomo and Piazza della Signoria. The first church on the site appeared around 750, an oratory nestled in the kitchen garden of a Benedictine monastery. The present name derives from these humble roots – a contraction of San Michele ad Hortum and then San Michele in Orto (*orto* still means 'vegetable garden' in Italian). The oratory was destroyed in 1239 to make way for a grain market, completed around 1280, possibly to a design by Arnolfo di Cambio. Religious associations, however, continued to cling to the site. The most notable was a fresco of the Virgin (painted on one of the market's pillars), an image whose supposed miracle-working powers attracted countless pilgrims to the area (see panel). In the end the Madonna's popularity led to the building of a small chapel and the founding of a religious confraternity.

Both market and Virgin, however, were victims of a great fire that swept Florence in 1304, destroying some 1,700 buildings. Rebuilding started in 1336, probably to designs by Francesco Talenti, who constructed an open loggia on the market's first floor (the upper storeys were set aside for emergency supplies of grain). In 1380, however, the market was relocated and the loggia's open arches bricked up. By this time it had been decided to retain the granary but turn the lower floor into a church – the present Orsanmichele.

Decoration of Talenti's new trade hall assumed an importance never before seen in Florence. As early as 1339 it was decided to provide each of the loggia's pillars with a statue, responsibility for the decoration being assigned to the city's leading guilds. Each was to commission a statue of its patron saint to fill the appropriate niche. Over the next 60 years, however, only one statue materialised (the Arte della Lana's *St Stephen*). In the meantime, most of the loggia – by now a church – had already received most of its interior decoration (see below). In 1408, exasperated by the delay, the city council set a 10-year deadline for completion of the outstanding statues, reserving the right to allocate niches to other guilds if the commissions remained unfulfilled.

The guilds' foot-dragging was to posterity's benefit. Instead of statues executed at a time when Florentine sculpture was in the doldrums, the niches were filled with work from the first wave of great Renaissance artists – Verrocchio, Ghiberti, Donatello, Luca della Robbia, and others. Not all the statues have remained in their intended places: some of the 14 niches are now either empty or filled with copies, though you can still admire the beautifully carved surrounds. The originals have been removed to a variety of galleries for safe keeping (see panel).

Orsanmichele's entrance is at the rear, tucked away from the bustle of Via dei Calzaiuoli. Inside is a dusky and peaceful oasis studded with indistinct patches of fresco peeping from shadowy, dark-stone walls. Most of the fragments depict the guilds' patron saints, painted to complement the statues outside. As your eyes become accustomed to the gloom, notice the bricked-up arches of the old loggia, its arcaded outline still clearly visible. Notice, too (not that it is easily missed), the glorious tabernacle to the rear, a glittering glass and marble masterpiece bathed in the soft yellow glow of candlelight. Created by Andrea Orcagna, and 11 years in the making (1348–59), it is the most beautiful work of its kind in Italy. It was financed by donations that flooded into Orsanmichele's religious confraternity. In its first year – 1348, the year of the great plague – these offerings amounted to more than the total sum raised by the city in taxes. At its heart lies a lovely *Madonna and Child* (1347) by Bernardo Daddi, said to have inherited miraculous powers from the fresco of the Virgin that was destroyed by the fire of 1304.

HIGH PRAISE

'Orsanmichele… is the complete, unravaged child of the Renaissance. There more than anywhere one can feel the continuity of the Florentine spirit, with all its seriousness, its humanity, and its unexpected level of beauty.' Kenneth Clark, *The Other Half* (1977)

Orcagna's Tabernacle

111

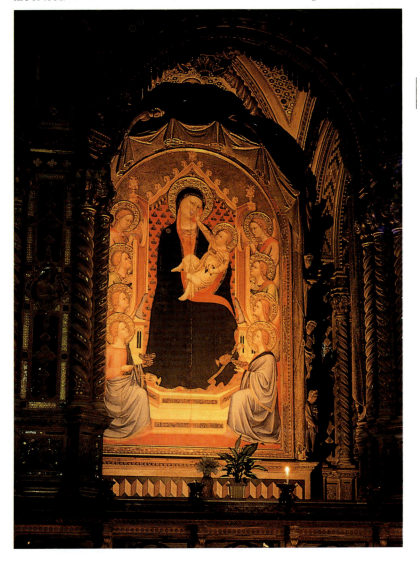

▶ Ospedale degli Innocenti IFCE5

Piazza Santissima Annunziata 12
Open: Mon, Tue, Thu–Sat 8.30–2. Sun 8.30–1. Closed Wed.
Admission charge

The Ospedale degli Innocenti (Foundling Hospital) is but one component (with the church of Santissima Annunziata – see page 155) of **Piazza Santissima Annunziata**▶, widely reported to be the most beautiful square in Florence. In reality, it does not quite live up to its billing, its Renaissance lines no match for some of Tuscany's medieval squares. Worse still, today its harmony is compromised by traffic, backpackers and junkies at night.

Begun by Brunelleschi in the 1420s, the piazza was then saddled with 200 years of minor modifications by architects from Ammannati to Antonio da Sangallo. Their additions did remarkably little to upset its overall unity, however. The equestrian statue at its heart is Giambologna's *Ferdinand I*, the sculptor's last work (1608). Less eye-catching, but more bizarre, are the two smaller fountains by Giambologna's pupil, Pietro Tacca – a pair of water monkeys spraying two bearded sea slugs.

The Ospedale degli Innocenti, along the piazza's eastern edge, was established in 1419 by the *Arte della Seta*, the Silk Weavers' Guild, and designed and built over the next seven years by Brunelleschi. Europe's first orphanage (and still operating as such), its function is advertised on the facade by Andrea della Robbia's medallions (1487) of blithe children wrapped in swaddling clothes. Under the nine-arched loggia (1432), one of the earliest creations of the Renaissance, notice the *rota* ('wheel') on the far left. Built in 1660, it contained a small revolving door used to receive abandoned children. This was bricked up in 1875.

Inside, you pay to see Brunelleschi's central Chiostro degli Uomini (Men's Cloister) and its narrow neighbour, off to the right, the Choistro delle Donne (Women's Cloister). The ticket also admits you to the Ospedale's small gallery, reached by stairs from the cloisters' left-hand corner. Among the paintings, only Domenico Ghirlandaio's *Coronation of the Virgin* and Botticelli's *Madonna and Child* stand out, together with a simple terracotta *Madonna and Child* by Luca della Robbia.

Pietro Tacca's bizarre fountain stands in front of Brunelleschi's Ospedale degli Innocenti, Europe's first orphanage

Gozzoli's Journey of the Magi *includes portraits of prominent Medici*

▶▶ Palazzo Medici-Riccardi   *IFCE5*

Via Cavour 1
Open: Mon, Tue, Thu–Sat 9–1 and 3–6; Sun 9–1. Closed Wed.
Admission charge

Amid the cacophony of Via Cavour, the seat of the city's greatest dynasty could easily be overlooked as just another grime-covered *palazzo*. Most people come here to see Benozzo Gozzoli's sublime fresco cycle, the *Journey of the Magi* (1459). Before seeing it, however, spare a moment for the palace itself, built by Michelozzo for Cosimo de' Medici in 1444. The design, with its heavy rusticated first-floor exterior (see panel), was to influence numerous buildings in the century of palace building that followed (notably the Palazzo Pitti and Palazzo Strozzi). It remained the Medici's principal residence until 1540, when Cosimo I moved to the Palazzo Vecchio.

Gozzoli's tiny frescoed chapel comes as a beautiful surprise after traipsing through the palace's bureaucratic gloom. Its frescoes, commissioned by Piero de' Medici, were painted in honor of the Compagnia dei Magi, one of the city's most prestigious religious confraternities (of which the Medici were members). The splendour of the figures in the paintings may also reflect the appearance of Greek and Ottoman visitors to the ecumenical Council of Florence, held in 1439. Several of the Medici are portrayed as kings and attendants, while the Magi's journey itself recalls the pageantry of the confraternity's annual procession through Florence.

Ignore, for a moment, the frescoes on either side of the altar (the landscapes are by Gozzoli) and concentrate on the chapel's three main walls. Each deals with one of the three kings. The first, on the right wall, depicts an immense procession, headed by a courtly figure on horseback – probably an idealised portrait of Lorenzo the Magnificent. Cosimo rides behind on another white horse, followed by his brother Lorenzo (in conical hat, riding a mule). Piero de' Medici, hatless, is between them. Head-on, behind the bowman, is Piero's younger son, Giuliano. The scene on the rear wall contains a lovely pastoral background of green hills and tower-filled villages. In the final scene the maroon-cloaked king astride a mule is surrounded by colourful details of the kind that make Gozzoli's work so appealing – leopards, monkeys, ducks, giraffes, and falcons with their bleeding prey.

RUSTICATION
According to Michelozzo, the purpose of rustication (building with huge, rough-hewn blocks of stone – to be seen all over Florence) was to 'unite an appearance of solidity and strength with the light and shade so essential to beauty under the glare of an Italian sun'.

113

FINDING THE WAY
Finding Gozzoli's frescos can be tricky. Walk through the first courtyard to the walled side garden (a rare survival of what was once a common feature of medieval *palazzi*). Buy your ticket and return to the courtyard. With your back to the entrance, take the first doorway on the right and climb the stairs to the third floor. To see the chapel's former altarpiece, take the second door on the right in the main courtyard as you enter from the street, and climb to the second floor. The picture, by Filippo Lippi, is in the triangular container off the windowed gallery.

SELF-PORTRAIT
Gozzoli has painted himself on the left of the crowded procession that follows the king in the fresco on the right-hand wall of the chapel. He stands a couple of rows from the rear in the ranks of red-hatted figures. His hat bears the words OP'S BENOTII ('Benoti's Work') in a gold-lettered band. This type of hat was favoured by scholars of the day.

Markets often lend heart and character to a city, and those of Florence are no exception. Choose between the Mercato Centrale's superb food stalls and the souvenir-oriented stalls of San Lorenzo, or between the rougher-edged bustle of Sant'Ambrogio and the more bohemian atmosphere of the markets in the Cascine and Piazza dei Ciompi.

PORCELLINO

'Little Pig' is the affectionate name given by Florentines to the bronze statue of a huge wild boar alongside the Mercato Nuovo. If you rub his polished snout and throw a coin in the fountain, tradition has it that you will return to Florence (all the money goes to charity). A copy of an ancient Roman statue now in the Uffizi, it was cast in about 1612 by Giambologna's pupil Pietro Tacca, the sculptor responsible for the eccentric sea-creatures in Piazza Santissima Annunziata (see page 112).

114

THE CASCINE

Florence's largest and busiest general market spreads through the gardens of the Cascine every Tuesday morning (7–1; see page 73).

San Lorenzo Florence's most central market, San Lorenzo is the one you will probably stumble on first. Usually thronged with visitors, including many foreigners, the sprawl of stalls fills the streets north of Piazza San Lorenzo. With its predictable panoply of fakes, clothes and leatherware, this market is more a spot to wander and soak up the atmosphere than a place for serious purchases (though there are bargains to be had). The open-air crowds make a welcome change from sight-seeing, but beware of pickpockets. *Open*: daily 8–7. *Closed* Sun and Mon in winter.

Mercato Centrale Situated at the heart of San Lorenzo's labyrinthine market, the Mercato Centrale is one of Europe's largest covered food halls. Built in 1874 and given an extra floor in 1980, it is a fantastic and flamboyant medley of colour and activity, crammed with fruit, vegetables, bread, meat, cheese, herbs, pasta, and seasonal specialities such as figs, truffles, wild boar, cherries, and plump *porcini* mushrooms.

Some of the city's best delicatessens are gathered in the Mercato Centrale, notably *Il Forteo* and *Baroni*, not to mention numerous bars, and cheap hole-in-the-wall trattorie like *Ottavino*, *Zà-zà*, and *Da Nerbone*. Whether you come to buy picnic supplies, or to revel in the atmosphere and sheer entertainment value, this is as essential a spot to visit as any of the city's museums and galleries. *Open*: Mon–Sat 7–2 (also mid-Sep–mid-Jun Sat 4–8).

Sant'Ambrogio Located to the northeast of Santa Croce in Piazza Lorenzo Ghiberti, Sant'Ambrogio is a more rambunctious and more down-at-heel version of the Mercato Centrale. Aimed at Florence's working population, it feels much more like a rural, small-town market. Wander around the food stalls, watch the people, and enjoy the atmosphere – and the prices, which are among the lowest in the city. The lunch counter and coffee bar inside the market are handy for refreshment stops. *Open*: Mon–Fri 7–2.

Piazza dei Ciompi Big-city flea markets these days rarely offer bargains, and Piazza dei Ciompi's modest *Mercato delle Pulci*, a couple of minutes' walk to the north of Sant'Ambrogio, is unfortunately no exception. Prices for its selection of books, coins, uniforms, and bric-a-brac are often as high as those in the city's antique shops.

Nonetheless, you can pick up the odd bargain and, as ever, it is fun to browse. If you do intend to haggle seriously, come to the much larger secondhand market held in the square on the first Sunday of every month (except July).

On the north side of the piazza is the Loggia del Pesce, built by Vasari for the fishmongers (*pesce* means 'fish') of the Mercato Vecchio when their market was moved in 1568. *Open*: Tue–Sat 8–1 and 3.30–7; last Sun of the month (except July) 9–7.

Mercato Nuovo The name may mean 'New Market', but a market has existed here, at the junction of Via Calimala and Via Porta Rossa, since the 11th century. Originally a covered market for silk and gold, it became a meeting place for shipping merchants with boats at Pisa and Livorno. (Notice the stone set in the floor, marking the spot where bankrupts and confidence tricksters were exposed before being pilloried.)

The market now deals in raffia goods, paper, leather, silks, as well as cheap souvenirs. Don't miss the famous *Porcellino* statue (see panel opposite). *Open*: daily 9–6. *Closed* Sun and Mon in winter.

MERCATO DELLE PIANTE
Florence's Flower Market is held weekly (Thursday 8–6) except in July and August under the post office loggia in Via Pellicceria (just off Piazza della Repubblica).

CRAFT MARKET
Piazza Santo Spirito has a small general market during the week but comes alive during the special craft market held here on the second Sunday of every month (except August).

Choose your market and then put together your picnic lunch

▶▶▶ Palazzo Pitti IFCD2

Piazza dei Pitti
Open: Galleria Palatina and Appartamenti Monumentali (combined ticket): Tue–Sat 8.30–6.50; Sun 9–2. Closed Mon. Museo degli Argenti and Galleria del Costume and Galleria d'Arte Moderna (combined ticket): Tue–Sat 8.30–1.50, plus 1st, 3rd and 5th Sun and 2nd and 4th Mon of the month. See panel on page 117 for ticket information

Few palaces or galleries come much larger than the Palazzo Pitti, home to the Medici for almost 200 years and now an eight-museum complex devoted to the family's insatiable (and sometimes tasteless) passion for paintings and fine art. Although intimidating on first acquaintance, the palace in fact boasts only two museums that definitely demand attention: the Galleria Palatina, home to a magnificent collection of paintings, and the Museo degli Argenti, a lavish assortment of Medici silverware and precious *objets d'art*.

The palace Few people linger to admire the Pitti's overbearing façade, variously described as a 'rusticated Stalinist ministry' (Dana Facaros), 'a rather expensive barracks' (Arnold Bennett), and a 'union of Cyclopean' massiveness [and] stately regularity' (George Eliot). Commissioned in 1457 by Luca Pitti, a wealthy banker,

The Parting of Venus from Adonis *(1707–8), a ceiling fresco by Sebastiano Ricci*

the palace's purpose was partly to put one over on the Medici, then the Pitti's implacable rivals. It was probably designed by Brunelleschi, who brought the plans to Pitti in a huff, having had them rejected by Cosimo de' Medici as too ostentatious. When Pitti died, in 1472, the palace remained unfinished, consisting of just seven central bays. Even at this modest juncture, however, its scale and grandeur were already attracting admiration from the likes of Vasari and Machiavelli.

Poor old Pitti was doubtless turning in his grave by 1549, when the family – now fallen on hard times – were forced to sell out to their old enemies, the despised Medici. Cosimo I bought the palace on his wife's prompting (she hated the Palazzo Vecchio, their previous home). Vasari was commissioned to unite the Medici holdings, the palace being linked to the Uffizi (the Medici's 'offices') by way of the Corridoio Vasariano (see page 129). Once installed, the family remained in residence for almost two centuries. In 1549 the palace was only one room deep, hemmed in by the slope of the Giardino di Boboli. This proved too modest for Cosimo's wife, Eleonora of Toledo, who engaged Ammannati to extend the palace in all directions. This was followed by several bouts of building in the 17th and 19th centuries, after which the façade had grown to three times its original width and the palace looked more or less as it does today.

117

The Galleria Palatina An unrivalled collection of 16th- to 18th-century paintings, the Palatine Gallery is packed with masterpieces by Raphael, Titian, Tintoretto, Giorgione, Velázquez, Murillo, Perugino, Rubens, Andrea del Sarto, and many others – as great a range of painters, in fact, as the Uffizi. Many complain that the works, though well labelled, are badly displayed – wedged as they are from floor to ceiling with no attempt at classification by period or provenance. In truth, the stacked arrangement was the way in which the Medici grand dukes chose to display their artistic possessions. It is also a vivid illustration of the collection's sheer scope.

Only the absolute highlights are given below, so be sure to put down the guide and spend time in front of paintings which simply catch the eye. The gallery's own catalogue numbers are included below in brackets.) Orientation can be confusing, both around the palace generally and within the Galleria Palatina in particular. To find the gallery, buy your ticket (see panel), walk to the rear right of the main courtyard, and climb the grand staircase to the Palatina's entrance. Beyond a stupendous chandelier, a hint of the splendour to come, walk straight on through the first two rooms (belvederes with lovely views of Ammannati's courtyard and the Giardino di Boboli). In the third room turn left. From here on, work down the six state rooms, all labelled, and then return down the seven parallel rooms to your starting point.

Room 1 (Sala di Venere) Note first the ceiling frescoes, the first of four masterpieces (continued in the following rooms) by Pietro da Cortona depicting allegorical and mythological scenes inspired by the Medici. Below them, look for [185] *The Concert* (c1510–12), [18] *Portrait of a Lady* (1536) and [54] *Portrait of Pietro Aretino* (1545) by Titian; two vast seascapes [4, 15] by Salvator Rosa; and a pair of

TICKETS
Separate tickets, from different ticket offices, are required to see the Pitti's various museums. One combined ticket admits you to the Galleria Palatina and the Appartamenti Monumentali (*Admission charge*). Another is valid for the Museo degli Argenti (*Admission charge*) and another for the Galleria de Costume and Museo delle Porcevane combined, the Galleria del Costume, and the Museo delle Porcellane (*Admission charge*). The last is in the Boboli gardens and can be seen only by prior arrangement with the ticket office. Tickets for the Giardino di Boboli (see pages 84–5) are purchased from a separate office immediately inside the palace.

One of Titian's best-known portraits, but the identity of the subject is unknown

HOSPITALITY ABUSED
Many writers left accounts of the high life to be enjoyed at the Pitti's Medici court – usually at the hosts' expense: 'Guests', observed Trollope, 'used to behave abominably. The English would seize plates of *bonbons* and empty the contents into their coat pockets. The ladies would do the same with their pocket handkerchiefs … I never saw an American pillaging … though I may add that American ladies would accept any amount of *bonbons* from English blockade runners … I have seen large portions of fish, sauce and all, packed up in newspaper, and deposited in a pocket. I have seen fowls and ham share the same fate, without any news paper at all. I have seen jelly carefully wrapped in an Italian countess's laced *mouchoir…*'

lovely landscapes [9, 14] by Rubens (*c*1637). The statue at the centre of the room is the Venus Italica, commissioned from Canova by a guilty Napoleon in 1812 to replace the famous *Venus de' Medici* which he removed to Paris (see the panel on page 164).

Room 2 (Sala di Apollo) This room's largest work is [237] Rosso Fiorentino's *Madonna and Saints* (1522), removed from Santo Spirito, but the masterpiece is [92] Titian's *Portrait of a Gentleman* (1540), one of the painter's most famous portraits. The sombre, dignified sitter is unknown, but was long believed to be the English Duke of Norfolk. To his left is [67] Titian's golden-hued and ripely sensuous *Mary Magdalen* (*c*1531). Van Dyck's portrait of *Charles I and Henrietta Maria*, tucked behind the door, may well be familiar. Henrietta, a Medici scion, was married to the English king.

Room 3 (Sala di Marte) Notice the balls of the Medici symbol on the ceiling, one of which, in an expression of the utmost conceit, has been painted as the Earth. The most eye-catching canvas is Rubens' huge [86] *Consequences of War* (1638), an allegory of the Thirty Years' War. The whole painting seems dragged to the right by its immense compositional force. Rubens explained that 'the grief-stricken woman in black [is] the unfortunate Europe, who, for so many years now, has suffered plunder, outrage, and misery'. Tintoretto's [83] *Portrait of Luigi Cornaro*, one of his finest works in the gallery, is outshone by [201] Titian's *Cardinal Ippolito de' Medici* (1532).

Room 4 (Sala di Giove) In its day this was the grand-ducal throne room. Now it is home to one of Raphael's finest portraits [245], the *Donna Velata* (Veiled Woman, *c*1516). The model was a Roman baker's daughter and, according to Vasari, the painter's mistress. By the exit door are [272] Andrea del Sarto's *John the Baptist* (1523), one of the most familiar paintings of the subject; [219] a Perugino *Madonna*; and [64] Fra Bartolomeo's *Deposition* (1516), one of his last and greatest works.

Room 5 (Sala di Saturno) Although [164] Perugino's luminous *Deposition* (1495) dominates, this room is filled with paintings by Raphael. His [151] *Madonna della Seggiola* (1515), encased in a gargantuan frame (all the gallery's frames are on an epic scale), has long been among the Pitti's most famous works (see panel). Raphael also painted [61] *Agnolo* and [59] *Maddalena Doni* (both 1505–6), portraits executed after their marriage (Michelangelo's only Uffizi painting, the Doni Tondo, celebrates the same union). Maddalena's pose is copied directly from that of Leonardo's *Mona Lisa*. Another half-dozen Raphaels line the walls, the most beautiful of which are [165] the *Madonna del Baldacchino* (1507–8) and [178] the sublime *Madonna della Granduca* (1504–5), so called because its owner, Ferdinand III of Lorraine, took it with him wherever he travelled.

Room 6 (Sala dell'Iliade) Elizabeth I of England makes a surprise appearance in [273] an anonymous portrait by a 16th-century English school (at one point the Medici attempted to make a collection of all the crowned heads of Europe). Also here are [229] Raphael's unusual *La Gravida* (Expectant Mother, 1504–8), showing the discreet bulge of pregnancy, and three works by Andrea del Sarto (well represented in the gallery), including [191, 225] two noted depictions of the Assumption (both *c*1527).

Rooms 7–11 These rooms on your return are smaller and less packed with obvious masterpieces. Again, however, certain paintings deserve special attention. The Sala della Stufa (7), formerly a bathroom, boasts an exquisite tile floor. The Sala dell'Educazione di Giove (8; entered before Room 7), boasts [96] Cristofano Allori's famous *Judith and Holofernes* (see panel) and [183] Caravaggio's *Sleeping Cupid* (1608), sporting a wonderfully ugly Cupid. Room 9 is a lovely bathroom. The Sala di Ulisse (10) has a late Raphael [94], the *Madonna dell'Impannata* (1514), a vivid display of the painter's range, and [338] a quiet, almost out-of-place *Death of Lucrezia* by Filippino Lippi (on the right wall). The Sala di Prometeo (11), last of the rooms, ends the gallery in style with a remarkable tondo [343], the *Madonna and Child* by Filippo Lippi (1452).

If you turn left here you enter a maze of rooms crammed with more minor paintings. Walk straight on, however, through the Galleria dei Poccetti and the Sala della Musica, to return to your starting point.

Museo degli Argenti The entrance to this museum is on the left of the main courtyard (separate ticket required). The so-called Silver Museum contains not only silverware but also any sort of precious object – whether exquisite or execrable – on which the Medici could lay their hands. Overwhelming as it is, the collection is only a fraction of that once owned by the family. Although Anna Maria, the sister of the last Medici, left the entire family collection to Florence, some of the most valuable pieces were sold to

THE MADONNA DELLA SEGGIOLA
According to legend the *tondo* (round panel) for this painting came from the end of a wine barrel. Raphael, it appears, was keen to master the demands of tondo technique, a traditional Florentine form. For centuries the work was one of the most popular depictions of the Virgin in Italian art. Would-be copyists in the 19th century had to join a five-year waiting list to study the painting. The bulging figures appear as if seen in a slightly convex mirror – one of the earliest conscious uses of illusionism in the Renaissance.

119

JUDITH AND HOLOFERNES
This was one of the most universally admired Florentine paintings of the 17th century. The figures are portraits of the artist Cristofano Allori, his mother, and his mistress. Despite the violence of the subject, few executions can have been so bloodless. Judith, a seductive, erotic figure dressed in spotless silks and gold satin, is immaculately coiffured, remaining sublimely indifferent to Holofernes' severed head.

GALLERIA D'ARTE MODERNA
This gallery boasts more than 30 rooms of Tuscan painting from about 1800 to 1945. Its undoubted highlights are the sunny Italians landscapes of the so-called Italian Impressionists (the Macchiaioli), a group who broke with tradition to produce colourful and realistic paintings after the manner of Corot and Courbet. Also on show are some immensely morbid and perverse sculptures, notably Room 19's *Suicide* and *Pregnant Nun*.

CAPPELLA RUCELLAI
Alberti designed this superb chapel (entrance at Via della Spada 18) for Giovanni Rucellai's tomb. It represents Alberti's idea of how Jerusalem's Holy Sepulchre might have looked when it was built by Emperor Constantine. The design also borrowed ideas from Florence's Baptistery, then believed to be a Roman building. *Open*: Sat 5.30 only, for Mass.

MUSEO MARINO MARINI
The Marini Museum lies behind the Palazzo Rucellai in Piazza San Pancrazio and houses 200 works by the modern sculptor Marino Marini (1901–66). *Open*: daily Mon, Wed–Sat 10–5, plus Thu 10 am–11 pm in summer. *Closed* Tue and Aug. *Admission charge*.

finance the wars of her family's Austrian relatives. The lavish salons on the first floor, which were used as reception rooms for important guests, boast exuberant and surprisingly charming baroque frescoes devoted – inevitably – to the Medici's unflagging prowess.

Off to the left of the first salon, in the Sala Buia, resides one of the museum's unquestioned masterpieces – a collection of 16 *pietre dure* vases owned by Lorenzo the Magnificent. They range from Roman and Byzantine pieces to medieval Venetian works. In an act of minor vandalism, Lorenzo engraved his monogram on each of the vases: 'LA V R MED'. Lorenzo believed that such items, along with gemstones, made better investments than paintings. Many precious stones in his collection, for example, were valued at over 1,000 florins, while a Botticelli painting could be had for less than 100.

Some of the collection's most magnificent and magnificently awful highlights reside on the museum's mezzanine and second floors. Everything is here – caskets, embroidery, rugs, ivory, painted glass, reliquaries, cutlery, furniture, and a host of articles to which you would be hard pushed to give a name. Make first for the superb jewellery exhibits on the mezzanine, then marvel at exotica such as tortoise butter dishes, ostrich egg chalices, mosaic stone portraits, Mexican feather mitres, buffalo-horn goblets, carved cherry stones, and sensationally tacky seashell figurines.

The **Galleria del Costume** (with Galleria d'Arte Moderna) is one for devotees of clothes and fashion. It illustrates the history of costume from the 18th century up to the 1920s. Displays are frequently changed, and the gallery hosts many special exhibitions.

▶ **Palazzo Rucellai**   *IFCD4*
Via della Vigna Nuova
Currently closed to the public except for temporary exhibitions
Rucellai was a wealthy merchant and scholar, whose fortune was made from *oricello*, the famous Florentine red dye (from which the family took its name). Proud of his patronage, he liked to say he earned more honour 'by having spent money well than by having earned it'. Much honour, then, must have accrued from his palace, built between 1446 and 1451, probably to a design by Leon Battista Alberti.

A great theorist, Alberti was an architect with firm ideas of what constituted good architecture. He particularly abhorred the fortresslike rustication championed by the Medici and Strozzi palaces (see below and page 113). 'Only the house of a tyrant can look like a fortress,' he chided, adding that palaces should be 'open to the world outside, beautifully adorned, and delicate and finely proportioned rather than proud and stately'.

His palace, still owned by Rucellai's descendants, was the first in the city to use the old classical orders. The pilasters on the first and top floors are decorated – like Rome's Colosseum – with Doric and Corinthian capitals, while the pilasters of the middle floor sport a Corinthian hybrid designed by Alberti himself. Alberti created only the façade's five left-hand bays: Rucellai added the other two, and might have added more but for a financial crisis brought on by the loss of two of his ships at sea. Notice the family's emblem on the façade – Fortune's sail – entwined with trios of Medici diamond rings, an allusion to the marriage of Rucellai's son to the granddaughter of Cosimo de' Medici.

The Palazzo Rucellai's ground floor now houses the **Museo di Storia della Fotografia Fratelli Alinari**, host to temporary photographic exhibitions and a collection tracing the history of the Alinari firm (founded in 1852), famous for its black-and-white photographs.

▶ Palazzo Strozzi   *IFC4D*

Piazza Strozzi
Open during temporary exhibitions
The style of palazzo so abhorred by Alberti (see above) is well exemplified in the nearby Palazzo Strozzi. Built for Filippo Strozzi, a powerful banker and head of Florence's anti-Medici faction, it was the last and largest of the 100 or so palaces raised in the city during the 15th century. It copies the **Palazzo Medici-Riccardi** (see page 113), offering almost nothing in the way of architectural nicety or innovation. Size is all here, the immeasurably ugly façade topped by a classically inspired cornice and faced in cyclopean blocks of rusticated stone. Only the inner courtyard might betray any hint of intimacy or delicacy – had it not been spoiled by the addition of an incongruous metal fire escape.

The Loggia dei Rucellai, probably built for a Medici wedding

LOGGIA DEI RUCELLAI
The loggia opposite the palace was the last of 26 such arcades built in medieval Florence. Noble families built a loggia in or close to their *palazzo* for weddings, meetings, and family entertainments. Alberti probably designed the Rucellai loggia (1460–6) for the marriage of Rucellai's son to Nannina Medici. Six properties were destroyed to create the site. Such profligacy was the death of loggias, which declined as building land became more expensive.

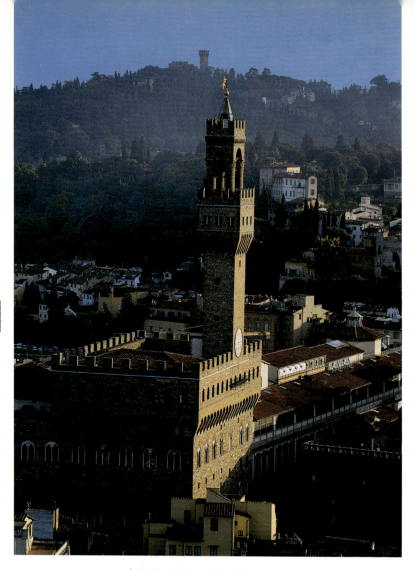

Guardian of the city

THE *SIGNORIA*
The nine *Priori* of the
Priorate or *Signoria*
(founded 1282) were
responsible for govern-
ment, law and diplomacy.
After a two-month term
of office, each was ineligi-
ble for reelection for three
years. While in office
the *Priori* received only
official visitors, and left
the palace only for mat-
ters of the gravest importance. They were paid a
modest wage.

▶▶ **Palazzo Vecchio**   *IFCE3*

Piazza della Signoria
Open: Mon–Wed, Sat 9–7, Sun 8–1. Closed Thu. Admission
charge. Combined ticket (Biglietto Cumulativo) available,
covering the Palazzo Vecchio, the Museo Bardini, the Museo di
Firenze com'era, and the Museo di Santa Maria Novella

'A stark … incarnation of the stern realities of medieval
times' was Stendhal's description of the Palazzo Vecchio
which dominates Piazza della Signoria and a stretch of the
Florentine skyline with its forceful tower and bristling
crenellations. The city's seat of government for seven centuries (and still the town hall), it was first mooted in 1285,
three years after the creation of the *Signoria* (see panel and
pages 34–5). Work started under Arnolfo di Cambio, who
at that time was also employed on the Duomo, and was
completed around 1302. Over the years the building
underwent several changes, the most notable in 1540,

when Cosimo I transferred the Medici court here from the Palazzo Medici. Ten years later, when Cosimo moved again – this time to the 'new' Palazzo Pitti – the palace took its present name (*vecchio* means 'old').

Between 1865 and 1871, while Florence was briefly Italy's capital, the palace housed the country's foreign ministry and parliament.

The courtyard The palace's grand *cortile* (1453), designed by Michelozzo, was later subjected to Vasari's dubious interior design talents. The result, as elsewhere in the palace, was a wearisome paean to Medici prowess. Some of the frescoes, rather oddly, depict views of Austrian cities; they were added to celebrate the marriage of Francesco, Cosimo's son, to Joanna of Austria.

The second floor Vasari's staircase leads to the palace's centrepiece, the cavernous but strangely soulless Salone dei Cinquecento. Built in 1495, it was designed to accommodate the 500-strong meetings of the *Consiglio Maggiore*, then the city's ruling assembly. In what might have been a Renaissance *tour de force*, Michelangelo and Leonardo da Vinci were lined up to fresco the walls. However, they were called away to Rome and Milan respectively, so neither progressed much beyond preliminary sketches. Vasari was commissioned to do the work instead, the result being six immense paintings (1563–5) of Florentine triumphs over Pisa and Siena. Few works of art can have been painted with such militaristic relish. More decorative excess washes over the ceiling (again courtesy of Vasari), where an orgy of paint and gilt celebrates the apotheosis of Cosimo I.

The third floor Steps opposite the Studiolo (see panel) lead to the palace's third floor. Halfway up, notice the fireworks fresco (1558), a view of Piazza della Signoria during the feast-day celebrations of St John the Baptist. Turn left at the top and you enter five rooms known as the Quartiere degli Elementi, each frescoed by Vasari and assistants. Beyond them is the more appealing Terrazza di Saturno, an open loggia with views over the rooftops to Santa Croce, San Miniato al Monte and the hills beyond.

Return to the stairs and turn right: an open balcony gives a view over the Salone below. Next comes the Quartiere di Eleonora di Toledo, the six-roomed apartment of Cosimo I's wife. The star turn here is the chapel (immediately on the right as you enter), a masterpiece of vivid Mannerist decoration by Bronzino (1540–45). Beyond the chapel you emerge into the larger Sala d'Udienza, with a beautiful ceiling and superb views of the Piazza della Signoria. Next door is the still larger Sala dei Gigli, its walls and tremendous ceiling swathed in the gold lilies that give the room its name (*giglio* means 'lily'). The palace's key work of art is here – Donatello's statue of *Judith and Holofernes* (1456–60). The one frescoed wall is by Domenico Ghirlandaio.

The two final rooms are the Cancelleria (off to the left), once used as an office by Machiavelli, and the lovely Sala delle Carte (or Guardaroba) to the right, filled with globes and 57 beautiful maps (painted on leather) of the known world in 1563.

123

STUDIOLO DI FRANCESCO I
Built for Cosimo I's gloomy son, Francesco I, the 'study' (1569–73) is a tiny, windowless room off the Salone dei Cinquecento, to the right of the entrance. It was decorated by 30 of Florence's leading Mannerist painters with scenes that reflected his scientific and alchemic interests. Each wall depicts allegorical episodes connected with Earth, Water, Air and Fire. The vault's facing figures are portraits by Bronzino of Francesco's parents. Francesco kept his more treasured knick-knacks hidden behind the oval-shaped lower paintings.

ROOM WITH A VIEW
The tiny room at the top of the Palazzo Vecchio's tower was known ironically as the *alberghettino* ('little guest house'). It was used for eminent prisoners such as Cosimo de' Medici (before his brief exile) and Savonarola, who stayed here between torture sessions gazing down over the piazza where he was later to be executed.

The name of Niccolò Machiavelli (1469–1527) has become a byword for intrigue and political cynicism. A look at his life and works, however, suggests that posterity has served him ill, for in reality he was a great political theorist, a superb stylist, and one of the foremost historians of his age.

Only one portrait of Machiavelli survives: an oil painting by Santi di Tito in the Palazzo Vecchio. From it 'Old Nick' gazes out with an expression that is anything but Machiavellian. Instead he looks simultaneously quizzical and sardonic, his features thin, neat and ascetic, his thinning hair swept back from a high forehead.

Deprivation and diplomacy Machiavelli came from noble stock, albeit from a family that – having once held high Florentine office – had recently fallen on hard times. 'I learnt to do without,' he wrote, 'before I learnt to enjoy'. Poverty was to limit his education, leaving him to his own devices, a hardship that perhaps honed, rather than hindered, his style and original thinking.

Entering political service after Savonarola's execution (1498), he became chancellor and secretary to the ruling council of the Florentine Republic. Entrusted with diplomatic missions, he spent five months at the French court (1500), receiving an object lesson in how a strong nation might be united under a single prince. The lesson was reinforced by visits to Switzerland and Germany, and by observing Cesare Borgia's attempts to carve out a principality in central Italy. Recording his observations, he noted – with the realism that was to become his trademark – that 'the world has always been inhabited by human beings who have always had the same passion'.

A smiling Niccolò Machiavelli, the only surviving portrait

Republic and Medici Rising through the ranks, Machiavelli became right-hand man to Piero Soderini, *gonfaloniere*, and chief magistrate under the city's Republican constitution. Having the ear of Florence's de facto ruler (the Medici having been temporarily deposed), he persuaded Soderini to create a militia in 1505, having seen at first hand the untrustworthiness of traditional mercenary armies. It was to be supervised by the Council of Nine (1506), with Machiavelli – who also led troops in the field – as its chief secretary.

Nemesis arrived in 1512 with the return of the Medici. Soderini was deposed and Machiavelli barred from the Palazzo della Signoria. When an anti-Medici plot was uncovered in 1513, Machiavelli, who was already under suspicion, was accused of complicity and imprisoned. Although tortured, he maintained his innocence and was eventually released. Limits were placed on his freedom, however, and without employment he was soon faced with destitution.

Machiavelli's writings It was at this point that he retired to write *The Prince* and the *Discourse on the First Ten Books of Livy* (both completed in less than six months). The books were masterpieces of political analysis, linking political science (the 'reason of state') with the study of human nature. They also proposed the idea of historical cycles, based on the premise that human behaviour remains immutable.

Reading the books today it is essential to see them as products of their time. Machiavelli loved Florence 'more than his own soul', and to see his beloved city descend into chaos inevitably coloured his thinking. His books and their proposed remedies, therefore, must be seen as the attempts of a patriot desperate to rescue his city, while doing so in a way that was compatible with human nature and with the vicissitudes of the age. His diabolic reputation and the moral backlash only came later (see panel).

After years in the political wilderness, Machiavelli gradually crept back into favour, serving as an adviser to Giuliano de' Medici and becoming the republic's official historian in 1520 (the *Istorie Fiorentine* were the result). When the Medici were again usurped in 1527, however, Machiavelli failed to regain his old post as chancellor – one final twist in the life of a man who raised the political twist to an art form.

Machiavelli's tomb in Santa Croce, by Innocenzo Spinazzi

BACKLASH
Machiavelli first came in for a critical mauling during the Counter-Reformation, when his ideas were singled out by the Inquisition for particular opprobrium. 'Machiavellianism', however, was originally a French term, coined to denigrate not Machiavelli, but all things Italian.

CALL TO ARMS

In times of crisis Florentines were summoned to a *Parlemento* in Piazza della Signoria by the tolling of the Palazzo Vecchio's famous bell, known as the Vacca (cow), after its deep, mooing tone. On hearing the bell, all males over the age of 14 had to gather in their separate wards and march behind banners to the piazza. When a quorum of two-thirds was reached, they were asked to approve the creation of a *balia*, a committee with full powers to deal with the crisis. The device was much used to subvert the normal processes of government.

Ammannati's Neptune

▶▶▶ Piazza della Signoria　　*IFCE3*

Florence kept the two chief pillars of medieval society well apart. While the Church busied itself in Piazza del Duomo, civic proceedings were confined to Piazza della Signoria. Lacking in architectural harmony, the latter is a less beautiful square than many in Italy. It has, however, witnessed key events in the city's history – Savonarola's execution in particular – and remains one of Florence's prime social meeting places. Of only modest size until the 14th century, the square was enlarged in 1307 as a setting for the Palazzo dei Priori (now the Palazzo Vecchio). Enlarged still further, it acquired more or less its present size when it was paved in 1385.

The piazza has always been a stage for political rallies and crowd-pleasing spectacles. Wild boar and lions, for example, were often released here for hunting and entertainment. On one occasion three men were killed by rampaging buffaloes. On another, a stallion was set loose among mares: the ensuing highjinks were described by one onlooker as 'the most marvelous entertainment for girls to behold', and by another as a spectacle that 'much displeased decent and well-behaved people'.

Political proceedings took place on the raised dais in front of the Palazzo Vecchio. It was known as the *arringhiera* – the origin of the English word 'harangue'.

Rallies often became heated. One meeting in 1343, for example, ended with a man reputedly being eaten by the inflamed mob. Cannibalism notwithstanding, high standards of behaviour were expected in the piazza. Carts and traffic were banned (as they are today), as were begging, gambling and prostitution. Crimes committed within its precincts were punished more severely than those committed elsewhere.

The piazza's key components are self-evident: the towered bulk of the **Palazzo Vecchio** (see pages 122–3) and the triple-arched **Loggia dei Lanzi** (see page 86). Between them lies the entrance to the **Uffizi** (see pages 160–5). Ranged across the piazza is a series of fountains and statues, some familiar, others – deservedly – more obscure. Most were erected during the 16th century to accentuate the approach to the Uffizi. (Michelangelo once proposed extending the Loggia's arches around the entire piazza to achieve the same effect.) From left to right as you face the Palazzo Vecchio the statues are as follows:

1. **Cosimo I** (1587–94) by Giambologna. This equestrian statue – the only one of its kind cast in the late Renaissance – was designed to emulate Rome's ancient statue of Marcus Aurelius, thus linking the 'glory' of Florence (and Cosimo) with that of classical Rome. The bas-reliefs describe three key events in Cosimo's career: the conquest of Siena (1555); his becoming Duke of Florence (1537); and Pope Pius V conferring on him the title of Grand Duke of Tuscany (1569).

2. **Neptune Fountain** (1565–75) by Ammannati. Neptune symbolises Cosimo I's ambitions for Florence as a naval power. Florentines call it *Il Biancone* (The Big White One), a river god turned to stone for spurning the love of women. When struck by the light of a full moon, it is said to wander the piazza conversing with other statues. It prompted a famous put-down (attributed to Michelangelo) 'Ammannato, Ammannato, che bel marmo hai rovinato' (what a beautiful piece of marble you have ruined). The better bronzes around the base are by Giambologna and others. A porphyry disc in front of the fountain marks the spot of Savonarola's execution.

3. **Il Marzocco.** A copy of Donatello's sculpture of Florence's heraldic lion (see panel). The original (1418–20) is in the Bargello (see page 59).

4. **Judith and Holofernes**. A copy of an original sculpture (1456–60) removed to the Palazzo Vecchio in 1980 (see page 123). Taken from the Medici palace after the family's fall in 1494, its role in the piazza was to symbolise the defeat of tyranny.

5. **David**. An 1873 copy of Michelangelo's original in the Accademia (see pages 52–3).

6. **Hercules and Cacus**. Bandinelli's statue, carved to partner David, simultaneously symbolises Cosimo I, Florentine fortitude, and the conquest of domestic enemies. The marble was originally offered to Michelangelo. Having been awaited with great expectation, Bandinelli's version was unveiled in 1534 to much disappointment. Cellini described it as a 'sack of melons'.

7. **Male Herm** by Vincenzo Rossi (1535).

8. **Female Herm** by Bandinelli (1535). The identity of the two herms is unknown. They served as posts for a chain across the entrance to the Palazzo Vecchio.

A detail of the Neptune Fountain

127

THE MARZOCCO
Florence's heraldic lion may have its origins in a mutilated Roman equestrian statue of Mars (*Martocus*) that stood at the end of the Ponte Vecchio until the 1333 flood. Or it may come from lions kept in the dungeons of the Palazzo Vecchio, whose behaviour was watched for auguries in times of crisis. From the 13th century onward, the symbol was raised in Tuscan towns conquered by Florence. Captured prisoners were customarily required to kiss its posterior. Donatello's lion was carved for a papal apartment in Santa Maria Novella and moved to the piazza in 1812 to replace a 14th-century version.

MEN ONLY
'I saw the pale crouching Duomo and in the thick moon-mist the Giotto tower...the Palazzo Vecchio with Michelangelo's *David* and all the statues of men we passed. "This is a men's town", I said, "not like Paris, where all the statues are women"'. Frieda Lawrence, *Not I, but the Wind* (1935)

Florence

Emblem of the city, and miraculous survivor

A BRIDGE TOO FAR
The Ponte Vecchio was the only Florentine bridge spared by the Nazis during the retreat of 1944. Harried by the American 5th Army, the Germans reneged on a promise to demilitarise the city and spare its artistic heritage (as had happened in Rome). All the Arno bridges were blown up, on 4 August, to hamper the Allied advance. Medieval quarters at either end of the Ponte Vecchio were also razed in order to block access to the bridge. Only the bridge itself survived, spared by Field Marshal Kesselring, possibly on direct orders from Hitler.

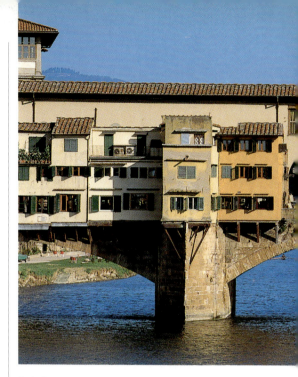

►►► Ponte Vecchio   *IFCD3*

With its evocative huddle of shops, the Ponte Vecchio is as much a symbol of Florence as the cathedral's dome or Michelangelo's *David*. As symbols go, however, it is one of the city's more crowded – so be prepared for hordes, hawkers, and souvenir-sellers.

Pitched close to the Arno's narrowest point and earliest crossing, the Ponte Vecchio is the last in a succession of bridges on the site that dates back to Roman times. Until 1218 it was the only bridge across the river, providing a vital lifeline between the old city and the Oltrarno. A wooden bridge, recorded here in 970 and reinforced in 1170, was swept away in the floods of 1333, some of the worst in the city's history. The bridge built to replace it in 1345 is the one that visitors flock to see today – a unique and miraculous survivor both of World War II (see panel) and (just) of the 1966 flood. Its name – the Old Bridge – was coined to distinguish it from the city's other medieval bridge, the Ponte alla Carraia (originally built in 1218).

Shops clung to the Ponte Vecchio from as early as the 13th century. Butchers and fish sellers were among its first occupants, attracted by the proximity of the Arno, a convenient sewer for their offal and other waste. Tanners were the next arrivals, a no less noxious bunch. They added to the communal stench by soaking hides in the river before tanning them in horse's urine. With the bridge awash in such delights, it was not long, inevitably, before a gap was made between the shops so that debris could be swept off the sidewalks into the river (the space is still there). Smells and detritus notwithstanding, the commercial potpourri was enriched over the years by barbers, blacksmiths, cobblers, hosiers, surgeons, and fruit and vegetable sellers.

The Ponte Vecchio is one of the best places to admire Vasari's much-vaunted **Corridoio Vasariano**, a covered aerial passageway built for Cosimo I in 1565 to link the Uffizi (the Medici offices) with the newly acquired Palazzo Pitti across the river. The corridor also served as a monument in celebration of the marriage of Cosimo's son, Francesco, to Joanna of Austria. It was built in just five months, and Vasari liked to boast that it might have taken others five years to complete. He also liked to allude to its classical antecedents, citing as his inspiration the passageway that reputedly linked the palaces of Priam and Hector in ancient Troy. He kept quieter about the five men killed as a result of the hasty construction work.

For Cosimo's part, the Corridoio allowed him to roam his domain without having to meet the Florentine hoipolloi. After crossing the Ponte Vecchio, for example, it snakes toward Santa Felicita (see page 144), passing over the church's portico in such a way that Cosimo could follow services without setting foot on a public street.

The corridor did not, however, offer enough protection to spare the nostrils and sensibilities of Cosimo's still more fastidious successors. By 1593 Ferdinand I had had his fill of the noxious odours and evicted the bridge's butchers and tanners – practitioners of what he termed 'vile arts'. In their place he introduced eight jewellers and 41 goldsmiths, practitioners of a traditional Florentine skill in which some of the finest Renaissance artists had been trained. This more decorous breed of craftsmen (more to the point, perhaps) allowed themselves to be cajoled into paying double the previous rents. To this day, jewellers have continued to monopolise the bridge's legitimate trade, hence its central bust (1900) of the most celebrated of Florence's goldsmiths, Benvenuto Cellini.

DICKENS'S VIEW
'… the Ponte Vecchio… is [a] most enchanting feature of the scene. The space of one house, in the centre, being left open, the view beyond is shown as in a frame; and that precious glimpse of sky, and water, and rich buildings, shining so quietly among the huddled roofs and gables on the bridge, is exquisite…'
Charles Dickens,
Pictures from Italy (1846)

The Arno is a fickle creature. In one breath Dante called it 'il bel fiume' (the beautiful river), in another 'la maladetta e sventurata fossa' (the cursed and luckless ditch). Its most malevolent side was certainly to the fore on 4 November, 1966, when it unleashed a deluge that created a human and artistic tragedy of unprecedented proportions.

THE 1884 FLOOD

Writers love a disaster because it makes good copy. Looking down from the Campanile at the submerged city in 1884, Anthony Trollope marvelled at the 'truly terrible and magnificent sight'. The river, he wrote, was 'one turbid, yellow, swirling mass … bringing down with it fragments of timber, carcasses of animals, and large quantities of hay and straw'. Later, Trollope had to travel by barge to his lodgings in a submerged Piazza Santa Croce. *What I Remember* (1887)

Top and below: in the wake of the flood – the morning after

Early floods Floods in Florence were nothing new. Early chroniclers traced the city's foundation back to Noah. A deluge in 1269 washed away the Carraia and Santa Trinita bridges. In 1333, the old Ponte Vecchio was destroyed after a four-day tempest – a storm so violent that the city's bells were tolled to exorcise the devils believed to be causing the cyclone. In 1557, flash floods submerged the city to a depth of 6m, moving so quickly that all but two children in a crowd on Ponte Santa Trinita were drowned before they could dash to safety. Stranded on a lone pillar, the surviving pair were fed for two days via a rope slung from the Palazzo Strozzi.

A city in the wrong place Surveying the Arno's muddy trickle in midsummer, it is easy to sympathise with Mark Twain's view that this 'great historical creek with four feet in the channel… would be a very plausible river if they would pump some water into it' (*The Innocents Abroad*, 1869). Had Twain made his observation in a different season, however, he would have realised that the Arno is more usually a torrent that holds Florence a watery hostage. Part of the fault lies with the city's position. Surrounded by hills, it sits helpless on a broad plain, the first flat ground downstream of the point where the Arno has been joined by the Sieve, its major tributary. Worse still, of course, the Arno rises in the Apennines, so is

A CITY IN CRISIS
The 1966 flood plunged Florence into chaos. Women and children were rescued from the rooftops by helicopter; men were left until the waters subsided. Food was short, and electricity and fresh water were cut off for days. Milk and bread were distributed from the Palazzo Vecchio. Total darkness enveloped the city at night, forcing the police to run patrols to discourage looting.

131

RUINOUS WATERS
'A tumultuous mass of water stretches from bank to bank... a snarling brown torrent of terrific velocity, spiralling in whirlpools and countercurrents that send waves running backward; its colour is a rich brown, a boiling *caffè-latte* brown streaked with crests the colour of dirty cream. This tremendous water carries mats of debris: straw, twigs, leafy branches, rags, a litter that the river sucks down and spews up again in a swelling turbulence', K K Taylor, *Diary of Florence in the Flood* (1966)

seasonally swollen by heavy rains and the meltwaters of countless mountain streams. Moving Florence, as has been said many times, is the only way to prevent Florentine floods.

Fateful morning By 4 November, 1966, it had been raining for 40 days and nights. Around 50cm of rain had fallen on Florence in the last 48 hours. Yet, as dawn broke on that fateful morning, and as the Arno rose, few people seemed aware of the imminent danger. Only upstream, where a reservoir threatened to burst, were the sluices opened. In the city itself only the Ponte Vecchio's jewellers stirred, warned in the small hours by a lone nightwatchman of the bridge's trembling. Two solitary policemen, apparently, watched in the darkness as they cleared their shops. Asked why they failed to raise the alarm they reputedly replied 'We have no orders'. In the words of the American writer, Francis Steegmuller, half the shops were soon 'gaping open – gutted by the tremendous force of a torrent that passed right through them' (*Stories and True Stories*, 1972).

Wake of the flood The Ponte Vecchio itself, miraculously, survived. The Arno's embankments were not so lucky. Shortly before dawn some 500,000 tons of mud and water tore through the sleeping city, moving with such ferocity that early-rising commuters in the station underpass were drowned where they fell. In all, 35 people lost their lives. Hundreds of homes and 16,000 cars were destroyed. In places the waters rose 6m above street level, filling cellars and flushing out heating oil that had just been delivered for the approaching winter. Five of Ghiberti's famous panels were torn from the Baptistery doors and later found a mile away. Watery mud filled the cellars of the Uffizi, home to 8,000 paintings. It lapped at Michelangelo's *David* and damaged 1½ million volumes in the Biblioteca Nazionale, a million of them beyond repair. It filled palaces, museums, and churches, devastating Santa Croce, whose ravaged *Crucifix* by Cimabue (see panel) has become a symbol of that terrible morning.

CIMABUE'S *CRUCIFIX*
In 1971 on the anniversary of the flood, Mayor Bargellini wrote in Florence's daily paper: 'When Cimabue's *Crucifix* was carried past, fatally wounded, on a tank going to Limonaia, even the most hardened men, the loudest blasphemers, stopped in their muddy labors and took off their hats in silence; every woman, however tough or dishonest, crossed herself with sincerity... It was as still and silent as on Good Friday'. *La Nazione*

Florence

PLANNING YOUR VISIT

The San Lorenzo complex can be confusing. First see Brunelleschi's church and the Sagrestia Vecchia. Then visit Michelangelo's Biblioteca Laurenziana. Move on to the Cappelle Medicee behind the church and Michelangelo's Sagrestia Nuova (see pages 64–5). Note carefully the opening times of the Biblioteca Laurenziana and the Sagrestia Vecchia (see page 135).

San Lorenzo and the street market alongside it

▶▶ San Lorenzo

IFCD4

Piazza San Lorenzo

An unfinished façade and San Lorenzo's market distract attention from what is one of Florence's oldest and most important churches. The first chapel here was consecrated in 393 by St Ambrose, Bishop of Milan, just 13 years after Christianity had been proclaimed the Empire's official religion. Dedicated to San Zenobius, it served as Florence's first cathedral until around the 7th century, when the bishop's seat was moved to Santa Reparata (itself later replaced by the present Duomo). A Romanesque church was built in 1060.

In 1419, eight parishioners led by Giovanni de' Medici offered to help finance a new church. The design went to Brunelleschi, who embarked first on the Sagrestia Vecchia (Old Sacristy), and in 1421 was given responsibility for the entire project (a distraction from the Duomo, on which he was also working). Twenty years of financial and political upheavals, however, meant that work faltered, recovering only when Giovanni's son, Cosimo de' Medici, provided 40,000 florins for the church's completion (at a time when 150 florins would keep a family for a year). In return the building became a Medici fiefdom and mausoleum (see also **Cappelle Medicee**, pages 64–5).

The church interior Praise is always heaped on Brunelleschi's downbeat interior, a landmark of early-Renaissance architecture (clearly influenced by the architect's study of classical buildings in Rome). A system of *creste e vele* (waves and sails) was used, with broad 'sails' of creamy wall stretched between expanses of gray *pietra serena*.

The two bronze pulpits (c1455–66), raised on marble pillars, were designed and partly executed by an elderly Donatello. Neither of these betrays any slackening of the artist's powers, each bristling with energy and rough-cast figures (particularly on the right-hand dais, where Donatello's hand is more evident). The scenes on this pulpit depict the Resurrection, while those on its neighbour show events from the life of Christ up to and including the Crucifixion. Sadly, however, the pulpits are too high for much detail to be easily discernible (the pillars were added in the 17th century). In his day, Savonarola used to thunder his sermons from these pulpits. Today, in keeping with their decorative theme, they are traditionally only used in Holy Week.

Close by, at the end of the south (right) nave, stands the *Pala del Sacramento* (1458–61) by Desiderio da Settignano. This was a highly influential work in its day: notice the perspectival tricks of its upper tabernacle (an echo of Masaccio's famous *Trinità* in Santa Maria Novella).

ROSSO FIORENTINO
Seven years after painting San Lorenzo's *Marriage of the Virgin*, Rosso abandoned Florence for France 'to raise himself', in Vasari's words, out of the 'wretchedness and poverty which is the common lot of those who work in Tuscany'. In France he became one of the country's most influential painters.

133

PIAZZA SAN LORENZO

PIAZZA MADONNA DEGLI ALDOBRANDINI

Chiostro

1. *Marriage of the Virgin* (1523) by Rosso Fiorentino (see panel).
2. *Pala del Sacramento* (1458–61) by Desiderio da Settignano.
3. and 4. Two bronze pulpits (c1455–66) by Donatello.
5. Tomb of Cosimo de' Medici.
6. *Martyrdom of San Lorenzo* (1565–69) by Bronzino.
7. *The Annunciation* (1440) by Fra Filippo Lippi.
8. Cenotaph to Donatello.
9. Sagrestia Vecchia (Old Sacristy).
10. Entrance to Biblioteca Laurenziana.
11. Ricetto (Vestibule), designed by Michelangelo.
12. Reading Room of Biblioteca Laurenziana.
13. Entrance to Cappelle Medicee (Medici Chapels).
14. Cappella dei Principi (see pages 64–5).
15. Sagrestia Nuova (New Sacristy – see page 65).

One of Donatello's two bronze pulpits

LORENZO
San Lorenzo (St Lawrence), one of Florence's patron saints, was a 3rd-century deacon of some character. When the Romans ordered him to hand over the treasures of the Church, he gathered all the sick and poor people he could find. The gesture was not appreciated and he was roasted alive on a gridiron, telling his executioners at one point they could turn him over: 'I am done on this side.' The scene is depicted in Bronzino's colourful fresco in the church (see the plan on page 133).

ST COSMOS AND ST DAMIAN
These early Christian martyrs feature prominently in Florentine art. They were the patron saints of doctors (*medici*) and, as the Medici were descended from doctors, the family adopted them as its own patron saints. By chance, Cosimo de' Medici was born on the saints' feast day, 27 September, so the pair are often to be seen in paintings that were commissioned by him.

Three brass grilles in front of the high altar mark the tomb of Cosimo de' Medici. The all-powerful city ruler, who died in 1464, is commemorated by the simple epitaph *Pater Patriae* (Father of the Fatherland). In the chapel just to the south is a cenotaph to Donatello, who died two years later and was buried, in accordance with his last wishes, close to Cosimo de' Medici, who had been his friend and patron. (*Open:* Mon–Sat 7–12 and 3.30–6.30, Sun 8–12.30, 3–6.30)

Sagrestia Vecchia A companion to Michelangelo's Sagrestia Nuova (see page 65), the Old Sacristy (1421) was the only structure designed by Brunelleschi to be completed during his lifetime. Dignified and simple – a perfect cube and hemispherical dome – it is far more satisfying than the church from which it is entered (note opening times below). On the left of the door as you enter stands the bronze and porphyry tomb of Giovanni and Piero de' Medici (Cosimo's sons), commissioned from Verrocchio by Lorenzo the Magnificent (1472). As a tomb, however, it is overshadowed by the marble table in the center of the room, the tomb of Giovanni and Piccarda de' Medici, Cosimo's parents and founders of the Medici fortune. Otherwise the decoration around the room is mostly by Donatello (1434–43), and was executed some 20 years before the church's pulpits.

Above the chapel's cherub frieze lie Donatello's eight tondi, four orange-pink in colour and four white against gray, the former striking for their surreal compositional effect. Between them they depict the Evangelists and scenes from the life of St John (Giovanni de' Medici's patron saint).

Over the two doors on the end wall are a pair of large reliefs, one showing St Lawrence and St Stephen (twin protectors of Florence), the other St Cosmos and St Damian, the Medici saints (see panel). Donatello's lively bronze doors below portray disputing martyrs to the left, Apostles and Church fathers to the right. The starry ceiling frescoes of the blue-painted dome depict the heavens as they were on 6 July, 1439, when the short-lived union of the Eastern and Western churches was declared at the

Council of Florence. The bust on the right as you enter is that of St Lawrence. (*Open*: Mon, Wed, Fri, and Sat 10–11.45, Tue and Thu 4–5.45. *Admission free*)

Biblioteca Laurenziana To reach the Laurentian Library leave the church beside the Bronzino fresco and in the cloister (having paused to enjoy the lovely views), take the stairs immediately on your right. Begun in 1524 on the orders of Pope Clement VII (Giulio de' Medici), the building was designed to house the 100-year-old Medici library (see panel). Michelangelo's Mannerist *ricetto* (vestibule) provides the entrance, a deliberately strange and revolutionary use of space designed to amuse, notable for its exaggerated design, his Medici patrons. Its lava-black staircase (completed by Vasari and Ammannati in the 1550s) contrasts with a fine wooden ceiling and the room's roughcast rendering. Among the eccentricities are pillars which carry no weight, and decorative brackets that support nothing but air.

The Reading Room, by contrast, is deliberately conventional. This, too, was designed by Michelangelo, who was responsible for virtually every detail. Notice the Medici symbol in every window, the date (1571) above the door (the year the library was opened to the public), and the fact that the only part of the vestibule visible from the Reading Room is a blank wall. Four rooms beyond contain glass cases displaying a handful of the library's thousands of volumes. The collection's oldest item is a 5th-century Codex of Virgil, but the oldest work on show is on the left as you enter the first room – a papal bull (dated 20 January, 1060) issued by Pope Niccolò II (formerly Bishop of Florence) authorising the reconsecration of San Lorenzo. (*Open* Mon–Sat 9–1. *Closed* Sun. *Admission free.*)

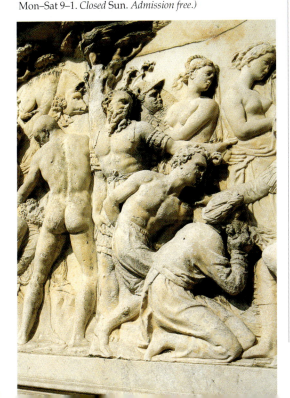

Carved detail from the statue of a Medici duke, Giovanni delle Bande Nere, located in Piazza San Lorenzo

BOOKS AND THE MEDICI

A 1418 inventory of Giovanni de' Medici's possessions mentions just three books. His son Cosimo, however, and Cosimo's son and grandson (Piero and Lorenzo), were avid bibliophiles and tireless collectors. Agents in search of books and manuscripts scoured Europe and the Middle East on their behalf. The Medici also founded libraries for the friars of San Marco and the Badia. The family library was confiscated in 1494 and moved (on Savonarola's advice) from the Palazzo Medici to San Marco. It was reclaimed and transferred to Rome in 1508 by the Medici Pope Leo X. Another Medici, Clement VII, restored it to Florence in 1534.

MICHELANGELO'S LOST CONTRACT

Michelangelo certainly knew how to mess up a contract. Having fought off competition from Sansovino and Giuliano da Sangallo to design San Lorenzo's façade (his winning model is in the Casa Buonarroti), he then argued with Pope Leo X over the choice of marble, wasted two years on building roads to carry stone from Carrara, antagonised his workmen, and finally found the quarrymen unwilling to cooperate. 'I am dying of grief', he wrote, tortured by the project: 'it is as though Fate is against me'. Exasperated by the delays, the pope cancelled the contract in 1520 and the façade was never actually built.

GETTING THERE

The best approach to San Miniato is on foot (see page 156). Failing that, take bus 13 to Piazzale Michelangelo, a fine but invariably crowded viewpoint from where the church is a short walk. Alternatively, take bus 12 (Via Porta Romana) to the steps on Viale Galileo Galilei leading to the church. Both services pick up at the Duomo and near the train station.

CAPPELLA DEL CARDINALE DEL PORTOGALLO

This chapel is dedicated to the 25-year-old Jacopo di Lusitania, the cultured nephew of King Alfonso V of Portugal. Sent to study law in Perugia, he became ambassador to Florence. After he died here in 1459, humanist admirers commissioned his tomb. Notice the angels flanking his tabernacle, one holding a virgin's crown (symbolising the cardinal's chastity), the other a palm (a symbol of his subjugation of earthly passion).

A late 13th-century mosaic of Christ and the Evangelists

▶▶▶ San Miniato al Monte   IFCF1

Viale Galileo Galilei

San Miniato is Florence's most beautiful and (after the Baptistery) most venerable church. Its multicoloured façade is a dazzling fixture on the green heights above the Oltrarno. St Minias was a merchant from the East (possibly a son of the Armenian king), who became a Christian and left his native land to seek penance in Rome. Moving to Florence around AD 250, he was caught up in the anti-Christian purges of the Emperor Decius. Being a member of royalty, however, he was offered numerous inducements to renounce his faith. He would accept none, and was executed on a spot close to the present-day Piazza della Signoria. Then, however, 'by a miracle of Christ', to quote chronicler Giovanni Villani, he picked up his severed head 'and set it again on his trunk, and on his feet passed over the Arno, and went up the hill where now stands his church.' The hill, the Mons Fiorentinus, was then crowded with pagan temples, and a 'little oratory in the name of the blessed Peter the Apostle, where many bodies of holy martyrs were buried'. Here Minias 'gave up his soul to Christ' and was buried.

The present church and convent were started in 1013 by Alibrando (Hildebrand), Bishop of Florence, on the orders of Emperor Henry II, who endowed it 'for the good of his soul'. Most of the building from this period is what is seen today. Initially run by the Benedictines, the church later became a Cluniac monastery, passing in 1373 to the Olivetans, its present incumbents.

The exterior It is hard to know which to admire first – San Miniato's exquisite façade or the magnificent view of Florence that unfolds below the church's lofty terrace. Like the Baptistery, whose patterned marbles it recalls, the façade (1090–1270) was often mistaken during the Renaissance for a Roman edifice. The mosaic of Christ, Mary, and San Miniato was added in 1260 (notice Christ's rather jolly oriental blue bolster). A gilded copper eagle (1401) clutching a bale of wool crowns the façade – the symbol of the Arte di Calimala, the guild responsible for

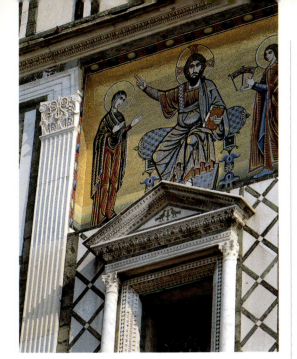

A close-up view of the façade showing the mosaic added to the green, grey and white marble in the 13th century

the church fabric since 1228. This may explain some of the decorative similarities between San Miniato and the Baptistery, a building also looked after by the Calimala.

The interior Few Florentine sights are as lovely as the first glimpse of San Miniato's Romanesque interior (1018–63). The famous inlaid pavement (1207), reputedly inspired by Sicilian fabrics, is patterned with lions, doves, and the signs of the zodiac, and the floor's date is inscribed in the zodiac panel. The painted wood ceiling dates from 1322 but was restored in the 19th century, along with the nave's columns, victims of some rather heavy-handed resurfacing. The capitals, however, are Roman and Byzantine originals.

Further highlights include the freestanding Cappella del Crocifisso (1448), designed by Michelozzo to house a miraculous *Crucifix* (now in Santa Trinita). It was one of the few commissions managed by Piero de' Medici during his short period at the city's helm. Steps beside the chapel lead up to the raised choir, dominated by a magnificent carved pulpit and screen (1207). The mosaic in the apse to the rear dates from 1297. Off to the right, the sacristy contains a fine fresco cycle by Spinello Aretino, *Scenes from the Life of St Benedict* (1387).

Back in the lower body of the church, see the Cappella del Cardinale del Portogallo (1460-8), a masterpiece of Renaissance collaboration off the north (left) aisle. It was designed by Manetti, a pupil of Brunelleschi (see panel opposite). The tomb is by Antonio Rossellino, the painting of the Annunciation (left-hand wall) by Baldovinetti, and the terracotta (and tiled) ceiling by Luca della Robbia. The altarpiece is a copy of a work by Antonio and Piero Pollaiuolo, now in the Uffizi. (*Open:* summer, daily 8–12, 2–7; winter, daily 8–12, 2.30–6.)

SAVED BY MATTRESSES
San Miniato's bell tower collapsed in 1499 and was replaced in 1523 by the present unfinished tower. During the siege of Florence in 1530 it was used as an artillery post, thus attracting the attentions of enemy gunners. Michelangelo, helping to organise the city's defence, had the tower covered in mattresses to protect it from enemy cannon-balls.

THE CRYPT
San Miniato's relics were transferred to the church's lovely crypt in the 11th century. The sanctuary is supported by four rough-hewn pillars and a forest of more delicate Roman columns. It also has a magnificent carpet of worn pavement tombs.

THE FIRST SANTA CROCE
Santa Croce's origins are slightly mysterious. It seems Franciscan friars preached in the vicinity at an oratory dedicated to the Holy Cross (Santa Croce). Florence was an early Franciscan centre, among the first towns after Assisi in which the Order established a foothold. In 1218, the Franciscans founded the hospital of San Gallo. In the same year, according to legend, St Francis personally founded the first Santa Croce. Fragments of a 13th-century chapel found after the 1966 flood lend the legend credence.

The dignified lines of Santa Croce soar above the rooftops

▶▶▶ Santa Croce

Piazza Santa Croce   IFCF3

'In Santa Croce's holy precincts,' wrote Lord Byron, 'lie/ Ashes which make it holier, dust which is/ Even in itself an immortality.' Some 270 eminent Florentines lie buried in the church, including such illustrious corpses as Galileo, Ghiberti, Michelangelo and Machiavelli. Alongside them are by Giotto and his followers, a small museum with Cimabue's famous flood-damaged *Crucifix*, and Brunelleschi's Cappella dei Pazzi, widely acknowledged as a masterpiece of the early Renaissance. Taken together, these attractions make Santa Croce the city's most important church.

History The church (1294–1450) was probably designed by Arnolfo di Cambio, architect of the Duomo and the Palazzo Vecchio (both begun at about the same time). Its Franciscan sponsors – theoretically members of an order dedicated to poverty – were determined from the outset to create one of Christendom's largest churches (equal in size to Rome's old St Peter's). In pursuing size for its own sake, the Franciscans were anxious not to be outdone by the Dominicans, then in the process of building the equally grandiose **Santa Maria Novella** (see pages 148–53). They were also being pressured by the *Comune* to create a church which, as well as 'benefitting the soul', would also 'do credit to the city'.

Both the city of Florence and private families sank vast sums into the project. Foremost among the latter were the members of banking dynasties, unsettled by their usurious practices and eager to ease their consciences by trying to purchase redemption. Clans like the Bardi, Peruzzi, and Baroncelli, in particular, sought spiritual deliverance by commissioning chapels around the church. It was also considered an act of humility – ironically, given the church's grandeur – to be buried amid the 'humble' Franciscans (hence Santa Croce's large number of tombs).

The interior A glance around Santa Croce's enormous interior suggests an intimidating sight-seeing prospect. Work methodically around the church, however, and the labor is not as daunting as it appears. The main features of interest are identified on the plan on pages 140–1.

The nave Before doing anything, be sure to sit and take in the atmosphere. The barnlike sense of space, not unlike that of the Duomo, is accentuated by high and graceful Gothic arches, leading the eye to a glorious and delicately strutted wooden ceiling. Patches of fresco adorn the walls, tantalising suggestions of how the church might once have appeared – fresco cycles by Orcagna in the nave were destroyed by Vasari in the 16th century to make way for side altars.

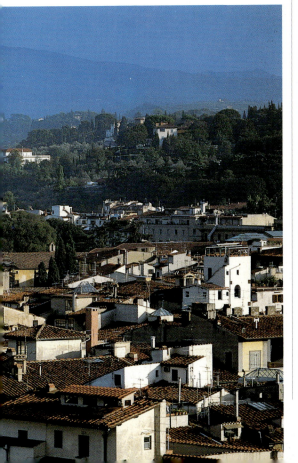

A FAÇADE AT LAST
After 150 years of building, Santa Croce was left without a façade. One was added in the 19th century, paid for by the Englishman Sir Francis Sloane. Even then it was a fake, designed by a charlatan who claimed to have discovered the long-lost plans for the 'original' façade. In fact, it is based on Orcagna's Tabernacle in Orsanmichele (see pages 110–11).

139

A PLEA FOR HUMILITY
St Francis would have been none too happy with Santa Croce. 'Small churches should be built,' he once wrote, 'for they ought not to raise great churches for the sake of preaching to the people or for any other reason, for they will show greater humility and give a better example by going to preach in other churches'.

DUBIOUS DUTIES
Despite St Francis's pacific principles, the Franciscans of Florence took over the duties of the papal Inquisition from the Dominicans in 1254. The Head Inquisitor was based at Santa Croce. Two armed friars roamed the city in the company of a lawyer hunting down heretics. 'Confessions' were often extracted with torture, and malefactors could be fined or burnt at the stake. One third of the fines went to the papacy and the Inquisition, one third to the city – they were spent on the city walls – and one third toward the building of Santa Croce and Santa Maria Novella.

MONUMENTAL SCULPTORS

The tomb of Leonardo Bruni in Santa Croce is the best-known work of Bernardo Rossellino (1427–79), an architect who was also responsible for planning the 'new town' of Pienza. His brother Antonio (1409–64) made the tomb of the Cardinal of Portugal in the church of San Miniato al Monte.

As you walk around the nave looking at some of the many monuments, it soon becomes clear that the finest memorials and the most famous names seldom go together. For example, Dante (though he died and was buried in Ravenna) is remembered here, but his memorial is an undistinguished affair dating from 1829 – even though Michelangelo had offered to carve a monument to the poet some three centuries earlier. Galileo, Michelangelo himself, and Machiavelli are all here, but their monuments are unexceptional in comparison with the magnificent Renaissance tombs of Leonardo Bruni and Carlo Marsuppini, eminent 15th-century scholars and humanists who are given places of honour at the head of the aisles. Bruni was a Chancellor of the Republic, author of the city's first history (a copy of which he is shown holding), and a translator of Plato, Aristotle, and Plutarch. He was also responsible for organising the competition to design the Baptistery doors. His tomb, by Bernardo Rossellino (see panel), was one of the most influential funerary monuments of the Renaissance. The human figure dominates for the first time in a secular tomb, lacking the figures of saints or virtues, with the Madonna and

1. *Madonna del Latte* (1478), a relief by Antonio Rossellino above the tomb of Francesco Nori, a victim of the violent aftermath of the Pazzi Conspiracy (see pages 74–5).
2. Tomb of Michelangelo (1570). (See the panel on page 143.)
3. Cenotaph to Dante (1829).
4. Pulpit (1472–6) by Benedetto da Maiano.
5. Monument to Vittorio Alfieri (1810) by Antonio Canova.
6. Tomb of Niccolò Machiavelli (1787; Machiavelli died in 1527).
7. *The Annunciation* (*c*1435) by Donatello.
8. Tomb of Leonardo Bruni (1446–47) by Bernardo Rossellino.
9. Monument to the composer Gioacchino Rossini (1792–1868) by Giuseppe Cassioli.
10. Cappella Castellani, with frescoes by Agnolo Gaddi (*c*1385)
11. Cappella Baroncelli, with frescoes by Taddeo Gaddi (1332–8).
12. Santa Croce's shop. Beyond the shop is a small leather workshop.
13. Cappella Medici, commissioned from Michelozzo by Cosimo de' Medici. The terracotta altarpiece is by Andrea della Robbia. Note: this chapel is usually closed for services.
14. Sacristy. Noted particularly for its 16th-century wood panelling and for the three fine frescoes on the south (back) wall: the *Crucifixion* (Taddeo Gaddi, *c*1340–55), the *Way to Calvary* (Spinello Aretino, *c*1400) and the *Resurrection* (Pietro Gerini, *c*1400).
15. Cappella Rinuccini. This tiny, grille-covered chapel is covered with frescoes of the lives of the Virgin and Mary Magdalene (*c*1365) by Giovanni da Milano, one of Giotto's more pioneering followers.
16. Cappella Velluti. The browny frescoes, by a follower of Cimabue, are overshadowed by Giovanni del Biondo's polyptych altarpiece.
17. Cappella Peruzzi, with frescoes by Giotto (*c*1326–30).
18. Cappella Bardi, with frescoes by Giotto (*c*1315–20).
19. Chancel. The extensive frescoes here depict the Legend of the True Cross. They and the stained glass are both by Agnolo Gaddi (*c*1380). The high altar polyptych is a composite of panels by different artists. Note: the chancel is often closed to visitors.
20. Cappella Bardi di Vernio. This chapel is superbly frescoed with scenes from the life of St Sylvester painted by Maso di Banco, one of Giotto's most sophisticated followers.
21. Cappella Bardi. The wooden *Crucifix* here, by Donatello, was reputedly denigrated by Brunelleschi for making Christ look 'like a peasant on a Cross'.
22. Monument to Leon Battista Alberti by Lorenzo Bartolini (early 19th century).
23. Tomb of Carlo Marsuppini (1453) by Desiderioda Settignano.
24. Monument to Galileo by Stefano Ricci (1737).
25. First cloister.
26. Cappella dei Pazzi.
27. Museo dell'Opera di Santa Croce.
28. Refectory.

The sacristy frescoes, dated to the 14th century

Santa Croce contains dozens of monuments, some dedicated to famous people (above, detail from Michelangelo's tomb) and some by famous sculptors

STENDHAL AT SANTA CROCE

The tourist who tries to see too much, warned the French novelist Stendhal, 'will develop a furious headache, and presently satiety and pain will render him incapable of any pleasure'. He appears to have had a turn of sorts himself after visiting Santa Croce: 'I was moved almost to tears', he wrote, 'I've never seen anything so beautiful... Painting has never given me so much pleasure. I was tired, my feet swollen and pinched in new boots – sensations which would prevent God from being admired in His glory...but I overlooked it...Emerging from Santa Croce I was seized with a fierce palpitation of the heart: I walked in constant fear of falling to the ground'.
Diaries (1811)

Child banished to a position high in the lunette. Desiderio da Settignano (see panel, page 59) took Bruni's tomb as his inspiration for that of Marsuppini, who lies in an equally prominent place, despite the fact that Marsuppini is said to have died without taking confession or communion. Near Bruni's tomb, note Donatello's outstanding *Annunciation*, an unusual work in gilded *pietra serena*.

Further down the nave, close to Benedetto da Maiano's lovely pulpit (see panel, page 59), with its five expressive panels intimately carved with scenes from the life of St Francis, another monument recalls the famous Italian poet and dramatist Vittorio Alfieri (1749–1803). Sculpted by Antonio Canova, the tomb was paid for by Alfieri's mistress, the Countess of Albany, former wife of Scotland's rebel prince Bonnie Prince Charlie. The countess modeled for the tomb's figure, a symbol of Italy bereaved by Alfieri's death.

The chapels Santa Croce's chapels were decorated with the lives of religious figures of particular relevance to the Franciscans. The **Cappella Castellani**'s patchy frescoes (*c*1385), by Agnolo Gaddi and assistants, depict (on the right) the stories of St John the Baptist and St Nicholas of Bari (the patron saint of children – he is shown saving girls from prostitution and reviving three murdered boys). On the left are episodes from the lives of St John and St Antony Abbot (Antony gave away his wealth in keeping with the Franciscan tradition of poverty). The frescoes (1332–8) in the nearby **Cappella Baroncelli** are by Agnolo's father Taddeo Gaddi, a pupil of Giotto. They depict scenes from the life of the Virgin. The panels contain the first night scenes in Italian painting. This chapel's altarpiece, *The Coronation of the Virgin*, is probably by Giotto, with Taddeo Gaddi and assistants.

Giotto was also responsible for the frescoes in the **Cappella Peruzzi** and the adjoining **Cappella Bardi** – two chapels which together form the church's artistic highlight. Motifs and scenes from both chapels were to be copied again and again by subsequent painters. Many of the panels are in poor condition, the result of Giotto having painted some scenes on dry plaster (see pages 98-9). Their condition was worsened in the 18th century, when both chapels were whitewashed and then badly repainted. Restoration in the 1950s repaired some of the damage. The frescoes in the Cappella Peruzzi (c1326–30) show scenes from the life of St John on the right wall and scenes from the life of St John the Baptist on the left. The Cappella Bardi's frescoes (c1315–20) are in better condition. Like Giotto's great Assisi cycle they depict scenes from the life of St Francis. The left wall has: *Francis Renouncing his Worldly Goods*; *Francis Appearing to St Antony of Arles*; *The Death of St Francis*. On the right wall are *Francis Issuing the Franciscan Rule*; *Francis's Ordeal by Fire before the Sultan*; *Francis Appearing to Friar Augustine and the Bishop of Assisi*. The vaults show allegories of Poverty, Chastity, and Obedience, the three qualities on which Francis founded his order. The entrance arch depicts *Francis Receiving the Stigmata*. Figures on the rear wall are Franciscan saints. Notice, in particular, *The Death of St Francis*, vividly portraying the touching and deeply felt emotions of the grieving friars. Around 150 years later Ghirlandaio used this as a model for his own version of the scene in **Santa Trinita**'s Cappella Sassetti (see page 154). (*Open*: summer, Mon–Sat 8–6.30, Sun 3–6; winter, Mon–Sat 8–12.30, 3–6.30. *Admission free*)

Cappella dei Pazzi and Museo dell'Opera di Santa Croce

Outside Santa Croce to the south are the church's convent buildings, home to two beautiful cloisters, the Cappella dei Pazzi and the Museo dell'Opera di Santa Croce. The **Cappella dei Pazzi** is perhaps the finest of Brunelleschi's smaller works, an even more complete encapsulation of Renaissance architectural ideals than San Lorenzo's Sagrestia Vecchia. Begun in 1430, its exterior remained unfinished at the time of the Pazzi Conspiracy (none of the Pazzi family is buried here). All is calm within, the interior based on the harmonious interaction of circle and square. Simple geometric forms are matched by simple decoration, with the repetition of similar elements. The 12 terracotta tondi of the Apostles are by Luca della Robbia (as is the decoration in the portico). The polychrome roundels in the upper corners have been attributed to Donatello and Brunelleschi.

Off the cloister on the right is the entrance to the small **Museo dell'Opera di Santa Croce**. Piazza Santa Croce is the city's lowest point: church and museum languished under 6 metres of water in the 1966 flood. Cimabue's damaged *Crucifix* hangs in the Refectory, together with a superlative fresco by Taddeo Gaddi of the Last Supper. Along the walls are fragments of fresco by Orcagna, saved from Vasari and removed from the main church. Centre-stage stands Donatello's redoubtable *St Louis of Toulouse*, commissioned for a niche in Orsanmichele (see pages 110–11). (*Open*: summer, Mon, Tue, Thu–Sun 10–12.30, 2.30–6.30; winter, Mon, Tue, Thu–Sun 10–12.30, 3–5. *Admission charge*)

FLORENCE NIGHTINGALE
In Santa Croce's first cloister is a monument to Florence Nightingale, who was born in Florence in 1820 and named after the city.

MICHELANGELO'S TOMB
Michelangelo's body was returned to Florence from Rome in 1574, 10 years after his death (and 34 years after he left the city). He wished to be buried near Santa Croce's entrance, it is said, so that on the Day of Judgment (when tombs would fly open), the first thing he set eyes on would be Brunelleschi's cathedral dome. Originally the tomb was to have included pieces of his own sculpture (such as the *Pietà* in the Museo dell'Opera del Duomo – see page 96). In the end posterity had to make do with a memorial by Vasari.

143

Figure from Vasari's 1570 tomb of Michelangelo

JACOPO PONTORMO

Pontormo (1494–1556) was one of Florence's more bohemian painters. Disturbed, reclusive, and terrified of disease, he lived in the top room of a house, which could only be reached by the ladder that he pulled up when he wished to be alone. His diary records both his parsimonious meals and the daily state of his bowels and kidneys. One writer claimed he 'kept dead bodies in troughs of water to make them swell' (in order to study them). Vasari said Pontormo had a morbid fear of death, and described his room as a 'beast's lair'. The artist worked only when the mood took him, which was infrequently, but he devoted the last 18 years of his life to a fresco cycle in San Lorenzo. It was totally destroyed in the 18th century.

The Cappella Capponi in Santa Felicita was designed by Brunelleschi

▶ Santa Felicita IFCD3

Florence's second oldest church (after San Lorenzo), Santa Felicita may have been founded as early as the 2nd century, perhaps by Syrian or Greek merchants who settled in the area and who may have been responsible for introducing Christianity to Florence. A 4th-century church certainly existed on the site, dedicated to St Felicity, an early Roman martyr. That building was replaced by new churches in the 11th and 14th centuries. Vasari added a portico in 1564 (to accommodate his *corridoio* – see page 129), and in 1736 all but the façade received a thorough remodelling.

In view of all these changes, it is small wonder that little in the interior of Santa Felicita suggests the church's antiquity. Instead, the inside is a miniature version of the gray-stone *pietra serena* interiors found all over the city. Only the **Cappella Capponi** (immediately to the right of the entrance as you enter) provides a compelling reason to go inside. Designed in 1420 by Brunelleschi (but later altered), the small chapel is famous for Jacopo Pontormo's extraordinary *Deposition* (1525–8), one of the supreme masterpieces of Mannerist painting (it is located above the main altar).

The painting's chief impact is in its remarkable colours: vivid purples, puce, cotton-candy pinks, and luminous Wedgwood blues. Christ, a pallid corpse, is the only realistically coloured figure. He is also the only conventional element in this *Deposition*. The thieves, cross, and Roman soldiers are all missing. In fact, the only extraneous characters are a set of strange, androgynous figures, while the only background detail is a solitary ghostly cloud. Pontormo may have included himself in the picture – the brown-cloaked figure on the extreme right is said to be a self-portrait.

The chapel's right-hand wall displays another work by Pontormo, an *Annunciation*, but it is tame by comparison, almost as if painted by another artist. The tondi of the Evangelists on the ceiling are also by Pontormo, with the exception of *St Mark*, which is a copy of an original by Bronzino.

▶▶▶ **Santa Maria del Carmine**   *IFCC3*

Piazza del Carmine
Cappella Brancacci open: Mon, Wed–Sat 10–5; Sun 1–5. Closed Tue. Admission charge

On its own, Santa Maria del Carmine would rank low in the roll of honour of Florentine churches. Built between 1268 and 1422, it was almost completely rebuilt after a disastrous fire in 1771. Among the areas that survived, however, was the **Cappella Brancacci**, which is decorated with one of the most important and influential fresco cycles in Western art (see pages 146–7). It was commissioned in 1424 by Felice Brancacci, a powerful patrician figure, shortly after his return from a period as Florence's ambassador to Egypt.

The painter Masolino da Panicale (1383–1447) set to work on the chapel in 1424, fresh from a stint working with Ghiberti on the bronze doors for the Baptistery. With him was a 22-year-old pupil, Tommaso di Ser Giovanni di Mone Cassai, better known by his nickname Masaccio (Mad Tom). The youngster's talent received fuller rein in 1426, when Masolino was recalled to Budapest, where he was employed as a painter to the Hungarian court. Left to his own devices, Masaccio demonstrated a mastery of perspective, narrative drama, and bold naturalism not seen in Florence since the days of Giotto. 'In a career of but a few years', wrote Bernard Berenson (in *Italian Painters of the Renaissance*, 1930), 'he gave to Florentine painting the direction it pursued to the end'. The frescoes became, in Berenson's words, 'the training school of Florentine painters'.

Masolino – now revealed as his pupil's inferior – returned to the chapel in 1427. He was called away again in 1428, this time to Rome. Masaccio followed him a few months later. Neither was to work on the frescoes again; the brilliant Masaccio died in the Holy City in 1428, aged just 27. After 1436, when Brancacci was exiled by Cosimo de' Medici, the frescoes remained untouched until 1480–5, when they were completed by Filippino Lippi in a style so carefully copied from that of the original artists that Lippi's work was only recognised in 1838.

145

NARROW ESCAPES
The Brancacci frescoes have survived against considerable odds. In 1680, Francesco Ferroni, the chapel's new patron, sought to remove 'these ridiculous men in their cassocks and old-fashioned outfits'. His attempt was thwarted only by the Accademia del Disegno and Vittoria della Rovere, wife of Ferdinand II. In the 1771 fire the frescoes' gilt frames caught fire, damaging their fringes and compounding damage inflicted by centuries of candle wax and revarnishing. By the time Bernard Berenson saw them in 1930, the frescoes were 'dust-bitten and ruined'.

All but two scenes of Santa Maria del Carmine's fresco cycle, the work of Masaccio, Masolino and Filippino Lippi, portray episodes from the life of St Peter, to whom the chapel is dedicated. The original plan for the series of paintings was probably drawn up by Masolino.

Plan of the frescoes in the Cappella Brancacci

146

PRACTICALITIES
The entrance to the Cappella Brancacci is through the cloister to the right of the church. During busy times a maximum of 30 people are allowed in the chapel for 15 minutes. For opening times, see page 145.

1. **The expulsion of Adam and Eve** (Masaccio). One of the most powerful images in Renaissance art, this traumatic fresco shows Adam and Eve distraught at their banishment from Paradise. Eve is half-hugging herself in grief and Adam – plunged into despair – trudges forward with his head in his hands. Notice the angel above them, an almost avenging figure brandishing the sword of righteousness. Compare this harrowing depiction of Adam and Eve with Masolino's far gentler and jollier portrayal of the pair opposite, in panel 6.

2. **The tribute money** (Masaccio). Three episodes are depicted here in the same scene. In the centre, Christ is asked by an official outside the gates of Capernaum to pay the tribute money owing to the city. He orders the apostles to: 'Render unto Caesar that which is Caesar's.' To the left, St Peter takes coins from the mouth of a fish for the tribute. To the right, St Peter hands over the money to the tax collector.

3. **St Peter preaching at Jerusalem on Pentecost** (Masolino).

4. **St Peter baptises the Neophytes** (Masaccio).

5. **St Peter heals the cripple and raises Tabitha** (Masolino). St Peter, in the company of St John, heals a cripple and brings Tabitha back to life. Note the

background view of 15th-century Florence, and the pair of well-dressed Florentines, blithely ignoring the miracles taking place to either side.

6. **The temptation of Adam and Eve** (Masolino).

7. **St Paul visits St Peter in prison** (Filippino Lippi).

8. **St Peter enthroned and the raising of Theophilus' son** (Masaccio and Filippino Lippi). Theophilus was the son of the Prefect of Antioch. St Peter raises him after he has been dead for 14 years. The people of Antioch, looking on, are converted to Christianity by the miracle. They build Peter a throne from which to preach. The three figures to the right of the throne are said to represent Masaccio, Alberti, and Brunelleschi.

9. **St Peter healing the sick with his shadow** (Masaccio). The lame are healed one by one as Peter's shadow passes over them. St John follows in St Peter's footsteps.

10. **The distribution of alms and the death of Ananias** (Masaccio). St Peter tells the people to give up their possessions to be distributed among the poor. Ananias retains some of his wealth and gives up his soul instead. Notice touching details such as the bottom of the child peeping out under its white smock.

11. **St Peter and St Paul before the Proconsul, and the Crucifixion of St Peter** (Filippino Lippi).

12. **St Peter freed from prison by an angel** (Filippino Lippi).

RESTORATION
Unsullied patches of the Cappella Brancacci's frescoes, showing what might lie beneath the grime, were found in 1932 under an altar installed in the 18th century. Restoration, however, only started 50 years later. Italian electronics company Olivetti paid for the cleanup, which was completed in 1988.

AN INSPIRATION TO OTHERS
'All the most celebrated sculptors and painters since Masaccio's day have become excellent and illustrious by studying their art in this chapel.' Vasari, *Lives of the Artists* (1550)

Left and top opposite: in Filippino Lippi's fresco, St Paul visits St Peter in prison

The polychrome Romanesque façade of Santa Maria Novella

▶▶▶ **Santa Maria Novella**   *IFCC4*

Piazza Santa Maria Novella
Open: Mon–Fri, Sun 7–12.15, 3–6, Sat 7–12.15, 3–5.

A certain squalour pervades Piazza Santa Maria Novella, a square where young people congregate during the day, and the scene of some seedy goings-on at night. It therefore comes as a relief to enter Santa Maria Novella, a church to rival Santa Croce in its scale and in the beautiful variety of its decoration. Originally a simple 9th-century chapel, it was rebuilt in 1094 as Santa Maria delle Vigne. In 1221, it was given to the Dominicans, who started a new church on the site in 1246. A series of Dominican architects saw the project through to its conclusion in 1360 (among them brothers Sisto and Cami, probably also responsible for much of the work on the Bargello).

The Romanesque façade remained half finished until 1456, when Leon Battista Alberti completed it in a harmonious Renaissance fashion for Giovanni Rucellai. Note Rucellai's name, picked out in Roman capitals, and his family emblem, the billowing sail of Fortune, woven into the façade's decorative friezes (as it is in the façade of his nearby Palazzo – see pages 120–1).

The interior A classic Gothic shell belies the fact that this was one of the first Italian churches of its kind to depart from the Cistercian model previously copied from France. Much of the original decoration was ruined in the 16th century by Vasari, who bleached numerous frescoes, removed the choir and rood screen, and shortened several aisle windows to accommodate new side chapels (he performed similar acts of vandalism in Santa Croce). Some of the damage was undone in the 18th century. In a trick of perspective, the nave's columns become closer together as you approach the high altar, making the already huge interior seem larger still. While in the nave, peep out of the doors on the east wall to see the lawns and Gothic-arched arcade of the *avelli*, a cemetery for the city's well-to-do medieval families. It is the only one of its kind in Florence.

1. *Annunciation* by Santi di Tito.
2. Fresco (Florentine School, late 14th century).
3. *Trinità* (c1428) by Masaccio.
4. Pulpit. It was from this pulpit (1443–1452), designed by Brunelleschi, that Galileo was first denounced by the Inquisition for espousing the Copernican theory of the heavens.
5. Three Gothic tombs. The simple classical tomb that precedes (6) is that of Paolo Rucellai.
6. Cappella Rucellai. This raised chapel contains a marble *Madonna and Child* by Nino Pisano, and Lorenzo Ghiberti's bronze tomb (1425) of Dominican General Leonardo Dati. *Note:* the chapel is often closed to visitors.
7. Cappella dei Bardi. The patchy 14th-century frescoes here are imprisoned behind a grille. The lunette murals of the Madonna Enthroned have been attributed to Cimabue, Giotto's first teacher.
8. Cappella di Filippo Strozzi, with frescoes by Filippino Lippi - (completed 1502).
9. Chancel, with frescoes by Ghirlandaio (1485–90).
10. Cappella Gondi. The chapel contains Brunelleschi's famous *Crucifix*, his only surviving work in wood. It was reputedly carved in response to Donatello's Santa Croce Crucifix (see page 141). Donatello is said to have been so struck on seeing his colleague's work that he dropped a basket of eggs.
11. Cappella Strozzi, with frescoes by Nardo di Cione (1351–57).
12. Sacristy. A Giotto *Crucifix* usually hangs here.
13. Entrance to Museo di Santa Maria Novella.
14. Chiostro Verde.
15. Frescoes by Paolo Uccello including *The Universal Deluge*.
16. Cappellone degli Spagnoli.
17. Chiostrino dei Morti.
18. Chiostro Grande.

CHARIOT RACES
Piazza Santa Maria Novella's pair of obelisks were raised in 1608 to emulate a Roman *circo*. They marked the winning posts in the *Palio dei Cocchi* (chariot races) that were held in the piazza on 23 June (the Eve of St John). Initiated by Cosimo I, the event was run annually between 1563 and the mid-19th century.

A detail from Masaccio's Trinità: *the kneeling figure on the right is the wife of judge Lorenzo Lenzi, the painting's donor*

Part of the avelli, *Santa Maria's communal cemetery*

PLAGUE VICTIMS
Fear generated by the plague prompted the commissioning of many chapels in Santa Maria Novella. At the beginning of his *Decameron*, Boccaccio describes his protagonists in Santa Maria Novella discussing the plague. 'Many dropped dead in the streets, both by day and night, while many others, though dying in their houses, drew their neighbours' attention to the fact by the smell of rotting corpses... How great a number of splendid palaces, fine houses and noble dwellings, once filled with retainers, with lords and ladies, were bereft of all who had lived there, down to the tiniest child. How many gallant gentlemen, fair ladies and sprightly youths, who would have been judged hale and hearty... having breakfasted in the morning with their kinsfolk... supped that same evening with their ancestors in the next world.'

Masaccio's *Trinità* Perhaps the single most important work of the early Renaissance, Masaccio's *Trinità* was one of the first paintings successfully to incorporate the ideals of perspective and classical proportion. Florentines lined up to see it on its unveiling, flabbergasted by a painting that appeared to create a three-dimensional chapel in a solid wall. The theme of the painting was suggested by the fact that the Dominican calendar began with the Feast of the Trinity.

A skeleton lies below the main picture bearing the none too cheerful motto: 'I was that which you are, you will be that which I am.' The fresco's sponsors, judge Lorenzo Lenzi and his wife, are the figures flanking the pair of painted pillars. Note how the painting's perspective and triangular composition deliberately underline the path of Christian redemption, drawing your eye from the Lenzi through the figures of the Virgin and John the Baptist (humanity's mystical link with the Holy Trinity) to Christ and God the Father at the triangle's apex. The coffered chapel behind owes much to Brunelleschi, whose architecture already applied the principles of perspective mastered here by Masaccio.

Frescoes Generations of visitors have come to Santa Maria Novella not only to marvel at the architecture but also to enjoy the many fine frescoes that escaped Vasari's whitewash. Filippino Lippi was commissioned to paint the **Cappella di Filippo Strozzi**, bought by the wealthy banker (see page 121) in 1486. Lippi's subject was the life of his saintly namesake, St Philip the Apostle. The cycle, different from anything in Florence at the time, was only finished in 1502, several years after Strozzi's death. Both its awkward style and its classical allusions looked ahead to the Mannerists. St Philip's crucifixion and his miracle in front of the Temple are depicted on the right wall. In the miracle, Philip kills the king's son by summoning forth an unholy stench, wonderfully depicted as orange smoke billowing from a monster's maw. The king's son, stricken and green-faced, collapses into the arms of his followers. On the left wall are *The Raising of Drusiana* and *The Martyrdom of St John* (he was martyred by being dipped in boiling oil); the vaults depict Adam, Noah, Jacob, and Abraham. Lippi also executed the chapel's stained glass and beautiful white *trompe l'oeil*. The superb tomb of Filippo Strozzi (1491–93) behind the altar is by Benedetto da Maiano.

Several of Santa Maria Novella's chapels were commissioned in the aftermath of the 1348 Black Death (notably the Cappella Strozzi; see page 152). The zealous Dominicans used the terror provoked by the pestilence, seen by many as a sign of divine ire, to cultivate a wave of religious fervour. It was in this chapel (before its frescoes were painted) that Boccaccio set the opening of the *Decameron*, a medieval literary masterpiece set in the period during and after the plague (see panels on this page and opposite).

During the period when Lippi was carrying out his commission for the Cappella di Filippo Strozzi, seven vast and very different frescoes were being painted on either side of the neighbouring **chancel**. They are the masterpiece (1485–90) of Domenico Ghirlandaio, who numbered the young Michelangelo among his many assistants. They replaced frescoes on the same theme by Orcagna, destroyed a century earlier by a bolt of lightning. Ostensibly scenes from the life of the Virgin (left wall) and the life of John the Baptist (right wall), they actually provide magnificent vignettes of daily life, costume, and customs in 15th-century Florence. They were commissioned by another banker, Giovanni Tornabuoni, and members of the Tornabuoni family are liberally sprinkled throughout most scenes. Such flattering glorification

BOCCACCIO'S DECAMERON
Boccaccio's 100-tale epic (1349–51), told over 10 days, opens in Santa Maria Novella's Cappella di Filippo Strozzi. It was here, one Tuesday morning after Mass, that 'seven ladies young and fair' decided to leave a city ravaged by the plague for the safety and tranquility of the countryside. There they would tell stories, 'hear the birds sing, and see the green hills, and the plains, and the fields covered with grain and undulating, like the sea, and trees of species manifold…'

NICE AND VULGAR
Ghirlandaio's chancel frescoes in Santa Maria Novella have often been criticised by serious art critics as superficial. John Ruskin believed 'if you are a nice person, they are not nice enough for you; and if you are a vulgar person, not vulgar enough'. *Mornings in Florence* (1875–7)

St Thomas Aquinas, to whom the Cappella Strozzi is dedicated, depicted in a stained-glass window by the di Cione brothers

Something for the sharp-eyed visitor to seek out in Piazza Santa Maria Novella – a tortoise creeps out from the base of the obelisk

LOOKOUT
The bell tower of Santa Maria Novella (*c*1330) was used for years as a watch-tower for spotting fires around the city.

A detail from Ghirlandaio's late 15th-century chancel frescoes, in which biblical scenes are depicted in a contemporary context

singled the paintings out for special vitriol during the sermons of Savonarola a few years later. Ghirlandaio (amid helpers) is shown in a red hat in the scene of the expulsion of St Joachim from the Temple (left wall, lower register). The painter, incidentally, is buried in one of the *avelli* outside the church (see page 149).

Much earlier frescoes, ruined but still highly appealing, adorn the **Cappella Strozzi**, whose patrons were Filippo Strozzi's ancestors. Stairs climb to this chapel, on the site of Santa Maria delle Vigne's earlier raised chancel. It is dedicated to St Thomas Aquinas, one of the Dominicans' top-ranking saints, and its frescoes (1351–57) are by Nardo di Cione. Most arresting of the frescoes is the crowded *Paradiso* on the left wall. The right wall depicts a maplike *Inferno*, a faded commentary on Dante's epic. Aquinas and the Virtues are shown in the vaults. Dante is one of the saved in the Last Judgment behind the altar (third row, second from the top). Signor and Signora Strozzi are also among the saved – they are shown being led by an angel into Paradise.

The magnificent altarpiece is by Nardo's brother, Andrea di Cione, better known as Orcagna, and shows Christ giving the keys to St Peter and the Book of Knowledge to St Thomas Aquinas (1357). Both brothers together were responsible for the stained glass.

Museo di Santa Maria Novella With its lovely cloister, Uccello frescoes, and magnificent chapel, this museum is much more than a mere afterthought to the main church. From the entrance (outside the church to the left of the façade), you reach the Romanesque **Chiostro Verde** (Green Cloister), named after the green terra verde pigment of its badly deteriorated fresco cycle.

The best-preserved panels are on the right-hand (east) side, notably Panel 4, Paolo Uccello's *Universal Deluge* (*c*1430), one of Florence's strangest Renaissance paintings. Its lurching compositional vortex vividly illustrates

Uccello's obsession with perspective. Notice the arks on either side, depicted before and after the Flood, and the wicker-ring hats, or *marzocchi*, whose 72-faceted structure allowed the painter to indulge his perspectival fixation to the full.

Off the cloister is the **Cappellone degli Spagnuoli** (Spanish Chapel), so called because it was used by the Spanish entourage of Eleanor of Toledo (wife of Cosimo I). It was funded by one Lapo Guidalotti, whose wife died in the 1348 plague. At one time it was the headquarters of the Inquisition (later transferred to Santa Croce).

Inside the chapel lies one of the city's least-known but most extensive fresco cycles (*c*1365), a sequence described by Ruskin as 'the most noble piece of pictorial philosophy in Italy'. It is the work of the little-known artist Andrea da Firenze. The left wall shows *The Triumph of Doctrine*, exemplified by Thomas Aquinas, who sits enthroned amid the winged Virtues and Doctors of the Church. The 14 figures below represent the Arts and Sciences; the figures at their feet are their historical embodiments.

The spectacular right wall shows *The Work and Triumph of the Dominican Order*. Note Florence's pink-purple Duomo (imagined 80 years before its completion) and (bottom right) St Dominic unleashing the 'hounds of the Lord' (*Domini canes*), a pun on the Dominicans' name. Above the kneeling pilgrims are portraits of Cimabue, Giotto, Boccaccio, Dante, Petrarch, and others. The four winsome women are the Four Vices, surrounded by scenes of dancing and other examples of unholy debauchery. A nearby friar gathers the saved, hearing confession before sending them heavenward toward St Peter.

Be sure also to walk into the Chiostrino dei Morti, the oldest part of the church convent, and peep into the Chiostro Grande, used as a police parade ground. (*Open*: daily 9–2, Sun 8–1. *Closed* Fri. *Admission charge. Biglietto Cumulativo* (combined ticket) available, also covering the Museo Bardini, the Palazzo Vecchio, and the Museo di Firenze com'era.

FARMACIA DI SANTA MARIA NOVELLA
This famous pharmacy lies just northwest of the church at Via della Scala 16. Founded in 1612, it is well known for its lovely 19th-century neo-gothic interior and its range of old-fashioned soaps, scents and potpourris. *Open*: Tue–Sat, 8.30–12.30 and 3–7; *Closed* Sun and Mon morning.

Old-world remedies on display in the Farmacia di Santa Maria Novella

▶▶ Santa Trinita IFCD3

Piazza Santa Trinita
Open: Mon–Sat 8–12, 4–6, Sun 4–6

Santa Trinita appeals not only by virtue of its superb fresco cycle, a masterpiece by Domenico Ghirlandaio, but also because of its oddly harmonious mixture of Gothic austerity and baroque exuberance. Founded in 1092 by Giovanni Gualberto (see panel), the church was rebuilt between 1258 and 1280, possibly by Nicola Pisano. The façade, by Buontalenti, dates from 1594.

In the atmospheric interior, make first for Domenico Ghirlandaio's frescoes (1483) in the **Cappella Sassetti** (the right-hand of the two chapels to the right of the altar as you enter). A series of scenes from the life of St Francis, they were commissioned by Francesco Sassetti to match those of his rival, Giovanni Tornabuoni, in Santa Maria Novella (also by Ghirlandaio). *St Francis Receiving the Rule*, in the lunette above the altar (the upper of the frescoes' three levels) is set in Piazza della Signoria and contains (right foreground) portraits of Sassetti between his son, Federigo, and Lorenzo the Magnificent (Sassetti worked for the Medici bank). On the stairs are the humanist Poliziano and three of his pupils, the sons of Lorenzo the Magnificent.

The chapel's altarpiece, *The Adoration of the Magi*, is also by Ghirlandaio. The epitome of a Renaissance painting, it fuses classical and Christian motifs, setting Mary and the Magi among ancient pillars, a Roman sarcophagus, and a triumphal arch transplanted from Rome's ancient forum. Sassetti and his wife are shown on either side, and it is they who occupy the black tombs located underneath the side arches.

The chapel to the left of the Cappella Sassetti contains the *Crucifix* that bowed its head to Gualberto (see panel). On the church's right wall (fourth chapel) are eye-catching frescoes by Lorenzo Monaco. To the left of the high altar, the second chapel on the left is graced by the tomb of Benozzo Federighi (a bishop of Florence who died in 1450), executed by Luca della Robbia. Finally, note Neri di Bicci's fresco of Gualberto pardoning his brother's assassin (fourth altar, north, left wall) and his lovely free-standing *Annunciation* (third altar).

GIOVANNI GUALBERTO
One Good Friday, so the story goes, Gualberto, an 11th-century Florentine nobleman, set out to avenge the murder of his brother, Ugo. On finding the murderer, however, Gualberto pardoned him in honour of the holy day. Entering San Miniato, he then knelt to pray. As he did, a *Crucifix* (now in Santa Trinita), miraculously bowed its head in approval of his merciful act. Gualberto went on to become a Benedictine monk and founded the Vallombrosan Order. In the 14th century, a 40,000-strong brotherhood dedicated to his memory, the Compagnia dei Bianchi, preached forgiveness in an effort to end acts of revenge.

Ghirlandaio's magnificent altarpiece, The Adoration of the Magi, *in the Cappella Sassetti*

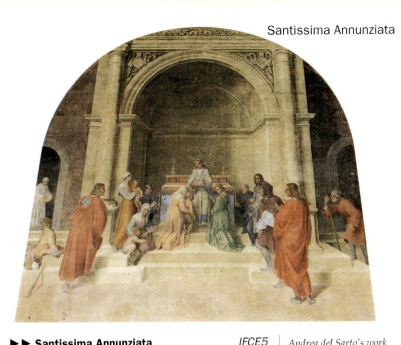

▶▶ Santissima Annunziata   IFCE5

Piazza Santissima Annunziata
Open: daily 7.30–12.30, 4–6.30

As a church celebrating the Annunciation, Santissima Annunziata has long played a special role in the life of the city, whose New Year, in the old Florentine calendar, started on the Feast of the Annunciation (25 March). It is also the mother church of the Servi di Maria (Servite Order), with whose history it is inextricably linked (see panel).

The order's fortunes changed dramatically in 1252, when a painting of the Virgin, started by one of the monks, was miraculously completed by an angel. By 1450 so many people were coming to venerate the image that a new church, paid for by the Medici, was commissioned from Michelozzo (the brother of the Servites' head prior). Via dei Servi was built at the same time to link Santissima Annunziata and the Duomo, the two most important churches in the city dedicated to the Virgin.

More changes ensued in 1516, when San Filippo Benizzi, a leading Servite saint, was canonised. To celebrate the event the church's entrance atrium, the covered **Chiostrino dei Voti**, was decorated with superb frescoes by Andrea del Sarto, Jacopo Pontormo, and Rosso Fiorentino. The church's interior decoration is among the city's most sumptuous – though there is little of real substance beyond the gilt-smothered ceiling and Michelozzo's magnificent Tempietto (on the left as you enter), which was built (1448–61) to shelter the church's miraculously painted *Virgin*. The second chapel on the north side contains Andrea del Castagno's noted *Holy Trinity with St Jerome*. Another more sombre work by the same artist, the *Vision of St Julian*, occupies the first chapel on the same side. Outside the church, visit the **Chiostro dei Morti**, entered through a portico on the left of the façade. Over the door in the far right-hand corner is Andrea del Sarto's *Madonna del Sacco*, one of his most famous works.

Andrea del Sarto's work in the Chiostrino

THE SERVITES
In 1234, seven noblemen abandoned Florence to live in poverty on nearby Monte Senario. They dedicated themselves to the cult of the Annunciation, taking the name Servants of Mary. On the site of the present church, they built a small oratory.

OFFERINGS TO THE VIRGIN
It became a tradition for pilgrims to leave wax votive offerings in honour of the Annunziata's Virgin. The images became so numerous that they were eventually hung from the nave ceiling and placed in the Chiostrino dei Voti. Most were life-size statues of the donors, many of them fully clothed and riding wax horses. The collection of 600 statues was renowned throughout Europe until 1786, when the images were melted down to make candles.

Walk

To San Miniato al Monte

An uphill walk in the Oltrarno, worth the effort for fine views of the city walls, across open countryside and over Florence (3km; allow 2 hours if you plan to visit the churches).

Start at the **Ponte Vecchio**▶ ▶ ▶ (see pages 128–9). Visit the church of **Santa Felicita**▶, known for its Pontormo frescoes (see page 144), before starting a steady climb on Via de' Bardi and Costa Scarpuccia – a pleasant alternative to the more direct route along Costa di San Giorgio.

Turn left uphill on Costa di San Giorgio. The house on the right at No 19 was the home of Galileo before he was condemned by the Inquisition (see pages 106–7). At Porta San Giorgio, the city's oldest surviving gate (1258), turn right into the **Forte del Belvedere** for views over Florence and the Giardino di Boboli (see the panel on page 84). Turn left down Via di Belvedere, which follows the line of the city walls, with views of olive groves and distant hills. At the bottom turn right for 150m until you see the steps of Via di San Salvatore del Monte on your left. Walk up the avenue of cypress trees and Calvary crosses, turning right at the top to visit **San Miniato**▶ ▶ ▶ (pages 136–7). Return downhill to Piazzale Michelangelo for more views. The No 13 bus takes you back to the centre.

▶ Santo Spirito

IFCC3

Piazza Santo Spirito
Open: 8–12, 4–8. Closed Wed 4–8.

You can have too much of a good thing. The piazza fronting Santo Spirito may be among the city's most pleasant – its shady trees and cobbles a welcome whiff of old Italy – but the church itself is one Brunelleschi-designed barn too many (even if Bernini did call it 'the most beautiful church in the world'). Behind its barren façade lies an interior of grey pillars, dour arches, and an almost impenetrable gloom. Although the effect is calming, it barely tempts you to explore the 38 side chapels in search of their hidden treasures (which, in fact, are actually very few).

Brunelleschi designed the building in 1434 to replace an earlier Augustinian church (1250–92). Work on the project commenced in 1444, two years before the architect's death, just one column in the nave being raised during his lifetime. Fire, financial shortfalls, and arguments over the design delayed final completion until 1487. The sandy-colored façade dates from the 18th century, its plaster obscuring earlier and, by all accounts, more prepossessing decoration. The interior, however, remains true to Brunelleschi's design, only the baroque high altar disturbing its bland unity of tone.

The church's artistic highlight is Filippino Lippi's age-blackened *Madonna and Child with Saints*, located in the south (right) transept (second chapel from the left of the four chapels on its south wall). Across in the north (left) transept, your eye is caught by an anonymous Madonna and Saints (first chapel on the right as you stand with your back to the altar). In the chapel to its left is the unmistakable *St Monica and Augustinian Nuns*, an unusual and strangely composed painting attributed to Andrea del Verrocchio. Paintings in this transept's other chapels are worth a quick look.

To the left is the entrance to the much-praised (but actually rather dowdy) vestibule (1489), where 12 columns are crammed into a tiny space. It was designed, like the adjoining sacristy, by Giuliano da Sangallo.

The peaceful piazza

157

COST-CUTTING
The building of Santo Spirito cost so much money that its Augustinian monks gave up one meal a day as a fund-raising example to others. The money saved went towards the church.

REFECTORY FRESCOES
The refectory of Santo Spirito's vanished 13th-century Augustinian monastery contains damaged but important frescoes attributed to Orcagna. One depicts the Last Supper, the other a large Crucifixion. The entrance is to the left of the main church at Piazza Santo Spirito 29. *Open* daily 9–2, Sun 8–1. *Closed* Mon. *Admission charge.*

THWARTED
Medieval architects had only limited influence. Brunelleschi wanted Santo Spirito to enjoy a view of the River Arno, but he was thwarted by the rich families whose homes would have had to be demolished.

The Florentine Renaissance of the 15th century was preceded by more than a century of artistic development across Tuscany and central Italy. Artists such as Giotto and Nicola Pisano steered art away from the stilted conventions of Byzantium, moving it gradually towards the more naturalistic style of the Renaissance.

GIOTTO DI BONDONE (c1266–1337)

Born of peasant stock in the hills above Florence, Giotto spent his early life tending his father's flock. According to legend it was thus that Cimabue found him, scratching pictures of his sheep on pieces of stone. He became a friend of Dante and Petrarch, the other great iconoclasts of the age. Fresco cycles in Rome and Naples are lost, while the true authorship of his famous work on the life of St Francis in Assisi is disputed. The frescoes in Santa Croce and in Padua's Cappella Scrovegni are his only universally attributed cycles.

DANTE ON GIOTTO

Dante described how Giotto surpassed his former teacher: 'Cimabue thought he held the field in painting, but now his fame is obscured and the cry is Giotto.' *Divine Comedy* (1321).

Top: a Giovanni Pisano pulpit, Pisa. Below: Sienese work: popes in the Duomo

New world, old art Byzantine art dominated Italy until the 12th century. Its reverential approach was typified by beautiful but highly stylised Madonnas, which eschewed real life, lacking naturalistic detail and almost any sense of movement, shadow, or depth. Imagine, then, how its exponents would have reacted to Renaissance paintings, whose attributes were outlined two centuries later in Alberti's treatise *Della Pittura* (*Of Painting*, 1436). 'Copiousness and variety', it suggested, should characterize a work of art, whose brief should embrace 'old, young, maidens, women, youths, young boys, fowls, small dogs, birds, horses, sheep, buildings, provinces …'

Much had obviously changed in 200 years. City-states, increased prosperity, and a wealth of new learning had all produced an increasingly sophisticated society. In the early part of the period, however, art still lagged behind the changes. It seemed to require some new or reinvented artistic language to match – and express – the advances in the civic domain.

Sculpture The first stirrings of this new language came with the sculptural work of Nicola Pisano (1220–84), whose great pulpits in Pisa's baptistery and Siena's cathedral took as their inspiration the realistic reliefs of Roman sarcophagi brought to Pisa from the Holy Land. Such reworking of classical forms was to be a cornerstone of Renaissance art, and one that Pisano's pupil, Arnolfo di Cambio (1245–1302), and his son, Giovanni Pisano (1248–1314), were to develop further. Giovanni's work on the façade of Siena cathedral, along with his pulpits in Pisa and Pistoia, incorporated startling new positions for figures – designs and forms never before seen in sculpture – and brought new vigour to formalised images: the Mother and Child ensemble, for

158

STEPHANVS IV   PASCHALIS I   EVGENIVS II   VALENTIN

example, began to suggest an emotional relationship in which maternal love received artistic expression.

Painting After lagging behind sculpture's advance, painting also began to shake off the strictures of Byzantine art. The transformation began in the late 13th century in Rome, where painters such as Pietro Cavallini turned from mosaic – very much a Byzantine tradition – to fresco, a medium more able to match sculpture's new realism and more complex compositions. His lead was taken up by the Florentine Cimabue (1240–1302), called by Vasari the 'father of Italian painting', who furthered the move toward naturalism with work in Assisi's Basilica di San Francesco. Here he was soon joined by his pupil, Giotto, born in about 1266.

Giotto Giotto revolutionised Italian art, forging a new style independent of both Byzantine and Gothic convention. Simply put, he introduced realism and naturalism into painting. His works had light and shade, depth and foreshortening. Events, now infused with narrative drama, turned to the real world for subject and inspiration. For the first time, people capable of movement and emotion were set in backgrounds informed by naturalistic details. In time Giotto's disciples – Maso di Banco, Agnolo di Gaddi, and others – were painting in their master's style around Florence's churches. Sienese painters, who had long adapted Byzantine motifs to their own brilliant use of colour and design, now fused the influence of Duccio, their school's founding father, with the space and realism of Giotto. The style that resulted, exemplified by men such as Simone Martini, Lippo Memmi, and Pietro Lorenzetti, was of immense influence, not only in Italy but also in France, Holland and England.

Santa Croce frescoes

GIOTTO IN FLORENCE
Giotto probably painted Santa Croce's Bardi and Peruzzi chapels between 1315 and 1330. He owned property in the city, and occupied a prominent position in the Arti Maggiori. He also requested a seat on the *Signoria*. A second spell in the city saw him appointed city architect and *capomaestro* of the Duomo (1334). He designed the Campanile, and may have planned some of its reliefs.

BOCCACCIO ON GIOTTO
'Giotto's art was of such excellence that there was nothing in nature that his pen or paintbrush could not exactly reproduce, not simply to make a likeness, but to be the very thing itself. His work was so perfect that a man standing before it would often find his visual senses confused, taking for real what was only painted.' *Decameron* (1349–51)

Long lines are a fact of life outside the Uffizi, which is Italy's most popular museum

▶▶▶ Uffizi, Galleria degli   *IFCD3*
Piazzale degli Uffizi
Open: Tue–Sat 9–7, Sun 9–2. Closed Mon. Admission charge

One of the world's great art galleries, the Uffizi contains not only the best Florentine paintings of the 14th and 15th centuries, but also masterpieces from elsewhere in Italy (Venice and Siena in particular) as well as four centuries' worth of works from the leading artists of Holland, Spain, and Germany. The gallery's building, begun by Vasari in 1560, was originally designed as a suite of offices (*uffizi*) from which to administer the Grand Duchy. In 1743 they were left to the city, along with the Medici art collection, by Anna Maria Luisa, sister of the last Medici grand duke, Gian Gastone.

Serious art lovers will want to visit the Uffizi at least twice, the high admission charge notwithstanding. If you are so tempted, your first visit should cover Rooms 1–15, dedicated to the Florentine Renaissance (and home to the most famous paintings). A second visit might deal with Rooms 16–27, devoted to the High Renaissance and Mannerism in Florence. Rooms 28–45 move out from the city to encompass later Italian and European paintings (the rooms are arranged in chronological order throughout the gallery).

Only highlights are given below, especially in later rooms, but do not be tempted to skim through the gallery's final stages. Its last three rooms, for example, contain masterpieces by Caravaggio, Rembrandt and Canaletto respectively.

The collection proper starts on the top floor (elevator or stairs). Downstairs, in rooms that formed part of an earlier church, are detached frescoes including portraits of illustrious Florentines by Andrea del Castagno and an *Annunciation* by Botticelli.

Room 1 (Roman statues; often closed) Statues were considered the Uffizi's main attraction until the last century, when many were removed to the Bargello. Shelley, for example, ignored the paintings altogether when he visited, and Gibbon made 12 tours of the gallery before even looking at a painting.

THE UFFIZI BOMB
The terrorist car bomb that exploded in an alleyway behind the Uffizi in the early hours of May 27, 1993 left five people dead and nearly 40 works of art damaged – some beyond repair. Miraculously, the Renaissance masterpieces are located on the eastern side of the gallery, away from the blast, and escaped the worst effects. Much of the collection was open again within a month, but many months of rebuilding and restoration were needed to repair wrecked rooms and staircases on the west side of the gallery.

Room 2 The Uffizi opens in majestic style, with three altarpieces of the Madonna Enthroned by Italy's greatest 13th-century artists – Giotto, Duccio, and Cimabue. Each reflects a stage in the development of Italian art away from the influence of Byzantium. Duccio's version (*c*1285), while rooted in the older tradition, suggests hints of what was to come in the folds of the Virgin's cloak and her delicately painted throne. Byzantium is uppermost in Cimabue's version (painted around 1280 for the church of Santa Trinita), though touches of perspective are used to create a sense of depth and volume. The throne, however, is cruder than Duccio's, and gold is used instead of light and shadow to pick out folds in the Madonna's cloak (a Byzantine device).

Compare both Duccio's and Cimabue's with Giotto's version, painted around 1310 for the church of Ognissanti. Light and shade (*chiaroscuro*) give body to the Madonna's clothing and, in a deft piece of realism, the Virgin even has the suggestion of breasts. Both the Madonna and her throne have solidity and depth, while the relationship between Mother and Child suggests genuine human tenderness. The surrounding angels and saints are standing, rather than floating rootlessly as they do in the works by Duccio and Cimabue.

Room 3 (14th-century Sienese School) Siena's art has been called 'poetry' to Florence's 'prose'. In this room are displayed some of the greatest Sienese paintings, including *The Annunciation* (*c*1333) by Simone Martini (the two flanking saints are by Martini's brother-in-law, Lippo Memmi), and works by the brothers Pietro and Ambrogio Lorenzetti, both of whom died in the 1348 plague. Ghiberti called Ambrogio a 'most famous and unique master', preferring him to Martini, whom the Sienese considered their finest painter.

Room 4 (14th-century Florentine School) Painters from this period shown here, such as Orcagna, Taddeo Gaddi, and Bernardo Gaddi, are better represented by the fresco cycles of Santa Croce and Santa Maria Novella.

VISITING THE UFFIZI
The Uffizi is the most visited museum in Italy (an estimated 1.5 million visitors a year). Long lines are almost inevitable. Weekends and between 11am and 3pm are the busiest times, so arrive early or late in the day if possible. For opening times see page 165. Tickets for entry at pre-set times – thus avoiding lines – can be booked in advance by calling 055 234 7941. A small booking fee is charged.

DOMENICO VENEZIANO
This Venetian artist is one of the rarest of painters. There are only 12 known paintings by him in the world (only two of them are signed), three of which are in Florence (though the one in the Uffizi is the only one on public view). Veneziano spent most of his life in Venice, but died destitute in Florence.

Giotto's Madonna Enthroned, *now in the Uffizi, was originally painted for Ognissanti*

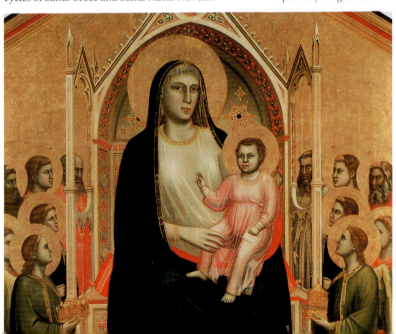

FEDERICO DA MONTEFELTRO

Duke Federico's court at Urbino was renowned throughout Europe for its culture and learning. His hooked nose is also one of the most familiar profiles of the Middle Ages. He is always depicted in left profile, for the right side of his face was badly disfigured in a jousting accident. The allegorical triumphs on the reverse of Piero's portraits depict the Cardinal Virtues (the Duke) and the Theological Virtues (the Duchess) carried on carts drawn by unicorns. The town in the Duchess's portrait is Gubbio (in Umbria), where she died giving birth to her ninth child and first son, Guidobaldo. The portrait was painted two years after her death.

PRIMAVERA

The meaning of Botticelli's painting has been debated for centuries. The central figure is Venus, goddess of spring and love. On the right, Zephyr, god of the west wind, chases the nymph Chloris, who is metamorphosed into the flower-decked Flora. On the left, Mercury wards off the clouds of winter while the Three Graces perform a dance under the threat of Cupid's arrow. The work may be an allegory of spring (*primavera*) or of all four seasons. Most critics believe, however, that it represents the Triumph of Venus, the Graces representing her beauty, Flora embodying her fruitfulness.

There is no escaping souvenirs of Botticelli's Birth of Venus

Rooms 5-6 (International Gothic) Florence's leading exponent of the courtly, highly embellished International Gothic style of painting was Lorenzo Monaco, though his *Coronation of the Virgin* (c1413), which dominates the room, is overshadowed by an exquisitely detailed *Adoration of the Magi* (1423) by Gentile da Fabriano, a painter from the Marches.

Room 7 (Early Renaissance) Renaissance pioneers here include Masaccio, Masolino, and Fra Angelico, but the most famous works are Veneziano's *Sacra Conversazione* (see panel on page 161) and Piero della Francesca's well-known portraits (see panel) of Federico da Montefeltro, Duke of Urbino, and his wife Battista Sforza (c1460). Piero was a pupil of Veneziano. Also here is one panel of Paolo Uccello's *Battle of San Romano*, painted 24 hours after the actual event in 1456 (its other two panels are in the Louvre in Paris and in London's National Gallery). It used to hang in Lorenzo de' Medici's bedroom in the Palazzo Medici. The painting displays an obsession with perspective shared by both Uccello and Piero della Francesca.

Room 8 Most paintings here are by Filippo Lippi, who, though brought up by monks, was consumed by earthly passions. Seduced nuns were among his models. His *Madonna and Child with Two Angels* (c1465) here is one of the loveliest depictions of the Madonna in the gallery.

Room 9 Much of this room is devoted to the brothers Antonio and Piero Pollaiuolo, who are better known as sculptors, engravers, and goldsmiths than as painters. The gallery's most infamous forgery is also here: *Man in a Red Hat*, long believed to be a self-portrait of Filippino Lippi, but actually a fraud perpetrated by an 18th-century English art dealer.

Room 10–14 Botticelli was virtually ignored until this century. Now this room (four smaller rooms run together) is the most popular in the gallery. The painter's most renowned works are collected here, notably *Primavera* (1478) and *The Birth of Venus* (1485), both profoundly influenced by humanist ideas (see panel on this page and opposite). Members of the Medici family feature in his *Adoration of the Magi*, Cosimo il Vecchio as the first king, his sons Piero and Giovanni as the other Magi. Lorenzo the Magnificent occupies the far left foreground. Botticelli has painted himself in a yellow robe on the right.

Bronzino's portrait of Cosimo I, who ruled Florence for more than 30 years

BIRTH OF VENUS'

This was the first 'pagan' nude of the Renaissance, and the last of Botticelli's mythological paintings. It was probably inspired by a poem by Poliziano, humanist, scholar, and friend of Lorenzo de' Medici. According to myth Venus rose from the sea after it had been impregnated by the castration of Uranus. The painting's allegorical meaning, therefore, suggests that beauty arose from the meeting of the spirit world (represented by Uranus) and the physical world. The supporting figures are the nymph Chloris and Zephyr, who, in the myth, blows the risen Venus to shore on a half-shell, where Hora hurries to robe her.

163

In later life Botticelli became increasingly religious, refusing to accept anything but devotional or 'improving' subjects. This more severe later period is reflected in less lyrical works such as *The Calumny of Apelles* (c1496). The room's large triptych by Hugo van der Goes was bought in 1488 by an agent of the Medici bank in Bruges. Its naturalism was to have a profound impact on Florentine painters.

Room 15 Florence has few confidently attributed works by Leonardo da Vinci. This room contains his sublime *Annunciation* and exotic *Adoration of the Magi*, the latter left unfinished when Leonardo left Tuscany for Milan in 1482 to paint *The Last Supper*. As an 18-year-old pupil he also painted the angel in Verrocchio's *Baptism of Christ* (begun c1470). Verrocchio confessed he himself could paint nothing as beautiful as his pupil's angel. Also in the room are wonderful works by Luca Signorelli and Perugino. The latter trained with Leonardo in Verrocchio's workshop.

Room 16 is a map room, the Sala delle Carte Geografiche.

Room 17 is often closed but contains a famous statue, *Hermaphrodite*, a 2nd-century BC copy of a Greek original.

Room 18 (The Tribune) This specially built octagon was designed in 1584 as an inner sanctum for the Medici's finest works of art. It also marks a convenient break in the gallery, ushering in the artists of Italy's High Renaissance. Paintings here include works by Bronzino and Raphael, and Pontormo's *Cosimo il Vecchio* (1519), one of the gallery's premier portraits. For centuries, however, the room's most famous work was the *Venus de' Medici*, long considered to be Europe's most salacious sculpture (see

Detail from Filippo Lippi's Madonna and Child with Two Angels

Florence

VENUS DE'MEDICI

The Medici Venus is a Roman copy of a 1st-century BC *Aphrodite of Cnidos*, considered to be antiquity's most erotic statue. Cosimo III kept it in Rome's Villa Medici, but removed it to Florence to prevent it from corrupting the city's students. Drawings and reproductions flooded Europe, and visitors grappled in prose with its sensual charge. Even the habitually miserable Smollett was moved by its famous buttocks: 'the back parts are executed so happily', he wrote, 'as to excite the admiration of the most indifferent spectator'.

BYRON ON THE VENUS

'We gaze and turn away, and know not where,/ Dazzled and drunk with beauty, till the heart/ Reels with its fullness... Chain'd to the chariot of triumphal Art/ We stand as captives and would not depart'. *Childe Harold's Pilgrimage* (1812)

THE DONI TONDO

Michelangelo considered easel painting to be drudgery in comparison with fresco or the more elevated art of sculpture. This is the only such painting he brought close to completion. Executed at the time of *David*, it was commissioned to celebrate the marriage of Angelo Doni and Maddalena Strozzi. Much of the content is still not fully understood, but the acid colours, contorted composition, and deliberately opaque meaning greatly influenced Mannerist painters such as Rosso Fiorentino.

panel). It was the only statue in Florence to be called to Paris after Napoleon's invasion of Italy.

Room 19 The paintings here include works by Perugino, Raphael's teacher, and Luca Signorelli, a pupil of Piero della Francesca.

Room 20 Among this room's pictures, mainly by German painters, is Albrecht Dürer's earliest work, *A Portrait of the Artist's Father* (painted when he was 19, in 1490). Dürer worked for a time in Venice, commenting: 'Here I am a lord, but at home I live as a sponger'.

Room 21 (Venetian School) Among works here by Giorgione, Carpaccio, Tura, and others, the most famous is Giovanni Bellini's baffling *Sacred Allegory* (c1495), whose strange symbolism has never been fully explained.

Room 22 (German and Flemish Schools) Works here include portraits by Memling, Joos van Cleve, and Hans Holbein the Younger.

Room 23 Correggio dominates the room, but in fact the finest paintings are three pieces by Andrea Mantegna, notably the three-panelled *Epiphany*, *Circumcision* and *Ascension* (1489).

Room 24 is given over to miniatures.

Room 25 Only when you are well over halfway around do you reach the only work by Michelangelo, *The Holy Family* (1504), or the Doni Tondo (see panel). Note the remarkable contrast with Raphael's *Madonna of the Goldfinch* (in Room 26), a quintessential late-Renaissance work painted at almost the same time, around 1505. Close by hangs Rosso Fiorentino's violently energetic *Moses Defending the Daughters of Jethro* (1523–4), one of the key works in the Mannerist canon. It was commissioned by a patron known for his violent temper.

Room 26 Here are to be found most of the Uffizi's Raphaels, notably his luminous *Madonna of the Goldfinch* (1506), a self-portrait, and a penetrating study (1518) of Medici prelates, *Pope Leo X* and *Cardinals Giulio de' Medici and Luigi de' Rossi*. Andrea del Sarto is also well represented here.

Room 27 Mannerism's leading lights – Bronzino, Pontormo and Rosso Fiorentino – dominate this room. Pontormo's *Supper at Emmaus* (1525) stands out, filled with artificial light, macabre shadows, and the virulent colours beloved of painters in this genre.

Room 28 Raphael's Medici portrait (Room 26) influenced Titian, whose portraits decorate this room. More notorious, however, is Titian's famous *Venus of Urbino* (1538), one of the best-known nudes in Western art. Byron thought her the definitive Venus. Mark Twain thought this 'the foulest, the vilest, the obscenest picture the world possesses'.

Room 29 Several devices that have given the Mannerist style a bad name are displayed in Parmigianino's famous *Madonna and Child with Angels* (1534–40) – the Virgin's unnaturally long neck, her peculiar posture (somewhere between sitting and standing), the column behind her, supporting nothing but thin air, and the compositional overloading of the left-hand side of the painting while the right-hand side is almost empty.

Rooms 30–35 Paintings from Emilia-Romagna, Venice, and the Veneto hang here, notably works by Lorenzo Lotto, Veronese, Tintoretto, and Sebastiano del Piombo.

Room 41 Painting by Rubens and Van Dyck claim this room, which is dominated by the former's sizable *Triumphal Entrance of Henri IV into Paris* (*c*1620). Henri's presence in the Medici collection is explained by his marriage to Maria de' Medici.

Room 43 Three paintings by Caravaggio make their mark here: an alarming *Medusa* (1596–8), a self-satisfied *Bacchus* (1593–4), and a violent depiction of the *Sacrifice of Isaac* (1594–6).

Room 44 Two Rembrandt self-portraits, young (1634) and old (1664), and his *Portrait of an Old Man* stand out in the gallery's penultimate room.

Room 45 Canaletto and 18th-century paintings bring the tour to a close. The Uffizi's cafeteria awaits beyond.

Note that several rooms that have been closed for a long time were opened to the public on the Uffizi's ground and first floors in 1998. Exhibits include lesser paintings from the gallery's collection.

Looking through the Arno façade of the Uffizi, designed by Vasari. The top floor was used by the Medici to display their works of art

The artistic reawakening of almost two centuries came to glorious fruition in Florence during the 15th century when the Renaissance (Rinascimento) was born against a background of wealth, patronage and the artistic, social and intellectual ferment of a great and cosmopolitan European city.

Why 'rebirth'? A combination of cultural and economic circumstances paved the way for the Renaissance. Initially, the rediscovery of classical texts and humanist scholarship, of the type promulgated by Lorenzo de' Medici's Platonic Academy, helped free art from its purely religious obligations. This led quite naturally to renewed interest in the classical ideals of art: form and harmony. Secular patronage – by successful laymen such as the Medici – fostered these new ideas in art and architecture, replacing a world in which art was sponsored by the Church – with all the rigidity and conservatism that that implied.

It was no accident that the mood of artistic and intellectual innovation came to fruition in Florence. By the 15th century banking and commerce, particularly textiles, had turned it into one of Europe's most prosperous cities. Creativity and individual genius flourished in its free-thinking atmosphere, enriched by the exchange of ideas among artists drawn together by its burgeoning artistic reputation.

166

Three angels visit Abraham – a detail from one of Lorenzo Ghiberti's panels for the east doors of the Baptistery, the 'Gates of Paradise'

The big three The Renaissance did not spring out of thin air (see pages 158–9). Nonetheless, it can be said to have been ushered in by three artists in three key disciplines. **Filippo Brunelleschi** (1377–1446) was its first great architect. Today he is chiefly remembered as the designer of Florence's cathedral dome, but his ideas were also vital to the new thinking on matters such as the ideals of design and the science of perspective. **Donatello** (1386–1466), perhaps the greatest of the early-Renaissance sculptors, overturned tradition with his extraordinarily lifelike figures; he also reintroduced the nude to the mainstream of artistic expression. **Masaccio** (1401–28), third of the triumvirate, was revolutionary in his use of perspective, producing paintings that stunned his contemporaries. His frescoes in the Cappella Brancacci became a point of pilgrimage for nearly every Florentine artist of their day.

Year one A date for the start of the Renaissance, as far as a date can be set, is often fixed at 1401, the year of a competition to design a second set of doors for Florence's Battistero. As a result, **Lorenzo Ghiberti** (c1378–1455) was to produce two pairs of doors permeated with the essentials of Renaissance style (allusions to classical sculpture, realistic portrayal of the human form, and the use of perspective to position figures in a naturalistic setting). Another notable sculptor, **Luca della Robbia** (c1400–82), perfected the art of glazed terracotta, a medium which his family spread, over the course of the century, throughout much of Tuscany. Other contemporary sculptors adopted the more joyful aspects of Donatello's often severe style – men like **Benedetto da Maiano**, **Bernardo Rossellino**, and **Desiderio da Settignano**.

The painters Nowhere does the Renaissance avalanche of hallowed names become more overwhelming than among the painters. Many, like Masaccio, were innovators, some only accomplished copyists, but all made their contribution to the body of beautiful work with which the Florentine *quattrocento* (15th century) is most commonly associated. One of the earliest, **Paolo Uccello** (1397–1475), was also one of the most taken with the new possibilities of perspective, driving himself to personal and artistic eccentricity with his newfound obsession. Challenging, almost visionary work was the result, best seen in Santa Maria Novella's *Universal Deluge* and the Uffizi's *Battle of San Romano*.

Top: detail from one of Ghirlandaio's frescoes on the life of St Francis in Santa Trinita church Below: Taddeo di Bartolo's Assumption of the Virgin, a glittering early-Renaissance work in the Duomo in Montepulciano

167

MICHELOZZO DI BARTOLOMMEO
After collaborations with Ghiberti and Donatello, Michelozzo (1396–1472) turned to architecture. He worked mainly for Cosimo de' Medici, designing a tribune for Santissima Annunziata, the Villa Medici at Fiesole, the library in the monastery of San Marco, and the highly influential Palazzo Medici-Riccardi.

Focus On   The Renaissance

LEON BATTISTA ALBERTI
A complete Renaissance man, Alberti (1404–72) was a scholar, writer, architect, and theoretician, whose tracts on painting and architecture – *Della Pittura* and *De Re Aedificatoria* – greatly influenced his Florentine contemporaries.

AGOSTINO DI DUCCIO
Possibly a pupil of the Sienese sculptor Jacopo della Quercia, Agostino (1418–81) worked on projects all over central Italy. His best work in Florence is in the Bargello.

One of Michelangelo's Four Slaves in the Accademia

Equally intense, but more spiritually elevated, was the heavenly inspiration of **Fra Angelico** (*c*1395–1455), a devout Dominican monk. His sublime work, intended as an aid to devotion, introduced innovative use of colour and composition. Few matched the ethereal blue of his palette, best seen in the frescoes of his own monastery, San Marco. Less profound, but no less beautiful, was Angelico's pupil, **Benozzo Gozzoli** (1420/22–97), who left examples of his highly decorated work in the Palazzo Medici-Riccardi (as well as in hill towns across Tuscany and Umbria).

More in keeping with Angelico's mystery and depth, if not his religious devotion, was **Filippo Lippi** (*c*1406–69), an errant friar who made a habit of seducing young women. A pupil of Masaccio, he soon instigated innovations of his own, introducing complex compositional groups, detailed colouring, and mystical paintings of poetic landscapes and wistful Madonnas. Another of Masaccio's pupils, **Andrea del Castagno** (1417/19–57), rigorously applied the rules of perspective, but added heroic figures to his striking, boldly painted frescoes (most notably in the Duomo's *Niccolò da Tolentino* and Sant'Apollonia's disturbing *Last Supper*). **Domenico Ghirlandaio** (1449–94) was perhaps the most prolific of Florence's painters (he offered at one point to cover the entire city wall with frescoes). His huge religious narratives set against classical and contemporary backgrounds epitomised the Renaissance approach (notably in Santa Trinita, Santa Maria Novella, and the Palazzo Vecchio's Sala dei Gigli).

Another spur to artistic progress came from **Antonio Pollaiuolo** (1433–1498), painter, engraver, sculptor, and goldsmith. Dedicated to the study of anatomy and movement, he also undertook a wide range of commissions, typical of the ever-widening interests developed by artists and patrons as the 15th century progressed. Also part of this trend was **Andrea del Verrocchio** (1435–88), a multitalented artist in his own right, but better known, like Pollaiuolo, as a teacher and head of a flourishing workshop (Leonardo was among his pupils). As the century spawned more artists, it moved towards its artistic climax, heralded by **Sandro Botticelli** (1444–1510), whose mythological paintings and mastery of line and colour are the epitome of Renaissance endeavour.

The High Renaissance Just as a trio of artists dominate the early years of the Renaissance, so three figures stand out at the climactic end of the era, the so-called High Renaissance. *The Last Supper*, painted at the beginning of the 16th century in Milan by **Leonardo da Vinci** (1452–1519), marks the start of the period, also underlining the fact that the glory of the Renaissance does not belong to Florence alone. Leonardo, born in Vinci (east of Florence) and trained in Verrocchio's workshop, now has only three works in the city, all of them in the Uffizi (see page 163).

Rome, too, saw its share of Renaissance greatness – not least in the work of **Michelangelo** (1475–1564), the consummate genius of his age. Though he spent the earlier part of his career in Florence, he was frequently lured to Rome, where papal patronage began to replace that of the Medici. Concerned primarily with sculpture, and with the nude in particular, Michelangelo's work is represented in Florence by the *David*, the Museo dell'Opera del Duomo's *Pietà*, the Medici tombs, and the Biblioteca Laurenziana. But it was Rome, ironically, that saw Michelangelo's greatest and most famous work – the frescoes in the Sistine Chapel. Urbino-born **Raphael** (1483–1520) was another Florence-trained genius lured to Rome – though he painted numerous masterpieces in Florence.

Mannerism After the sack of Rome in 1527, Renaissance self-confidence gave way to the more self-conscious art that became known as Mannerism. Partially inspired by Raphael and Michelangelo, artists of the genre followed some of the techniques, but not the spirit, of their masters, in a way which perhaps allowed artifice to dominate over art. Established conventions of scale, colour, and composition were ignored. Mannerism was a style in which homegrown artists continued to excel, its leading lights being **Rosso Fiorentino** (1495–1540), **Jacopo Pontormo** (1494–1556), **Andrea del Sarto** (1486–1531) and **Agnolo Bronzino** (1503–72). In sculpture the style was embraced by **Bandinelli** (1493–1560) and **Ammannati** (1511–92), and by the more accomplished **Giambologna** (1529–1608) and **Benvenuto Cellini** (1500–71). Examples of their work decorate the Bargello and open spaces of the Piazza della Signoria.

The atrium of Santissima Annunziata has a series of Mannerist frescoes. Above: an Andrea del Sarto

RENAISSANCE TALENT OUTSIDE FLORENCE
Piero della Francesca (1416–92), from the Tuscan town of Sansepolcro, painted mysterious pictures that combined ethereal beauty with compositional precision. In Cortona, his pupil Luca Signorelli (c1441–1523) began a career later distinguished by the powerful *Last Judgement* in Orvieto cathedral in Umbria. Umbria also had Perugino (1446–1523), Raphael's teacher, known for his harmonious religious paintings. Siena boasted sculptors like Jacopo della Quercia (c1374–1438), and painters such as Sassetta (c1392–1450) and Giovanni di Paolo (c1403–82).

Florence

THE PERFECT VILLA

Alberti's *De Re Aedificatoria (About Building)* described the perfect villa: it sat on a hill to enjoy the best views, its rooms radiated from a central atrium, and its windows were large and numerous to admit light and air. Its garden – considered more important than the house – was based on geometric formality and was linked to the villa by a central path. Secondary paths crossed it to create a grid, and squares, arcs, and circles were introduced as complementary motifs. In short, said Alberti, 'the harmony and concord of all the parts [should be] achieved in such a manner that nothing could be added or taken away or altered except for the worse'.

Gargoyle from the Villa della Petraia

THE KING'S TREE HOUSE

The upper terrace of the Villa della Petraia's garden contains a famous 400-year-old ilex. It was King Vittorio Emanuele II's favourite tree, and he built the tree house that is still here today.

▶ Villa Medicea di Careggi   IBCD5

Viale Pieraccini 17 (5km north of city centre)
Bus: No. 14c from train station
Open: grounds only, Mon–Fri 8–6, Sat 8–2. Closed Sun.
Admission free

The Villa di Careggi is now a nurses' home, but in its day it was the first and most famous of the Medici's several villas – elegant country homes, within easy reach of Florence but offering a rural alternative to the family *palazzo*. Acquired by the Medici in 1417, and altered by Michelozzo in the 1430s, it was to the Villa di Careggi that Cosimo de' Medici returned after his Venetian exile (1434), and here that Cosimo, his son Piero, and his grandson Lorenzo (the Magnificent) all came to die. Under Lorenzo the house also became the meeting place of the Platonic Academy, the informal gathering of poets, scholars, and philosophers that promulgated Florence's humanist movement. When the Medici left Florence in 1494, the villa was ransacked and badly destroyed by fire. It was restored by Cosimo I and in the middle of the 19th century by the Englishman Sir Francis Sloane.

▶▶ Villa Medicea di Castello   IBCD5

Via di Castello 47 (6km northwest of city centre)
Bus: No 28 from train station to Piazza di Careggi and then 400-metre walk
Open: gardens only, Nov–Feb 9–4.30; Mar and Oct 9–5.30; Apr, May and Sep 9–6.30; Jun–Aug 9–7.30. Closed 2nd and 3rd Mon of the month. Admission charge includes Villa Medicaea della Petraia

The Villa di Castello's gardens are among the finest in Tuscany. The building was bought in 1477 by Giovanni and Lorenzo di Pierfrancesco de' Medici, second cousins of Lorenzo the Magnificent and principal sponsors of Botticelli. Sacked during the siege of Florence in 1530, it was restored by Cosimo I. It was given to the state in 1919, and now houses the Accademia della Crusca, founded in 1582 to promote the study of the Italian language.

The gardens were laid out for Cosimo I in 1537 by Niccolò Tribolo, a pupil of Michelangelo. Although his work was continued by Buontalenti, who also restructured the villa, the planned arrangement of over 50 sculptural tableaus was never realised. The gardens dazzled visitors nonetheless, among them Montaigne, who described them as the most beautiful in Europe. Surrounded by their lemon trees, labyrinths, and geometrically arranged hedges, the centrepiece is the marvellous Grotto degli Animali (*c*1570), encrusted with false stalactites, shell mosaics, and a menagerie of birds and plaster animals (Giambologna's bronze animals in the Bargello were removed from here). The upper terrace has fine views, and there is a large orangery, Tribolo's triple-bowled fountain, and Ammannati's chilly statue, *January*.

▶ Villa Medicea della Petraia   IBCD5

Località Castello (6 km northwest of city centre)
Bus: No 28 from train station
Open: same hours as Villa Medicea di Costello.
Admission charge; includes Villa di Castello

One of the last Medici villas, the Villa della Petraia was originally a castle owned by the Brunelleschi family. Only its tower was retained when Ferdinando I bought and rebuilt the property in 1575.

Today, the area suffers badly from its proximity to Florence. Matters are made worse by the interior, reappointed in poor taste by King Vittorio Emanuele II in 1864. Only a handful of 17th-century frescoes (tracing the Medici's history), some tapestries, and a statue of Venus by Giambologna make a visit worthwhile. The beautiful park and gardens are more enticing, however.

▶ Villa Medicea di Poggio a Caiano   IBCC5

Piazza dei Medici 12 (18 km west of city centre)
Bus: COPIT bus (every 30 minutes) from Piazza Santa Maria Novella to Poggio a Caiano village
Open: Nov–Feb 9–3.30; Mar and Oct 9–4.30; Apr, May, Sep 9–5.30; Jun–Aug 9–6.30. Guided visits to the interior of villa leave hourly on half-hour from 9.30. Admission charge

Poggio a Caiano – the best-preserved of the Medici retreats – is the place to visit if you have time for only one villa. Bought as a farmhouse by Lorenzo the Magnificent in 1480, it was converted by Giuliano da Sangallo, becoming the first building designed as a villa since antiquity (and Lorenzo's only architectural commission). Despite later additions (notably the entrance loggia added by Lorenzo's son, Giovanni, later Pope Leo X), the villa retains a classical elegance that owes much to Alberti's blueprint for the ideal country house (see panel opposite).

The interior is magnificent, its *pièce de résistance* being a two-storey *salone*, described by Vasari as the most beautiful room in the world. Among its frescoes are Andrea del Sarto's *Caesar Receiving Egyptian Tribute* and Pontormo's sunny *Vetumnus and Pomona*. The Romans in the latter are the Medici in disguise, while the historical scenes of the former depict events parallel to those connected with the family.

A Medici rural retreat: the Villa Medicea della Petraia

STRANGE DEATHS
Poggio a Caiano contains the apartment of Bianca Cappello, second wife of Francesco I. She left her Venetian lover to be with Francesco, but was banned from Florence by Francesco's first wife. As his second wife she became a social outcast, shunned by Florentine society. In 1587, both she and Francesco died within hours of each other at the villa, possibly from a virulent illness, or as a result of being poisoned.

Doing Florence in style: one of the city's top-class luxury hotels

NOISE

The only way to escape Florence's cacophony – car horns, wailing sirens, motor scooters, domestic discord, buses, early-morning street cleaners, late-night bars – is to stay in a soundproofed hotel or flee the city altogether. You could spare yourself some of the racket, however, by avoiding the main streets and piazzas, and by asking for rooms either away from the front of the hotel or facing into a central courtyard. Better still, invest in earplugs.

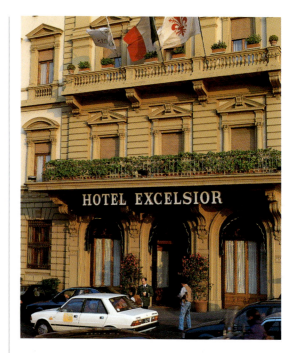

LAST-MINUTE BOOKINGS

If you arrive without a room booked, try the ITA (Informazioni Turistiche Alberghiere) office on the train station concourse (*open* daily 9–9; tel: 055 282 893). They charge a modest fee for finding a room, depending on the category of hotel. Other ITA offices (*Open* Apr–Nov) are located at the Chianti Est service station (on the A1 expressway tel: 055 621 1349) and the Agip service station at Peretola (on the A11 expressway to the coast, tel: 055 421 1800).

Accommodation

Florence's limitless stream of tourists has spoiled its hoteliers. Certain of customers, they are often able to pass off lacklustre rooms at premium prices. Exceptions to this rule are well known, so to be sure of a bargain, or even of value for money, you need to book well in advance. Location is not of prime importance, except in the budget bracket, where most of the options cluster in the rather drab streets around the station. Cheaper hotels also lurk close to the Duomo, however. More stylish hotels can be found in most neighbourhoods.

Noise, as in any Italian city, is invariably a problem. So, too, is summer heat. Opting for a quieter hotel in Fiesole or the Florentine hills is an alternative possibility. You might look even farther afield if hotels are full: train rides of less than an hour make day trips to Florence feasible from Arezzo, Pistoia, Prato, and Pisa.

Booking That much-vaunted commodity, a room with a view, is not usually to be found at the last minute – unless you are very lucky or very rich. Florence's peak season is between Easter and the end of October, but the city's 400 or so hotels are always well booked. The bargain establishments and the better hotels are well known, so reservations are essential whatever you are paying. Some hotels will accept a credit card reservation over the phone, but to be absolutely sure of a booking expect to send some sort of deposit. The Italian State Tourist Office in your home country will help with booking. International Money Orders (available from post offices) are also useful.

A day or two before your planned arrival, always telephone to confirm a reservation – most receptionists speak some English. If you arrive without a booking, try one of the agencies on the spot (see panel opposite), but make sure you are not given a room a long way from the central districts. If you have no reservation, be certain to arrive early in the morning, for most spare rooms will have gone by mid-afternoon. Do not accept offers from touts at the train station.

Prices Italy's hotels are classified into five categories from one-star (basic) to five-star (luxury). The prices charged in each category are set by the local tourist office and must, by law, be displayed in each room. Although this arrangement clearly protects the visitor, an EU directive of June 1993 unfortunately outlawed the legal obligation as unfair 'price-fixing'. Whether this will lead to runaway prices remains to be seen, but for the moment most hotels seem to be adhering to the old system.

Prices for different rooms can vary within a hotel, so if one room is too expensive do not be afraid to ask for another, cheaper one (the chances are you will be offered the most expensive rooms first). Single rooms cost about two-thirds the price of doubles, and to add an extra bed to a room increases the rate by 35 per cent. Even nicer hotels may have a few cheaper rooms without bathrooms. Some hotels will offer reduced rates between November and March, though few admit to a low season. Taxes and service charges should be included in the room rate, but hotels can charge supplements for showers (in cheaper places) and for air conditioning (as much as L30,000 a day). Places with restaurants invariably demand you take half-pension (bed, breakfast, and a main meal) and many hotels insist you pay for breakfast, whether you want it or not.

PRICES

Hotel rates are high in Florence. For hotels listed as 'Expensive' in the Hotels and Restaurants section (pages 273–281), expect to pay between L250,000 and L500,000 for two people in a double room. 'Moderate' rates are roughly L125,000–L250,000; 'Budget' L70,000–L125,000.

173

A riverside setting and rooms with a view

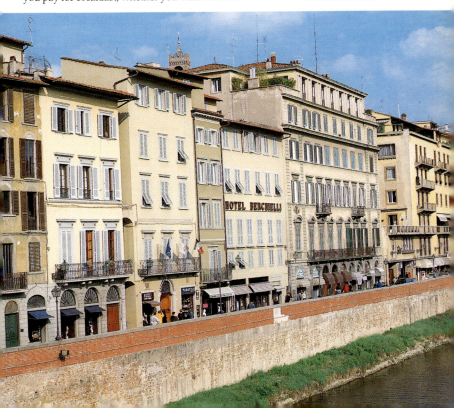

FAST FOOD

Hamburger joints are becoming increasingly common. One of the biggest is on the train station concourse. Florence's traditional fast food is bread rolls filled with tripe and pig's intestine. If you have the stomach, stalls selling them can be found in the Mercato Centrale and Piazza dei Cimatori.

SMOKING

Italians smoke more than most nationalities, and Italy has no real anti-smoking lobby. Very few bars or restaurants have nonsmoking sections.

Le volpi e l'uva

Piazza De' Rossi - 50125 Firenze
Tel. e Fax 055/2398132

Food and drink

Most centrally located restaurants in Florence are crowded. Something is probably badly wrong with any that are not. The food served by some of them, however, is little more than tourist fare. The better places are all well known, so either book or arrive early to be sure of a table. (See pages 277–8 for recommendations.)

Only the most expensive restaurants require a jacket and tie, but Italians usually dress. Dress code for most places can best be summarised as casual elegance.

Types of restaurant Little difference exists these days between a *ristorante* and a *trattoria* (a *ristorante* used to be more expensive and fancier). An *osteria*, once extremely basic, now often indicates somewhere chic and expensive. A *pizzeria*, of course, is what it says, though it will usually offer pasta and some main courses as well as pizzas. The *tavola calda* and the *rosticceria* (places serving hot or cold local fast foods) are now something of a rarity, but both serve hot snacks throughout the day, usually to take out. *Enoteca*, *vinaio*, and *fiaschetteria* are all names for a wine bar, which often serves snacks. A *gelateria* serves ice-cream, a *pasticceria* cakes and pastries.

Main meals Breakfast (*prima colazione*) is a straight-forward stand-up affair of *cappuccino* and plain, cream- or jam-filled croissants (*brioche* or *cornetti*). Stocks of *cornetti* in the best bars last until about 10am. Lunch (*pranzo*) – from around 12.30 – is no longer the over-blown affair of days gone by. You may find it best to buy a picnic or bar snack at midday (see page 175) and save the main meal until evening. Dinner (*cena*) starts around 7.30.

Menus Traditionally, lunch and dinner run through *antipasto* (starters) of ham, salami, and *crostini* (toasts); a course consisting of soup, risotto, polenta, or pasta (*il primo*); a meat or fish course (*il secondo*); salad or vegetables (*insalata* or *contorni*); and dessert (*dolce*), cheese (*formaggio*), or fruit (*frutta*). Coffee, liqueurs, and *digestivi* round things off. Naturally you need not wade through all the courses. Upmarket restaurants, however, will take a dim view if you order only a salad and a glass of wine. Note that the main course (*il secondo*) is à la carte: salad and vegetables are served and billed separately. When ordering fish and the famous *bistecca alla fiorentina* you usually pay by the *etto* (100g) or *hectogram* (400g). Items thus priced are usually marked $S Q$ or *hg*.

Paying The bill (*il conto*) invariably includes a per person cover charge (*pane e coperto*) and a 10–15 per cent service charge (*servizio*). Tip around this amount if service is not included. Remember that bars and restaurants are required by law to give you a proper receipt (*una ricevuta*). Illegible scrawl on a scrap of paper may mean someone is

*Taking it easy in a
Florentine café*

HOLIDAYS AND CLOSING
Most restaurants close for
their annual holidays in
August. They may also be
closed on public holidays.
All must, by law, close
one statutory day
(*chiusura settimanale*)
each week, often Monday.
Many also close on
Sunday evening. First
orders for lunch are at
about 12.30, for dinner
around 7. Few places stay
open for late-night dining
(after 11), and to have an
unhurried meal you must
be at the restaurant by
9.30 at the latest, espe-
cially on weekdays.

cheating you. Always check the bill carefully. You can
keep costs down by skipping *antipasti* and desserts – go to
a *gelateria* for an ice-cream instead. Alternatively, opt for a
fixed-price *menù turistico*, usually a basic pasta, main
course, fruit, and half bottle of wine and water per person.
The food will be filling rather than exciting. The slightly
different *prezzo fisso* is a set-price menu that usually
excludes cover, service, and beverage charges.

Snacks Head for markets, corner shops (*alimentari*), or
supermarkets for picnic supplies. Most bars serve a variety of sandwiches (*tramezzini*) or filled rolls (*panini*). Slices
of pizza (*pizza taglia*), sold everywhere, are good value,
but check the quality of the topping first. A *rosticceria* will
provide you with anything from chips to a whole roast
chicken, while a *tavola calda* confines itself to a few soups
and basic pastas. Wine bars also offer snacks and cold cuts
to accompany a glass or bottle of wine.

VEGETARIANS
Florence has only a hand-
ful of vegetarian restau-
rants. Many *antipasti*,
pizzas, and pastas, how-
ever, will suit vegetarians
(though soups may be
made with meat stock). If
you eat neither meat nor
fish, your main course
may have to be an
omelette (*una frittata*).

Caffè Gilli

TEA

Tea with lemon (*tè al limone*) is common in Italy. Tea with milk is a combination that still raises eyebrows, so be sure to ask for it specifically (*un tè con latte*). Make sure the milk is cold (*latte freddo*). Chamomile (*camomilla*) is common and popular before bed, and iced tea (*tè freddo*) is available in summer.

APERITIFS

Fortified wines such as Martini, Cinzano, and Campari are common aperitifs. Campari Soda comes ready mixed in its own bottle. The artichoke-based Cynar is another popular aperitif.

BRANDY

The best Italian brandies, both widely drunk, are Vecchia Romagna and the second-ranked Stock.

Fast food, Italian-style

176

Bars Florence has a bar on nearly every street corner. Many are functional places for coffee, snacks and an after-work *aperitivo*. You pay a premium to sit down, inside or out, though a single purchase allows you to sit and watch the world go by almost indefinitely, otherwise you stand at the bar. Sitting down usually implies waiter service. The normal procedure otherwise is to pay for what you want at the cash desk (*la cassa*) and take your receipt (*lo scontrino*) to the bar. A L100 tip slapped down when repeating your order usually guarantees prompt service. It is a good idea to take breakfast in bars (invariably cheaper and better than hotels), and they are also ideal for lunchtime snacks.

Coffee A good cup of coffee is a certainty almost anywhere in Italy. Breakfast means a milky *cappuccino*, named after the brown robes and white cowls of Capuchin monks. At other times the *espresso*, a small kick-start of caffeine, is the coffee of choice (usually known as *un caffè*). Decaffeinated coffee is *caffè Hag*, iced coffee *caffè freddo*, and American-style coffee (weaker and in a larger cup) *caffè Americano*. Other varieties include *caffè corretto* (with a dash of grappa or brandy), *caffè latte* (an espresso with extra milk), and *caffè macchiato* (an espresso 'stained' with a drop of milk). If you are really particular, the mark of a good bar is one that uses fresh (not longlife) milk. Italians, incidentally, never drink tea or coffee with meals, and rarely touch *cappuccino* after midday and *never* after a meal.

Wine Most middle- to upper-price-bracket restaurants should have a good selection of Tuscan wines (see pages 212–3). Cheaper places may only have a house wine (*vino della casa*), usually a Chianti or one of its close cousins. Ask for a bottle (*una bottiglia*), half bottle (*mezzo litro*) or quarter flask (*un quartino*). Better restaurants should also have a variety of other Italian wines, and in some cases, a

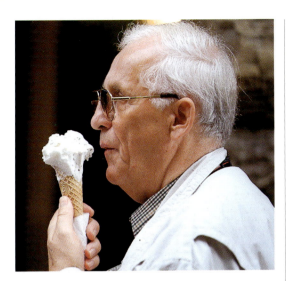

Florence has some of the best ice-cream in Italy

few of French or German origin as well. The famous Enoteca Pinchiorri, one of Europe's greatest cellars (see page 278), has 80,000 bottles of French and Italian vintages. At the other extreme, you can sample wine by the glass in any bar (*un bicchiere di vino*).

Beer The cheapest way to buy beer (*birra*) is from the keg (*una birra alla spina*). Be sure to specify the size you want – *piccola* (25cl) or *media* (50cl). A *grande* (litre) is getting serious. Usually you will be served light, lager-style beer, though dark British-type ale (*birra scura*) is becoming more common. Italian bottled beer (*birra nazionale*) is reasonably priced. Peroni, Dreher, and Nastro Azzurro are the most common brands. Again, specify the size you want. The 25cl Peroncino ('little Peroni') is a good thirst-quencher. Foreign beers are fashionable, and consequently expensive.

Water Florence's tap water (*acqua normale* or *acqua dal rubinetto*) is perfectly safe. Nonetheless, Florentines usually reserve it for washing dishes or watering the flowers. In its place they drink mineral water (*acqua minerale*), either fizzy (*gassata*) or still (*liscia, naturale,* or *non gassata*). Ask for a litre (*un litro*), half a litre (*mezzo litro*), or a glass (*un bicchiere*).

Soft drinks Freshly squeezed orange juice (*una spremuta*) in spring or early summer (when Sicily's oranges are in season) is the best accompaniment to breakfast. Lemon (*limone*) and grapefruit (*pompelmo*) juice are usually also available. Alternatively, ask for bottled fruit juices (*un succo di frutta*), available in flavours such as pear (*pera*), peach (*pesca*), and apricot (*albiccoca*). Lemon Soda, a bitter lemon drink, is popular and widely available. Also be sure to try a fresh milk shake (*un frullato* or *un frappé* if made with ice-cream). *Granita* is crushed ice covered in a syrup (usually coffee). Sodas, of course, are ubiquitous. *Crodino*, a nonalcoholic aperitif, is also popular. Ice is *ghiaccio*; a slice of lemon is *uno spicchio di limone*.

GRAPPA
Usually drunk after a meal, Italy's most famous liquor is a clear firewater made from the mulch of skins and stalks left over after wine making. The best known come from Bassano del Grappa in the Veneto. Fruit- and herb-flavoured versions are common, but frowned on by purists.

LIQUEURS
The best-known Italian liqueurs outside Italy are Sambuca, a sweet aniseed-based drink, and Amaretto, a sweet almond-flavoured concoction. In Italy itself the most common after-dinner tipple is *amaro*, a bitter medicinal brew of herbs, wines, and secret ingredients. The best brands (in ascending order of bitterness) are Montenegro, Ramazotti, Averna, and Fernet-Branca.

Florence

OPENING TIMES
Most shops open daily 9–1 and 3.30–7, with slight seasonal variations. Downtown shops, however, are increasingly remaining open during the afternoon especially department stores and supermarkets. Virtually everything closes on Sunday, and many stores also shut on Monday morning. Food stores also close for one additional afternoon a week, usually Wednesday in winter and Saturday in summer.

SHIPPING
If you need purchases shipped home, contact Fracassi, Via Santo Spirito 11 (tel: 055 289 340).

MAPS AND GUIDES
Libreria Il Viaggio (Borgo degli Albizi 41r) specialises in tourist guides and maps.

BOOKS IN ENGLISH
The Paperback Exchange (Via Fiesolana 31r) has over 10,000 new and second-hand books in English, and offers a trade-in exchange on your old paperbacks.

Shopping

Florence ranks second only to Milan as a source of Italian high fashion, also scoring highly for its range of luxury and leather goods (shoes, bags and gloves). Craft items and antiques are other specialities, together with art books and the marbled paper for which the city is famous. Quality does not come cheap, but reproductions of many goods can be found in supermarkets and street markets (see pages 114–15).

The centre forms the heart of shopping country – Piazza della Repubblica, Via de' Tornabuoni, Ognissanti, and around the Duomo. Shops of certain types, however – leather and antiques shops in particular – can be found dotted throughout the city.

Clothes The top names in Italian design cluster in the city's most fashionable shopping street, Via de' Tornabuoni – which has **Versace**, **Gucci** and **Ferragamo** – and its surrounding streets, such as Via della Vigna Nuova, home of **Valentino**, **Armani** and **Pucci**. Notable exceptions include **Luisa**, first choice for *alta moda* (high fashion), which can be found at Via Roma 19–21. More affordable **Max Mara** is at Via de' Pecori 23r, while glamourous Romano, for men and women, operates from Piazza della Repubblica. Other streets with less exalted names and more reasonably priced stores include Via de' Cerretani, Via del Corso, Via Roma, and Via Calimala. Also worth a look are the department stores **Coin** (Via dei Calzaiuoli 56r), **Principe** (Via degli Strozzi 21–9r) and the stylish, more upmarket **Rinascente**, Piazza della Repubblica 1.

Leather goods Florence has hundreds of shops and market stalls selling leather handbags, gloves, belts and other

Head-turning Florentine fashion

accessories. For quality and real craftsmanship, you have to go for the big names, of which **Ferragamo** (Via de' Tornabuoni 16r) and **Gucci** (Via de' Tornabuoni 73r) are the best known. A better-kept secret, beloved of Florentines, is **Cellerini** (Via del Sole 37r), generally considered the best shop of its type in the city. Everything from gloves to lizard-skin handbags is made on the premises, closely supervised by the firm's family founders. Items here are as stylish, as skillfully made, and as steeply priced as they come. Close behind comes **Raspini**, as renowned in Florence as Gucci but with the difference that they have no foreign outlets, only licensees. They have three branches (Via Roma 25–9r, Via Martelli 5–7r, and Via Por Santa Maria 72r).

As ever, you can cut costs by visiting the markets (San Lorenzo in particular) or one of the better chains, among which **Beltrami** (for shoes, clothes, and accessories) receives most plaudits (branches at Via dei Calzaiuoli 31r and 44r, Via de' Pecori 16, Via Calimala 9, and Via de' Tornabuoni 48r).

Antiques 'Antique' in Italy does not always mean what it says. Under Italian law, an antique need not be old. In the case of furniture, for example, it needs only to be made from wood that is old. Much of what you see in Florence, therefore, is reproduction work – albeit very beautiful reproduction work, for this is a craft at which Florentines have excelled for centuries. Good buys, over and above furniture, include picture frames, jewellery, ceramics, statues, and paintings. Specialist shops congregate on Borgo Ognissanti (and its side streets Via dei Fossi and Via della Porcellana) and in the Oltrarno around Borgo San Jacopo and Via Santo Spirito (and their side streets). Via Maggio, also in the Oltrarno, is known for its small-scale dealers, and for the auction house **Casa d'Aste Pitti** (Piazza Ridolci, Via Maggio 15; tel: 055 287 138).

Jewellery Jewellers have had a virtual monopoly on trade across the Ponte Vecchio for almost four centuries. Still the most famous source of jewellery in Florence, shops on

A better class of souvenir on sale in the Oltrarno

LEATHER WORKSHOPS
To see leather goods being made, visit the workshops in the church of Santa Croce or the Santo Spirito district.

FABRICS
Florence's most beautiful and expensive fabrics come from Lisio Tessuti d' Arte (Via dei Fossi 45r). *Closed* Saturday afternoon and Monday morning. No credit cards. (tel: 055 212 430). Also try Casa de Tessuti, Via de' Pecori 20r (tel: 055 215 961), or Loretta Caponi, Piazza Antinori 4r (tel: 055 213 668).

ART AND ARCHITECTURE

Centro Di (Piazza dei Mozzi 1r), despite its hidden basement location, is one of Italy's most important art bookshops and publishers. Salimbeni (Via M. Palmieri 14–16r) is a highly reputable art and antiquarian bookshop.

PERFUMES AND TOILETRIES

No shopping trip in Florence is complete without visiting the Farmacia di Santa Maria Novella (Via della Scala 16). Founded in 1612, its lovely antique interior is as famous as its products, which include soaps, face creams, and medieval herbal remedies. Less well known but equally beautiful is the Antica Farmacia di San Marco (Via Cavour 146r), best known for its colognes, rose water, and medieval remedies.

HERBS AND FLOWERS

De Herbore (Via del Proconsolo 6a) sells more than 400 herbs and a wide selection of dried fruit, vegetables, herbal teas and dried flowers.

PORCELAIN

Tuscany's most famous porcelain is made by Ginori in the town of Sesto Fiorentino. The firm has a shop in Florence at Via Rondinelli 17r (tel: 055 210 041).

the bridge offer reliable quality and an impressive range of specialities. **Melli** (Nos 44–46r), **Piccini** (No 23r) and **Mannelli** (No 14r) are among the top names. The gold jewellery, in particular, is outstanding, a legacy of Florence's long tradition in the craft (Cellini, Ghiberti, Brunelleschi, and Verrocchio all trained as goldsmiths). Prices are usually high.

Top names elsewhere include the Milanese firm of **Buccellati** (Via de' Tornabuoni 71r) and **Settepassi** (Via de' Tornabuoni 25r), one of the grandest and longest-established Italian jewellers. **Bijoux Cascio** (Via de' Tornabuoni 32r and Via Por Santa Maria 1r) has a reputation stretching back over 30 years for good costume jewellery. **COI**'s upstairs showroom at Via Por Santa Maria 8r, deals in high-volume, low-cost gold jewellery.

Food Markets such as the **Mercato Centrale** (San Lorenzo) and **Sant'Ambrogio** (Piazza Lorenzo Ghiberti) provide excellent starting points in the hunt for edible souvenirs such as olive oil, truffles, and dried *porcini* mushrooms. Street-corner food shops (*alimentari*) sell perfectly good olive oil, brands such as Monini (from Umbria) being the staple of most Italian households. Alternatively you could go for 'designer-label' oils (such as Antinori, sold at Piazza degli Antinori 3) or buy directly from open terracotta pots at **Vino e Olio** (Via de' Serragli 29r).

Leading delicatessens include **Alessi** (Via delle Oche 27–9r), **Vera** (Piazza Frescobaldi 3r), and **Pegna** (Via dello Studio 28r). The top restaurant **Cibrèo** also has a shop selling fine foodstuffs on its premises at Via dei Macci 118r. Among the more specialised shops, **Porta del Tartufo** (Borgo Ognissanti 133r) is the place to find truffle products, and (see page 200) **Dolce & Dolcezze Corti** (Piazza Beccaria 8r) is the last word in high-calorie sweets (cream, pastries, butter, chocolate and cheesecake are the most populara specialities).

At the other extreme, ordinary supermarkets sell Italian basics at keen prices.

Wine Wine can be bought at most grocery shops (*alimentari*) and at the old-fashioned *Vino e Olio* shops (a dying breed). Other specialist shops are known as *cantine, fiaschetterie,* or *mescite* (from *mescere*, which means 'to pour'). In most of these places except *alimentari* you should be able to buy snacks and wine by the glass to taste before buying. **Alessi** (Via della Oche 27–9r) has the best selection of Tuscan wines (with one room devoted to nothing but varieties of Chianti). **Zanobini Fratelli** (Via Sant'Antonio 47r) is also well known for its Tuscan selection (and has the advantage of being close to the Mercato Centrale). For northern Italian vintages and further local varieties, go to **Biagini** (Via de' Banchi 55–7r) and the **Cantinone del Gallo Nero** (Via Santo Spirito 5r), a Chianti specialist. Or try Casa del Vino, Via dell'Ariento 16, close to the Mercato Centrale; the Enotecci Baldovino, Via San Giuseppe 18r, just behind Santa Croce; or Fuori Porta, Via del Monte all Croci, en route for San Miniato.

Paper Florence is renowned for its marbled paper, the product of a craft first brought to Venice from the Orient in the 12th century. The city's most venerable outlet (and *the* place to buy) is **Giannini e Figlio** (Piazza Pitti 37r), a beautiful little shop founded in 1856. **Pineider** has shops all over Italy, but the one at Piazza della Signoria 14r was the first. As well as handmade papers, it sells expensive pens and miscellaneous stationery. There is a second outlet at Via de' Tornabuoni 76r. Other outstanding but more reasonably priced shops include **Il Torchio** (Via dei Bardi 17) and **Il Papiro**, which has branches at Via Cavour 55r, Piazza del Duomo 24r, and Lungarno degli Acciaiuoli 42r. Market stalls also sell marbled paper products.

ARTISTS' MATERIALS
Zecchi (Via Maggio 34r) sells a huge range of artists' materials, many of them unavailable anywhere else in Europe. *Closed* Monday morning. No credit cards.

181

Shopping al fresco *in Piazza Santo Spirito*

Florence

MAIN CONCERT HALLS

Teatro Comunale (Corso Italia 16; tel: 055 211 158; buses 1, 9, 12, 26 or 27); Teatro della Pergola, Via della Pergola 18 (tel: 055 247 9651; buses 6, 12, 14 or 23); Teatro Verdi (Via Ghibellina 101; tel: 055 212 320).

The Teatro Comunale, Florence's main concert venue

Nightlife

Florence has all the nightlife you would expect of a medium-sized city. Films and theatre will probably be beyond non-Italian speakers, but classical concerts, night-clubs, and a quiet dinner *al fresco* are within everyone's grasp. The centre of Florence may appear staid at times, but a large student population ensures some lively venues. If your dancing days are behind you, a stroll across the Ponte Vecchio or a summer evening's drink may be all the nightlife you need. Farther afield lies Fiesole (see pages 82–3), a favourite spot at night to admire the lights of the city below.

Information Listings of all daily events (music, theatre, films etc.) are in Florence's daily newspaper, *La Nazione*, or in monthly magazines such as *Time Off* and *Firenze Spettacolo*. The main tourist office (Via Cavour 1r; tel: 055 290 832/3 or 055 276 0381) has pamphlets and posters detailing events. So, too, does the city council information office at Bargo Santa

Croce 29r (tel: 055 234 0444 or 055 226 4524). Tickets can be bought directly from box offices or through travel agents and larger hotels.

There are also several central ticket agencies, notably **Box Office** (Via Faenza 139r; tel: 055 210 804) and Chiasso dei Soldanieri 8r, off Via Porta Rossa on the corner of Via de'Tornabuoni (tel: 055 219 402).

The sun sets behind the Ponte Santa Trinita

Music festivals Florence's big classical music event is the annual **Maggio Musicale Fiorentino**, perhaps the most important such event in all Italy. Held between May (*Maggio*) and early July, it embraces opera and ballet as well as classical concerts and smaller recitals. It has its own orchestra, chorus, and ballet troupe, and performances are given by visiting international companies. Most big events take place in the **Teatro Comunale** (Corso Italia 16; tel: 055 277 9236). This is also the festival's main box office. More modest recitals use the Teatro's smaller auditorium, the **Ridotto** (or *Piccolo*); the **Teatro della Pergola** (Via della Pergola 18; tel: 055 247 9651); and the **Teatro Verdi** (Via Ghibellina 101; tel: 055 212 320).

The other big festival is Fiesole's **Estate Fiesolana**, a series of chamber and symphony concerts held between June and late August. Like the Maggio Musicale, it also offers peripheral opera, ballet, theatre and film presentations. Most events take place in Fiesole's **Badia Fiesolana** or in the open-air **Teatro Romano** (the old Roman theatre. Others are staged in Florence, usually in **Santa Croce** or the courtyard of the **Palazzo Pitti**. (Bus No 7 will take you to Fiesole.)

Classical music As well as the summer festivals, Florence hosts several seasonal concert series. The **Amici della Musica** organises concerts most Saturday and Sunday afternoons (Jan–Apr and Oct–Dec) and/or evenings at the **Teatro della Pergola**. Their office is at Via Sirtori 49 (tel: 055 608 420 or 055 607 440). The **Orchestra da Camera Fiorentina** (Via Enrico Poggi; tel: 055 783 374) performs a season of concerts, usually two or three times weekly

THEATRE
Florence's main classical theatre is the Teatro della Pergola, host to leading Italian companies between October and May. One of the city's oldest theatres, the Teatro Niccolini (Via Ricasoli 3; tel: 055 213 282 or 055 239 6653), comes a close second. For cabaret or more experimental work try Teatro di Rifredi (Via Vittorio Emanuele II 303; tel: 055 422 0361).

Cinemas are plentiful, but most films are dubbed into Italian

DANCE

Florence's best ballet and modern dance is to be found at the two summer festivals – the Maggio Musicale and Estate Fiesolana. Visiting companies also perform at the Teatro Comunale and the Teatro della Pergola.

(Mar–Oct), often in the churches of Orsanmichele and the Badia Fiorentina. Tickets from box office or churches up to an hour before performances. As well as the Maggio Musicale's big events, the **Teatro Comunale** stages its own cycle of concerts. These take place between mid-September and December, in tandem with the city's main opera season, which finishes in mid-January. From January to April, the **Teatro Verdi** mixes opera and ballet with its theatrical productions. Finally, members of the **Orchestra Regionale Toscana** (tel: 055 424 767 or 055 234 355) present regular chamber concerts once or twice monthly (December to May) usually on Saturday or Wednesday in the Teatro Verdi. Tickets from box office or Teatro Verdi.

Films The only cinema regularly showing English-language films is the **Cinema Astro** (no phone) at Piazza San Simeone (near Santa Croce and opposite Gelateria Vivoli). It is closed on Mondays. Film clubs occasionally show original-language films; these include **Spazio Uno** (Via del Sole 10; tel: 055 283 389) and **Atelier Alfieri** (Via dell'Ulivio 6; tel: 055 240 720). For a unique experience, try films in the open air at the **Pianeta Cinema** in the Forte del Belvedere (summer only). More devoted film goers can try Florence's three international film festivals. The **Festival dei Popoli**, based at Via Castellani 8 (tel: 055 294 353), is the best known, but the **Florence Film Festival**, established in 1983, is gaining ground, as is the festival of women's films in movies and television, the **Incontro Internazionale Cinema Donne**. For details of the three festivals, contact the Atelier Alfieri (see above).

Rock, pop and jazz The names that follow include the current clubs of choice, as well as some of the larger and longer-established spots. Nearly all are in the suburbs, involving a bus ride there and possibly a long walk back late at night. Big international acts use the **Palasport** stadium at Viale Paoli (reached by bus No 10). Bands or solo singers who draw smaller crowds use the **Teatro Verdi** (Via Ghibellina 101; tel: 055 212 320) and the **Teatro Tenda** (Lungarno Aldo Moro; tel: 055 650 4112; bus No 14). Indie bands have an annual festival, the 'Meeting', held during the summer at the **Palazzo dei Congressi** (Viale F Strozzi). Best known of the more intimate venues, featuring bands of all persuasions, is **Auditorium Flog** (Via Michele Mercati 24; tel: 055 490 437; bus No. 4).

Jazz fans are not so well served as in Milan or Rome, but Florence's Auditorium Flog (see above) still manages to attract many of the top international names. More specialised clubs include the **Jazz Club** (Via Nuova dei Caccini 3; tel: 055 247 9700; buses 6, 12, 14, or 23) and **Be Bop** (Via des Servi 281; no phone) a smart place within walking distance of the centre between the duomo and ss Annunziata. Jazz club also hosts events organised by the Toscana Jazz Pool, a jazz festival held in several Tuscan cities.

Clubs and discos Like music venues nightclubs drop in and out of fashion. Four of the city's older discos have achieved almost historic status. **Tenax** (Via Pratese 46a; tel: 055 308 160) is the most popular, attracting locals and foreigners alike; it also presents new and established live bands (*Open* nightly Tue–Sun). **Meccanò** (Viale degli Olmil–Piazzale delle Cascine; tel: 055 331 371) is the city's most famous disco, attracting clubbers from across Tuscany (*Closed* Sun, Mon, Wed and two weeks in Aug). The other two are more intimate: **Andromeda** (Piazza de' Cerchi 7a; tel: 055 292 002; *Open* nightly except Mon) and **Space Electronic** (Via Palazzuolo 37; tel: 055 293 082; *Open* nightly. *Closed* Mon in winter). More sedate clubs and piano bars include **Jackie O** (Via dell'Erta Canina 24a; tel: 055 234 2442/3) and **Full Up** (Via Vigna Vecchia 21r; tel: 055 293 006), both popular with the older set. At the other extreme, try the Latin-influenced **Maxcal Club** (Via Ghibellina 69r; tel: 055 248 0609. *Closed* Mon and Wed); the dark, ultra-cook **Maramao** (Via de'Macci 79r; tel: 0550244 341; daily); and excellent club-bar **Rex** (Via Fiesolana 23r; tel: 055 248 0331; *Closed* Jul–Aug).

185

GAY AND LATE-NIGHT BARS
Gay clubs include the Crisco, a men-only pub (Via Sant'Edidio 43r) and the Samtamassa Bar (Via dei Pandolfini 26).
If you want to burn the midnight oil, the following bars and cafés stay open later than most:
Il Rifrullo (Via San Niccolò 55r)
La Dolce Vita (Piazza del Carmine) and Rex Bar (Via Fiesplana 23r).

Florence is full of small, chic clubs and discos

Florence

A good map is always a worthwhile investment

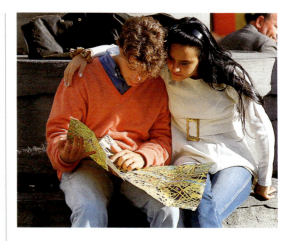

186

MAIN BUS ROUTES

Most buses can be picked up either at the bus station (right next to the train station) or in Piazza del Duomo.

1 Duomo, Stazione, Viale Talenti
6 Duomo, San Marco, San Frediano
7 Stazione, Duomo, San Marco, Fiesole
10 Stazione, Duomo, San Marco, Settignano
11 Duomo, Porta Romana, Poggio Imperiale
12 Duomo, Porta Romana, San Miniato al Monte
13 Stazione, Duomo, Piazzale Michelangelo (San Miniato al Monte)
14 Duomo, Stazione, Careggi
17 Cascine, Stazione, Duomo, Salviatino (for the youth hostel)

Practical details

Information Before setting foot in a museum, visit one of Florence's **tourist offices** to collect a free city map, a list of events, and a full list of gallery opening times and up-to-date admission prices. The most convenient is at **Via Cavour** 1r (tel: 055 276 0381 or 055 290 832/3), close to the Palazzo Medici-Riccardi and the Duomo. In the east of the city, the most convenient office is the **Comune di Firenze** office just two minutes' walk from Santa Croce at Borgo Santa Croce 29r (tel: 055 234 0444 or 055 226 4524). A third office can be found outside the **train station**; it is at the bottom of the row of buses on your left as you leave the station building (tel: 055 238 1226 or 055 212 245).

Via Cavour and Borgo Santa Croce is open Mon–Sat 8.30–7.15; Via Cavour also opens Sun 8.30–1.45. Piazza della Stazione opens Mon–Sat 8.30–1.45. Times may have slight seasonal variations.

Buses Much of what visitors come to see in Florence is easily reached on foot. However, you may wish to take a bus when visiting San Miniato al Monte and Piazzale Michelangelo, the Cascine, and the Museo Stibbert. Longer trips to Fiesole and to the Medici villas (see pages 82–3 and 170–1) can also be made by bus from downtown. General public transportation information is given in **Travel Facts** (see pages 257–9).

The city bus company is called ATAF (Information tel: 055 565 0222). There are four basic ticket types: one valid for any number of trips within an hour; a similar one valid for two hours; a similar one valid for 24 hours; and a 'carnet' of four one-hour tickets. Tickets must be purchased before boarding the bus, and are available from bars, newsstands, or tobacco shops displaying an orange ATAF sticker (saying '*Biglietti Abbonamenti Qui*'). Automatic ticket machines also dot the city, notably at the bus station itself, the Fortezza da Basso, and Piazza San Marco (where there is also an ATAF kiosk).

You can enter buses through either the front or the rear doors, where you must validate tickets in the small machine. Leave by the central doors. Buses run to and from Florence's Peretola airport roughly every hour, seven days a week. The trip takes about 15 minutes, and buses leave from Via Santa Caterina da Siena (just west of the train station). If taking the bus from Peretola, you have to buy a ticket at the bar above the departure lobby.

Crime and safety No large city is entirely free of crime. Florence is no exception, its many tourists a source of rich potential pickings for the unscrupulous. Despite all this, Florence is hardly a den of vice, and basic precautions and common sense should ensure a trouble-free trip.

Late at night avoid the Cascine, Piazza Ognissanti, and the backstreets around the station: all are red-light areas of dubious repute. The same goes for the *Viali*, the busy roads on the city outskirts. Women on their own may be propositioned in quieter city streets.

Use common sense to guard against pickpockets. Buses and street markets (especially San Lorenzo) are the thieves' favourite hunting grounds. Never keep money or valuables in a back pocket or an easily opened handbag. Put them in a pouch or money belt. Carry bags and cameras across your chest, not over your shoulder, and never put them down on café tables. Reduce temptation by leaving anything that can be snatched, such as necklaces and bracelets, in the hotel safe. Never leave your luggage or radio-cassette players in cars.

Addresses Florence has a confusing double-number address system. Business addresses (which usually include bars and restaurants) are followed by the letter 'r' for *rosso* (red), as in 'Via Confusione 32r.' Numbers are usually marked in red on a white background. Most hotels and residential addresses simply have a number, occasionally followed by a blue or black 'b.' Matters are further complicated by the fact that the two sets of numbers are independent of each other. Via Confusione 32r, therefore, will probably be some distance from Via Confusione 32b, or 31r for that matter.

TOURIST PASS
Non-residents can buy a special Carta Arancio, a seven-day pass valid for all trains and buses within the province of Florence (which does not include Siena). It must be used with valid identification such as a passport, and is available from ATAF (Piazza della Stazione) or SITA (Via Santa Caterina da Siena 15) or CAP (Via Nazionale 13) or COPIT (Piazza Santa Maria Novella 22).

187

An ATAF bus: core of Florence's public transport system

188

A13
Malalbergo
Portomaggiore
Comacchio
Reno
Molinella
Argenta
Valli di Comacchio
Búdrio
Medicína
Consélice
Alfonsine
Bagnacavallo
Ravenna
Lugo
A14dir
Russi
Montone
Castel San Pietro Terme
Imola
Faenza
A14
Forlì
Cérvia
Brisighella
Castrocaro Terme
Forlimpopoli
Cesenático
Modigliana
Méldola
Cesena
Bellária-Igea Marina
Marradi
Predáppio
Savignano sul Rubicone
Rímini
Rocca San Casciano
Santarcángelo di Romagna
Riccione
Gabicce Mare
Dicomano
Santa Sofia
Bidente
Mercato Saraceno
Verúcchio
SAN MARINO
San Marino
mèdicea
aréggi
etraia
astéllo
1654m
Mte Falterona
Sársina
Bagno di Romagna
Novalféltria
San Leo
Morciano di Romagna
Montelábbate
Stia
Camáldoli
Badia Prataglia
Montefeltro
Pennábilli
Fóglia
Sassocorvaro
ontassieve
Vallombrosa
Chiusi della Verna
M A R C H E
Reggello
Poppi
1591m
Bibbiena
Pieve Santo Stefano
Urbino
Fossombrone
Fíglline Valdarno
Caprese Michelangelo
Sant'Angelo in Vado
Acqualagna
Grópina
San Giovanni Valdarno
Subbiano
Sansepolcro
Apécchio
Cagli
Montevarchi
Anghiari
Arezzo
Monterchi
San Giustino
Cantiano
1701m
Mte Catria
Búcine
A1
Città di Castello
Monte San Savíno
Castiglion Fiorentino
1566m
Mte Cucco
Brólio
Montécchio
Gubbio
Rapolano Terme
Fóiano della Chiana
Cortona
Umbértide
Abbazía di Monte Sinalunga Olivéto Maggiore
Tórrita di Siena
Passignano sul Trasimeno
Gualdo Tadino
Buonconvento
Lago Trasimeno
Magione
Perúgia
Valfábbrica
San Quírico
Montepulciano
Castiglione del Lago
Nocera Umbra
Montalcino
Pienza
Assisi
1290m
Mte Subásio
Bagno Vignoni
Chianciano Terme
Chiusi
Torgiano
Spello
Abbazía di Sant'Antimo
1738m
Mte Amiata
Cetona
Città della Pieve
Deruta
Bevagna
Folígno
Arcidosso
Marsciano
Montefalco
Trevi
Roccalbegna
U M B R I A
Todi
Spoleto
Acquapendente
A1
Orvieto
Montéluco
Albegna
Sorano
Monti Volsini
Acquasparta
Sovana
Grádoli
Lago di Bolsena
Bolsena
Civita
Lugnano in Teverina
Terni
Pitigliano
Manciano
Capodimonte
Montefiascone
Amélia
Canino
Marta
Bomarzo
Orte
Narni
Tuscánia
L A Z I O
Bagnáia
Viterbo
Vignanello
Montalto di Castro
L di Vico
Caprarola
Magliano Sabina
1288m
Tarquinia
Vetralla
Ronciglione
Blera
Sutri
Castellana Nepi
Tévere
Monti Sabini
Tolfa
Lago di Bracciano
Mti Sabatini
Trevignano Romano
D
E

Veterinary services advertised on an old Tuscan street sign

SCENIC DRIVES
Tuscany has numerous drives worth following for their own sake. These are a few of the best:
· SS 146/451 Montepulciano, Pienza, San Quirico (Montalcino), Buonconvento, Monte Oliveto Maggiore.
· SS 222 (the *Chiantigiana* wine road), Siena, Castellina, Greve, Florence.
· SS 68 Volterra (San Gimignano), Colle di Val d'Elsa.
· SS 70/208 (Florence), Pontassieve, Poppi, Camaldoli , Bibbiena, Chiusi di Verna.
· SS 324 Castelnuovo di Garfagnana, San Pellegrino, Pievepelago, San Marcello, Pistoia.
(See also pages 198–9 and 242–3.)

For many people, Tuscany *is* Italy. Its vineyards and soft-edged hills, its red wines and balmy summers, its quiet villages and cypress-ringed villas weave a spell that can be hard to resist from Florence's traffic-clogged streets. Resist it, however, many visitors do – some simply because they are short of time, others perhaps because they are reluctant to leave the city's protective cocoon. It takes a courage of sorts, after all, to tackle public transportation or face the perils of Latin drivers and Italian roads. You should not, however, be fainthearted. Most Tuscan towns of note, including nearly all those featured in this A–Z section, can be reached in no more than an hour from Florence. In the case of the big three – Siena, Lucca, and Pisa (not to mention Arezzo, Prato, and Pistoia). The trip requires no more than the simplest of train rides. If Florence is your base, all such towns can be seen as day trips; if not, many make ideal springboards for the type of leisurely exploration that will ultimately reveal the best of the region.

Towns The attractions of most Tuscan towns make each one worthy of a whole day's sightseeing. **Siena** deserves at least that, its calm medieval ambience the perfect antidote to Florence. Little-known **Lucca** comes next, as graceful and civilised a town as any in Italy. Nearby **Cortona**, by contrast, seduces with its views, its galleries, and its quiet medieval streets. Much the same goes for **Montepulciano**, as attractive for its own sake as for any surfeit of art and architecture. **Volterra**, too, has its views and its medieval moments, as well as a wealth of Roman and Etruscan remains. The largely modern **Pisa** attracts by virtue of its Campo dei Miracoli (but can be curiously disappointing thereafter). **Arezzo** might be similarly lacklustre but for Piero della Francesca's great fresco cycle. **Pistoia** and **Prato** are perhaps too industrialised for immediate visitor appeal, but each has a sprinkling of masterpieces and monuments within easy reach of Florence.

The façade of San Michele in Foro, Lucca

Vineyards chequer the hills of Chianti, Tuscany's most famous region

191

Villages The siren call of Tuscany's towns could well leave little time for its villages. No trip to the region, however, would be complete without a visit to **San Gimignano** and its famous towers. Fewer people find their way to **Pienza**, a tiny Renaissance jewel, or to **Montalcino**, heart of the famous Brunello wine region (see pages 212–13 and 242–3). More are discovering Monteriggioni, a short hop from Siena, and perhaps the most perfect of Tuscany's fortified villages (see panel on page 239). Close by stand three beautiful **abbeys** – Sant'Antimo, San Galgano, and Monte Oliveto Maggiore (see pages 232–3) – all fascinating monuments to Tuscany's long monastic tradition.

Landscapes Try to visit **Chianti**, of course – the most famous of Tuscany's landscapes – but try also to see the similar but less praised areas of the Mugello, the Pratomagno, and the Casentino. All three are mountainous regions smothered in huge forests, each a far cry from the pastoral images often associated with other parts of the Tuscan heartland. Departing farther from Tuscany's gentler side are the marble-streaked summits of the **Alpi Apuane**, part of the great mountain range that rears up behind Pisa, Lucca, and the Versilian coast. Too distant, perhaps, for many visitors to Florence, this spectacular country still deserves exploration, particularly the green Garfagnana Valley and the flower-strewn meadows of the Orecchiella.

Less immediately appealing is the Maremma, a rather melancholy coastal plain, but nonetheless one of Italy's more unspoiled shores, with the Parco Naturale della Maremma as well as a couple of Tuscany's best beaches. South of Siena and closer to home are the Crete. Here will be found some of the region's strangest landscapes – bare clay hills chequered with dusty fields and prairies of rippling wheat.

ESCAPE
'I'd had my fill of Florence, lovely but indigestible city. My eyes were choked with pictures and frescos, all stamped one on top of the other, blurred, their colours running. I began to long for those cool uplands, that country air, for the dateless wild olive and the uncatalogued cuckoo'. Laurie Lee, *I Can't Stay Long* (1975).

The sloping Piazza Grande in Arezzo

TOURIST INFORMATION
Arezzo's main tourist office is outside the station at Piazza della Repubblica 28 (tel: 055 0575/377 678).

CASA DI VASARI
Giorgio Vasari was born in Arezzo in 1511. Best known for his *Lives of the Artists* (1550), he was also the court painter and architect to Cosimo I. Few of his works have stood the test of time, and churches such as Santa Croce and Santa Maria Novella in Florence lost numerous earlier frescoes through his ill-considered interventions. His house (1540), at Via XX Settembre 55, is decorated with some of the better examples of his work. *Open* daily 9–7. *Admission free.*

▶▶ Arezzo IBCF4

Arezzo would probably have few fans, were it not the home of one of Tuscany's most celebrated fresco cycles. Largely modern in appearance, the town relies for its prosperity on furniture making and on one of Europe's largest gold and jewellery industries. In days gone by it was a leading member of the Etruscans' 12-city federation. Trans-Apennine trade routes maintained Arezzo's importance under the Romans and it became an independent city state during the Middle Ages before falling to Florence in 1384.

The church of San Francesco and its frescos (see below) will probably take most of your time, but leave an hour or so to see the precipitous **Piazza Grande▶**, flanked by Vasari's 1573 loggia and the **Palazzetto della Fraternità dei Laici**. The latter, built for a lay confraternity, sports a Gothic ground floor (1377) and a Renaissance upper storey by Bernardo Rossellino (1434).

To the right of the palazzetto stands the arcaded apse of the **Pieve di Santa Maria▶▶**, which is one of the region's finest Romanesque churches. The Pisan-inspired façade looks out onto Corso Italia, its portal decorated with touching reliefs (1210) that illustrate the months of the year. Inside the church, the high altar has a grandiose polyptych by Pietro Lorenzetti.

Wander past the Casa di Petrarca (Petrarch's House) to take in the **Duomo▶** (*Open* daily 7.30–12, 3–6.30. *Admission free*) with its small fresco of Mary Magdalene by Piero della Francesca (end of the north aisle) and, alongside it, the superb tomb of Bishop Guido Tarlati (d 1327), possibly sculpted to a design by Giotto. The nearby church of **San Domenico** has fresco fragments, an *Annunciation* by the local artist Spinello Aretino and a *Crucifix* painted by the 20-year-old Cimabue.

San Francesco ▶▶▶

(Open daily 8–12, 2–6.30, until 7 in summer. *Admission free).* Although it was built in 1320, Arezzo's Franciscan church only received its great fresco cycle in the 1450s. Commissioned by the Bacci, one of the town's leading families, the paintings were started by Bicci di Lorenzo, who, at his death, had completed only the choir's vaults (decorated with scenes of Hell, Heaven, and Purgatory). Piero della Francesca, who continued the cycle, adopted a new theme taken from *The Legend of the*

GETTING THERE
Arezzo is a major stop on the Florence–Rome train line (40 minutes).

MUSEO ARCHEOLOGICO
The archeological museum (Via Margaritone 10) has lovely examples of the Roman *coralline* ceramics for which Arezzo was famed. *Open* Mon–Sat 9–2; Sun 9–1.30. *Admission charge.*

ANTIQUES FAIR
One of Italy's foremost antiques fairs, the Fiera Antiquaria, is held in Arezzo's Piazza Grande over the weekend of the first Sunday in the month.

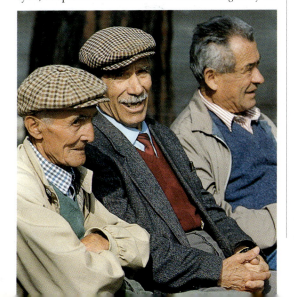

Three wise men: Arezzo locals

Piero della Francesca's True Cross *cycle*

THE PIERO TRAIL
Piero della Francesca's
Madonna del Parto, the
only pregnant Madonna in
Italian art, stands in
Monterchi's former
school-house (*Open*
Tue–Sun 9–1, 2–7;
shorter hours in winter.
Admission charge), 25km
east of Arezzo. Farther
east, the Museo Civico
(Open daily 9.30–1, 3.30-
6.30. Admission charge)
in Sansepolcro, Piero's
birthplace, contains two
minor and two major
works.

True Cross, a series of stories first collected in the 13th century by Jacopo da Voragine, Archbishop of Genoa. By
Piero's time, the tales had become an international best-
seller, reprinted in countless editions in all the major
European languages.

Cleverly linking the story of Adam and Eve and original
sin with the story of humanity's redemption, this narrative charts an unlikely series of events in which the tree
from which Eve plucked the forbidden fruit becomes the
cross of Christ's crucifixion.

The story had already been painted, notably by Agnolo
Gaddi in Florence's Santa Croce and by Cenni di
Francesco in Volterra's San Francesco. Piero's version,
however, is more complicated – not to say more accomplished – than its predecessors. This is partly because he
was a better painter, and partly because he takes his story
from two versions of the *Legend*. It was further complicated by Piero's insistence on artistic rather than narrative
logic. Two battle scenes, for example, are placed opposite
one another, their positions designed for compositional

Plan of the San Francesco frescoes

impact rather than narrative explanation. Similar symmetries are repeated in the Queen of Sheba's courtly retinue, which appears twice, and in the identical portraits of the queen and the empress Helena.

The narrative sequence of the frescoes is as follows:

1. Adam announces his death and implores his son Seth to seek the 'oil of mercy' from the Angel of Paradise.

2. The angel instead sends a twig from Paradise's Tree of Knowledge, which Seth plants in his father's mouth.

3. The twig has become a tree over Adam's grave. Solomon intends to use it in his temple, but instead orders a bridge to be built from its wood. The Queen of Sheba, visiting Solomon, kneels in prayer, sensing the bridge's divine importance.

4. The queen foresees the Crucifixion and the fate of the Jews, whose realm 'shall be defaced and cease'. She tells Solomon of her prophecy.

5. Solomon orders the beam's burial (the scene deliberately echoes Christ's carrying of the cross).

6. The Roman emperor, Constantine the Great, asleep on the eve of battle, has a vision telling him to look for the sign of the cross. An angel announces 'Under this sign shall you be victorious'.

7. The victory of Constantine over his rival emperor, Maxentius. Constantine asks the meaning of the cross and is baptised.

8. Under torture, the Levite Judas (kept in a well for six days) reveals to the empress Helena, mother of Constantine (and an inveterate collector of relics), the location of Calvary's three crosses.

9. The crosses are found: the True Cross is revealed when it touches a dead man and brings him back to life. The city in the background (meant to be Jerusalem) is Arezzo.

10. Thirty years later, the Persian king, Chosroes, steals a portion of the cross, using it to build a throne on which he sets himself up as a god. Chosroes is defeated by Heraclius, emperor of the Eastern Empire.

11. Heraclius returns the cross to Jerusalem.

12. Prophet (by an assistant to Piero).

13. Prophet.

14. Annunciation.

PASSEGGIO DEL PRATO

Arezzo's public garden, next to the Duomo, is the nicest place in town for a walk or picnic. The ruined Fortezza Medicea, above the park, has magnificent views over the surrounding countryside.

GIOSTRA DEL SARACINO

After a morning of processions in medieval costume, a pair of knights from each of Arezzo's four quarters take turns charging at the Buratto, a figure recalling the days when Saracen pirates menaced Tuscany and the Tyrrhenian coast. In one hand the Buratto bears a numbered shield (scores depend on where the knights' lances strike), in the other a cat-of-nine-tails that swings round when the shield is struck. The winner receives a golden lance. The event is traditionally held on the first Sunday in September in Piazza Grande. Recently it has become so popular that repeat performances are held throughout the summer. Contact the tourist office for dates.

Tuscany's rural patchwork of hills and valleys offers many pockets of beautiful countryside. Some are less well-known versions of Chianti's classic scenery; other, wilder places are areas of outstanding natural beauty and enjoy protection as regional or national parks.

196

BIRD-WATCHING

Tuscany's best bird watching sites are the Ombrone estuary in the Parco Naturale della Maremma; the Worldwide Fund for Nature (WWF) oasis at Albinia, on the Orbetello lagoon; the WWF reserve at Lago di Burano, 10km southeast of Orbetello; and the WWF reserve at Bolgheri, near Cecina about 40km south of Livorno. WWF reserves are usually open only from September to May on Thursday and Sunday, but many birds can also be seen in these areas outside the reserves.

Sunflowers and vines in the Chianti hills are part of the gentler face of Tuscany

Mugello, Pratomagno and Casentino It can only be a matter of time before this great arc of countryside north and east of Florence begins to share the popularity of the more famous (but scenically inferior) Chianti hills to the south of the city. A tour of the **Pratomagno**, a great bowed dome of meadow-topped hills, should start at Vallombrosa, whose mighty forests were immortalised in the opening book of Milton's *Paradise Lost*. Milton describes the rebel angels, fallen from Heaven, lying 'Thick as autumnal leaves that strow the brooks/ In Vallombrosa, where th'Etrurian shades/ High over-arched, embow'r'. In 1638 the poet stayed at the village's famous monastery, now largely modern in appearance but still at the heart of some magnificent scenery.

Further west, another old monastery village, Camaldoli, makes a good focal point in the **Casentino**, an area famed since antiquity for its mountains and huge, wind-blown forests. The biggest region of all, the **Mugello**, has enough byways for days of exploration, best accomplished – as elsewhere in these regions – on the scenic mountain roads well away from the towns and semi-industrialised valleys.

Alpi Apuane and Orecchiella Tuscany's most spectacular scenery – and its best walking country – gathers north of Pisa in two mountain ranges flanking the Garfagnana Valley. To the west the **Alpi Apuane** rise from the sea with almost Alpine splendour, dotted with marble quarries whose snowlike streaks glisten on the slopes above Massa and Carrara. Countless marked trails crisscross the hills, well-worn tracks weaving through thick chestnut forests or cresting the panoramic and craggy-topped summit ridges. The mountains are well mapped (unlike much of Italy) and refuges provide picnic supplies and overnight stops – maps and refuge information are available from Massa, Carrara, and most coastal towns. As a result, day hikes in this area, and several long-distance paths, are some of the easiest in Tuscany to tackle without too much planning ahead. The best starting points are the villages of Stazzema and Levigliano on the western flanks. If you wish to drive instead, a network of tiny roads crisscrosses the mountains, providing superb views.

The **Orecchiella**, east of the Garfagnana – higher and wilder than the Alpi Apuane – offers almost equally good scenery and walking country. Visit Barga for its honey-coloured cathedral, and the well-managed Parco Naturale, whose park centre at Orecchiella (a hamlet 15km north of Castelnuovo di Garfagnana) is the starting point of several easy marked trails. Castelnuovo di Garfagnana and

Corfino are the best bases for the area. Excellent, readily obtainable maps allow you to explore under your own steam. Driving, too, is a delight, a particularly good target being the excellent folk museum at San Pellegrino in Alpe (16km northeast of Castelnuovo).

Maremma A stretch of fertile coastal lowlands under the Etruscans and the Romans, the Maremma deteriorated into a malaria-ridden swamp during the Middle Ages. It remained that way – and all but uninhabited – until recla-mation began in the 18th century. Today, the region's finest sweep of unspoiled landscape is protected by the Parco Naturale della Maremma (a proposed national park). The hills of the park, the Monti dell'Uccellina, are topped by coastal watchtowers and have caves that have yielded some of Italy's oldest prehistoric remains. The shores are the least spoiled in Tuscany, while forests of umbrella pine, coastal dunes, marshes, and Mediterranean maquis provide cover for a fantastic assortment of flora and fauna. Only the superb beach at Marina di Alberese is open to cars. Otherwise, you have to park at Alberese, 20km south of Grosseto, and take the park bus (see panel). Alternative access is on foot from Talamone, an appealing village at the park's southern edge.

PARK BUS
For access to the Parco Naturale della Maremma, leave your car at Alberese and buy a bus ticket from the main square's park kiosk (hourly, Wednesday and weekends only). The bus drops you in the heart of the park (there are no other roads). From here you can walk almost at random; the lovely beach is about 20 minutes' walk away. The last bus out leaves at 5.30.

197

*Top: the Maremma.
Below: the jagged peaks of
the Alpi Apuane near the
marble town of Carrara*

The heart of Chianti

A circular tour from Siena (see pages 234–41) through Chianti's hills, villages and most famous vineyards (approximately 110km).

Chianti is not only the home of Italy's most famous red wine, but also a region whose vineyards and wooded hills evoke the quintessential image of Tuscany. Thousands of visitors swarm to its villas and farmhouses. Some villages are tarnished by the influx: others, like Radda and Gaiole, are spoiled by a surprising amount of light industry. The region's real pleasures, therefore, lie in driving its winding back roads, exploring the smaller hamlets, and in sampling wine at any one of the hundreds of vineyards open to the public.

Leave Siena by SS 408 (signed to Montevarchi), joining it beyond Siena's train station. Turn right after 10km onto the minor road past San Giusto alle Monache and San Felice. **Castello di Brolio**▶▶ offers tours around one of Chianti's best vineyards. The estate has been in the Ricasoli family since 1167, and Barone Bettino Ricasoli, Italy's second prime minister, established Chianti Classico's formula in 1870.

Rural and rambling: a typical Chianti farmhouse

For marvellous views of the Chianti hills, take SS 484 south of Brolio. Continue north past the hamlets of San Gusmé, Campi, and Linari before rejoining SS 408 beyond the castle of Meleto. This loop adds 27km. If you are short of time, drive west from Brolio for 5km to meet SS 408, 2km south of Meleto.

Continue to **Gaiole**▶ – not the prettiest of Chianti villages, though its single main street is pleasant enough, and there is the novelty of a stream (often dry) through the village centre. Further on, a short detour from the main road (worthwhile for the views alone) leads to **Badia a Coltibuono**. The lovely (but rarely open) Romanesque church, San Lorenzo, is part of an abbey complex owned by one of the more commercially minded Chianti estates. Its wine, honey, and oil are exported to delicatessens all over Europe, but you can also buy produce directly from Da Gianetto, the estate's stylish restaurant.

The road west to **Radda in Chianti** is particularly panoramic, and though Radda's outskirts are unappealing, the village's medieval centre, Piazza Ferrucci, is more picturesque. If you have time to spare, drive the 15km loop north to the fortified hamlet of **Volpaia**, whose evocative towers and castle are the legacy of its role as a vital military look-out in the 16th century.

Continue west to **Castellina in Chianti►**, another walled village whose main concern these days is wine production. Be sure to visit the Bottega del Vino Gallo Nero at Via della Rocca 13, a showcase for the region's wine and olive oils. They will also advise on local vineyards offering tours and tastings.

Return to Siena on SS 222, or turn right off SS 222 800m south of Castellina at Malafrasca to visit the superbly preserved village of **Monteriggioni** (see page 239), off SS 2 (10km southeast of Poggibonsi).

►► Cortona

Cortona may become one of your favourite Tuscan hill-towns. Magnificently situated, with olives and vineyards creeping up to its walls, it commands enormous views over Lake Trasimeno and the plain of the Valdichiana. Its two fine galleries and scattering of churches are relatively unvisited, and its delightful medieval streets are a pleasure to wander for their own sake. Last but not least, pleasant hotels and restaurants make the town a good overnight base.

Cortona may be one of Italy's oldest towns – 'Mother of Troy and Grandmother of Rome', in popular speech. Tradition claims it was founded by Dardanus, the founder of Troy (after whom the Dardanelles are named). He was fighting a local tribe, so the story goes, when he lost his helmet (corythos) on Cortona's hill. In time, a town grew up that took its name (Corito) from the missing headgear. By the 4th century BC the Etruscans had built the first set of town walls, whose cyclopean traces can still be seen in the 3km sweep of the present fortifications. A member of the Etruscans' 12-city Dodecapolis, it became one of the federation's leading northern cities. An important consular road, the Via Cassia, which passed the foot of its hill, maintained the town's importance under the Romans. Medieval fortunes waned, however, as the plain below reverted to marsh. After holding out against neighbours like Perugia, Arezzo, and Siena, the *comune* was captured by King Ladislas of Naples in 1409 and sold to the Florentines two years later.

Cortona's steep streets make you pay for your pleasure, but any amount of puffing and panting is worth it to enjoy their views and medieval vignettes. Only one lane is level: the main Via Nazionale (linking Piazza Garibaldi and Piazza della Repubblica), referred to by locals as the *Ruga Piana* (Flat Street). Areas well worth seeking out include Via Guelfa and Via Ghibellina, the main streets of the old town, both sprinkled with a mixture of medieval

GETTING THERE

Trains to Cortona from Florence (90 minutes) stop at Terontola or Camucia-Cortona. Both stations are several kilometres from the town. Shuttle buses connect them roughly every 30 minutes to Piazza Garibaldi. The town centre is closed to cars, so use the parking lots near San Domenico or at Porta Colonia and Piazza del Mercato. LFI buses run from Piazza Garibaldi to Arezzo and Castiglion Fiorentino.

SPECIAL EVENTS

Cortona's lively weekly market takes place on Saturday. An annual antiques and furniture fair is held in late August and September.

Santa Margherita is the highest church in this lovely hill town

200

and Renaissance architecture; Via Janelli, a picturesque thoroughfare of 14th-century timber-framed houses below Piazza del Duomo; and Via Maffei, lined with a parade of 16th-century Renaissance *palazzi*. Also in this last street is the church of **San Francesco**, the first church established by the Franciscans outside Assisi. The third altar on its left (north) wall has an unfinished *Annunciation* (1669) by Pietro da Cortona, a poor substitute for the painter's best work, which is divided among Rome's baroque churches and the Palazzo Pitti in Florence, whose state rooms feature the ceiling frescoes that brought the artist fame (see page

Time on his hands: a Cortona watchmaker

TOURIST INFORMATION
Cortona's tourist office is at Via Nazionale 42 (tel: 0575 630 352).

Wash day and a pause for thought – a timeless scene in Cortona

VIEWS
Visit the Fortezza Medicea and the public gardens near San Domenico for Cortona's best views. Come at dusk, when lights twinkle across the huge plain below the town.

HANNIBAL
At Tuoro sul Trasimeno, just a few miles east of Cortona, you can visit the site of one of antiquity's most famous battles. In 217 BC, Hannibal and his army defeated a Roman army under the consul Flaminius. Some 16,000 Romans were killed after a cunningly planned ambush. A drive and a marked trail have been laid out around the site.

117). The church's crypt is believed to contain the tomb of Cortona's other famous painter, Luca Signorelli (1441–1523).

Northeast of the town centre, be sure also to visit the cypress-shaded **San Nicolò**, known for an unusual double-sided painting by Signorelli. One face shows a fine *Deposition*, the other a *Madonna and Child*. Ask the custodian to operate the intriguing pulley system that turns the painting around. Fra Angelico's old church, **San Domenico**, has a faded fresco by the painter over its portal. A chapel to the right of the high altar contains a *Madonna and Saints* (1515) by Signorelli and a detached fresco of San Rocco by Bartolomeo della Gatta. The striking altarpiece, *The Coronation of the Virgin* (1402), is by Lorenzo Gerini. To the east of the church the **Giardini Pubblici** (public gardens) offer lovely walks with superb views (see panel).

Museo dell'Accademia Etrusca▶▶ (*Open* Tue–Sun, 10–1 and 4–7; winter, 9–1 and 3–5; *closed* Mon. *Admission charge*). Cortona's civic museum at Piazza Signorelli 9 offers a fascinating and eclectic collection that goes beyond the Etruscan limits suggested by its name. The *Accademia*, a historical institute founded in 1727, numbered Voltaire among its early members. The museum occupies one of the town's more impressive medieval palaces, the 13th-century Palazzo Casali (or Palazzo Pretorio), which was former home to Cortona's leading medieval family.

The main hall contains a famous and unusual 5th-century BC chandelier. The largest object of its kind ever found, it consists of a gorgon's head surrounded by dolphins and stylised waves, its 16 small oil lamps formed by alternating male and female figurines. Attic vases, bronze figures, and Roman statuettes line the walls, together with paintings by Pietro da Cortona and Luca Signorelli, both natives of Cortona (as well as works by Pinturicchio, Cristofano Allori, and more minor artists). Rooms off the hall include further paintings, notably a triptych by Bicci di Lorenzo, as well as (poorly labelled) fans, ivories, weapons, porcelain, miniatures, coins and jewellery. Best of this miscellany are several medieval ceramics and an Egyptian collection amassed in 1891 by the Vatican's Egyptian legate.

Museo Diocesano►►► (*Open* Tue–Sun, 9–1 and 4–7; winter, 9–1 and 3–5; *closed* Mon. *Admission charge*). Piazza del Duomo's main draw is not so much its lacklustre Duomo as the museum opposite, a rather gloomy former church whose interior is enlivened by a small but prestigious collection of Renaissance paintings. Perversely, however, it opens with a 2nd-century Roman sarcophagus, whose carved centaurs and battle scenes were apparently much admired by Donatello and Brunelleschi. The fresco fragments here include *The Way to Calvary* by the Sienese master, Pietro Lorenzetti.

Two paintings by Fra Angelico dominate the gallery proper – a sublime *Annunciation* (1428–30) and a triptych of the *Madonna and Child with Saints*. Both were painted during the artist's 10-year sojourn in Cortona's Dominican monastery (the triptych's predella depicts scenes from the life of St Dominic).

The room also contains three works that would be outstanding in any other company: a *Crucifix* by Pietro Lorenzetti; Sassetta's *Madonna and Child*; and Bartolomeo della Gatta's *Assumption of the Virgin*. Lorenzetti has another beautiful painting in the room beyond, a *Madonna Enthroned*. Local painter Luca Signorelli is also well represented by a *Deposition* and *Communion of the Apostles*.

SANTA MARIA DEL CALCINAIO
This outstanding 15th-century Renaissance church is located on the winding approach road to Cortona (3km from Porta Sant'Agostino). It was built on the site of a tannery (known as a *calcinaio* after the lime used in the tanning process) to house an image of the Virgin that had miraculously appeared on the tannery walls. Similar High Renaissance churches, built on the Greek cross plan and with a central dome, are to be found at Prato, Montepulciano, and Todi (in Umbria).

203

Part of a Roman sarcophagus in Cortona's Museo Diocesano

Tuscany

The city's Roman grid of streets, glimpsed from the Torre Guinigi

GETTING THERE

Lucca is easily reached by bus or train from Pisa (30 minutes). Hourly trains from Florence on the Viareggio line take 70–90 minutes. The train station is in Piazza Ricasoli, just outside the walls to the south of the city. Local and long-haul CLAP and Lazzi buses use the terminal in Piazza G Verdi, in the west of the city. There are regular fast buses to Florence (1 hour). Cars are severely restricted in the centre of Lucca. The best parking lot is Le Tagliate, outside Porta San Donato.

TOURIST INFORMATION

Lucca's main tourist office is in the northern corner of Piazza G Verdi (tel: 0583/419 689).

LUCCA IN LITERATURE

Lucca's surrender to Napoleon features in the opening lines of the great Russian novel, Tolstoy's *War and Peace*: 'Eh bien, mon prince, so Genoa and Lucca are now no more than private estates of the Bonaparte family.' (Anna Pavlovna Scherer to Prince Vasili, July 1805)

▶ ▶ ▶ Lucca   *IBCB5*

No city in Italy is as quietly urbane as Lucca. Its ring of walls encloses dozens of tiny Romanesque churches, quiet paved streets, steadfast defensive towers, and numerous museums and monuments – the sort of place, in the words of Henry James, that is 'overflowing with everything that makes for ease, for plenty, for beauty, for interest and good example' (*Italian Hours*, 1909). The city centre is closed to traffic, and the local people, prosperous and courteous, have responded by taking to bicycles (though you can walk across the city in less than 20 minutes). If you are pressed for time the essential sights are the Duomo; San Michele and San Frediano; the Museo Nazionale Guinigi; and the Torre Guinigi and Piazza Anfiteatro. If possible, leave time also to walk at least part of the way around the city's magnificent walls.

Lucca prospered as a Roman colony, whose gridiron plan is still reflected in the city's streets. It became Tuscany's first Christian town (the city's first bishop, Paulinus, was a disciple of St Peter) and then capital of Tuscany (Tuscia) under the Lombards and the Franks. Later it was ruled by the Margraves, who eventually moved to Florence. Its medieval wealth, second only to that of Florence, was based on banking and a thriving silk industry (underwear is still a major money earner). Under the dashing Castruccio Castracani the town dominated western Tuscany, capturing Pisa and Pistoia: only Castracani's untimely death prevented the capture of Florence as well. Lucca remained independent until 1799 under successive noble families (notably the Guinigi). Nemesis came in 1805 in the shape of Napoleon (see panel), who presented the city to his sister, Elisa Baciocchi. In 1817, it passed to Marie Louise de Bourbon, becoming part of the Tuscan Grand Duchy in 1847.

Duomo di San Martino▶▶▶ (*Open* Apr–Oct Tue–Sun 10–6; Nov–Mar 10–2. *Admission charge*: includes entry to Roman excavations beneath nearby Church of San Giovanni). Lucca's cathedral was consecrated in 1070 by Pope Alexander II (previously the city's bishop), and built in fits and starts over the next 400 years. The delays were to present several problems. When the 13th-century façade was added, for example, it had to be married uncomfortably with the existing bell tower, whose lower half was built in 1060 as a defensive tower. This resulted in a

Such seasonal tasks as threshing, fruit picking and wine making are depicted in the Labours of the Months *relief sculptures beside the Duomo's central doorway*

Jacopo della Quercia's tomb of Ilaria del Carretto

206

JACOPO DELLA QUERCIA
This greatest of Sienese sculptors was working at the same time as Donatello and Ghiberti and was one of the unsuccessful entrants in the competition to design Florence's Baptistery doors. Other works are to be found in Siena and San Gimignano.

VOLTO SANTO
According to myth, Lucca's prized holy relic came to the city in 782 of its own volition, journeying by boat from the Holy Land before being guided to Lucca, on an oxcart, by divine will. In truth, it is probably a 13th-century copy of an 11th-century work, copied in turn from an 8th-century Syrian original. It is perhaps no coincidence that it brought huge wealth to the church of the time, or that it appeared during the reign of Lucca's Bishop Anselmo, later to become pope. Revered for centuries, its fame was enormous. King William Rufus of England swore by it – '*per sanctum vultum de Lucca*'.

decidedly lopsided frontage (the tower's upper section was added in 1261). Asymmetry notwithstanding, the façade remains dazzling, the apotheosis of Pisan-Romanesque architecture – all arches, arcades, and decorated columns – for which the city is renowned. Note in particular the stunning entrance colonnade and its three portals (1233), the carvings on the left door – notably an *Annunciation* and an *Adoration of the Magi* – probably early works by Nicola Pisano (and possibly his first works in Tuscany). Reliefs beside the central door depict the life of St Martin and the Labours of the Months (note, in particular, the wonderfully graphic boar-hunting scene).

The interior is dominated by Matteo Civitali (1435–1501), a barber-turned-sculptor almost unknown outside his native Lucca. He was responsible for the inlaid pavement, the pulpit, a pair of water stoups, two beautiful tombs (in the south transept), and for the huge gilt-and-marble *Tempietto* midway down the nave. The last was built to house the famous *Volto Santo* (Holy Face), a cedarwood crucifix, reputedly a true effigy of Christ carved by Nicodemus after the Crucifixion (see panel). In a separate room off the south (right) aisle, is the tomb of Ilaria del Carretto (1410), the masterpiece of Sienese sculptor Jacopo della Quercia (justifiably described by John Ruskin as 'the loveliest Christian tomb in Italy'). It consists of a raised dais and the sculpted body of Ilaria, second wife of Paolo Guinigi, one of the city's medieval overlords. Note the touching addition of the family's favourite dog at its mistress's feet. The large statue of St John in the north aisle is by the same sculptor. The church's surprisingly good paintings include a *Madonna and Child* (1509) by Fra Bartolomeo (immediately before the Carretto tomb); Bronzino's *Presentation of the Virgin* (first chapel on the left); a garish *Last Supper* by Tintoretto (third altar on the right); and a *Madonna Enthroned* by Domenico Ghirlandaio (on the left wall of the sacristy). Outside the Duomo, the Museo dell'Opera del Duomo is worth seeing for its collection of medieval silverware.

San Michele in Foro▶▶▶ With its poetic confection of tiny arcades and delicately twisted columns, San Michele's sublime façade – surely one of Tuscany's most beautiful – draws you time and again to Piazza San Michele (once the city's Roman forum, or *foro*). The church took some 300 years to build, during which time money for the project ran out, a shortfall that left the interior bereft of its projected splendour. Its only works of note are a della Robbia *Madonna and Child* and Filippino Lippi's *Saints Jerome, Sebastian, Roch, and Helena* (at the end of the right nave).

While in the area, make for **Via Fillungo**, the city's appealing main street. Be sure to visit the **Caffè di Simo** (Via Fillungo 58), a café famous for its beautiful turn-of-the-century interior. It is close to the Torre delle Ore, the city's clock tower since 1471. The whole of Via Fillungo is full of other lovely art-nouveau shop fronts and interiors. Also worth a brief stop is the church of **San Cristoforo**, burial place of Matteo Civitali and a monument to Lucca's war dead, whose names are etched into the walls. The church is now used as an art gallery.

San Frediano▶▶ The third of Lucca's big three churches, San Frediano (1112–47) substitutes a glorious 13th-century mosaic for the columns and arcades of the city's other Romanesque façades. An evocative twilight bathes the interior, the gloom half-concealing the Fonta Lustrale,

GIACOMO PUCCINI
The composer Puccini (1858–1924) was born in Lucca, at Corte San Lorenzo 9 (off Via di Poggio). His family were organists in the Duomo for four generations, and he himself was a chorister at San Michele. His house now contains a small museum of memorabilia – scores, piano, photographs, and even his overcoat. *Open* Tue–Sun, summer 10–6; winter 10–1, 3–5. *Closed* Mon year round. *Admission charge.*

The magnificent Fonta Lustrale in San Frediano

207

A detail of the mosaic from the façade of San Frediano

208

OLIVE OIL
Much of Lucca's prosperity derives from its rich agricultural plain – 'half-smothered in oil and wine and corn and all the fruits of the earth', in the words of Henry James, who was much taken with Lucca (*Italian Hours*, 1909). Its olive oil is regarded as some of the best in Italy.

MARKETS
Lucca's main market takes place in Piazza Anfiteatro every Wednesday and Saturday (8–1).

a stupendous 12th-century font decorated with reliefs of the apostles, the months of the year, the shepherds, the prophets, and scenes from the life of Moses (note the relief depicting the crossing of the Red Sea, its Egyptian soldiers depicted as medieval knights).

Behind the font is an *Annunciation* by Andrea della Robbia, festooned with garlands of glazed terracotta fruit. The adjoining Cappella di Santa Zita holds the body of St Zita (patron saint of servants), who was given to smuggling bread from her household to give to the poor. Challenged one day as to what was in her apron, she replied 'only flowers and roses', into which the bread was miraculously transformed.

The Cappella Trenta (the fourth chapel of the north aisle) contains two pavement tombs and a carved altarpiece (1422) by Jacopo della Quercia. The north aisle's second chapel boasts Lucca's best frescoes (1508–9) – Amico Aspertini's *Life of St Augustine*, *The Arrival of the Volto Santo* (see panel on page 206), and *The Legend of San Frediano* (Frediano was a 6th-century Irish monk who saved Lucca from flood).

Piazza del Anfiteatro►► This piazza's oval of tall, rather ramshackle buildings reflects the shape of the Roman amphitheatre that stood here until the 12th century. Stone from the theatre was used to build the city's churches and palaces, but some still remains embedded in the piazza's buildings, particularly on its north side. This part of the city, quiet and interesting, is a pleasure to explore. Its worthwhile targets include Sant' Agostino, Palazzo Pfanner, and the Romanesque façade of San Pietro Somaldi. Also try to pop into the cavernous San Francesco on your way to the Museo Nazionale.

Museo Nazionale Guinigi► (*Open* Tue–Fri 9.30–12.30, Sat–Sun 9.30–12.30, 3.30–6.30. *Closed* Mon. *Admission charge*). Although Lucca's museums pale beside those of Florence or Siena, the 20 rooms of this gallery in the Via della Quarquonia offer a pleasingly eclectic collection. The lower floor is given over largely to archeology and sculpture. Highlights are finds from Roman Lucca (Room 1), a tomb slab by Jacopo della Quercia (Room 2), and several works by the ubiquitous Matteo Civitali (Room 5). Upstairs the paintings of relatively anonymous Lucchese masters dominate, leavened by Sienese works and Fra Bartolomeo's *Madonna della Misericordia* and *God the Father with Mary Magdalene and St Catherine* (both in Room 14).

Torre Guinigi▶ (*Open* Mar–Sep, 9–7.30; Oct, 10–6; Nov–Feb, 10–4.30. *Admission charge*). Lucca's eastern margins are duller than the rest of the city, so cut back from the Museo Nazionale to Via Sant'Andrea, where the Torre Guinigi constitutes one of the city's more eccentric landmarks. The 14th-century tower, part of the Guinigi's rambling redbrick palace, is topped by a grove of ilex trees whose roots have grown into the room below. Climb the tower to see this oddity and to enjoy some tremendous views of the city and surrounding countryside.

Leave time to take in **Santa Maria Forisportam** just to the south, so called because until 1260 it was outside the city walls. The façade is captivating, while the interior has a couple of good works by Guercino (in the north transept and on the north aisle's fourth altar).

City walls▶▶ No visit to Lucca is complete without walking at least part of the way around its impressive ramparts (the total circuit measures 4km). Tree-lined and closed to traffic, the walls were built between 1500 and 1650, prompted by advances in weapon technology that had rendered the old (1198) walls obsolete. The moats are 35m wide, with 11 bastions defending ramparts 12m high and 30m wide.

A surrounding swathe of green, 200m wide, was created to deprive an enemy of cover. The defences, among the finest in Europe, were never defended in anger; the only time they were used was in 1812, when the three original gates were shut to protect against a flood. Napoleon's sister, Elisa Baciocchi, had to be hauled over the ramparts by crane. Her successor, Marie Louise de Bourbon, transformed the rampart walks into tree-shaded gardens.

SPECIAL EVENTS
A large antiques market takes place in the streets around the Duomo over the third weekend of every month. September sees the Settembre Lucchese, a monthlong festival of music and the performing arts. An outdoor festival of Puccini's operas, the Festival Pucciniano, takes place in July and August in Torre del Lago Puccini, 18km west of Lucca. The Festival di Marlia (opera and classical music) is held at the Villa Reale near Marlia, 8km east of the city.

209

Make time to enjoy the tree-shaded walk around Lucca's city walls

Poverty was the mother of culinary invention through the long centuries of peasant tradition that have shaped Tuscany's contemporary cuisine. As a result the region's cooking – like most Italian cooking – relies on simple ingredients and a refreshingly down-to-earth approach to preparation and presentation.

CHEESE

All sorts of national and regional cheeses are available in Tuscany. Some of the most typical are the many varieties of pecorino, a sheep's cheese that comes in soft (*dolce*) or matured (*stagionato*) versions. Another sheep's cheese, ricotta, is a delicious soft creamy cheese. It can be eaten either savoury (with olive oil, salt, and pepper) or sweet (with honey and cinnamon).

Antipasti The simplicity of Tuscan cooking is apparent from a meal's first mouthful. *Antipasti* (starters) are nothing if not straightforward. Ham (*prosciutto*) and salami are both common *antipasti*, with specialities such as *finocchiona* (fennel-flavoured salami) and *prosciutto di cinghiale* (air-cured wild boar ham). Ordinary hams are also commonly served – perhaps with melon or figs – either *crudo* (raw) or *cotto* (cooked). Equally widespread are *crostini* – small pieces of toast drizzled with warm oil and covered with a savoury paste made from anchovy, or pine nuts with cheese and basil, or liver and capers. *Bruschetta* (or *fettunta*) is similar, but tends to be plainer – just toasted slices of bread rubbed with garlic and brushed with warm olive oil.

Primi First courses traditionally consist of pasta, rice, soup or polenta – originally a means of filling up before the main meat or fish dishes to follow. Tuscany naturally has its pasta dishes – the most famous being *pappardelle alla lepre* (noodles with a hare sauce) – but it puts more enthusiasm into its soups. Most ubiquitous of these is *ribollita* (literally 'reboiled'), a hearty mix of vegetables, beans, cabbage and bread, so reduced as to be more like a thick casserole than a liquid soup. Equally warming and also vegetable-based is the well-known *minestrone*. *Pappa al pomodoro* is a rich tomato soup, thickened with bread and seasoned with basil. Egg is whisked into *acquacotta* (literally 'cooked water') – an onion, celery, and mushroom soup served over toasted bread. Bean soup (*zuppa di fagioli*) and onion soup (*carabaccia*) are other favourites. On the coast, every restaurant has its own version of *cacciucco*, a fish soup with more than a passing resemblance to the French *bouillabaisse*.

A risotto flavoured with Tuscany's prized porcini *mushrooms*

The art of making tagliatelle

If pasta is your preference, most Italian staples are usually available. Try to venture beyond the old favourites – meat and tomato sauces (pasta *al sugo* or *al pomodoro*) – and experiment with local specialities like *pici* (handmade pasta found around Siena), or *tortelli* (ricotta- and spinach-stuffed pasta from the Maremma).

Secondi Meat and fish provide the centrepiece of any Italian meal. Nowhere in Italy is the meat grander than in Tuscany, whose best-known dish is the redoubtable *bistecca alla fiorentina*. These days you have to pay a lot for the real thing – a vast T-bone steak from the white cattle of the Valdichiana near Montepulciano. Cooked in the traditional way it is unbeatable – dripped with olive oil, seasoned with herbs, and grilled over the perfumed embers of a chestnut-wood fire. Grilled meats (*alla griglia*) are generally a Tuscan staple, whether lamb (*agnello*), pork (*maiale*), or chicken (*pollo*). The same meats are also served roasted (*arrosto*), often presented together as a mountainous mixed roast (*arrosto misto*). They may also be prepared *alla cacciatore*, a rich casserole of meat, tomatoes, and olives 'in the style of the hunter'. Tuscan *scottiglia* is similar, a stew of poultry, white wine, and veal (*vitello*). Less immediately appealing to many visitors, but one of the great Florentine specialities, is *trippa alla fiorentina* – tripe in a tomato sauce. A notch more appetising, perhaps, are *baccalà* (salted cod in a tomato sauce) and *cibreo* (chicken liver and egg stew). All types of fish and seafood are available on the coast (and occasionally inland). Vegetables and salads, it goes without saying, are almost invariably excellent.

Dolci Restaurants often disappoint over desserts, too many of which are made off the premises and over-sweetened with some virulent liqueur. Fruit can be a wiser choice – especially grapes, cherries, and strawberries in season. Better still, indulge in an ice cream from a *gelateria* during an after-dinner stroll. Special desserts worth a try are *cantuccini*, almond biscuits dipped in dessert wine (*Vin Santo*), or more readily available specialities such as Siena's tooth-rotting *panforte* (a cake of nuts and candied fruit).

SEASONAL FARE
Autumn adds game to the Tuscan menu, usually boar (*cinghiale*), but also hare, rabbit, pheasant, partridge, and guinea fowl. Other seasonal delicacies include truffles (from Umbria) and mushrooms, especially the highly prized *porcini*, eaten grilled or added to pasta and risottos.

211

TRATTORIA «DA GUIDO»

Via Faenza 34/r · FIRENZE
☎ 055 / 289746

IN CENTRO STORICO
FRA LA STAZIONE FF.SS.
E IL MERCATO DI
SAN LORENZO

MERCOLEDI CHIUSO
GIOVEDI APERTURA POMERIDIANA

Tuscan wine no longer means a straw-covered flask of old-fashioned Chianti. Attention these days is more likely to focus on Brunello and Vino Nobile, central Italy's finest reds, and on the cultish 'Super Tuscans' of the region's more visionary producers.

A hard sell for San Gimignano's well-known white wine

212

THE DOC SYSTEM

Italy's DOC (*Denominazione di Origine Controllata*) classification system, modelled on the French *Appellation Contrôlée* equivalent, is now largely outdated and discredited. A radical over-haul is currently under way. A DOCG (*Denominazione di Origine Controllata e Garantita*) label, for example, is being awarded to the finest wines. Many producers, however, ignore both systems, producing excellent wines under the humblest classi-fication of all – *vino da tavola* (table wine).

A new breed Tuscan wine is enjoying a renaissance, reju-venated by the adoption of French grape varieties and by the grafting of foreign techniques onto traditional produc-tion methods. Foremost among the resulting vintages has been Sassicaia, a wine that eschews Tuscany's traditional grape, the red Sangiovese, in favour of 100 per cent Cabernet Sauvignon. In its wake have come imitators like Antinori's Tignanello and the reliable Carmignano, both blends of native grapes with foreign varieties such as Merlot, Cabernet, and Pinot Noir. Whites have wedded Chardonnay and Sauvignon to Tuscany's indigenous Trebbiano. Many of the new wines have jumped onto what is proving to be a lucrative band-wagon, and prices for some are out of all proportion to their quality (though Italians have proved willing to pay for novelty and for being fashionable). The innovations over-all, however, have been a good thing, enhancing the range and quality of the region's wines.

Chianti Tuscany's most famous wine has been forced to look to its laurels by the region's viticultural revolution. No wine was previously in greater disarray, its 700 or more varieties ranging from the sublime to the substan-dard. Chianti's name, perhaps derived from an Etruscan family, first appears in the 14th century when it referred to a group of nobles known as the Chianti League. Its first mention as a wine comes in 1404, in the diaries of Francesco Datini, the entrepreneurial subject of Iris Origo's famous biography *The Merchant of Prato*. In 1716, under a grand ducal decree, Chianti became part of Europe's first wine zone. These days its wines are grouped into seven areas, the best by far the original Classico area, whose bottles bear the distinctive *Gallo*

Nero (Black Cockerel) symbol. Rufina is the second-ranking zone, but such is Chianti's variety that there are few hard and fast rules to help you pick a reliable wine.

Brunello Montalcino's vineyards produced what was – before the advent of brash new rivals – Tuscany's most majestic wine. The best Brunello is still outstanding, though you occasionally pay an unnecessary premium for the top names. Over and above the prestigious Biondi Santi (the earliest producers), the tiny Case Basse estate receives high plaudits, so too Lisini, Altesino, Carpazo, Il Poggione and Villa Banfi. The Fattoria dei Barbi is also well known as much for its restaurant as for its wine. For more leisurely drinking, Brunello's younger cousin, Rosso di Montalcino, is an increasingly good buy.

Vino Nobile Montepulciano's ancient Vino Nobile – the 'king of wines' – is also riding the crest of Tuscany's wine revival. Standards are rising (in what was, in most cases, already a fine wine). Top names, both new and old, to look for here include the mass-produced but excellent-value Vecchia Cantina (a cooperative), Poliziano, Cantucci, Bindella and Le Casalte.

White wines Tuscany's big reds have long overshadowed its more humble whites. In days gone by the region's most famous *bianco*, the Vernaccia di San Gimignano, might have stood comparison with its *rosso* rivals. Now, overproduction and slipshod standards have besmirched its once lofty reputation (in 1966 it was the first wine to be awarded a DOC classification). Several producers do retain an excellent name, notably Roberto Guicciardini's 1,000-year-old Cusona estate, producers of Vernaccia since the 15th century. Even better (and more expensive) are Teruzzi & Puthod's Carmen and Terra di Tufo, closely followed by Falchini's Casale and Vigna a Solatio. (Be warned that most of the wine available in San Gimignano's shops is insipid tourist fodder, made in one of several large cooperatives.) Other reasonable whites include the ubiquitous Galestro and Bianco di Pitigliano.

NOBLE LINEAGE
Many Tuscan wine producers come from ancient noble families. The Ricasoli trace their association with wine making to 1141, the Frescobaldi to 1300. Antinori, one of the region's finest estates, has been in operation for 600 years.

POETRY AND WINE
Poet Fulvio Testi paid effusive tribute to the 'Etruscan Chianti that kisses you and bites you and makes you shed sweet tears'.

TUSCAN WINE IN HISTORY
Viticulture in Tuscany blossomed under the Etruscans, but fell away under the Romans, who preferred the heavier wines of southern Italy. Monks guided its re-emergence in the Middle Ages, quickly making wine a staple part of their daily diet.

213

Tuscany produces some of Italy's finest red wines

GETTING THERE

Montepulciano's nearest railway station is 11km away at Chiusi-Chianciano, from where hourly buses run to the town's Porta al Prato. Regular buses run to Pienza and there is a twice-daily service to Siena. By car, the quickest approach is on the A1 expressway (leave at the Chiusi exit, 16km from Montepulciano). Park outside the town walls.

TOURIST INFORMATION

Montepulciano's tourist office is at Via Ricci 9 (tel: 0578/757 985 or 758 687).

SAN BIAGIO

This cool and harmonious Renaissance church (1518–45) stands in open countryside about a mile southwest of Montepulciano. It is the masterpiece of Antonio da Sangallo the Elder, and compares with similar churches in Prato, Cortona, and Todi (in Umbria).

Tempted by home-made produce

►► Montepulciano   IBCF2

Montepulciano, like nearby Pienza, represents an attempt to impose Renaissance architectural ideals on an ancient Tuscan hill town. It also offers magnificent views (it is one of the region's highest towns), the chance to wander quaint medieval streets, and opportunities to taste and buy its famous red wine, Vino Nobile di Montepulciano (see page 213), or sample the homemade preserves that are a local speciality.

Historically, the town was bandied around between Siena and Florence during the Middle Ages. Siding with Florence for good in 1511 was the cue for its Renaissance overhaul, an orgy of building that employed some of the era's leading architects – Antonio Sangallo the Elder, his nephew Sangallo the Younger, and (a little later) the Mannerist master, Vignola.

Montepulciano sits along the ridge of a long, narrow hill. The best way to explore it – and take in the town's best Renaissance palaces – is to clamber up the **Corso►►**, a serpentine main street that follows the hill's north-to-south axis. (Be sure to duck into the smaller lanes along the way.) In effect a single street, it nevertheless changes its name three times (from Via di Gracciano to Via di Voltaia and Via dell'Opio).

The Porta al Prato, Sangallo's first commission, marks the town entrance and the start of the Corso. Immediately inside the gate is a statue of the Marzocco, Florence's heraldic emblem (see the panel on page 127) – an 1856 copy of a 1511 original now in the Museo Civico. The best of the Corso's many palaces include the Palazzo Cocconi (No 70), attributed to Antonio Sangallo, and the Palazzi Tarugi (No 82) and Avignonesi (No 91), both of which are attributed to Vignola. Palazzo Bucelli (No 73) is unmistakable, its lower walls inset with numerous ancient Etruscan funerary urns.

The church of **Sant'Agostino►** stands 120m up from the Porta al Prato on the right. Designed by Michelozzo, one of the Medici's favourite architects, it contains a high altar *Crucifix* attributed to Donatello and a couple of good paintings – by Lorenzo di Credi (third altar on the north

The church of San Biagio, a Renaissance masterpiece

wall) and the Sienese painter Giovanni di Paolo (second altar on the south wall).

At the Loggia del Mercato, 120m beyond Sant' Agostino, a right turn onto Via di Poggiolo will take you directly to the tourist office and offers a shortcut to Piazza Grande. The churches of **Santa Lucia** and **San Francesco** en route are both worth a look, the former home to a superb *Madonna* by Signorelli.

The longer route to Piazza Grande, along the Corso, brings you to the church of the Gesù (120m up on the left), a baroque conversion created by Andrea del Pozzo, the architect of many similar renovations in Montepulciano and elsewhere. More palaces line the street, which bends around the Fortezza at the town's southern flank to enter Montepulciano's oldest and most interesting quarter.

At the summit of the Corso, the main square, the **Piazza Grande**▶▶, is dominated by the 13th-century **Palazzo Comunale**▶. Its façade was added by Michelozzo, and its tower commands views that stretch to Siena in one direction and over Lake Trasimeno in the other. Sangallo designed a couple of palaces here, one of which, the **Palazzo Cantucci**, has a cantina where you can taste and buy Vino Nobile di Montepulciano (similar outlets are dotted around the town).

The plain-faced **Duomo**▶▶ is redeemed by Taddeo di Bartolo's high altar *Assumption*, and by fragments of the dismantled tomb of Bartolomeo Aragazzi (1427–36) by Michelozzo. Reliefs and statues from the tomb are scattered to the right of the door and around the high altar: two of its angels even found their way to London's British Museum. The nearby **Museo Civico** (Via Ricci 15; *Open* Apr–Sep, Tue–Sun 10.30–12.30, 4–7. *Closed* Mon and winter) is disappointing, its best pieces being some della Robbia terracottas and a handful of Sienese paintings.

SPECIAL EVENTS

August in Montepulciano is one long festival. The well-known Cantiere Internazionale d'Arte (early August) specialises in the performance of new works in theatre, dance, and music, often coinciding with Montepulciano's highly regarded jazz festival, which attracts top performers. Exhibitions of local handicrafts and the Baccanale wine festival are also held in August, along with performances of *Bruscello*, a local form of street theatre with masks, over Ferragosto (14–16 August). The oldest festival is the Bravio delle Botti, in which pairs of men from the town's eight quarters race uphill, pushing 80kg barrels, from Piazza Marzocco to Piazza Grande (last Sunday in August). The town's patron saint, St Agnes, is celebrated with a fair on her feast day, 1 May.

GETTING THERE
Buses run to Pienza from Montepulciano (nine daily), Siena, and Buonconvento (seven daily). By bus or car you arrive at Piazza Dante, outside Porta al Murello, from where Corso Rossellino leads to Piazza Pio II, the main square.

TOURIST INFORMATION
Pienza's tourist office is in the Palazzo Civico, Piazza Pio II (tel: 0578/748 502).

MUSEO DELLA CATTEDRALE
Housed in the Palazzo Borgia, or Palazzo dei Vescovi (Piazza Pio II) at Via Casello 1, the cathedral museum contains illuminated manuscripts, Flemish tapestries, Pius II's famous *Opus Anglicanum* (a copy made in England), and several fine paintings by Duccio, Sassetta, Fra Bartolomeo, Vecchietta, Bartolo di Fredi, and Pietro Lorenzetti. *Open* summer Tue–Sun 10–1, 2–6; winter Sat–Sun 10–1, 2–6. *Admission charge*.

PIEVE DI CORSIGNANO
This lovely little Romanesque church stands alone in an olive grove 800m west of Pienza's Porta al Ciglio. It has an unusual tower, fine views of Pienza, and an old font that was used to baptise Pius II.

▶▶ Pienza   IBCE2

Pienza owes its appearance to Aeneas Sylvius Piccolomini, who, as Pope Pius II, had grand plans to transform his home village into a model Renaissance town. Born in 1405 of an exiled Sienese family, Piccolomini set about the reconstruction of Corsignano – as it then was – a year after his election to the papacy in 1459. The man entrusted with the transformation was Bernardo Rossellino, a protegé of the great Renaissance theorist Leon Battista Alberti. His mandate was to create a cathedral, a papal palace, and a town hall (plus miscellaneous buildings) that adhered to his master's principles. Gothic and Renaissance styles were to be fused, and the buildings were to be decorated with Sienese and Florentine paintings, as well as incorporating ideas picked up by Pius II during his travels overseas. The net result was to be a project that expressed Renaissance ideals of art, architecture, and civilised good living in a single scheme.

After the completion of the Duomo and its flanking palaces (in just three years), Pius renamed the town in a papal bull, adding the caveat that not a single detail of the cathedral should be changed (he considered it the 'finest in all Italy'). The plan was then for a city to sprout of its own accord, nurtured by sycophantic cardinals who would be encouraged to build their own palaces. In the event, Pius died just two years later, relieving his successors of the responsibility for a 'city' that was a monument to one man's dreams (only Pius's nephew, Pius III, showed any further interest in the project). As a result, the planned metropolis scarcely extended beyond the village's piazza.

Pienza's main square remains a Renaissance jewel – despite its occasionally empty and windswept appearance – and, with lovely countryside on its doorstep, makes an ideal place to spend a quiet morning. Start a tour at the **Duomo**▶▶▶ (Piazza Pio II), the heart of Pius's planned folly. Its classically inspired frontage, one of Tuscany's earliest, features Pius II's garlanded coat of arms in the upper pediment. Pius's hand is further evident in the interior, whose barnlike appearance was inspired by the *Hallenkirchen* (hall churches) he had admired during visits to Germany. The tall windows were also a papal whim, commissioned to produce a *domus vitrea* (house of glass), a symbol of the age's humanist enlightenment.

Five specially commissioned 14th-century altarpieces by Sienese masters grace the interior, all depicting the Madonna and Child with a variety of saints: the artists concerned are Giovanni di Paolo (south aisle); Matteo di Giovanni (north aisle); and Matteo di Giovanni, Vecchietta, and Sano di Pietro (in the apse's first, fourth, and fifth chapels respectively). Note the lovely stalls (1462) and the crypt's baptismal font (carved by Rossellino). The various fragments of Romanesque sculpture come from Santa Maria, an earlier church on the site. Note, too, how the church has been shored up at its eastern end. The cramped site meant that Rossellino had to build on sandstone supported only by an unstable substratum of clay. Cracks, now widening alarmingly, appeared in the building even before its completion.

The **Palazzo Piccolomini**►► (*Open* guided tours every half hour, Tue–Sun: summer 10–12.30, 4–7; winter 10–12.30, 3–6. *Admission charge*), Pius II's palace (finished by his nephew, Pius III), stands to the right of the Duomo. Rossellino's masterpiece, it owes much to Alberti's Palazzo Rucellai in Florence (see pages 120–1) – though its rear three-tiered loggia was an inspired innovation. The second-floor apartments (entered from the right of a magnificent courtyard) were occupied by Piccolomini's descendants until as recently as 1968.

An entrance to the left off the courtyard leads to the hanging gardens, a beautiful mixture of box hedges and small trees unaltered since the days of Pius. They offer sweeping views over the Val d'Orcia toward the distinctively shaped Monte Amiata – a dramatic embodiment of Alberti's idea that gardens should provide a link between architecture and nature.

CHEAT

Rossellino cheated Pope Pius during the building of Pienza, embezzling funds and spending three times his original budget. The pope forgave him because he had 'built these glorious structures which are praised by all except those consumed by envy'.

The town of Pienza lords it over the hills of southern Tuscany

217

Part of Nicola and Giovanni Pisano's Gothic Baptistery

▶▶ Pisa

IBCB5

There is more to Pisa than its Leaning Tower – but not much more. The city offers surprisingly little temptation to linger after the tower and its companion pieces, the Duomo, the Battistero (Baptistery), and the Camposanto. Nearby Lucca is more deserving of your time. Access from Florence is straightforward, however, so a trip to Pisa need take no more than a morning.

Though settled around 1000 BC, the city first flourished under the Romans and the Lombards. By the 11th century it was one of Italy's four great maritime republics (with Amalfi, Venice, and Genoa). War with the Saracens won Pisa, Corsica, Sardinia, and the Balearic islands (between 1050 and 1100). The 12th century saw a building boom and the emergence of pioneering sculptors such as Nicola and Giovanni Pisano. This was also the heyday of Pisa's Romanesque architecture, whose Moorish-inspired hybrid of columns, blind arcades, and coloured marbles influenced churches as far afield as Arezzo and Sardinia. War with Genoa and defeat at the Battle of Meloria (in 1284) marked the city's fall from grace. By 1421 both the port – by then silting up – and the city had fallen to Florence. Pisa's modern and frequently ugly appearance is the result of bomb damage in 1944, when much of the great medieval city was lost.

Leaning Tower▶▶▶ Pisa's foremost monuments gather together in the **Campo dei Miracoli** (The Field of Miracles), a remarkable expanse of meadow in the city's northwestern corner. Few medieval groupings are as beautiful, and few so beautifully framed by their surroundings. Only the sprawl of souvenir stands detracts. The key component is the Campanile, better known as the

GETTING THERE
Trains leave Florence hourly for Pisa Centrale (for the city) and Pisa Aeroporto (1 hour). From outside Pisa station, bus No 1 goes directly to the Campo dei Miracoli (tickets from the forecourt kiosk). Allow about 25 minutes if you prefer to walk.

TOURIST INFORMATION
Tourist offices are outside the station at Piazza della Stazione 11 (tel: 050/42 291) and in the corner of the Campo dei Miracoli (tel: 050/560 464).

Candlelight inside Pisa's Duomo

Leaning Tower (*Torre Pendente*). Begun in 1173, the tower started to lean almost immediately, precipitated by the area's sandy subsoil (this part of the coast, once beneath the sea, is mostly sand and silt). Successive architects attempted to correct the tilt, all to no avail, and since the tower's completion (around 1350) the lean has reached a giddy 5m from the vertical.

The tower these days is so dangerous that it has been closed to visitors (though only after considerable opposition from Pisans worried at losing valuable tourist revenue). A tilt which was increasing by 1mm a year for decades has now started to lurch by the same amount every few weeks. With the tower's 14,000 tonnes showing alarming cracks, an international commission is struggling to agree on a possible remedy. Steel cables and lead weights were inserted in the tower's base in 1992. Current proposals involve trying to reverse the tilt of the tower slightly by extracting material from beneath one side while using cables to stabilise it.

Duomo▶▶▶ Even without the Leaning Tower, visitors would flock to Pisa simply for its cathedral. Begun in 1063, it represents the archetype of all Pisan Romanesque churches, and was the first to be decorated in the black and white stripes typical of the style. The entrance is usually through the south transept's Portale di San Ranieri, whose celebrated bronze doors (1180) were cast by Bonanno, the Leaning Tower's first architect. Much of the

Tuscany

A detail of the Duomo's interior, heavily restored after a fire at the end of the 16th century

CAMPO DEI MIRACOLI

The five major monuments on and around the Campo dei Miracoli – Duomo, Battistero, Camposanto, Museo dell'Opera del Duomo, and Museo delle Sinopie – are all open daily at the same time: currently 8am–7.30pm, though this is subject to change. You can buy tickets for two, three, four or five monuments.

SANTA MARIA DELLA SPINA

A thorn (*spina*) from Christ's crown sits at the heart of this lovely Romanesque-Gothic church near the Ponte Solferino. In 1871, the whole building was moved brick by brick from a site nearer the Arno to protect it from floods.

PALAZZO DELL' OROLOGIO

The palace stands on the north side of Piazza dei Cavalieri, Pisa's main medieval square, designed by Vasari (about 1560). In 1288, Count Ugolino, a Pisan military leader, was starved to death in the palace's old tower (along with his sons and grandsons), falsely accused of treachery during the Battle of Meloria. Dante consigned him to the Eighth Circle of Hell for eating his children in a vain attempt to ward off starvation. A number of other important Renaissance buildings stand on Piazza dei Cavalieri including Palazzo dei Cavalieri and Santo Stefano dei Cavalieri.

interior was restored after a disastrous fire in 1595 (hence its rather lacklustre decoration), though several masterpieces survived the conflagration. Most noteworthy are the tomb of Emperor Henry VII (1315), by Tino da Camaino (in the south transept's left corner); an ornately framed *St Agnes* by Andrea del Sarto (on the choir's right-hand entrance pier); and Giovanni Pisano's impressive pulpit (1302–10), decorated with reliefs of New Testament scenes (top of the left aisle).

Battistero (Baptistery) ▶▶▶ Begun in Romanesque mode in 1152, Italy's largest baptistery received its Gothic finishing touches from Nicola and Giovanni Pisano between 1270 and 1290 (the 120-year delay was caused by a financial shortfall). The echoing interior contains a lovely octagonal font by Guido da Como (1246) and a groundbreaking pulpit (1260) by Nicola Pisano, carved 50 years earlier than his son's pulpit in the Duomo. The work was the sculptor's first major commission, and its departure from Romanesque convention marked a step towards more recognisably Renaissance forms. Pisano was inspired by classical models, notably the Roman sarcophagi brought by Pisan ships from the Holy Land and reused as tombs by Pisa's more recherché citizens. Many examples can be seen in the Camposanto.

Camposanto▶▶ Before it was severely damaged by incendiary bombs in 1944, John Ruskin described the Camposanto as one of Italy's three most precious buildings (the Sistine Chapel and Venice's Scuola di San Rocco were the others). Begun in 1278 and completed in the 15th century, the marble-walled cemetery was reputedly filled with soil brought from the Holy Land (which, it was claimed, could rot down a corpse to a skeleton in less than 24 hours). At one time the vast internal cloister was covered in some 1950sq m of fresco. Now only a few fragments survive, fossils of works by Gozzoli, Taddeo Gaddi, and Spinello Aretino. A few surviving sketches have been displayed in the new, rather dull Museo delle Sinopie nearby. For all its vanished splendour, the cemetery is still worth a visit, if only to enjoy its myriad tomb sculptures – an insight into the Pisan way of death.

Museo dell'Opera del Duomo▶▶ The Duomo's old chapter house displays works removed from the cathedral, the Battistero, and the Camposanto. The 23-room collection is variable, but the highlights more than justify the admission charge. Look for the 11th-century Islamic bronze griffon (Room 1); Nicola Pisano's *Christ, Madonna and St John* (Room 2); Giovanni Pisano's ivory *Madonna and Child* (Rooms 9–10); and the colossal figures of the Prophets, Evangelist, Madonna and Child by Nicola and Giovanni Pisano (at the portico by the museum exit).

Museo Nazionale di San Matteo▶▶ Pisa's main museum suffers from poor displays and a gloomy atmosphere, but contains paintings by Lippo Memmi, Simone Martini and Masaccio, Sculptures include a bust by Donatello, works by Nicola and Giovanni Pisano, and Andrea and Nino Pisano's *Madonna del Latte*.

A FAMOUS EXPERIMENT
During his sojourn at Pisa University, Galileo (see pages 106–7) dropped balls of different weight from the Leaning Tower to disprove Aristotle's theories on the acceleration of falling bodies.

221

The Duomo and Italy's most famous tower – built in 1173 and still leaning

The art, architecture and landscapes of Tuscany have long provided a refuge for the world-weary poets, painters and writers of colder and more hellish climes. In the 19th century, Shelley was to describe the region as a 'paradise of exiles'. His rapture was not shared by all who wrote of their Tuscan travels.

FIRST THOUGHTS

'I think it is the most beautiful city I have ever yet seen ... Domes and steeples rise on all sides ... On the other side there are the foldings of the Arno above: first the hills of olive and vine, then the chestnut woods, and then the blue and misty pine forests, which invest the aerial Apennines, that fade in the distance ... I have seldom seen a city so lovely at first sight as Florence.' Shelley (1792–1822), *Letter*

Top: Percy Bysshe Shelley (1792–1822) Below: Robert Browning (1812–89), poet and exile

Unfashionable Florence Early exiles passed Florence by. Cervantes and Chaucer, for example, shunned the city on their Italian journeys. Travellers of Protestant stamp, notably Goethe, ignored its Renaissance charms, preferring the relics of classical Rome. Montaigne, the first notable writer to record his impressions (1580), fails to mention even Raphael or Michelangelo. Thomas Gray and Hugh Walpole (1741) called Florence 'one of the dullest cities in Italy' – though for this pair (if Gray's journal is to be believed) sightseeing was hardly a priority. Describing their day, Gray wrote: 'We get up at twelve, breakfast till three, dine till four, sleep till six, drink cooling liqueurs till eight, go to the bridge [the Ponte Vecchio] till ten, sup till two, and so sleep till twelve again.'

The beginnings of tourism By the early 19th century, Florence was attracting more discerning visitors. The reasons they came are many – the obvious ones of art, history, health, beauty, scholarship, creative inspiration, and the more obscure ones of escape – from failure, from doomed relationships, from the strictures of the home country. The seductions of love and lust were undoubtedly a factor: hundreds were emboldened by the idea of a warm climate stimulating the passions to greater heights, a hypothesis summarised in a couplet from Byron's *Don Juan*: 'What men call gallantry, and gods adultery,/ Is much more common where the climate's sultry.'

Literary visitors At one time or another Tuscany played host, among others, to Milton, Trollope, George Eliot, Robert and Elizabeth Browning, Tennyson, Dostoevsky, John Ruskin, Stendhal, James Fenimore Cooper, Nathaniel Hawthorne, Mark Twain, Henry James, Aldous Huxley, E M Forster, and D H Lawrence – not to mention the countless less famous exiles who set up residence in countryside villas (much

'Little Englander' Tobias Smollett and (below) Aldous Huxley

223

as they do today). The region proved particularly alluring to the Romantics, tempting the likes of Shelley, who fled here to escape 'the shadows of his first marriage ... the tumult of humankind, and the chilling fogs and rains of our own country'.

The down side Not everyone's Italian journeys were blessed with success or recorded with enthusiasm. Joseph Addison arrived at Calais and promptly fell in the harbour; Petrarch was injured by a horse; Walpole's dog was eaten by a wolf; Casanova was sexually assaulted by a policeman. Tobias Smollett, surely the world's most miserable traveller, found dirt, disease, and disillusion at every turn. Italian women, for example, he thought the most haughty, insolent, capricious and revengeful females on the face of the earth; accommodation was universally 'execrable'; he 'fared wretchedly at supper'; and he thought that services were offered with the most 'disagreeable importunity'.

For Aldous Huxley, the spectacle of Florence, 'that second-rate provincial town with its repulsive Gothic architecture and its acres of Christmas card primitives almost made me sick'. The good life also became too much for Dylan Thomas, who found the city 'a gruelling museum' and became 'sick...of drinking chianti in our marble shanty, sick of vini and contadini and bambini'. Laurie Lee bemoaned 'the streets laden with odours of meat and frying oil'...and abhorred the 'brick-faced British tourist' in the 'cheaper cafés...sweating and counting their crumpled money'. But then, as Goethe wisely observed, in an alien country 'every foreigner judges by the standards he brings with him'.

A GILDED CITY
'Oh! How much beauty, when on a fair, clear morning, we look ... on Florence. See where it lies before us in the sunlighted valley, bright with the winding Arno, and shut in by swelling hills: its domes, and towers, and palaces, rising from the rich country in a glittering heap and shining in the sun like gold'. Charles Dickens, *Pictures from Italy* (1840)

FED UP
'This is a pestilential place, smug little hills domed over with villas, and museums and churches that have been so much photographed and written about that one is fed up to the eyes with them long before one sets foot inside'. Violet Trefusis, *Letter* to Vita Sackville-West (1921)

A Madonna and Child over the doorway of Andrea Pisano's octagonal Baptistery

▶▶ Pistoia   IBCC6

Pistoia is probably the least visited of Tuscany's first-rank towns. Its Duomo, Battistero and Campanile, however, stand comparison with similar buildings in Pisa and Siena, and are complemented by the bonus of tremendous Romanesque pulpits in three of Pistoia's other churches. The city traditionally enjoyed a reputation for violence: Michelangelo called its citizens 'enemies of Heaven', while Machiavelli thought them 'brought up to slaughter and war'. In the 16th century, pistols are said to have taken their name from the city's small *pistolese* daggers. Pistoia's ferocious reputation, however, failed to trouble Florence, to whom it remained subservient for most of its medieval history. Today, its trade is in ornamental trees and shrubs, its nursery gardens being among the largest in Italy.

Piazza del Duomo▶▶, Pistoia's beautiful main square, is a revelation. The **Campanile**, once a Lombard watch-tower, dazzles at its centre. The Gothic **Battistero** (1338–59) is also lovely to look at – the design was by Giovanni Pisano – but rather lacks interior interest. Other buildings include the Palazzo dei Vescovi, home to the **Museo della Cattedrale** (*Open* tours Tue and Thu at 8.30, 10, 11.30 and 3.30; also same hours Sat, plus 2.30 and 4.45. *Admission charge*), whose prize piece is a Reliquary of St James by Ghiberti (1407). The nearby Palazzo Comunale houses the **Museo Civico** (*Open* Tue–Sat 10–7, Sun 9–12.30. *Closed* Mon. *Admission charge*), packed with six centuries' worth of mostly minor paintings.

A tiled porch and a lovely *Madonna and Child* by Andrea della Robbia usher you into the **Duomo**▶, whose interior attractions include a font (entrance wall) by Benedetto da Maiano and the tomb (1337) of Cino da Pistoia, diplomat, teacher, poet and friend of Dante (right aisle). Overshadowing both, however, is the St James Altar (1287–1456), perhaps Italy's finest silver altarpiece (in the Cappella di San Jacopo, off the right aisle). Weighing almost a ton, and decorated with 628 figures, its sculptors included Brunelleschi, who created the two *Prophets* on the work's left-hand side. Other highlights of the cathedral include the Cappella del Sacremento (to the left

GETTING THERE
Trains from Florence on the Viareggio line take 35–45 minutes to reach Pistoia. Buses to and from Florence, Lucca, and Pisa use the terminal at the train station. If you are driving, note that the town center is closed to traffic. Use the parking lots off Via Pacinotti, north of the station.

TOURIST INFORMATION
Pistoia's central tourist office is at Piazza del Duomo 4 (tel: 0573/21 622). Information on the province of Pistoia is available from the Azienda Promozione Turistica Abetone, Pistoia, Montagne Pistoiesi. Their office is at Via Marconi 16 in San Marcello Pistoiese, a village towards Abetone.

OSPEDALE DEL CEPPO

This working hospital takes its name from the hollowed-out tree trunk (*ceppo*) used by 13th-century Franciscan monks to collect alms (the name was later applied to many charitable foundations). The 15th-century façade, a copy of Brunelleschi's Ospedale degli Innocenti in Florence (see page 112), is famous for its *Seven Works of Mercy* – colourful terr-cottas by Giovanni della Robbia (1514–25). Contemporary figures, including pilgrims, prisoners, the sick and the deceased, are depicted with startling realism.

225

of the high altar), decorated with a bust of Donato de' Medici by Antonio Rossellini and a *Madonna and Saints* (often covered), started by Verrocchio and finished by Lorenzo di Credi.

See Pistoia's other lovely churches in the following order and you will be able to follow the chronological development of three pulpits whose carving marked a watershed in Italian sculpture. Each piece reveals the growing confidence of craftsmen whose revival of classical idioms was to pave the way for the Renaissance. The 12th-century church of **San Bartolomeo▶** has a pulpit by Guido da Como (1250).

San Giovanni Fuorcivitas▶▶ stood outside the city (*fuori città*) in its 8th-century incarnation. Inside is a pulpit (1270) by Guglielmo da Pisa, a pupil of Nicola Pisano, father of Giovanni (Giovanni carved the water stoup's *Four Cardinals*). Note also Luca della Robbia's terra-cotta *Visitation* on the left wall. **Sant'Andrea▶▶** contains the best of the pulpits, a work of 1301 by Giovanni Pisano, superior even to the pulpit he began carving for Pisa's cathedral a year later.

BLACK AND WHITE

An accident in Pistoia allegedly caused the famous split of the Guelph ranks into Black and White factions. A child, so the story goes, was sent to apologise for hurting his friend while playing with a sword. The friend's father chopped off his hand, saying 'Iron, not words, is the remedy for sword wounds'.
The punishment divided Pistoia into rival camps – *Neri* and *Bianchi* (Black and White) – the ancestral names of the families concerned. The names were taken up by rival factions of Florence's divided Guelphs.

Pistoia's daily market takes place in Piazza della Sala, one of the town's oldest squares

GETTING THERE

Prato is an easy day-trip from Florence. Trains from Florence on the Viareggio line takes just 25 minutes (the station is 800m east of the centre). Regular CAP buses from Florence stop at Via Magnolfi, just off Piazza del Duomo. Cars are banned from the centre, but parking is available at Piazza Mercatale and Piazza dei Marcelli.

TOURIST INFORMATION

Prato's tourist offices are behind the church of Santa Maria delle Carceri at Via Cairoli 48 (tel: 0574/24 112). Note that the actual entrance to the office is at Piazza Sorita Maria delle Carceri 15.

Datini, the wealthy 14th-century Merchant of Prato

Prato is Tuscany's most prosperous but least obviously pretty city. However, its unappealing industrial outskirts (where some 75 per cent of Italy's textiles are produced) surround a tight historic core, a noted Renaissance church, and one of Tuscany's most captivating fresco cycles.

Woollen mills first appeared in Prato in 1108, some 56 years earlier than in Florence. Unable to control its political factions, the medieval city placed itself under the protection of Naples' Anjou rulers in 1313. Besieged in 1350 by the Florentines, who were concerned at Prato's commercial ascendancy, the city found itself sold out to Florence by the Queen of Naples a year later. Thereafter its fortunes followed those of its neighbour. Today, however, the stories are reversed, with Prato much the more commercially dynamic of the two former rivals.

Once through Prato's ugly suburbs, you find old Prato huddled within a hexagon of medieval walls and watched over by the **Castello dell'Imperatore** ▶ (*Open* Jun–Sep, Mon, Wed–Sun, Jun–Sep 9.30–12.30, 3.30–7; Oct–May, Mon, Wed–Sun 8.30–12.30, 3.30–5.30. *Closed* Tue. *Admission free*). The castle, built in the 13th century for Emperor Frederick II, served as a base for imperial armies travelling between Germany and the emperor's dominions in Sicily and southern Italy. Now heavily restored, its walkways provide a good spot from which to enjoy an overview of the city. Concerts are held here in the summer.

To the north of the castle stands **Santa Maria delle Carceri**, an early Renaissance church begun in 1485 by Giuliano da Sangallo. With its piazza, it takes its name from the prison (*carceri*) that used to stand here. The church was built to honour a miraculous talking Madonna painted on one of the prison walls, the Madonna delle Carceri. The church betrays the influence of Brunelleschi and Alberti, its interior of the blandly harmonious type so familar in Florence. Decorative relief is provided by a fine enamelled frieze and tondi of the Evangelists (1490) by Andrea della Robbia.

Piazza del Duomo, Prato's broad main square, lies a few blocks north of the church and castle, flanked by Piazza del Comune and a garland of attractive medieval palaces. The **Duomo** ▶ ▶, which was begun in 1211, is distinguished by a lovely exterior pulpit designed by the artists Donatello and Michelozzo (1428–38) for ceremonial displays of the Virgin's girdle, Prato's most sacred holy relic (see panel opposite). The dancing putti (by Donatello) are copies, the originals now on display in the **Museo dell'Opera del Duomo** (*Open* Mon, Wed–Sun 9.30–12.30. *Closed* Tue. *Admission charge*), along with Maso di Bartolomeo's *Reliquario della Cintola* (Reliquary of the Holy Girdle). Above the main portal is a lovely terracotta lunette (1489) by Andrea della Robbia of the Madonna and Saints Stephen and Lawrence. The unusual, half-striped façade dates from 1385 to 1457. Immediately on the left inside is the Cappella della Cintola (1385–90), built to house the sacred girdle. Its redoubtable bronze screen partly conceals an altar statuette of the Madonna and Child (a masterpiece by Giovanni Pisano) and a fresco cycle by

Agnolo Gaddi, *The Legend of the Holy Girdle* (1392–5). The nave's left-hand aisle contains a pulpit by Antonio Rossellino and Mino da Fiesole. The highlight of the interior, however, is Fra Filippo Lippi's superlative fresco cycle (1452–66) in the choir behind the high altar, considered one of the great cycles of the early Renaissance. The left wall depicts scenes from the life of St Stephen, the right wall scenes from the life of John the Baptist. The dancing figure of Salome in the latter (*The Banquet of Herod*) is a portrait of Lucrezia Buti, the nun seduced by Lippi, who was himself a monk. Ironically, Lippi seduced her during a ceremony to honour the Virgin's girdle. She subsequently became the painter's mistress and mother of their son, Filippino Lippi, himself an accomplished artist.

Donatello and Michelozzo's Pulpit of the Sacred Girdle

THE SACRED GIRDLE
According to tradition, the Virgin Mary tossed her girdle (*cintola*) to Thomas the Apostle at the moment of her Assumption as she hurtled heavenwards. He, in turn, bequeathed it to a priest, one of whose descendants married Michele Dogomari from Prato, who visited the Holy Land as a Crusader and remained there as a merchant. When the couple returned to Prato, the girdle accompanied them as part of the girl's dowry. It is displayed from Donatello's pulpit five times a year (on Easter Day, 1 May, 15 August, 8 September, and Christmas Day).

Ferdinando Tacca's 17th-century Fontana del Bacchino in Prato

The famous 'medieval Manhattan': San Gimignano's towers

▶ ▶ ▶ San Gimignano

IBCC4

San Gimignano may be among Tuscany's best-preserved medieval villages but it is far from being one of its least-discovered. During the summer, tour buses by the score roar in for their occupants to admire its famous towers. To enjoy the ambience to the full, aim either to come out of season or to spend a night here. If time forces you to join the crowds, allow at least a morning to take in not only the towers and the little back streets, but also the glorious fresco cycles of the village's two main churches, the Collegiata and Sant'Agostino.

San Gimignano was inhabited by both the Etruscans and the Romans (though it is named after a 4th-century bishop of Modena). Its position on the Via Francigena, an important pilgrimage route between Rome and northern Europe, brought it to medieval prominence. The towers took root from about 1150, some 72 of them sprouting to create what is now, famously, dubbed a 'medieval Manhattan' (only 15 of the originals are still here). Built as status symbols – the higher the better – and as defensive outposts, the towers played a prominent part in the internecine feuds that ultimately proved to be the town's undoing. When nobles were not dousing one another in boiling pitch, or hurling rocks at their neighbours, they were kept busy fighting off the challenge of towns like Volterra and Poggibonsi. Weakened by such bickering, the town eventually put itself under Florence's protection (in 1348), a move that broke the nobles' power, rendering the towers obsolete – otherwise they might not have been allowed to survive. Thereafter, San Gimignano became a sleepy backwater (another factor in the towers' survival). Its only later claim to fame was a fictional appearance as 'Monteriano' in E M Forster's *Where Angels Fear to Tread*.

GETTING THERE

Take a train or SITA bus from Florence to Poggibonsi (80 minutes) and then a TRA-IN bus from close to the station forecourt to San Gimignano. The village is 53km from Florence by road. Parking is provided outside the walls on Viale Garibaldi.

TOURIST INFORMATION

San Gimignano's tourist office is at Piazza del Duomo 1 (tel: 0577/940 008). The village has just three central hotels but many private rooms for rent. For help in finding accommodations, contact the Co-operativa Turistica, Via San Giovanni 125 (tel: 0577/940 809).

The present village is a pocket-sized place – less than 15 minutes' walk from one end to the other. Enter either by Porta San Matteo or by the fine southern gate, the Porta San Giovanni (1262). Then walk up Via San Matteo or Via San Giovanni to the interconnecting main squares – Piazza del Duomo and Piazza della Cisterna (named after its 13th-century well). Piazza del Duomo contains most of the action – the Collegiata and the Palazzo del Popolo, the latter home to the Museo Civico and Torre Grossa (the only tower you can climb). Be sure to brave the backstreets as well, wandering to the walls and the Rocca (castle) for fine views and quiet spots away from the crowds.

Collegiata►►► (*Open* Cappella di Santa Fina, Tue–Sun 9.30–12.30, 3–6; winter, 2.30–5.30. *Closed* Mon. *Admission charge. Biglietto Unico* available, see panel for details). San Gimignano's cathedral in all but name (the village no longer has a bishop), the Collegiata was consecrated in 1148 and enlarged by Giuliano da Maiano between 1466 and 1468. Little in the plain Romanesque façade prepares you for the splendid interior, whose decorative scheme has no fewer than four major fresco cycles. The first, on the right-hand (south) wall, is a 22-panel sequence of scenes from the New Testament (*c*1381), long attributed to Barna da Siena, a follower of the great Sienese painter Simone Martini. Barna reputedly died in a fall from

A homey corner in San Gimignano

229

BIGLIETTO UNICO

A single ticket (*Biglietto Unico*) is available, covering admission to San Gimignano's Museo Civico, the Cappella di Santa Fina, the Museo d'Arte Sacra, and the small Museo Ornitologico.

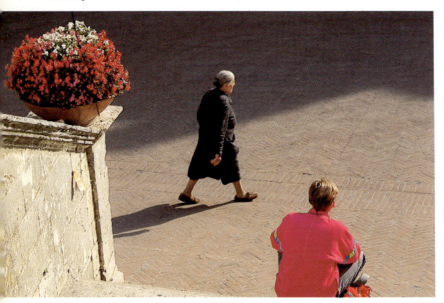

Just watching life go by: a visitor enjoys the sunshine in this charming little town

scaffolding while working on the cycle. Most critics, however, now credit the work to Lippo Memmi and his assistants (1333–44).

The Old Testament cycle on the left wall is less contentious, being signed and dated (1367) by Bartolo di Fredi. Its 26 episodes describe the stories of Genesis, Noah, Abraham, Joseph, Moses, and Job. Biblical narrative aside, the paintings are remarkable for their human and incidental detail, full of ideas copied from Ambrogio Lorenzetti's influential frescoes, the *Allegories of Good and Bad Government*, in Siena (see page 237).

The Collegiata's third cycle, on the rear wall, is Taddeo di Bartolo's *Last Judgment, Paradise, and Hell* (c1393) – perhaps the most entertaining of the three, if only for the wonderfully gruesome execution of its more lurid scenes. Close to the rear wall are two painted wooden statues of the Virgin Annunciate and the Angel Gabriel by Jacopo della Quercia (1421).

Off the south aisle, the Cappella di Santa Fina (1468), a Renaissance masterpiece by Giuliano da Maiano, contains a ciborium and altar bas-reliefs (1472–7) by Giuliano's better-known brother, Benedetto da Maiano. Here, too, you will find the Collegiata's fourth fresco cycle (c1475), Domenico Ghirlandaio's depiction of episodes from the life of Santa Fina, one of San Gimignano's most revered saints (see panel opposite).

MUSEO D'ARTE SACRA
This small museum, entered to the left of the Collegiata, contains a collection of Etruscan finds, church silver, old wooden statues, valuable 13th-century crucifixes, and a *Madonna and Child* by Bartolo di Fredi. *Open*: Tue–Sun, Mar–Oct 9.30–8, Nov and Jan 9.30–11, 2.30–5, Dec 9.30–1.30; *Closed* Mon. *Admission charge*; *Biglietto Unico* available (see panel on page 229).

Museo Civico▶▶ (*Open* Tue–Sun, Apr–Sep, 9.30–7.30; Mar and Oct, 9.30–6; Nov–Feb, 9.30–12.50, 2.30–4.50; Dec 9.30–7.30. *Closed* Mon. *Admission charge. Biglietto Unico* available, see panel, page 229). Climb the Palazzo del Popolo's tower and then explore its civic museum and picture gallery. The palace's frescoed main hall, the Sala del Consiglio or Sala di Dante, is where Dante tried to persuade San Gimignano to join an alliance with Florence in 1300 (see pages 70–1). The room is dominated by Lippo

Memmi's magnificent (but damaged) *Maestà* (1317), a not dissimilar work to Martini's superb fresco in Siena's Palazzo Pubblico. Upstairs are countless valuable paintings, including winsome pieces by Gozzoli, Pinturicchio, Filippino Lippi, Taddeo di Bartolo, and others. San Gimignano's most endearing pictures, though, are the so-called *Wedding Scene* frescoes by the more obscure Memmo di Filippuccio.

Various interpretations have been placed on these 14th-century paintings, which are tucked away in one of the museum's smaller rooms. Some say they are a warning against the wiles of women, others that they are a harmless sequence of nuptial scenes. They show a wife riding on her husband's back, and a couple taking a shared bath before climbing into bed.

Sant'Agostino▶▶ Barnlike, in the manner of most Augustinian churches, Sant'Agostino (1298) is known for the beautifully detailed frescoes (1464–5) in the choir. The work of Benozzo Gozzoli, a painter born in San Gimignano, they depict scenes from the life of St Augustine. The church has an altar (1495) by Benedetto da Maiano (in the Cappella di San Bartolo, to the right of the main door); frescoes of the life of the Virgin (1374) by Bartolo di Fredi (south apse); a resounding *Coronation of the Virgin and Saints* (1483) by Piero Pollaiuolo (over the high altar); and *Four Bishops*, a marble relief by Tino da Camaino. The third altar in the north aisle contains a redoubtable fresco of St Sebastian, commissioned from Benozzo Gozzoli in 1464 to celebrate the passing of a plague epidemic.

SANTA FINA

Fina led a strange life. Born in San Gimignano in 1238, she desperately repented her sins after contracting a fatal illness at the age of 10 (her worst lapse, apparently, had been to accept an orange from a boy). She passed the next five years lying on a wooden board awaiting her death, which had been announced to her in a vision by St Gregory. In the meantime, she kept busy by working miracles (some shown in Ghirlandaio's Collegiata frescoes): she healed her nurse's paralysed hand; restored a choirboy's sight; and caused angels to ring the Collegiata's bells. At her death, violets blossomed from her board and wallflowers sprang from a tower in the village.

231

PIEVE DI CELLOLE

This beautiful 13th-century Romanesque church, one of the area's finest, lies 4km northwest of San Gimignano on the Certaldo road.

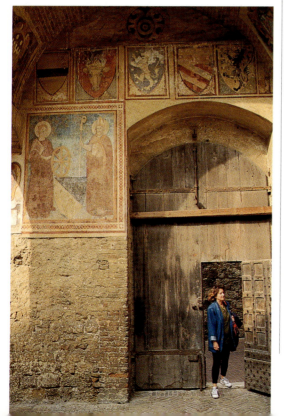

Little frescoed nooks and crannies: all part of the charm of San Gimignano

There have been monasteries scattered across Tuscany for over a thousand years, tucked away in the folds of forested slopes far from the debilitating cares of a decadent world. Three of the most beautiful lie close together in the tranquil countryside south of Siena.

232

ST GALGANO GUIDOTTI
The abbey of San Galgano honours St Galgano Guidotti (1158–81), a monk whose old hermitage forms part of the circular chapel (1182–5) on Monte Siepi, the hill above the abbey. At the entrance to this chapel is a sword he thrust into a stone to symbolise his renunciation of his former knightly career (after his family and fellow knights had come to try and tempt him back to his old way of life). He was made a saint by Pope Urban III in 1185 as an example to other Christian knights. Around the chapel's walls are faint frescoes (1344) by Ambrogio Lorenzetti showing scenes from Galgano's life.

Monte Oliveto Maggiore Tuscany's most-visited abbey was founded in 1313 by the Olivetans, or 'White Benedictines', a breakaway group who sought to return to the simple ideals of the earliest Benedictines. Today its buildings are mainly institutionalised affairs restored in the last century, but its setting is one of Tuscany's loveliest, secluded amid thick woodlands in the deep-cut hills south of Siena.

Most people come here to enjoy a fresco cycle that ranks with Tuscany's best. Located in the main cloister, the Chiostro Grande (1426–74), it was started by Luca Signorelli, who painted nine panels (1497–8) depicting scenes from the life of St Benedict. Several years later (1505–8) the remaining 27 panels were completed by Il Sodoma, a remarkable painter who was invariably surrounded by a coterie of young boys and a menagerie of 'badgers, apes, dwarf asses, horses…magpies, dwarf chickens, tortoises, Indian doves…' The painter's own letters also spoke of three wives and 30 children.

Before you leave the abbey, be sure to go into the main church to see the beautiful inlaid woodwork of the choir (dating from 1503). The abbey is 9km east of Buonconvento on SS 451 (*Open* daily 9.15–12.30, 3.15–6.30. *Admission free*).

San Galgano Few places in Tuscany are as romantic as San Galgano. Roofless, its grassy nave looks to the heavens, its empty windows a playground for darting swifts. Vegetation curls across its ruined frescoes, and the wind idles around its crumbling columns. Founded in the 13th

Monte Oliveto Maggiore: details from the monastery – (top) interior and (right) exterior

century, and once Tuscany's largest Cistercian abbey (and one of the two largest in Italy), it was begun jointly by Italian monks and Cistercians from the order's mother house at Citeaux (hence its amalgam of French and Italian architectural styles). Its abbots – who grew wealthy from the sale of wool – arbitrated in disputes between Tuscan cities, oversaw the building of Siena's Duomo, and held posts as *casalinghi* (accountants) on Siena's council.

By the end of the 14th century after years of intercity strife, San Galgano's population of monks had dropped to a mere handful. Renewed settlement was thwarted by corruption, most notably the sale of its roof leading, a scam (worked by one of its abbots) that led to the nave's collapse in 1786. Thereafter the abbey mouldered and fell into disuse. Some of the buildings are restored and reoccupied by an Olivetan order of nuns. *(Open* daily dawn to dusk. *Admission free*). The abbey is 32km southwest of Siena off the Grosseto road (SS 73).

Sant'Antimo Sant'Antimo's considerable appeal is both scenic and architectural. The first abbey here was reputedly founded by Charlemagne in 781, though most of the present Romanesque church – one of Italy's finest – dates from the beginning of the 12th century. The abbey declined during the 14th century, and was suppressed by Pope Pius II in 1462.

The exterior and interior sculpture is outstanding, particularly the nave capitals, which show a combination of French, Lombard, and even Spanish influences. The sacristy (rarely open) forms part of the primitive Carolingian church, its entrance flanked by 9th-century pilasters. The small vaulted crypt dates from the same period. Above the nave runs a *matroneum* (women's gallery), an unusual feature once used to segregate the congregation. Equally unusual is the ambulatory, whose three radiating chapels (rare in Italian churches) were probably copied from French models. Sant'Antimo is 10km south of Montalcino (*Open* Mon–Sat 10.30–12.30, 3–6.30, Sun 9.15–10.45, 3–6; 2–4 in winter. *Admission free*).

Cypresses gird the abbey of Monte Oliveto Maggiore

GREGORIAN CHANT
Sant'Antimo is maintained by a small community of French Cistercian monks who sing a haunting Gregorian Mass every Sunday at 11am. Organ concerts are also held in the church during July and August.

Tuscany

The intricate façade of Siena's cathedral

GETTING THERE
Regular trains run to
Siena from Florence
(some involve changing at
Empoli). Services run
roughly every hour, and
take 90 minutes. Once in
Siena, cross the road
from the station for buses
to Piazza Matteotti, near
the centre (tickets are
available from the station
atrium). The centre of
Siena is completely
closed to traffic. Parking
lots are well signposted
on the approaches to the
city, but spaces can still
be difficult to find.

TOURIST INFORMATION
Siena's tourist office is at
Piazza del Campo 56 (tel:
0577/280 551). *Open*
winter, 8.30–1 and
3.30–7; summer,
8.30–7.30; *Closed* Sat
afternoon and Sun.

HOTEL HELP
For assistance in booking
a hotel, contact either the
tourist office or Siena
Hotels Promotion, Piazza
San Domenico (tel:
0577/288 084).

▶▶▶ **Siena**   *IBCD3*

Italy's loveliest medieval city (the perfect foil to Florence),
Siena is the one trip you should make in Tuscany if you
make no other. A breathtaking piazza, the Campo, forms
Siena's heart and is the setting for the Palio, Italy's most
famous festival (see pages 240–1). The towering Palazzo
Pubblico contains masterpieces of painting from the
Sienese School, a genre further represented in the
Pinacoteca Nazionale, one of Italy's leading provincial
galleries. Siena's Duomo ranks among Europe's great
Gothic buildings, and is filled with treasures ranging
from Pinturicchio's vivid fresco cycle to sculptures by
Pisano, Donatello, and Michelangelo. The Museo
dell'Opera del Duomo offers the most majestic of all
Sienese paintings, Duccio's *Maestà*, not to mention a glorious aerial view of the city. Finally, Siena's streets
harbour several churches, shops and restaurants, and
some of the area's loveliest medieval nooks and crannies.

Siena was reputedly founded by Senius, son of Remus,
one of the two legendary founders of Rome – hence the
many statues of the she-wolf, who suckled Romulus and
Remus. A small Etruscan settlement was superseded by
Saena Julia, a Roman colony founded by Augustus. By
1125, Siena was a free comune – though already sunk in
the rivalry with Florence that was to dominate its

medieval history. The old enemy was defeated in 1260 at the Battle of Montaperti, the high point of a century during which its wealth made Siena one of Europe's major cities. Sienese bankers figured among the continent's wealthiest, and Sienese painters – men such as Duccio, Martini, and the Lorenzettis – were at the cutting edge of Italian art. From 1287 to 1355, the city was ruled by the quasi-democratic Council of Nine, under whom the Duomo, the Campo, and the Palazzo Pubblico were completed.

The Black Death of 1348, during which three quarters of Siena's population died, was a blow from which the city never fully recovered. Two charismatic saints emerged to dominate the ensuing period of spiritual uncertainty: St Catherine of Siena (1347–80) and St Bernardino (1380–1444). In the political sphere, Siena struggled against a succession of papal, imperial, and autocratic rulers, owing allegiance to Charles V (from 1530) before suffering a devastating siege at the hands of Florence, and eventually succumbing to the military might of the Grand Duchy of Tuscany in 1559. After that, the city languished for centuries in a period of neglect. Today the outlook is rosier, the town a bustling provincial centre grown rich on banking, agriculture, and tourism.

The Campo▶▶▶ Siena sits on a Y-shaped ridge, ranged over three hills. At its heart, on the site of the Roman

WINE TASTING
Siena's Forte di Santa Barbara, also known as the Fortezza Medicea, houses the Enoteca Italiana Permanente, a national wine library that claims to possess a bottle of every wine produced in Italy. Its bar offers wine by the glass or bottle. Views from here are superb, especially at sunset. *Open* daily 3–midnight. *Closed* Sun.

NANNINI

Siena's favourite café is Nannini at Banchi di Sopra 22–24. The same family runs Nannini Gelateria on the corner of Banchi di Sopra and Piazza Matteotti.

OSPEDALE

Be certain to visit the Ospedale di Santa Maria della Scala, the large building opposite the cathedral façade. For some 800 years this was Siena's main hospital. Today it is being converted into the city's principal cultural and exhibition centre. Pride of place goes to a magnificent fresco cycle (1440) by Domenico di Bartolo on the history and function of the hospital. *Open* daily, summer 10.30–6; winter 11–5. *Admission charge.*

The Duomo she-wolf, Siena's emblem – one of many that can be seen in the city

forum, lies the Campo, a huge piazza. Its medieval rebuilding under the Council of Nine explains the nine sections of its fanlike brick pavement (also intended to symbolise the Madonna's cloak, sheltering Siena under its protective embrace). Cafés and restaurants on the perimetre of the Campo are expensive, but it is worth indulging in at least one expensive *cappuccino* to enjoy the square's street life. The piazza's fountain, the Fonte Gaia, is a largely 19th-century copy of a 15th-century original.

Palazzo Pubblico▶▶▶ (*Open* Mar–Nov 5, Mon–Sat 9.30–6.30, Sun 9.30–1.30; Nov 6–Feb 28, Mon–Sat 10–5, Sun 9.30–1.30. *Closed* Dec. *Admission charge*). The Campo's southern flank is dominated by this great civic palace, built between 1297 and 1310 and still housing the city's municipal offices. From the courtyard an entrance to the left leads to the tower, the Torre del Mangia (102m high, with over 500 steps), allegedly named after its first bell ringer, Giovanni di Balduccio, a renowned glutton and wastrel (whose nickname, *mangiaguadagni*, means 'eat the profits'). The views are outstanding.

The ticket office on the right of the courtyard provides access to the **Museo Civico** (*Open* same hours as Palazzo Publico. *Admission charge*), on the palace's upper floor. Quality is variable across the gallery's 18 rooms, but the highlights represent some of the greatest of Tuscany's Sienese paintings.

To start, go past the ceramics and 16th- to 18th-century paintings) and turn left into the Sala di Balia, frescoed by Spinello Aretino (1407) with scenes from the life of Pope Alexander III. Ahead lies the Anticamera del Concistoro, covered in frescoes and *sinopie*, and beyond that the Sala del Concistoro, whose ceiling frescoes (1529–35) by Beccafumi (see panel opposite) consist of a series of allegories on the virtues of Siena's medieval government (an artistic brief imposed on most of the Palazzo's painters over the centuries).

Doors off the anticamera lead through the vestibule and anticappella respectively, the latter frescoed by Taddeo di Bartolo. To its left is the *cappella* (chapel), unmistakable behind an iron screen (1435–45) designed by Jacopo della Quercia, Siena's leading medieval sculptor. The frescoes, *Scenes from the Life of the Virgin* (1407–8), are also by Taddeo di Bartolo. The altarpiece is by Il Sodoma. The large Sala del Mappmondo beyond contains two of the palace's highlights, Simone Martini's huge *Maestà* (1315–21) on the left wall, and his *Equestrian Portrait of Guidoriccio da Fogliano* (1328) on the right wall (though the attribution of this is disputed).

Through to the right (in the Sala della Pace) are two more famous frescoes, Ambrogio Lorenzetti's wonderfully detailed (though somewhat damaged) *Allegories of Good and Bad Government* (1338), once considered the most important cycle of secular paintings of the Middle Ages.

Duomo▶▶▶ *(Open mid-Mar–Oct, daily 9–7.30; Nov to mid-Mar, daily 10–1, 2.30–5. Admission charge).* A church has existed on the cathedral's current site since at least the 9th century. The present building dates from 1215 to 1376 – a period that also saw an aborted plan to extend the cathedral, a scheme whose half-finished results are still clearly visible to the right of the Duomo.

Giovanni Pisano designed much of the fine lower façade (1285), though most of his original statuary now resides in the Museo dell'Opera del Duomo (see page 238). The façade's upper half, a less harmonious undertaking, was added in the 14th century; the upper gable mosaics date from the 19th century.

The interior of the Duomo is even more dazzling than the façade. Its pavement, partly covered for protection, comprises 56 panels, designed between 1369 and 1547 by 40 of Siena's leading artists. Midway down the left aisle (fourth altar) is the Piccolomini altar, whose four lower-niche statues are early works by Michelangelo (1501–4).

Frescoed vaulting and part of the font in the Battistero

DOMENICO BECCAFUMI
The outstanding Sienese painter of his time, Domenico Beccafumi (1484/6–1551) worked in Rome before returning to Siena to work in the Mannerist tradition of Bronzino and Andrea del Sarto. His best work is in Siena's Duomo and Palazzo Pubblico.

SAN DOMENICO
This huge, redbrick 12th-century church is known for the only authentic portrait of St Catherine of Siena (located to the right of the entrance). Also worth seeing are the frescoes by Sano di Pietro, Pietro Lorenzetti, and Matteo di Giovanni, and Sodoma's *St Catherine in Mystical Ecstasy* (right nave). Catherine's house and sanctuary can be visited nearby on Costa di San Antonio.

COMBINED TICKETS
Combined entry tickets are available for the Libreria Piccolomini, Museo dell'Opera, and Battistero and – at a small fee – for the Oratorio di San Bernadino.

CHURCH AND ORATORY
The church of San Francesco's cavernous interior contains frescoes by the brothers Pietro and Ambrogio Lorenzetti. To the right of the church is the Oratorio di San Bernardino, built on the spot where the Franciscan St Bernardino used to preach. Upstairs there is a fine Mannerist fresco cycle by Sodoma and Beccafumi. *Open* Apr–Oct only, daily 10.30–1.30 and 3–5.30. *Admission charge.*

Immediately to its right is the entrance to the Libreria Piccolomini, beautifully frescoed by Pinturicchio with scenes from the life of Aeneas Piccolomini, better known as Pope Pius II (see pages 216–17). The frescoes (1502–9) were commissioned by his nephew, Pius III, who was pope for only 10 days.

Nicola Pisano's Gothic pulpit (1268), at the end of the left aisle, is the Duomo's masterpiece. To its left, in the corner chapel, seek out Tino da Camaino's tomb of Petroni (d.1313), copied throughout the 14th century, and, below it, the bronze pavement tomb (1426) of Bishop Pecci by Donatello.

The hexagonal Cappella di San Giovanni Battista occupies a corner of the left transept, home to more frescoes by Pinturicchio and a bronze statue of St John the Baptist (1457) by Donatello.

Outside the Duomo, be sure to see the **Battistero** (Baptistery) (*Open* mid-Mar–Sep, 9–7.30; Oct, 9–6; Nov–mid-Mar, 10–1, 2.30–5. *Admission charge*), which was built in 1317–82 is reached down steps to the right and rear of the building. Inside, beneath the beautiful vaulting, stands a hexagonal font (1417–30) that is one of the most important sculptural works of the early Renaissance. Most of its bronze panels, depicting scenes from the life of John the Baptist, were cast by Donatello, Lorenzo Ghiberti, and Jacopo della Quercia. Most of the frescoes are by Vecchietta.

Museo dell'Opera del Duomo▶▶ (*Open* Jan–mid-Mar and Nov–Dec, daily 10–1, 2.30–5; mid-Mar–Sep daily 9–7.30; Oct daily 9–6. *Admission charge*). Siena's excellent cathedral museum opens downstairs with the Galleria

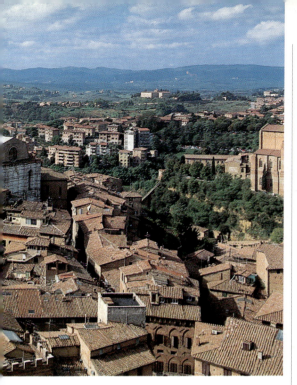

THE PERFECT VILLAGE
The village of Monteriggioni, a few kilometres north of Siena, is perhaps the most perfectly preserved fortified village in Italy. Its towers and fortifications are evocative from afar, and within its walls are a tiny huddle of streets, a four-star hotel, and a couple of good restaurants.

239

Below: the Torre del Mangia overlooks the Campo

delle Statue, whose central exhibit is an ochre-coloured tondo of the Madonna and Child by Donatello. Close by is a *Madonna and Child with Saints* by Jacopo della Quercia. The heavyweight wall statues – the work of Giovanni Pisano – were removed from the façade. A reverentially lit room on the second floor contains Duccio's magnificent *Maestà* (1308–11). Allow plenty of time to study both the main altarpiece and its many predella panels, all but three of which have been recovered after the painting was split up in the 18th century. Also here are Duccio's *Madonna and Child* and Pietro Lorenzetti's *Birth of the Virgin* (1342).

Further Sienese paintings grace the gallery's second floor, notably Beccafumi's *St Paul*, Simone Martini's *Blessed Augustine*, and the bizarre but influential *Madonna degli Occhi Grossi* (Madonna of the Large Eyes), an anonymous work by the so-called 'Maestro di Tressa' (1220–30). Absolutely not to be missed is the superb view from the museum's external tower and balcony (signed *Ingresso al Panorama*).

Pinacoteca Nazionale▶▶▶ (*Open* Tue–Sat 9–7, Sun 8–1, Mon 8.30–1.30. *Admission charge*). This extensive 36-room gallery at Via San Pietro 29 is a must if you enjoy the golden-hued and beautifully coloured paintings of the Sienese School. The one caveat is its preponderance of paintings depicting the Madonna and Child – over half the pictures commissioned in Siena between 1350 and 1550 were of the Virgin, and the *Maestà* – the Virgin Enthroned – was a Sienese invention. Paintings are arranged chronologically, and include works from all Siena's leading names.

Siena's world-famous Palio is not staged just to entertain its visitors. The twice-yearly horse race – Italy's most spectacular pageant – gives colourful expression to the fierce rivalries that have raged for 700 years among the town's 17 medieval districts, the contrade.

Bound for glory: the start of another Palio

SEEING THE PALIO
Only the most determined visitor is likely to get a reasonable view of the Palio. Even if you arrive several hours before the race, the Campo will be hot, noisy, and very crowded. Balcony places around the piazza are sold for high prices months beforehand. For advance booking you could try contacting Palio Viaggi, Piazza Gramsci 7 (tel: 0577/280 828) and some hotels may be able to obtain tickets if you ask well in advance. The only way to guarantee a cheap and comfortable view of the Palio is to watch the live broadcasts on national television. Alternatively, watch one of the practice runs that take place in the week before the big event.

A time-honoured tradition The Palio has taken place in some shape or form virtually every year since the 13th century. It takes its name from the *pallium*, an embroidered banner awarded to the winning *contrada*, and is held in honour of the Madonna. For this reason, the first race is run on the festival of the Visitation (July 2), the second (instigated in 1659) on August 16, the day after the Feast of the Assumption. (Races are also occasionally run to honour a special event – see panel opposite.) The contest originally took place around the city streets, usually from an outer gateway to the Duomo. Regular races only began to be held in the Campo in 1656.

Siena's *contrade* Since the 13th century, Siena has been divided into three administrative districts (*terzi*) – the *Terzo di Città*, the *Terzo di Camollia*, and the *Terzo di San Martino* (corresponding roughly to the city's three hilly spurs). Each *terzo* is divided into smaller wards, or *contrade*, of which there were 42 in the 14th century, reduced to 23 in the 16th century. Today there are 17 *contrade*, each with its own church, social club, museum, fountain, flag, and heraldic animal motif (from which the *contrade* take their names). Allegiance to the *contrada* is absolute: after a conventional baptism, for example, children are rebaptised in their *contrada* fountains. Each *contrada* is run by an assembly, elected democratically by all those born within that *contrada* and aged over 18. Special heralds attend weddings and funerals of *contrada* members, and signs of the *contrade* are visible everywhere as you walk around Siena. Each *contrada* holds an annual parade, and the *alfiere*, the famous flag throwers (not to mention the *tamborini*, the drummers), can often be seen practising in the streets.

Preparations for the Palio No more than 10 *contrade* take part in each Palio, so lots are drawn to make the selection. Horses and starting positions are also drawn by lot, though each *contrada* selects its own jockey, many of whom are drawn from the *butteri*, the traditional cowboys of Tuscany's Maremma region. Thereafter, anything goes. Horses are sometimes drugged, and jockeys bribed or ambushed. Alliances are forged and broken. Huge amounts of money change hands. Small wonder that jockeys are guarded day and night, allowed to communicate only through their bodyguards.

Rehearsals, processions, and boundless pageantry fill the days before a race. A *contrada* banquet is held on the eve of battle. The following morning, horses are taken to church to be blessed – 'go, little horse, and return a winner' are the priest's words (dung produced at this point is seen as an excellent omen). At around 5pm the pages, *tamborini* (drummers), equerries, and *alfieri* (flag throwers) of each *contrada* process to the Campo. In front of them march city officials and representatives from the old towns of the Sienese Republic.

The race At about 7pm the race is ready to roll. All but one of the horses are penned into a corner of the Campo, which is covered in sand and lined with mattresses to lessen the dangers to horse and jockey. The lone rider charges when the group least expects it, and the race is under way. Jockeys beat their horses (and each other) with whips made from calf phalluses. Ninety seconds and three laps of the piazza later it is all over. Winning jockeys drink to victory, while losers drown their sorrows. The winning horse is the guest of honour at the celebratory feast. Celebrations go on for days, recriminations for decades.

SPECIAL EVENTS
Of the 600 Palios run since the 17th century, around 60 have been held to celebrate special events. For example, races took place in 1809 to mark Napoleon's victorious return to Paris; in 1849 to celebrate the opening of the Siena–Empoli railway; in 1945 to mark the end of World War II; in 1947 to record the sixth centennial of St Catherine's birth; and in 1969 to acknowledge the first lunar landing.

241

NON-EVENTS
It takes a lot to stop the Palio. Races were not held during the two world wars or during a cholera outbreak in 1885. In 1900, they were called off after the assassination of King Umberto I, and again in 1798 after a devastating earthquake (though this time only the July race was cancelled). During violent political rioting in 1919, Siena's left- and right-wing factions set aside their differences for the duration of the Palio.

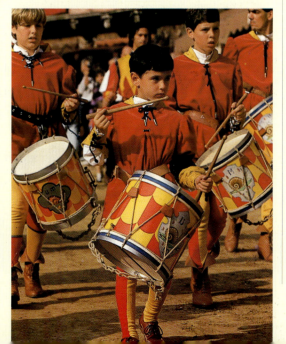

Local rivalries start young in Siena: these tamborini, *members of one of the* contrade, *will practice all through the year*

Drive

Siena to Montepulciano

A drive through the heart of the beautiful Tuscan countryside, visiting vineyards, ancient abbeys, Roman baths, and several historic hill towns on the way (approximately 120km one way).

Leave Siena by SS 326 and after about 5km take SS 438 for Asciano. This road passes through the crete, the so-called Sienese 'badlands' – a region of eroded clay hills covered in summer with sunflowers and rolling wheatfields.

Modest **Asciano**▶ is a partially walled hill town with two museums: the Museo d'Arte Sacra, home to a dozen or so important Sienese paintings, and the Museo Archeologico, filled with Etruscan finds from the surrounding area. Continue south from Asciano, passing **Monte Oliveto Maggiore**▶▶▶, Tuscany's most beautifully situated monastery (see page 232).

From here follow the road southwest toward **Buonconvento**▶ (*Open* Tue and Thu 10–12; Sat 10–12 and 4–6; Sun 9–1. *Admission charge*), which has an excellent and little-known museum of medieval paintings, the Museo d'Arte Sacra at Via Soccini 17. The drive south along the Ombrone Valley to **Montalcino**▶▶ passes through delightful countryside. More verdant than the often eerie desolation of the *Crete*, the landscape is rippled with the Brunello vineyards for

*The hot springs (*terme*) that are now the focal point of the medieval piazza in Bagno Vignoni have been used since Roman times*

which the region is famous (see page 213). The village's *rocca* (castle), with its glorious views, has a lovely *enoteca* where you should stop to sample local wines. For nonalcoholic refreshment, visit the Fiaschetteria Italiana, an untouched turn-of-the-century café in the main square.

Some 10km south of Montalcino, set amid olive groves and ilex-covered hills, is the 12th-century abbey of Sant'Antimo, one of the region's most enchanting Romanesque buildings (see page 233).

Continue southeast on minor roads before turning north beyond Ansidonia toward San Quirico. After the hilltop hamlet of Castiglione d'Orcia and the junction with SS 2, watch for the sign to **Bagno Vignoni**▶▶. The steaming sulphur pool in the village's main square is one of Tuscany's most memorable sights. The arcaded Renaissance *piscina* was built by the Medici, but the spa has been used since Roman times. More hot springs

emerge near the Posta Marcucci hotel, where nonresidents can bathe in the hotel spa.

Return to the main SS 2 and drive north to **San Quirico**▶, which, despite its rather moribund appearance, merits a brief stop if you have time to explore its Collegiata, a pretty Romanesque church with outstanding carved portals, a good Renaissance choir, and a lovely 15th-century triptych of the Madonna and Saints by Sano di Pietro.

The final stretch of the drive follows SS 146 eastward through **Pienza**▶▶▶, one of Tuscany's most interesting small towns (see pages 216–7). The hilltop town of **Montepulciano**▶ is even more appealing (pages 214–5). Both towns are convenient places to spend the night. To return to Siena take the main road north from Montepulciano, to Nottola. Turn north to drive through Torrita to Sinalunga. Here pick up SS 326 for Siena (42km).

Room for two more on one of Viareggio's well-groomed beaches

GETTING THERE
Trains run to Viareggio directly from Florence roughly every hour. The trip takes about 90 minutes.

TOURIST INFORMATION
Viareggio's tourist office is at Viale Carducci 10, one block back from Viale Regina Margherita, the seafront promenade (tel: 0584/962 233). A summer-only kiosk operates at the station (Piazza Dante, tel: 0584/463862).

▶ **Viareggio**　　　　　　　　*IBCA5*

Viareggio, to all intents and purposes, is Florence-by-the-Sea. It is known for its carnevale celebrations, reputed to be second to Venice. Almost any train bound here on a summer's morning is likely to be teeming with Italians heading for a day on the beach. The town marks the southernmost point of the **Versilia**, a mountain-backed riviera of beach resorts that stretches almost to the Ligurian border. As the Biarritz of this Tuscan riviera, Viareggio is the place to choose if you want an easily organised day by the sea from Florence. It is also the best of the resorts, rivalled only by **Forte dei Marmi**, an unaccountably chic little enclave beloved of writers, artists, and would-be celebrities. In fact, any of the Versilian resorts will do if all you want is an hour of sun and a dip in the sea. All are commercialised, and all are dominated by the so-called *stabilimenti*, private stretches of beach that charge for access and rent out towels, changing rooms, and sun loungers. This may sound a grim arrangement, but the sand is guaranteed to be clean and groomed (even if the water sometimes fails some safety standards). If you blanch at the thought of paying, the shore is also dotted with public beaches (*spiaggia libera*).

The beaches of Viareggio will be far from empty, and the *stabilimenti* rates are pretty steep, but the town has an elegant and relaxed atmosphere and the sand is excellent (over 100m wide and several kilometres long). The town is among Italy's oldest resorts, its long seafront promenade – fronting a gridiron street plan – having been built in 1860. A fire in 1917 changed its appearance somewhat, the original boardwalk and wooden buildings giving way to palm-fringed boulevards and a number of lovely Liberty-style buildings. The most notable of these is the Gran Caffè Margherita (near the marina), which was designed by Italian art-nouveau iconoclasts Galileo Chini and Alfredo Belluomini.

Prices for most things in Viareggio are on the steep side, particularly in the seafood restaurants – though these are some of Italy's best if you want to treat yourself. Even the seafront pizzerias will land you with eye-opening bills. Picnic provisions can be bought from the market in Piazza Cavour, which is midway between the train station and the seafront.

If you have time, be sure to head south and follow the famous Via dei Tigli – a 6km-long avenue of linden trees – to the lakeside village of **Torre del Lago Puccini▶** (accessible by bus from Viareggio's Piazza d'Azeglio). Giacomo Puccini, born in nearby Lucca, spent the second half of his life here, composing all his best-known operas (with the exception of *Turandot*) on the edge of Lago Massaciuccoli. It was the lake, incidentally, that attracted Puccini, who came here to hunt, or – as he put it – to practise 'my second favourite instrument, my rifle'.

The composer's house, the **Villa Puccini▶** (*Open* guided tours only, every 30 minutes, summer, Tue–Sun 10–12, 3–7.30; winter, Tue–Sun 10–12.30, 3–5.30. *Closed* Mon. *Admission charge*), is now a museum, set back from the lake and rather hidden behind trees and high iron railings. Its rooms contain numerous musical mementoes, including Puccini's favourite instrument, his piano. Nothing has been changed since the composer's death. The mausoleum of Puccini and his wife is placed, rather aptly, between the piano room and the gun room.

The popular Festival Pucciniano takes place in venues around Torre del Lago Puccini during August Concerts of the master's works are given in the village's open-air theater. Details of the current year's programme can be obtained from the festival office, Piazzale Belvedere Puccini (tel: 0584/359 322).

SHELLEY'S DEATH
The English poet Shelley moved to Italy in 1818, age 26, accompanied by his second wife Mary, author of *Frankenstein*. After four years in his 'Paradise of Exiles' (he coined the phrase), he drowned while sailing from Livorno to meet up with his fellow poet and exile, Byron. His corpse was washed up two weeks later at Gombo, just south of Viareggio. Byron and other friends cremated Shelley's body on the spot, 'pouring libations of wine, salt, and frankincense on to the red-hot ashes'. Trelawney, one of the friends present, observed that 'the brains literally seethed, bubbled and boiled as in a cauldron … [but] what surprised us all was that the heart remained entire'. The said heart was returned to England, where it was laid to rest in Bournemouth. The poet's ashes were buried in Rome's Protestant cemetery.

245

Art-nouveau architecture is one of the many pleasures of Viareggio

Few ancient peoples were as enigmatic yet as culturally sophisticated as the Etruscans. Between 800 BC and 400 BC – when their civilisation was at its height – they controlled much of central Italy (Etruria) through a loose but prosperous confederation of cities.

Top: Etruscan vase (c500 BC), showing boxers fighting

ROMAN BULLIES?
'Because a fool kills a nightingale with a stone, is he therefore greater than the nightingale? Because the Roman took the life out of the Etruscan, was he therefore greater than the Etruscan?' D H Lawrence, *Etruscan Places* (1932)

246

ETRUSCAN SITES
Etruscan sites and museums in Tuscany can be found in Arezzo, Florence, Volterra, Chiusi, and Grosseto. Some of the most interesting tombs that are regularly open to the public dot the countryside around Sovana in the south of the region.

Uncertain origins Where the Etruscans came from is one of history's great mysteries. They believed themselves to be Italy's indigenous people. Their alphabet has links with Chaldean Greek, suggesting roots in Asia Minor. Motifs in their funerary art suggest contact with Buddhism, while their tomb figures have a distinctly Asiatic cast. The Etruscan caste system and priestly oligarchy show parallels with the Brahmanism of 10th-century BC India. Scholarly evidence today suggests mixed roots – a blend of seafarers and indigenous tribes, with ethnic links to Asia Minor and trading ties with Greece. Trying to unravel the Etruscans' origins today, however, is rather like an archeologist 3,000 years in the future trying to untangle the ethnic roots of the average 20th-century Englishman or American, where no single source can easily be isolated.

Etruscan cities The first Etruscan cities were probably established around the 8th century BC. Over the next 200 years the most powerful, which were known as 'lucomonies' (autonomous kingdoms), came together to form a loose 12-city federation, the Dodecapolis. Some of the cities – including Arezzo, Cortona, Chiusi, and Volterra – are still important towns (as are Orvieto and Perugia in Umbria, and Cerveteri and Tarquinia in Lazio). Others, such as Vulci, Roselle, and Vetulonia, are now little more than scattered ruins. Although most of the cities were concentrated in central Italy, Etruscan outposts spread as far south as Pompeii, and to Ravenna and Bologna in the north.

Etruscan fortunes took a turn for the worse in 474 BC, a fateful year that saw the Etruscans defeated by the Greeks at the Battle of Cumae. After that, territory was

An Etruscan plate in the Museo Nazionale Etrusco in Chiusi, one of several museums in Tuscany that is packed with Etruscan artifacts excavated from tombs

Tuscany is riddled with hundreds of Etruscan tombs. The half-hidden one pictured here is located near Volterra

also lost to the Gauls and Samnites. Cities then fell in fairly rapid succession to the Romans. Veio was one of the first to go (in 396 BC), Perugia one of the last (in 309 BC). Some fought, others went quietly. Some, for a while, maintained a benign independence. All, however, were eventually assimilated, their people and customs absorbed by force or through intermarriage.

The Etruscan legacy Wander the streets of Volterra, it is said, and you encounter faces that might have come straight from the town's Etruscan tombs. Since so little else of Etruscan culture has survived, genetic continuity may appear at first glance to be one of the Etruscans' few historic bequests. History, however, has been side-tracked by the Romans, who deliberately set out to appropriate the culture of their predecessors and absorb it into their own. Etruscans, for example, were probably Rome's first settlers, and provided its first kings. Their alphabet passed into Latin, and thus into later European languages. The Romans also inherited many of the Etruscans' gods and divinations, and even their circuses, rituals, and gladiatorial games.

Much of the Etruscans' material culture has been lost because their cities were made mostly of wood. Almost all that remains are necropoli, the great 'cities of the dead' that surrounded every Etruscan settlement. Almost everything found (or known) about the Etruscans, there-fore, comes from tombs (the Etruscans, like the Egyptians, buried their dead equipped with everything they might need in the afterlife). This has given them an undeserved reputation for gloom and an obsession with death. In truth, they were lively and imaginative – 'effer-vescent as flowers,' in the words of D H Lawrence – and possessed of highly developed social, cultural, and political systems.

LIFE AND DEATH
'Death ... to the Etruscans was a pleasant continuance of living, with jewels and wine and flutes playing for the dance. It was neither an ecstasy of bliss, a heaven, nor a pur-gatory of torment. It was just a natural continuance of the fulness of life. Everything was in terms of life ... the things they did, in their early centuries, are as natural and easy as breathing.' D H Lawrence, *Etruscan Places* (1932)

PRACTICALITIES

A branch line runs from the main Pisa-Rome rail line at Cecina to Saline di Volterra, 10km from the town centre. Shuttle buses run from there to Piazza Martiri della Libertà. Volterra's tourist office is at Via G Turazza 2, off Piazza dei Priori (tel: 0588/86 150).

OPENING TIMES

The Museo d'Arte Sacra, Pinacoteca and Museo Etrusco have the same opening hours (*Open* daily summer 9–7, winter 9–2). A reduced price joint ticket is available.

BALZE

Volterra's plateau is slowly crumbling away. The best place to see its famous cliffs and chasms is beyond Porta San Francesco. On the way, drop into the church of San Francesco, known for its fresco cycle of 1315, *The Legend of the True Cross* by Cenni di Francesco. Most of its scenes are similar to Piero della Francesca's famous cycle in Arezzo (see pages 192–5).

MUSEO D'ARTE SACRA

The tiny museum next to the Duomo (entrance at Via Roma 13) contains a collection of sculptures, bas-reliefs, bells, furnishings, vestments, silver-ware, and illuminated manuscripts. The best of the paintings are Rosso Fiorentino's *Madonna of Villamagna* and Daniele da Volterra's *Madonna of Ulignano*.

Looking down on Volterra's extensive Roman remains

▶ Volterra

Commentators invariably describe lofty Volterra as grim and forbidding – a city, in the words of D H Lawrence, 'that gets all the wind and sees all the world…a sort of inland island, still curiously isolated and grim'. On the wrong sort of day this atmosphere is all-pervasive. Hunched behind medieval walls, the town is still inward-looking; perched above a ring of brown-gray hills, it continues to be lord of all it surveys. At other times, Volterra can be a delightful place, not only for its tremendous views, but also for its superb Roman remains, numerous parks and gardens, fine medieval buildings, and one of the country's top Etruscan museums.

As Velathri, Volterra was one of the Etruscans' 12 cities, its early prominence based on mining and an impregnable position. In the 3rd century BC it became Roman Volaterrae. A thousand years later, it was briefly the capital of the Lombard kings. Florence subdued the city in 1361, then again in 1472, when Lorenzo de' Medici hired mercenaries to defend Florentine claims to the town's alum mines (alum was used as a fixative for dyes and was therefore vital for Florence's textile trade). A terrible siege and sack ensued: the resulting slaughter was one of three 'crimes'. Lorenzo confessed to Savonarola on his deathbed. Volterra remained a Florentine vassal and part of the Grand Duchy of Tuscany until unification in 1860.

The town's main square, **Piazza dei Priori▶▶**, is straight out of the Middle Ages. Its **Palazzo dei Priori** (*Open* summer, Mon–Sat 9–1, 3–7; winter, Mon–Sat 9–1. *Closed* Sun. *Admission free*), Tuscany's first civic palace (dating from 1208–1257), is still the town hall. The Sala del Consiglio, on the second floor, boasts a large fresco of the *Annunciation* by Orcagna (1383). Opposite stands the **Palazzo Pretorio**, known for its Torre del Porcellino

(Piglet's Tower), named after the quaint carved boar to the right of the entrance.

The 12th-century Pisan-style **Duomo▶** has several noteworthy works of art. On the high altar stands a 1471 tabernacle by Mino da Fiesole. The pulpit to the left was assembled from 13th-century Pisan fragments in 1584. A chapel in the south transept contains a polychrome *Deposition* (1228), a redoubtable work in wood by an unknown Pisan sculptor. On the left (north) wall the second altar has a lovely *Annunciation* (1497) by Fra Bartolomeo. A separate room, off the north aisle, displays 15th-century terracotta figures depicting the Nativity and the Adoration of the Magi, the latter with a frescoed background by Benozzo Gozzoli.

Volterra's **Pinacoteca▶** (art gallery) is housed in the Palazzo Minucci-Solaini at Via dei Sarti 1. Most of its works have been salvaged from churches around the town, including San Giusto al Bostro, a church swallowed up by the town's crumbling cliffs, the *balze* (see panel opposite). Highlights among the Sienese and Florentine paintings are works by Taddeo di Bartolo, Ghirlandaio, and Luca Signorelli. The main treasure is Rosso Fiorentino's *Deposition* (1521), a masterpiece of Mannerist painting (in Room 12, on the first floor).

Given its worthy reputation, the old-fashioned layout of the **Museo Etrusco Guarnacci▶▶** may be a disappointment. The sheer surfeit of urns can seem overwhelming – there are some 600 of them ('an open book of life', in the words of D H Lawrence). Etruscan devotees, however, will find much to keep them happy. Particularly eye-catching is the *Ombra della Sera* (the 'Shadow of the Night'), an elongated 5th-century bronze figurine (used as a poker by the farmer who found it in 1879). The most famous work is Room 20's *Gli Sposi* (The Married Couple), a tomb cover that is reproduced on postcards.

FORTEZZA AND PARK
Volterra's castle is two castles – the Vecchia (1343) and the Nuova (1475). The latter, also known as *Il Maschio* (The Male), after its battlemented tower, was built by Lorenzo de' Medici after the 1472 siege. It is linked to *La Femmina* (The Female) by a double rampart. Parts are currently used as a prison. The nearby Parco Archeologico (*Open* daily 10–12, 4–one hour before dusk. *Admission free*) is the best place in the town to enjoy a picnic or a siesta.

TEATRO ROMANO
Volterra's Roman theatre is one of the best preserved in Italy. Although it has been closed for some time, you can enjoy a view of it and the surrounding excavations north of Porta Fiorentina on Via Lungo le Mura del Mandorlo.

Florence

250

WEEKEND ITINERARY
Rather than trying to 'do it all', combine a few of the main sights with time spent strolling, relaxing, and enjoying the city's restaurants and shops. Introduce yourself to the city on Saturday morning with the walk on page 54, perhaps lingering awhile in Piazza della Signoria and visiting the Museo della Casa Fiorentina Antica and Santa Maria Novella. Have lunch in a restaurant near the centre, then visit the Uffizi before crossing the Ponte Vecchio and walking up to San Miniato al Monte in the early evening (page 156).

Begin Sunday with a visit to the Bargello, then see one of the great churches: Santa Croce and its museum, or San Lorenzo and the Cappelle Medicee. After lunch, see Piazza del Duomo and climb Giotto's Campanile, marvelling at the view as you plan a more leisurely return visit to the city.

Itineraries

These suggested itineraries should save you unnecessary legwork and valuable time spent in working out where to go when (to check opening times, see under individual entries in the A-Z sections and also pages 268–9.)

One- or two-week itinerary
First week
Sunday Begin with the introductory walk on page 54, stopping at the tourist office, the Palazzo Vecchio, and the Museo della Casa Fiorentina Antica. Fortify yourself with a restaurant lunch, then return to Piazza del Duomo to climb the Campanile and explore Piazza del Duomo.
Monday Start at the Museo di Firenze com'era, then visit Casa Buonarroti before buying a snack or a picnic lunch in the Mercato di Sant'Ambrogio (pages 114–5). Visit Santa Croce and its museum, then stroll to the Ponte Vecchio and enjoy an early evening walk (page 156) up to San Miniato al Monte. Take bus No 12 or 13 back.
Tuesday Take a train to Lucca or Pisa for the day.
Wednesday Devote the morning to the Uffizi. Spend the afternoon in Piazza del Duomo, visiting the Duomo and the Battistero and the Museo dell'Opera del Duomo.
Thursday Start with a browse on and around the Ponte Vecchio, then walk to the Palazzo Pitti. Spend the rest of the morning looking at pictures there, then relax (perhaps with a picnic lunch) in the Giardino di Boboli. Walk to Santa Maria del Carmine to see the Brancacci Chapel frescoes, then visit Santo Spirito before finding a pleasant Oltrarno restaurant for dinner.
Friday Make an early start and take a long half-day over the walk in the north of the city (page 94), visiting as many of the churches and museums as you can. After a late lunch, rest your legs by taking the circular tour from Piazza San Marco on bus No 15 (see panel on page 186). If you still have the energy, get off the bus in Via de' Tornabuoni for some window-shopping.
Saturday Visit the Bargello and the Badia Fiorentina in the morning and then pick up a pizza for lunch on the way to visit Santa Maria Novella and perhaps also Santa Trinita in the afternoon.

Second week
Sunday Spend the morning at the Museo Archeologico and the afternoon on a bus trip to one of the Medici villas (pages 170–1).
Monday and Tuesday Hire a car (see page 256) and visit San Gimignano and Siena, staying overnight and perhaps fitting in one of the drives on pages 198–9 or 242–3.
Wednesday Spend a leisurely day in Fiesole.
Thursday Visit the Museo della Fondazione Horne and the Museo Bardini, then in the afternoon either revisit the Uffizi or do some shopping.
Friday Take a train to either Arezzo or (for a longer day) Cortona for the day.
Saturday Spend a scientific last morning visiting the Museo Zoologico–La Specola and, back across the Ponte Vecchio, the Museo della Storia di Scienza. The afternoon is left free for shopping, revisiting places of special interest, packing – or just relaxing.

Travel Facts

Arriving and departing

Entry formalities Citizens of the US and the British Commonwealth require passports, but visas are not necessary for visits to Italy that do not exceed three months. Passports or Visitor Cards will suffice for citizens of most European Union (EU) countries. Visas are required for longer stays and for nationals of other countries. It is a good idea to carry some form of identification (with a photo) at all times in Italy.

By air: The increasingly popular small Peretola or 'Amerigo Vespucci' airport (tel: 055 373 498) on the north-western outskirts of Florence handles scheduled direct daily flights to and from London, Paris, Brussels, and other European cities. Travellers from the US will have to change in Rome (Fiumicino) or Milan (Malpensa), and it may be easier for them to change at London Heathrow.

SITA buses connect Peretola and Florence about every hour and the journey takes 15 minutes. Buses arrive in Via Santa Caterina da Siena (behind the station). Tickets should be bought at the airport bar and punched on the bus.

Pisa's larger Galileo Galilei airport (tel: 050 28 088, 050 500 707 or 050 216 073) handles international flights, with numerous daily connections on national and charter airlines to most major cities in Italy and Europe. Hourly trains (taking 1 hour) connect Pisa Aeroporto with Florence's main train station.

Bologna airport (1 hour by road or rail from Florence) has scheduled flights from London, Paris, and other European cities.

By train: Florence's main railway station, Santa Maria Novella, lies at the heart of central Italy's rail network. Direct international trains arrive here from Paris, Calais (summer only), Brussels, Amsterdam, Basel, Munich and other European cities. Fast main-line connections are also available from Rome (2 hours), Milan (3 hours), Pisa (1 hour), Bologna (1 hour), Verona (2 hours), Venice (3 hours), Genoa (2 hours) and Turin (4 hours). For train information, tel: 166 105 050 or 147 888 088.

The station has left-luggage, exchange, restaurant and hotel-booking facilities. City buses leave

Pointing the way: road signs in Pisa

from the concourse on its eastern side (to the left as you go out). Taxis depart from the front of the station. It is about 10 minutes' walk to the Duomo and Piazza della Signoria. A small tourist office (tel: 055/212 245) is located at the southern end of the bus bays in Piazza della Stazione, to the east of the railway station (the left as you leave).

A few trains (mostly night sleepers) use Florence's two minor stations, Rifredi (north of the city) and Campo di Marte (to the east).

By car: Florence sits on Italy's main A1 motorway, the Autostrada del Sole. To the north it links to Bologna; to the south it links to Arezzo and Rome.

The closest exits to the city centre are Firenze–Certosa and Firenze–Signa. A fast motorway-standard road leaves the A1 south of the city at Firenze–Certosa to connect with Siena. The A11 motorway leaves the A1 at Firenze–Nord to connect with Prato, Pistoia, Lucca and the west-coast A12 motorway (for Genoa and La Spezia).

A new superstrada (not yet marked on many maps) runs parallel to the A11 to the south, linking Florence with Pisa, Livorno and the A12 motorway.

By bus: Tuscany is served by several long-haul bus companies (see under

Fast and flashy, but unsuitable for Florence's traffic-clogged streets

Public Transport on pages 258–9 for details). Most have their terminals on or close to the main railway station in Florence. CLAP and Lazzi all arrive at Piazza della Stazione. COPIT uses Piazza Santa Maria Novella, just to the south. SITA is based in Via Santa Caterina da Siena, immediately off the western edge of Piazza della Stazione.

Customs Since July 1999 people travelling within the European Union are no longer entitled to import duty-free goods. However, travellers from outside the EU can bring in duty-free goods up to the current EU allowances:
● 200 cigarettes or
100 cigarillos or
50 cigars or
250g of tobacco
● 1 litre of alcohol (over 22° vol) or
2 litres of alcohol (not over 22° vol)
● An additional 2 litres of still table wine
● 60ml perfume,
250ml toilet water.

Travel insurance

It is highly recommended that you take out fully comprehensive travel insurance before travelling to Italy. EU citizens should take out a form E111 (see page 263).

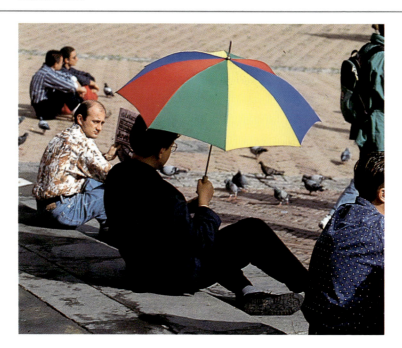

Essential facts

Don't leave your umbrella at home: it has its uses, rain or shine

Climate
Despite its generally mild winters and warm summers, Florence has a surprisingly varied and extreme climate. Summers can be uncomfortably hot and oppressive, whilst winter temperatures often match those of northern European cities. Rainfall can be high until well after Easter, and tumultuous summer thunderstorms are fairly common (particularly in September). The best months for sightseeing are May, June and September. The wettest months are January and November, followed by October and April.

FIRENZE

October–December

May–August

When to go
Try to avoid July and August, Florence's hottest and busiest months, and plan a visit for May, June, September or October instead. Hotels will be busy from May to September. The Tuscan countryside is at its best in May, when spring flowers are in full bloom. September's landscapes have a different beauty, burnt brown and gold by the summer sun.

National holidays
Shops, banks, offices and schools close on the following national holidays: 1 January (New Year's Day); 6 January (Epiphany); Good Friday; Easter Sunday; Easter Monday; 25 April (Liberation Day); 1 May (Labour Day); 15 August (Assumption); 1 November (All Saints' Day); 8 December (Immaculate Conception); Christmas

Day; 26 December (Santo Stefano).
The feast of St John, Florence's patron
saint, is celebrated on 24 June as a
local holiday.

Accommodation is usually in short
supply around the public holidays,
and roads and railways will be
especially busy.

Time differences

Italy is 1 hour ahead of GMT in winter, 2 hours ahead in summer. US
Eastern Standard Time is 6 hours
behind Italy: Sydney is 8 hours ahead
in summer. Note that these time differences may vary by an hour for
short periods in spring and autumn,
since the time change takes place on
different dates in different countries.

Money matters

On 1 January, 1999, the euro became
the official currency of Italy and the
lira became a denomination of the
euro. Italian lira continue to be legal
tender during a transitional period.
Euro bank notes and coins are likely
to start to be introduced by 1 January,
2002. The lira is issued in the following denominations:
• **Bills** – L1,000; L2,000; L5,000;
L10,000; L50,000; L100,000; L500,000.
• **Coins** – L5 and L10 (both rare); L50;
L100; L200; L500; L1000. The L200
telephone token (*gettone*) can be used
as a coin.

Foreign exchange Many Florentine
banks offer over-the-counter
exchange (*cambio*) facilities (see page
264 for opening times). Increasing
numbers have external automatic
tellers that exchange all major foreign
banknotes into lire.

Exchange kiosks are also common.
Those with the longest opening
hours include the office in the train
station ticket hall and **Exact** (*open
daily from 8.30 until the evening*;
branches at Via dei Calzaiuoli 42r,
Via Por Santa Maria 3r, and Via
Alamanni 9r). The **American Express**
office is at Via Dante Alighieri 22r
(tel: 055 50981). Major stores will
advise on reclaiming value added
tax (VAT).

Credit cards Cash still reigns
supreme in Italy, but the credit card
(*carta di credito*) is gradually gaining
acceptance. Most Florentine hotels
and restaurants accept cards, though
there may be more reluctance in
smaller Tuscan towns. Credit cards
are accepted at some service stations
in cities, but are seldom accepted for
petrol purchases elsewhere. The most
commonly recognised cards are
American Express, Diner's Club,
MasterCard and Visa.

*Exchange machines help reduce the
queues of visitors in banks*

255

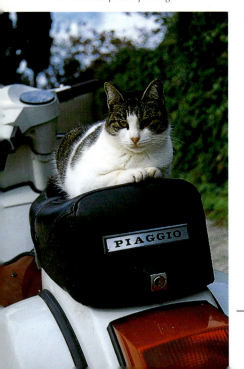

Getting around

Driving

Car-hire To hire a car you must be over 21 and hold a valid driver's licence. The big firms have offices at Pisa and Peretola airports. Enquire about fly-drive deals at travel agents before leaving home. All agencies are listed in the Yellow Pages (*Pagine Gialle*) under *Autonoleggio*. Be sure to

A contented pillion passenger

Two wheels are quicker than four

read the small print, and to satisfy yourself that insurance cover is adequate and that you are aware of all extra charges (accident waiver, additional insurance, VAT).

The main car-hire offices in Florence are as follows:
Avis Borgo Ognissanti 128r (tel: 055 213 629 or 055 39 8826); airport (tel: 055 315 558)
Europcar Borgo Ognissanti 53r (tel: 055 236 0072/3); airport (tel: 055 318 609)
Hertz Via Maso Finiguerra 33r (tel: 055 282 260 or 055 239 8205)
Italy by Car Borgo Ognissanti 134r (tel: 055 93 021 or 055 287 161).

Car breakdown

If your car breaks down, switch on the hazard warning lights and place a warning triangle 50m behind your car. Then call the Automobile Club d'Italia (ACI) emergency number (tel: 116) and give the operator your location and the car's make and registration. The car will be towed to the nearest ACI-affiliated garage. This service is free for foreign-registered cars. ACI have a special assistance number in Florence at Viale G Amedola 36 (tel: 24 861).

Driving tips

Whilst narrow and winding roads will probably be your only problem in rural Tuscany, note that Florence has a complicated one-way system and that much of the city centre is completely closed to traffic for most or all of the day.

Documents Visitors bringing their own (foreign-registered) cars to Italy must be at least 18 years of age and carry the vehicle's registration and insurance documents and a full driving licence (*patente* in Italian). A green UK, red Eire or other European licence is acceptable if accompanied by a translation (available from ACI offices or the Italian State Tourist Office or motoring organisations in your country of origin). Translations are not required for the new (pink) EU driving licences.

Rules of the road Italian traffic rules are allied to the Geneva Convention and Italy uses European standard road signs (motorway signs are green, others blue). Driving is on the

A picturesque but expensive way to see Florence

right and you should give way to traffic from the right unless otherwise indicated. Tolls are payable on motorways (*autostrade*). The speed limit in urban areas is 50kph; outside urban areas it is 110kph on dual carriageways, unless otherwise marked, and 90kph on secondary roads. The limit on motorways is 130kph for vehicles over 1100cc and 110kph for vehicles under 1100cc. The wearing of seat belts is compulsory. Police can impose heavy fines and take away your driving licence for many offences.

Accidents If you have an accident (*un incidente*) place a warning triangle 50m behind your car. Call either the ACI (tel: 116) or the emergency services (tel: 112 or 113). Do not admit liability or make statements that might incriminate you later. Ask unloading only (so hotels with private garages are at a premium). New peripheral car parks (*parcheggi*) are opening in Florence (notably at Piazza della Stazione). The most central long-term car park is at the Fortezza da Basso (linked to the centre by bus no 15). Other smaller car parks include Piazza Beccaria, Piazza Porta Romana, Piazza Libertà and Lungarno della Zecca Vecchia. Illegally parked cars may be towed away; call Parco Auto Requisite (tel: 355 321) to arrange recovery.

Public transport

By air: Alitalia and its domestic affiliate ATI fly from Pisa to most national and international destinations (see pages 252–3). Prices are high and within Italy it is cheaper and often more convenient to travel by rail. Students and passengers aged between 12 and 25 qualify for 25 per cent reductions on certain Alitalia flights. There are also 30 per cent discounts on some night flights, plus 50 per cent savings for family groups (spouse and/or children travelling with you). For airport inquiries at Pisa Galileo Galilei, tel: 050/500 707. For Florence Peretola, tel: 055/373 498.

By bus: (For information on buses within Florence, see page 186). About 10 bus companies serve Florence and Tuscany. For tickets and information on prices and timetables for long-haul buses (*autobus* or *pullman*), visit tourist offices or the offices below:
SITA Via di Santa Caterina da Siena 15r (tel: 284 661)
Lazzi, Piazza della Stazione 4 (tel: 298 840)
CAP (Northern Tuscany) Via Nazionale 13 (tel: 214 637)
CLAP (Northern Tuscany) Piazza della Stazione 15 (tel: 283 734)
COPIT (Northern Tuscany) Piazza Santa Maria Novella 22r (tel: 215 451)
CAT (Central and southern Tuscany) Via Fiume 2 (tel: 283 400)
TRA-IN (Siena province) Piazza San Domenico, Siena (tel: 0577/221 221)

any witness(es) to remain. Make a statement to the police and exchange names, addresses, car details and insurance companies' details with any other driver(s) involved.

Petrol Petrol (*benzina*) in Italy is some of the most expensive in Europe. Diesel (*gasolio*) is cheaper. Petrol stations follow normal shop hours (closed 1–3.30pm and after 7pm) and many close all day Sunday and for the month of August (except on motorways). Do not rely on paying by credit card.

Parking Parking is extremely difficult in the centres of all Tuscan towns. Where street parking exists, it is seldom free except in areas with disc schemes, where you can park for a specified short period if you display your time of arrival. Town centres are often classified as limited traffic zones (ZTL or zona di traffico limitato), open only to public transport, residents' cars and taxis. In these areas (such as central Florence), visitors may park outside hotels for

Train: Florence sits astride the main Rome–Milan line (connections to Bologna and Arezzo) and is the terminus for two lines to the west (one to Livorno via Pisa and Empoli, the other to Viareggio via Prato, Pistoia and Lucca). Direct lines run to Siena (sometimes with changes at Empoli) and Faenza in Emilia-Romagna. Italy's main west-coast route runs through Tuscany linking Orbetello in the south with Livorno, Pisa, Viareggio and Massa in the north (connections to Rome, Genoa and Turin).

● **Network** Except for a few private lines the Italian rail network – cheap, comprehensive and efficient – is run by the Ferrovie dello Stato (FS).

● **Trains** There are five basic train categories: *Pendolino* and *Inter/Euro City* stop only at major stations and require you to book in advance and pay a supplement (*un supplemento*). *Espressi* and *diretti* make more stops, while *locali* halt at every station. Two new categories – *Regionali* and *Inter-Regionali* – are being introduced.

● **Tickets (*biglietti*)** These are available as single (*andata*) or return (*andata e ritorno*) in first (*prima*) or second class (*seconda classe*).

● **Fares** Fares are calculated on a kilometric basis and are among the cheapest in western Europe. Return tickets offer a 15 per cent discount on distances up to 250km.

● **Validity** Return tickets are valid for one day from the day of purchase for journeys up to 250km. They acquire an extra day of validity for each additional 200km up to a maximum of six days.

Tickets are generally valid for two months from date of purchase until punched in platform machines. Such validation is compulsory before you travel. You will be heavily fined if you fail to do so.

● **Reservations** Stations usually have separate ticket windows for reservations (*una prenotazione*) and sleepers (*una cucetta*).

● **Reductions** Discounts of 20 per cent are available for families with a *Carta Famiglia* (Family Card); for travellers between 12 and 26 with a *Carta Verde*; and for those over 60 with a *Carta d'Argento*. Cards can be purchased from main-line stations and are valid for a year.

● **Passes** The FS issue two main passes: the *Chilometrico*, valid for 3,000km of travel over a maximum of 20 journeys; and the 'Italy Railcard', a first- or second-class travel-at-will card available for periods of 8, 15, 21 or 30 days. Note that passes are not valid on high-speed *Pendolino* trains, and that supplements must be paid as with normal tickets for Inter-City and Euro-City trains.

● **Timetable** Be sure to buy the *Pozzorario*, a cheap bi-annual timetable widely available from bookshops and station kiosks.

Taxis Drivers are usually honest, but make sure the meter is switched on at the start of the journey. There is a standard minimum fare, and supplements apply to baggage, night services, and journeys to the airport. If you call a taxi, the meter starts when you make the phone call.

259

Santa Maria Novella station

Communications

Media

Florence's favourite newspaper (*giornale*) is *La Nazione*, a national broadsheet with its roots in Tuscany (much as *La Stampa* belongs to Turin, *La Repubblica* to Rome, and so on). It produces local editions with supplements for most Tuscan towns, plus full listings of daily events. Other widely read quality papers are the centre-left *La Repubblica* (which produces a lively Florentine edition) and the more conservative *Corriere della Sera*. Two sports-based papers are also popular, the *Gazzetta dello Sport* and the *Corriere dello Sport*. News magazines enjoy a large readership, notably *L'Espresso* and *Panorama*.

Foreign newspapers and magazines are readily available in Florence, usually from late afternoon on the day of issue (the railway station kiosks are the most reliable source).

Italian radio and television are both deregulated, and both offer a vast range of national and local stations. Standards are often low, with most Tuscan networks devoted to advertising, pop music and old films. National stations are a little better, dividing equally between the three channels of the state RAI network and the stable of channels part-owned by Silvio Berlusconi (Canale 5, Rete 4 and Italia Uno).

Post offices

Florence's most central post office is at Via Pellicceria 8, tel: 216 122 (*Open*: Mon to Fri 8:15–7 and Sat 8:15–noon). There is another big post office at Via Pietrapiana 53–5; tel: 27 741 or 212 305 (same hours). Small town post offices (*ufficio postale*) usually open Mon to Fri 8–2 and Sat 8–noon, longer in larger cities. All post offices close at noon on the last working day of the month.

● **Stamps** (*francobolli*) These can be bought either from post offices or from tobacconists (*tabacchi*) displaying a blue 'T' sign.

● **Post-boxes** These are small and red and marked *Poste* or *Lettere*. Many have two slots: one for local mail (*Città*), the other for further afield (marked *Altre Destinazioni*).

An Italian post-box. Mail services can be very slow

● **International mail** Mail sent to and from Italy can take up to three weeks to arrive. You might speed matters by sending mail *espresso* (express) or *raccomandata* (registered).

● ***Poste restante*** Letters can be sent *poste restante* to the main post office by addressing them Fermo Posta, followed by the name of the town. Counters 23 and 24 at Florence's Via

Telephones in Italy are easy to use

Pellicceria office deal with *poste restante* mail. Take a passport when collecting mail and be prepared to pay a small fee (around L300 per item). Filing can be haphazard, so ask staff to check under your first and last names.

● **Telex, fax and telegrams** These can be sent from Florence's main post offices (the telegram office at Via Pellicceria is open until 10pm).

Telephones

Italy's main telephone company Telecom Italia (previously SIP) provides public telephones in bars, on the streets and in special offices. All are marked by red or yellow signs showing a telephone dial and receiver.

In Florence, booths at the railway station are open 8am–8pm, while the main Telecom Italia (SIP) office at Via Cavour 21r is open 24 hours.

Most phones accept L100, L200 and L500 coins, as well as a L200 token known as a *gettone*. The last are often given as change or can be bought from bars and *tabacchi*.

The oldest phones (often in bars) usually only accept these tokens. Public phones are increasingly being modified to accept cards (schede *telefoniche*).

Cards are available in L5,000, L10,000 and L15,000 denominations from *tabacchi*, Telecom offices, automatic dispensers or shops displaying a Telecom (SIP) sticker. Remember to tear the corner off the card before using it.

Making a point: portable phones are Italy's latest status symbol

● **Timing of calls** Peak period on weekdays is 8.30am–1pm. The cheapest rate is 10pm–8am all week, while other times are classified as either standard (such as weekdays 1–6.30pm) or off peak (such as weekday evenings and Sundays). The cheap international rate covers all day Sunday, and 10pm–8am on other days for calls in Europe, 11pm–8am for the rest of the world.

● **Tones** The dialling tone on public phones is a sharp hum. A series of rapid pips means you are being connected, while long beeps indicate a ringing telephone at the other end. More rapid beeps mean 'engaged'.

● **International calls** Use a phone card or a *telefono a scatti* – a kiosk where you speak first and pay when your call is over; these are found in some bars, hotels, post offices and tourist offices and in most Telecom offices. Dial 00 for an international line followed by the country code: 44 for the UK; 1 for the US; 61 for Australia and so on. (The code for Italy when calling from abroad is 39.)

● **Reversing the charges** To make a reverse-charge (collect) call, dial 15 (Europe) or 170 (Intercontinental) and ask to make *una chiamata con pagamento a destinazione*.

● **Area codes** The area code for Florence is 055 (omitted in this book on the assumption that you will be telephoning from Florence). Area codes are included for other towns.

Emergencies

Crime and the police The sheer number of visitors to Florence makes them an obvious target for the unscrupulous. In this city as in others, all sorts of horror stories circulate of unwitting tourists fleeced by the criminal elite. Whilst crime certainly exists in Florence, few such tales have much basis in fact, and common sense and a few precautions should keep you safe.

Report any theft to your hotel and then to the police at the Questura, Via Zara 2 (tel: 49 771). They have a special department to deal with visitors' problems. They will also issue you with a special document (*una denuncia*) to forward with any insurance claims. Report loss of passport to the police and your nearest consulate or embassy.

● To contact the police in an emergency, telephone 112 or 113.
● Always carry cash in a belt or pouch – never in a pocket.
● Do not carry large amounts of cash. Use credit cards or travellers' cheques.
● Wear your camera and never put it down on café tables. Beware of strap-cutting thieves.
● Do not flaunt valuables. Better still, leave them at home.
● Leave jewellery in the hotel safe (not in rooms), especially items like chains and earrings which can easily be snatched.
● Hold bags across your front as the Florentines do – not hung over one shoulder where they can more easily be rifled or grabbed.
● Be careful of pickpockets on crowded buses, in street markets or anywhere where large groups of tourists congregate.
● After dark, avoid non-commercial parts of town, parks, and the area around the railway station.
● When driving always lock your car, and never leave luggage, cameras or valuables inside.

Consulates
● **Belgium** Via dei Servi 28 (tel: 055 282 094)
● **Denmark** Via dei Servi 13 (tel: 055 211 007)
● **France** Piazza Ognissanti 2 (tel: 055 230 2556)
● **Netherlands** Via Cavour 81 (tel: 055 475 249)
● **Norway** Via G Capponi 26 (tel: 055 247 9321)
● **Sweden** Via della Scala 4 (tel: 055 239 6865)
● **UK** Lungarno Corsini 2 (tel: 055 284 133)
● **USA** Lungarno Amerigo Vespucci 38 (tel: 055 239 8276)

The art of gentle persuasion. Italy has several different police forces

Travellers from Ireland, Australia, New Zealand and Canada should contact their embassy in Rome.

Emergency telephone numbers
Police (*Carabinieri*) 112
Emergency services (Police, Fire, Ambulance) 113
Fire (*Vigili di Fuoco*) 115
Car breakdowns 116
Questura (Florence Police Station) 49 771
Medical emergency(24-hour central number for all of Tuscany) 118
24-hour tourist medical centre 475 411

Lost property
• ATAF city buses: Via Circondaria (tel: 055 367 943; Mon–Wed and Fri–Sat 9–12).
• Trains: Santa Maria Novella station, platform 16 near left luggage (daily 4:15am–1.30am)
• Peretola airport (tel: 055 373 498)
  Report losses of passports to the police and your consulate. Report general losses to the police at the Questura, Via Zara 2.

Health
The chief everyday health hazards are likely to be too much sun, air pollution (especially for asthma and allergy sufferers) and biting insects and snakes. Water is safe to drink unless marked *acqua non potabile*. Condoms (*profilattici*) are available over the counter from pharmacies and some supermarkets.

Be certain to take out health insurance before travelling (and keep all receipts for medicine and treatment). Free treatment is available to citizens of EU countries, but to be eligible you must bring the necessary documentation (Form E111) to Italy with you from your country of origin.

Pharmacies A chemist's shop (*farma-cia*) is identified by a green cross. Pharmacies have the same opening hours as shops, but some take turns to stay open late and all night (the rota is displayed on pharmacy doors). Regular late-night outlets include the pharmacy at the railway station; Molteni, Via dei Calzaiuoli 7r; All'Insegna del Moro, Piazza San Giovanni 20r; and Paglicci, Via della

Italian pharmacists can advise on minor medical problems and dispense a wide variety of medicines

Scala 61. Staff are well qualified to give advice on minor ailments, and can dispense many medicines over the counter, including some normally only available on prescription in other countries. Remember to bring any prescriptions or doctor's notes that might be required to obtain medicine. Better still, bring with you from home enough medication to last the duration of your stay.

Doctors If you need a doctor (*un medico*) ask first at your hotel, telephone 118, or contact the Tourist Medical Service, Via Lorenzo il Magnifico 59 (tel: 055 475 411), which has multilingual doctors on 24-hour call. For first aid (often given free) or hospital treatment visit the Ospedale di Santa Maria Nuova, Piazza Santa Maria Nuova 1 (tel: 055 27 581).

Vaccinations Vaccinations are not necessary for entry into Italy unless you are travelling from a known infected area.

Other information

Camping and self-catering

Most Tuscan campsites are on the coast. They tend to open seasonally (typically June to September) and are extremely busy during the peak months of July and August, when you must book ahead or arrive before 10am to have any hope of finding a place. Tourist offices have lists of sites and current prices. You might also invest in the widely available *Campeggi e Villaggi Turistici*, an exhaustive list of sites published by the Touring Club of Italy. Freelance camping is usually acceptable, but ask the landowner's permission first, and do not light fires.

Countless agencies rent villas or farmhouses in Tuscany. Most advertise in Sunday newspapers. Agencies and local tourist offices in Italy can also be helpful. Prices are considerably higher than for equivalent properties in France or Spain. Check matters such as whether you will be sharing your swimming pool (often you are) and whether the owner (or caretaker) lives on or near the property. It is essential to know what is included in the hire price (water, electricity, maid service, cleaning and linen can all be extra). Water shortages can be a problem in summer.

Visitors with disabilities

Matters are improving but Florence, with its narrow, car-crowded streets and antiquated hotels and galleries, is still not the easiest of cities for visitors with disabilities. Lists of hotels from tourist offices usually indicate places suitable for the disabled. Italian state tourist offices abroad also provide lists of appropriate hotels and the addresses of Italian associations for travellers with disabilities in various towns and cities. Specific information is also provided in the British publication *Access in Florence*, available for a small fee from OUSA Office, Sherwood House, Sherwood Drive, Bletchley, Milton Keynes MK3 6AN (tel: 01908/71 131).

New public buildings in Italy must all be wheelchair-accessible, and museums generally are gradually improving their accessibility. A few

Inter City trains, particularly on the Rome–Milan line, now have special wheelchair facilities. Staff at airports, stations and in galleries are usually helpful. Parts of central Florence usually closed to traffic are open to drivers with disabilities, and there are also special parking places. Restaurants present few problems, though it is advisable to call ahead to reserve a convenient table.

Opening times

Opening hours can be a problem in Florence, where most of the 'sights' are churches, museums and galleries. Be sure to obtain a list of current opening times (*Orario di Apertura*) from one of the city's tourist offices.
- **Banks** Open weekdays 8.20–1.20. Some larger branches may also open 3–4pm.
- **Churches** No two Florentine churches seem to have the same opening times. Generally most open at 7 or 8am and close at noon or 12.30. They re-open between 3 and 4pm, closing finally between 6 and 7.30. Notable exceptions include the Duomo (open all day), Santa Croce (open all day in summer) and the Battistero (open afternoons Monday to Saturday, but Sunday morning).
- **Museums and galleries** Opening times are given under individual entries in the A-Z sections of this book and (for Florence only) on pages 268–9. Most large (usually state-run) galleries open 9–2 Tuesday to Sudayn and close on Monday (a few close at 1pm). Notable exceptions are the Uffizi and the Museo dell'Opera del Duomo. Some other museums open in the morning and perhaps also in the afternoon (though Sunday is usually a half-day) and some of these museums close an hour or two earlier in the afternoon between about October and March. Closing days of smaller museums vary.
- **Parks** Public parks and gardens usually open from 9am to an hour before dusk, but both the Giardino dei Semplici and the Giardino di Boboli have more restricted opening hours.
- **Post offices** Open Monday to Friday 8–2, Saturday 8–noon. Smaller post offices may not open on

Saturday. Main post offices often stay open for some services until 8pm. All post offices close at noon on the last working day of the month.

● **Restaurants** All restaurants have a statutory weekly closing day (*la chiusura settimanale*), often Monday. Many also close for one evening. Most close for part of August (sometimes July). See also page 175.

● **Shops and offices** These are normally open from 8.30 or 9am to 1pm, re-opening between 3 and 4pm, and closing at 7.30 or 8pm. Food shops close (for most of the year) on Wednesday afternoon. Most other shops are closed on Monday morning (except for the period from mid-June to mid-September when many stores close on Saturday afternoon). Many garages close on Sunday (except on motorways). Supermarkets and department stores usually open 9am–8pm (closed Sunday).

Places of worship
● Church of England St Mark's, Via Maggio 16 (tel: 294 764)
● American Episcopal Church St James's, Via Rucellai 9 (tel: 294 417)

Opening times of sights such as the Battistero can be unusual, so check before paying a visit

● Synagogue Via L C Farini 4 (tel: 245 252/3)

Toilets
Public conveniences are rare in Florence, and are often grim. They are to be found at the railway station, in the basement of the Palazzo Vecchio and off the courtyard of the Palazzo Pitti. Otherwise you will probably have to use the facilities in bars and cafés. These are free, but are intended for the use of customers so you will be more welcome if you buy something first. Ask for *il gabinetto* or *il bagno*, and do not confuse Signori (Men) with Signore (Women). Some facilities may have an attendant and a small dish for gratuities – leave around L200.

Photography
Shops are always ready to serve Florence's countless visitors with films and various photographic paraphernalia. A film is *una pellicola*, slides are *diapositive*.

High fashion meets High Renaissance in one of Florence's luxury shops

Tipping

A 10–15 per cent service charge (*servizio*) is usually included in restaurant bills, but waiters expect a small tip on top. For quick service in bars, do as the locals do and slap down a L100 or L200 coin with your till receipt when ordering.

Theatre usherettes expect a small tip for showing you to your seats, and it is a good idea to give around L500 per visitor to custodians or sacristans who open up churches or museums out of hours. In taxis, round the fare up or tip 10 per cent. Tip hotel staff at your discretion.

Electricity

Current in Italy is 220 volts AC (50 cycles). Plugs are of the two-round-pin variety: a travel adaptor is useful. Some sockets have a third (central) earth socket, but will still accommodate the standard two-pin plug.

In some older hotels and houses you may find there are still two-pin plugs of different specifications. Here you will need to buy (or borrow) an Italian adaptor.

CONVERSION CHARTS

FROM	TO	MULTIPLY BY
Inches	Centimetres	2.54
Centimetres	Inches	0.3937
Feet	Metres	0.3048
Metres	Feet	3.2810
Yards	Metres	0.9144
Metres	Yards	1.0940
Miles	Kilometres	1.6090
Kilometres	Miles	0.6214
Acres	Hectares	0.4047
Hectares	Acres	2.4710
Gallons	Litres	4.5460
Litres	Gallons	0.2200
Ounces	Grams	28.35
Grams	Ounces	0.0353
Pounds	Grams	453.6
Grams	Pounds	0.0022
Pounds	Kilograms	0.4536
Kilograms	Pounds	2.205
Tons	Tonnes	1.0160
Tonnes	Tons	0.9842

MEN'S SUITS							
UK	36	38	40	42	44	46	48
Rest of Europe	46	48	50	52	54	56	58
US	36	38	40	42	44	46	48

DRESS SIZES						
UK	8	10	12	14	16	18
France	36	38	40	42	44	46
Italy	38	40	42	44	46	48
Rest of Europe	34	36	38	40	42	44
US	6	8	10	12	14	16

MEN'S SHIRTS						
UK	14	14.5	15	15.5	16	16.5	17
Rest of Europe	36	37	38	39/40	41	42	43
US	14	14.5	15	15.5	16	16.5	17

MEN'S SHOES						
UK	7	7.5	8.5	9.5	10.5	11
Rest of Europe	41	42	43	44	45	46
US	8	8.5	9.5	10.5	11.5	12

WOMEN'S SHOES						
UK	4.5	5	5.5	6	6.5	7
Rest of Europe	38	38	39	39	40	41
US	6	6.5	7	7.5	8	8.5

Etiquette

● **Churches** Do not wear shorts, mini skirts or skimpy tops in churches, and do not intrude while church services are in progress. Many churches and galleries forbid the use of flash, or ban photography altogether.

● **Smoking** There are few non-smoking areas in restaurants or public places. Smoking is banned on buses.

● **Topless sunbathing** This is usually tolerated on out-of-the-way beaches.

● **Bargaining** This is no longer appropriate in shops, though in markets (except food markets) and budget hotels you may be able to negotiate.

● **Hotels, restaurants and bars** Do try to speak Italian; it will be appreciated – however bad. Children are more than welcome in most hotels, bars and restaurants.

Women travellers

Women visiting Tuscany and Florence are likely to receive fewer uninvited approaches from 'Latin lovers' than in Rome or southern Italy. Such advances, while irritating, are unlikely to turn violent. The best remedy is to walk away. Resorting to put-downs or a well-chosen Italian swear word invariably makes matters worse. At night it is best to avoid areas such as the Cascine, the streets around the station and Santa Maria Novella. On trains, choose a compartment with other women.

Tourist offices

Visit a tourist office early in your stay to collect free information: maps, lists of events, museum opening hours and charges. The most convenient office in Florence is the one close to the Duomo and the Palazzo Medici-Riccardi at Via Cavour 1r (tel: 276 0381or 290 832/3). Details of other tourist offices in the city appear on page 186, and details of offices in other Tuscan towns appear on the relevant pages of the Tuscany A-Z section (pages 192–249). There is at least one tourist office open in Florence daily all year (see page 186 for exact times) . Elsewhere, especially in villages, they may close in the afternoon out of season.

Italian State Tourist Offices abroad

Australia and New Zealand Orient Overseas Building, Suite 202, 32 Bridge Street, Sydney, NSW 2000 (tel: 02/247 7836)

Canada 1 Place Ville Marie, Montréal, Québec H3B 3M9 (tel: 514/866 7667)

Irish Republic 47 Merrion Street, Dublin 2 (tel: 01–666 397)

United Kingdom 1 Princes Street, London W1 8AY (tel: 0171–408 1254)

United States 630 5th Avenue, Suite 1565, Rockefeller Center, New York NY 10111 (tel: 212/245 4822).

A postcard home from the Ponte Vecchio

As an aid to planning your time in Florence, this chart gives the opening hours for the city's most important galleries, museums, and churches.

Page		Mon–Sat	Sun	Closed
Galleries and museums				
52	Accademia	8.30-6.50	8.30–1.50	Mon
56	Bargello	8.30–1.50	8.30–1.50	Mon*
135	Biblioteca Laurenziana	9–1	—	Sun
146	Cappella Brancacci	10–5	1–5	Tue
64	Cappelle Medicee	8.30–1.50	8.30–1.50	Mon*
68	Casa Buonarroti	9.30–1.30	9.30–1.30	Tue
69	Casa di Dante	9–6 (winter 10–4)	9–6 (winter 10–4)	Tue
100	Cenacolo di S Apollonia	8.30–1.50	8.30–1.50	Mon
102	Chiostro dello Scalzo	9–1 Mon and Thu	—	Fri to Sun, Tue, Wed
84	Forte di Belvedere	9–8 or dusk if earlier	9–8 or dusk if earlier	
87	Museo Archeologico	9–2	9–1	Mon/Sun
88	Museo Bardini	9–2	8–1	Wed
85	Museo Botanico	*closed temporarily*		
90	Museo della Casa	*closed for restoration*		
92	Museo di Firenze com'era	9–2	8–1	Thu
93	Museo della Fondazione Horne	9–1	—	Sun
121	Museo di Fotografo Alinari	10–7.30 (11.30PM Fri and Sat)	10–7.30	Wed
120	Museo Marino Marini	10–5 (winter 10–1)	10–7 (winter 10–1)	Tue and Aug
85	Museo di Mineralogia	9–1	—	Sun
96	Museo dell'Opera del Duomo	9–6.50; (winter 9–6.20)	—	Sun
143	Museo dell'Opera di Santa Croce and Capella dei Pazzi	10–12.30, 2.30–6.30 (winter 3–5)	10–12.30, 2.30–6.30 (winter 3–5)	Wed
85	Museo di Paleontologia	9–1 Tue to Thu, Sat; 2–6 Mon	—	Sun, Fri
100	Museo di San Marco	8.30–1.50	8.30–1.50	Mon*
152	Museo di Santa Maria Novella	9–2	8–1	Fri

Page		Mon–Sat	Sun	Closed
102	Museo Stibbert	9–1	9–1	Thu
104	Museo di Storia della Scienza	9.30–1; (also 2–5 Mon, Wed, Fri)	—	Sun
108	Museo Zoologico– La Specola	9–1	9–1	Wed
	Waxworks	9–12 (Tue and Sat)		
112	Ospedale degli Innocenti	8.30–2	8.30–1	Wed
113	Palazzo Medici-Riccardi	9–1, 3–6	9–1	Wed
116	Palazzo Pitti	8.30–6.50	9–2	Mon*
122	Palazzo Vecchio	9–7	8–1	Thu
160	Uffizi, Galleria degli	9–7	9–2	Mon

269

Churches

Page		Mon–Sat	Sun	Closed
55	Badia Fiorentina	Under long-term restoration—check times locally		
60	Battistero	1.30–6.30	8.30–1.30	—
63	Campanile	9–6.50 (winter 9–4.20)	9–6.50 (winter 9–4.20)	—
	Cappella Brancacci	see under Galleries and museums opposite		
	Cappelle Medicee	see under Galleries and museums opposite		
76	Duomo	10–5	10–5	—
76	Crypt	10–5	—	Sun
80	Dome	10–5	—	Sun
110	Orsanmichele	9–12, 4–6	9–12, 4–6	1st/last Mon of month
134	Sagrestia Vecchia (San Lorenzo)	10–11.45 (Mon Wed, Fri, Sat); 4–5.45 (Tues, Thu)	—	Sun
132	San Lorenzo	7–12, 3.30–6.30	8–12.30, 3–6.30	—
136	San Miniato al Monte	8–12, 2–7 (winter 8–12, 2.30–6)	8–12, 2–7 (winter 8–12, 2.30–6)	—
138	Santa Croce	8–6.30 (winter 8–12.30, 3–6.30)	8–12.30 (not winter), 3–6.30	—
148	Santa Maria Novella	7–12.15, 3–6 (Mon–Fri) 7–12.15, 3–5 (Sat)	7–12.15, 3–6	—
154	Santa Trinita	8–12, 4–6	4–6	—
155	SS Annunziata	7.30–12.30, 4–6.30	7.30–12.30, 4–6.30	—
157	Santo Spirito	8–12, 4–8	8–12, 4–8	Wed 4–8

*open same hours 1st, 3rd, 5th Mon of each month

Glossary

These pages explain some of the artistic and architectural terms used in the book.

aedicule	decorative niche framed by columns
ambo	simple medieval pulpit, often with marble inlay
anfiteatro	amphitheatre
apse	semicircular recess behind church altar
architrave	a supporting beam above a column
atrium	inner entrance court of early house or church
baldacchino	a canopy on columns, usually over a church altar
battistero	baptistery
campanile	bell tower
campo	square
camposanto	cemetery
cantoria	choir loft
capital	top of a column
cappella	chapel
cartoon	full-size preliminary sketch for a fresco or painting
chancel	part of church containing altar
chiaroscuro	exaggerated light and shade effects in a painting
chiesa	church
chiostro	cloister
colombarium	part of a tomb, with wall niches for the dead
comune	administrative department of an Italian town, city, or village
confessio	crypt beneath a church's high altar
cornice	top of a classical façade
cortile	courtyard
Cosmati work	marble with inlay of coloured stones and glass
crypt	burial place of a church, usually under the altar
cupola	dome
diptych	two-panelled painting
duomo	cathedral
fresco	wall-painting on wet plaster (see pages 98–9)
graffito	incised decoration on a building or wall
intarsia	mosaic or inlay work in wood or stone
loggia	roofed gallery or outside balcony
lunette	semicircular space above door, window or vaulting

Italy's finest piazza: the Campo in Siena

Maestà	representation of the Madonna and Child in majesty
matroneum	women's gallery in early churches
narthex	vestibule of a church
nave	central space of a church
palazzo	palace, large house, or apartment block
pendentives	four curved triangular elements on piers supporting a dome or cupola
peristyle	courtyard surrounded by colonnades
piano nobile	main floor of a palace
piazza	open space or square in a town or village
Pietà	image of the Madonna mourning the dead Christ
pietra serena	a light-coloured stone
pietre dure	semiprecious stones such as agate and amethyst
pinacoteca	picture gallery
porta	gate
portico	covered doorway
predella	small panel below the main part of an altar-piece
putto	cherubic child in painting or sculpture
sinopia	wall sketch for a fresco
stele	vertical headstone
stemma	coat of arms
teatro	theatre
terme	baths

The courtyard of the Palazzo Vecchio, with decoration by Vasari

tondo	round painting or relief
torre	tower
transept	transverse arms of a church
tribune	raised gallery in a church or the apse of a basilica
triptych	painting on three panels
trompe l'oeil	tricks using perspective to create the illusion of depth in a painting

Stemme (the coats of arms of those who held public office) are found on many buildings

Italians respond well to foreigners who make an effort to speak their language. Many Italians speak a little English, and upscale hotels and restaurants have multilingual staff.

All Italian words are pronounced as written, with each vowel and consonant sounded. The letter **c** is hard, as in 'cat', except when followed by **i** or **e**, when it becomes the soft ch of 'children'. The same applies to **g** when followed by **i** or **e** – soft in *giardino*, as in the English 'giant'; hard in *gatto*, as in 'gate'. Words ending in **o** are almost always masculine in gender (plural ending –**i**); those ending in **a** are feminine (plural –**e**). In the Floretine dialect, hard '**c**' is often pronounced as '**h**', so that **cosa** (what?/thing) is 'hosa'.

Use the polite, third person (*lei*) to speak to strangers: use the second person (*tu*) to friends or children.

Italians usually appreciate visitors' attempts to speak their language, so don't be afraid to try out a few phrases

272

Courtesies

good morning **buon giorno**
good afternoon/good evening **buona sera**
good night **buona notte**
hello/goodbye (informal) **ciao**
hello (answering the telephone) **pronto**
goodbye **arrivederci**
please **per favore**
thank you (very much) **grazie (mille)**
you're welcome **prego**
how are you? (polite/informal) **come sta/stai?**
I'm fine **sto bene**
I'm sorry **mi dispiace**
excuse me/I beg your pardon **mi scusi**
excuse me (in a crowd) **permesso**
you're welcome **prego**

Basic vocabulary

yes **sì**
no **no**
I do not understand **non ho capito**
left/right **sinistra/destra**
entrance **entrata**
exit **uscita**
open **aperto**
closed **chiuso**
good/bad **buono/cattivo**
big/small **grande/piccolo**
with/without **con/senza**
more/less **più/meno**
near/far **vicino/lontano**
hot/cold **caldo/freddo**
early/late **presto/ritardo**
here/there **qui/là**
now/later **adesso/più tardi**
today/tomorrow **oggi/domani**
yesterday **ieri**
how much is it? **quant'è?**
when **quando**
do you have …? **avete …?**

Emergencies

help! **aiuto!**
Where is the nearest telephone?
Dov'è il telefono più vicino?
There has been an accident.
C'è stato un incidente.
Call the police.
Chiamate la polizia.
Call a doctor/an ambulance.
Chiamate un medico/un'ambulanza.
first aid **pronto soccorso**
Where is the nearest hospital?
Dov'è l'ospedale più vicino?

Hotels and Restaurants

The recommended hotels in this section have been divided into three price categories:
(£) = budget: a double room for under L125,000
(££) = moderate: a double room for L125,000–250,000
(£££) = expensive: a double room for over L250,000
Telephone numbers are given in the form you would use if phoning in Florence. Note that all Italian hotels and classifed by law from five star (luxury) down to one star. Prices are also set by law, and must be displayed at reception, and in each room. Restaurant recommendations begin on page 278 and, for Florence, a selection of cafés and bars is also given.

HOTELS

FLORENCE

Central covers the area immediately around Piazza del Duomo and Piazza della Signoria. The other districts are **West**, **East**, and **North** (of Piazza del Duomo) and **Oltrarno** (south of the Arno).

Central

Bavaria (£) (one star)
Borgo degli Albizzi 26 tel: 055 234 0313
Reliable cheap option in a 16th-century palazzo, but becomes booked quickly.
Brunelleschi (£££)
Piazza Santa Elisabetta 3 tel: 055 290 311
Fine new four-star hotel incorporating beautifully converted medieval tower; in a quiet location behind Via dei Calzaiuoli.
Della Signoria (£££)
Via delle Terme 1 tel: 055 214 530
Modern three-star hotel with views of the Ponte Vecchio from upper floors. Nice breakfast terrace.
Helvetia e Bristol (£££)
Via de' Pescioni 2 tel: 055 87 814
Close to the Duomo, this five-star hotel dates from the 18th century, but was completely restored in 1989 with the aim of creating the finest of all Florence's central hotels. It has largely succeeded, with its elegant and exclusive atmosphere, attention to period detail, evocative wood and marble bar, and a high-quality in-house restaurant. Rooms are large and well-appointed, and most of the marble-tiled bathrooms have hot tubs. Very expensive.
Hermitage (££)
Vicolo Marzio 1, Piazza del Pesce
tel: 055 287 216
Very well-known three-star hotel on the Arno overlooking the Ponte Vecchio. Fine terrace. Rooms on the street are double-glazed but the rooms to the rear are quieter.
Maxim (£) (one-star)
Via de' Medici 4 tel: 055 217 474
Immediately behind Via dei Calzaiuoli, a minute from the Duomo. Very friendly, multilingual owners. Many quiet if basic off-street rooms.

Pendini (££)
Via degli Strozzi 2 tel: 055 211 170
Busy but well-run and friendly 42-room three-star hotel near Piazza della Repubblica.
Porta Rossa (££)
Via Porta Rossa 19 tel: 055 287 551
A wonderful, old-fashioned three-star hotel founded in the 14th century, with large if often spartan rooms and fine period decoration. Byron and Stendhal both stayed here.
Savoy (£££)
Piazza della Repubblica 7 tel: 055 283 313
Most central of the city's big four-star hotels: expensive, efficient, but rather impersonal.

West

Aprile (££) (three-star)
Via della Scala 6 tel: 055 216 237
Excellently converted former Medici home with many original features. Some rooms are modern, some medieval in flavour. There are some cheaper rooms, but these are very small.
Beacci Tornabuoni (£££) (three-star)
Via de' Tornabuoni 3 tel: 055 212 645
Hotel on the top three floors of a 14th-century *palazzo*. Rooms vary in quality – some are small and sparse. Dull dining room but excellent terrace for breakfast and drinks.
Bretagna (£–££)
Lungarno Corsini 6 tel: 055 289 618
Airy two-star rooms in charming pensione with excellent view over the Arno.
Excelsior (£££)
Piazza Ognissanti 3 tel: 055 264 201
The city's grandest hotel: old-world, spacious, and 158 comfortable five-star rooms, some of which overlook the river. The piazza, though, is not one of Florence's prettiest. Very expensive.
Grand Hotel (five-star)
Piazza Ognissanti 1 tel: 055 288 781
Smaller (107 rooms) but otherwise similar to the Excelsior opposite. Rooms are often more modern but they have less character. Luxurious and very expensive.
Kraft (£££)
Via Solferino 2 tel: 055 284 273
Quiet, comfortable, four-star rooms in choice of modern or traditional styles. Mannered rather than charming atmosphere. Fine upper terrace, moderate restaurant, and small rooftop swimming pool with grand views.
La Mia Casa (£)
Piazza Santa Maria Novella 23
tel: 055 213 061
Popular and probably the best of the many one-star budget options on this piazza (21 rooms).
Principe (£££)
Lungarno Vespucci 34 tel: 055 284 848
Small, elegantly old-world four-star. Many of the 20 rooms have terraces overlooking the Arno. Small garden. Popular with US visitors.
Residenza (££)
Via de' Tornabuoni 8 tel: 055 218 684
Fine, no-frills old-world three-star hotel on the top four floors of a 17th-century palazzo. Good value given the location, though street-front rooms can be noisy (24 rooms).

East

Balestri (££)
Piazza Mentana 7 tel: 055 214 743
Spacious and comfortable if short on style, this welcoming three-star hotel has been in the same family over four generations since 1888. It stands on a piazza just off the Arno between the Uffizi and Santa Croce (50 rooms).

Hotel J & J (£££)
Via di Mezzo 20 tel: 055 234 5005
An intimate and quiet little four-star hotel in a 16th-century monastery close to Santa Croce. Stylish and tasteful rooms are all different, some with painted ceilings, others with terraces, small courtyard, or views over the rooftops; attracts select clients from the world of fashion and design (18 rooms).

Liana (££)
Via V Alfieri 18 tel: 055 245 303/4
Old two-star villa hotel in the former British Embassy (1864–70). Fading and rather tastelessly decorated, but good value. Most of the 18 rooms face onto a peaceful garden.

Plaza & Lucchesi (£££)
Lungarno della Zecca Vecchia 38 tel: 055 26236
Stylish four-star hotel on the Arno. Modern rooms with good bathrooms (97 rooms).

Regency (£££)
Piazza Massimo D'Azeglio 3 tel: 055 245 247
Intimate five-star luxury and exclusive clublike hotel with slick, rather vividly decorated rooms (though some are small for the price). The quiet piazza is 15 minutes' walk from the centre of Florence.

Santa Croce (£)
Via Bentaccordi 3 tel: 055 217 000
Inexpensive, small and modern two-star hotel near Santa Croce, with just 10 rooms.

North

Ariston (£)
Via Fiesolana 40 tel: 055 247 6980
Inexpensive two-star choice east of Piazza della Santissima Annunziata with 20 rooms.

Le Due Fontane (££)
Piazza della Santissima Annunziata 14 tel: 055 210 185
A comfortable and modern, if rather bland, three-star hotel on one of Florence's best-known piazzas (57 rooms).

Loggiato dei Serviti (££–£££)
Piazza della Santissima Annunziata 3 tel: 055 289 592
A lovely three-star hotel in the vaulted interior of the Servites' 16th-century confraternity. The refined rooms are calm, cool, and spacious. Advance booking is essential at busy times of the year.

Monna Lisa (£££)
Borgo Pinti 27 tel: 055 247 9751
Excellent public spaces belie the quality of the private rooms in this popular but now overpriced four-star hotel, which is part of a 15th-century Renaissance palace. Some of the 30 rooms overlook a courtyard and garden.

Morandi alla Crocetta (££)
Via Laura 50 tel: 055 234 4747
Small, atmospheric, and charming family-run three-star hotel in part of the old 16th-century Crocetta convent. Warm welcome and good value. Just 10 rooms.

Rudy (£)
Via San Gallo 51 tel: 055 475 519
Quieter than some of the cheap one-star hotels in this area (notably those on nearby Via Cavour). No private bathrooms in double rooms. 1am curfew. 12 rooms.

Sampaoli (£)
Via San Gallo 14 tel: 055 284 834
Much the same as the Rudy, but without the curfew. (One-star; 12 rooms.)

Splendor (£–££)
Via San Gallo 30 tel: 055 483 427
Reasonably priced, modest family-run three-star hotel with 31 bright, if unexceptional, rooms within walking distance of San Marco and the Accademia.

Oltrarno

Annalena (££)
Via Romana 34 tel: 055 222 402
Long-established, famous, and much sought-after *pensione*-style three-star hotel – part of an old Medici *palazzo* – situated opposite the Boboli gardens. Beautiful public rooms. Most of the 20 large bedrooms boast antiques and painted furniture; some have terraces and pleasant garden views.

Bandini Sorelle (£–££)
Piazza Santo Spirito 9 tel: 055 215 308
This old-fashioned one-star hotel's charm, value for money, and location mean that its 10 rooms are often fully booked months in advance.

Lungarno (££–£££)
Borgo San Jacopo 14 tel: 055 272 611
A modern four-star hotel occupying a new building and the 13th-century Torre Marsili. The 66 rooms are cosy and comfortable; 14 have river views; 13 are in the old tower.

Pitti Palace (££–£££)
Via Barbadori 2 tel: 055 239 8711
This modern and delightful 72-room three-star hotel, part of an upscale chain, is a favourite with American and British visitors. Lovely sitting room and terrace, but bedrooms are not the best you could obtain for this price, and some can be noisy.

Silla (£–££)
Via de'Renai 5 tel: 055 234 2888
Fine old *palazzo* on the river, with a superb terrace looking over the Arno and a small park. Good value three-star with 32 rooms.

Villa Cora (£££)
Viale Machiavelli 18 tel: 055 229 8451
Although it is some way from the centre (there is a free shuttle service), this five-star luxury hotel is among the Florentine élite. A fine villa in its own grounds, with stunning décor and attentive service, it also has very high prices (48 rooms).

275

Hotels and Restaurants

TUSCANY

Arezzo

Astoria (£)
Via Guido Monaco 54 tel: 0575 24 361
Central two-star hotel close to San Francesco.
Cecco (£)
Corso Italia 215–17 tel: 0575 320 986
Extremely convenient and central if rather
bland two-star hotel.
Continentale (££)
Piazza Guido Monaco 7 tel: 0575 320 251
Modern, comfortable, and convenient three-
star hotel.
Ostello Villa Severi (£)
Via Redi tel: 0575 299 047
HI youth hostel in an old villa out of town (bus
No 4 from the train station).

Chianti

Castello di Spaltenna (££–£££)
Via Spaltenna, Gaiole in Chianti
tel: 0577 749 483
Very pretty converted monastery just outside
Gaiole; popular restaurant.
Relais Fattoria Vignale (££–£££)
Via Pianigiani, Radda in Chianti
tel: 0577 738 300
Highly elegant hotel with renowned restaurant.
Located in a villa on a wine estate.
Salivolpi (££)
Via Fiorentina, Castellina in Chianti
tel: 0577 740 484
Welcoming family-run hotel.
Tenuta di Ricavo (££–£££)
*4km south of Castellina in Chianti on San
Donato road tel: 0577 740 221*
Medieval hamlet transformed into a fine
Swiss-run hotel.

Cortona

Athens (£)
Via San Antonio tel: 0575 630 508
One-star budget option.
Italia (£)
Via Ghibellina 5 tel: 0575 630 254
Reasonable three-star hotel on one of
Cortona's nicer streets.
Ostello San Marco (£)
Via Maffei 57 tel: 0575/601 392
Central HI youth hostel.
Sabrina (£)
Via Roma 37 tel: 0575 630 397
Three-star facilities in tiny, central hotel.
San Luca (££)
Piazza Garibaldi 1
tel: 0575 630 460 or 0575 630 504
Near a busy piazza on the southern edge of
town; the hillside setting guarantees fine views
from the reception areas, but rooms are simple
and straightforward.
San Michele (££)
Via Guelfa 15 tel: 0575 604 348
Fine four-star and Cortona's top choice if price
is not important.

Fiesole

Villa Bonelli (££)
Via F Poeti 1 tel: 055 59 513 or 598 941
One of Fiesole's more intimate hotels; a three-
star with 20 modestly but nicely furnished
rooms, some with fine views of Florence.
Villa San Michele (£££)
Via Doccia 4 tel: 055 59 451
This is one of Italy's most luxurious four-star
hotels. The villa, set in its own extensive
grounds and with a swimming pool, is said to
have been designed by Michelangelo. While
some of the 28 rooms are small and somewhat simple given their price, meals can be
taken outdoors in a glorious loggia with
stunning views over Florence.
Villa Sorriso (£–££)
Via Gramsci 21 tel: 055 59 027
Finding a cheap place to stay in Fiesole is a
problem; this one-star establishment is the
most reasonable of those close to the centre.

Lucca

Diana (£)
Via del Molinetto 11 tel: 0583 492 202
First choice among the cheaper two-star
hotels. Close to the Duomo.
La Luna (££)
Corte Compagni 12 tel: 0583 493 634
Three-star hotel nicely located just west of
Piazza Anfiteatro.
Piccolo Hotel Puccini (££)
Via de Poggio 9 tel: 0583 55421
Modern rooms in a Renaissance building at the
heart of the historic quarter of the city.
Universo (££)
Piazza del Giglio 1, near Piazza Napoleone
tel: 0583 493 678
An air of old-world, slightly faded elegance per-
vades Lucca's top central hotel: Standards
(and views) vary from room to room.

Montepulciano

Duomo (£)
Via San Donato 14 tel: 0578 757 473
The best mid-range choice.
Il Borghetto (££)
Via Borgo Buio 7 tel: 0578 757 354
Montepulciano's top hotel; located off the
Corso near Piazza Michelozzo.
Marzocco (£)
Piazza Savonarola 18
tel: 0578 757 530 or 0578 757 262
A good mid-range choice situated just inside
the town walls at the lower end of the Corso.

Monteriggioni

Hotel Monteriggioni (££–£££)
Via Maggio 4 tel: 0577 305 009
This four star is one of the finest hotels in this
part of Tuscany: beautifully appointed and
located at the heart of one of Italy's most perfectly preserved medieval villages: a good
out-of-town alternative to staying in Siena.

Pienza

Dal Falco (£)
Piazza Dante Alighieri 7 tel: 0578 748 551
A restaurant with a few cheap rooms to rent.
Il Chiostro di Pienza (££)
Corso Rossellino 26 tel: 0578 748 400
A conversion of the former San Francesco monastery, this beautiful three-star hotel has modern rooms, good views, and a cloister. Patches of fresco remain in parts of the hotel.
Il Corsignano (£)
Via della Madonnina 11 tel: 0578 748 501
Pienza's best choice as a mid-range (three-star) hotel: it is modern and is situated just outside of the town.

Pisa

Amalfitana (£)
Via Roma 44 tel: 050 29 000
Pleasant and well-located two-star hotel just south of the Campo dei Miracoli.
Grand Hotel Duomo (££)
Via Santa Maria 94 tel: 050 561 894
This four-star establishment is the best of the town's modern and luxurious hotels if you wish to do Pisa in style.
Gronchi (£)
Piazza Arcivescovado 1 tel: 050 561 823
First choice among the cheaper hotels near the Campo. A one-star with 23 rooms.
Jolly Hotel dei Cavalieri (££)
Piazza della Stazione 2 tel: 050 43 290
Modern four-star hotel convenient for the station (and for the airport) but not for much else.

Pistoia

Firenze (£)
Via Curtatone e Montanara 42 tel: 0573 23 141 or 21660
Pistoia's only two-star hotel; quiet and close to Piazza del Duomo.
Il Convento (££)
Via San Quirico 33, Santomato tel: 0573 452 651 or 453 578
Peaceful hotel 5km northeast of Pistoia near Ponte Nuovo. A converted 18th-century convent, with a swimming pool.
Patria (£)
Via Crispi 6–8 tel: 0573 25 187 or 21 247 or 368 168
Three-star hotel conveniently situated between the centre and the train station.

Prato
Flora (£)
Via Cairoli 31 tel: 0574 33 521
Modern, middling three-star near Santa Maria dei Carceri.
President (££)
Via Simintendi 20 tel: 0574 30 251
A four-star hotel, aimed at business people.
San Marco (£)
Piazza San Marco 48 tel: 0574 21 321
Convenient three-star hotel located between the train station and Castello.

Stella d'Italia (£)
Piazza del Duomo 8 tel: 0574 27 910
Perfect position for a formerly grand but now faded, central, two-star hotel.

San Gimignano

Bel Soggiorno (££)
Via San Giovanni 91 tel: 0577 940 375
There is little to choose between this three-star hotel and the Leon Bianco – though you may have to eat all your meals here in high season.
La Cisterna (££)
Piazza della Cisterna 24 tel: 0577 940 328
The oldest and perhaps the nicest three-star hotel in San Gimignano.
Leon Bianco (££)
Piazza della Cisterna 13 tel: 0577 941 294
A fine old hotel on the main square.
Le Vecchie Mura (£)
Via Piandornella 15 tel: 0577 940 270
One of the best budget choices after the youth hostel; friendly management and rooms – some with views – above a restaurant in the south-east corner of the village.
Ostello della Gioventù (£)
Via delle Fonti 1 tel: 0577 941 991
HI youth hostel in the north of the village.
Villa San Paolo (££–£££)
tel: 0577 955 100
One of several country villas dotted around the countryside close to San Gimignano; located on the road for Certaldo, 4km north of the village. Beautiful hillside setting,; ample terraces, tennis court and swimming pool.

Siena

Athena (££)
Via P Mascagni 55 tel: 0577 286 313
Modern three-star hotel just outside the city walls to the south. Most rooms have views.
Duomo (££)
Via Stalloreggi 38 tel: 0577 289 088
Ideally placed and perfectly comfortable three-star hotel situated south of the Duomo.
Il Palio (£)
Piazza del Sale 19 tel: 0577 281 131
Large two-star (a better chance of vacancies).
Locanda Garibaldi (£)
Via Giovanni Duprè 18 tel: 0577 284 204
Modest but excellent and budget-friendly choice just off the Campo.
Palazzo Ravizza (££–£££)
Pian dei Mantellini 34 tel: 0577 280 462
Quiet three-star hotel at the southern end of Via Stalloreggi, but the owners usually insist on full board (three meals a day).
Piccolo Hotel Etruria (££)
Via delle Donzelle 1–3 tel: 0577 288 088
Central, two-star hotel just off Via di Città.

Volterra

Etruria (£)
Via Matteotti 32 tel: 0588/87 377
A three-star on the main street. Probably the best overall choice, with good value for money.

Nazionale (££)
Via dei Marchesi 11 tel: 0588 86 284
D H Lawrence stayed in this three-star while researching *Etruscan Places*. Modernised since then, but rooms are small.
San Lino (££–£££)
Via San Lino 26 tel: 0588 85 250
Volterra's best hotel; four-star.
Villa Nencini (££)
Borgo Santo Stefano 55 tel: 0588 86 386
Pleasant hotel with pool and garden, just outside the city walls.

RESTAURANTS

FLORENCE

Most of the restaurants listed are within 10 minutes' walk of Piazza del Duomo. The areas covered are **North**, **West**, and **East** (of Piazza del Duomo and Via dei Calzaiuoli) and **Oltrarno** (south of the Arno).

North

Antellesi (£)
Via Faenza 9r tel: 055 216 990
Inexpensive, charming, and inviting place close to the Cappelle Medicee. Simple wooden tables and easygoing atmosphere. Arrive early to be sure of a table. *Closed* Sun.
Beatrice (££–£££)
Via del Proconsolo 31r tel: 055 239 8123).
The Italian-International cuisine here is not exceptional, but the dining room and its glorious painted wooden ceilings is probably one of the most beautiful places to eat in the city.
Cafaggi (££)
Via Guelfa 35r tel: 055 294 989
A two-roomed *trattoria* that has been in the Cafaggi family for 60 years. Many ingredients, such as wine and olive oil, come from the family's Chianti estate. Fish dishes are good.
Closed Sun evening, Mon lunch, and August.
La Taverna del Bronzino (££–£££)
Via delle Ruote 27r tel: 055 495 220
Oriented toward expense accounts: top-notch cooking, rarefied but unstuffy atmosphere. *Closed* Sun.
Le Fonticine (££)
Via Nazionale 79r tel: 055 282 106
A noted Florentine institution whose owners give added refinement to classic local dishes such as *cervello fritto* (fried brains), and *pappardelle di cinghiale* (thick ribbon pasta and wild boar).*Closed* Sun, Mon, and August.
Mario (£)
Via Rosina 2r tel: 055 218 550
No dessert or coffee, just basic Tuscan fare served to students and market traders. Arrive early. *Open* for lunch only. *Closed* Sun.
Palle d'Oro (£)
Via Sant'Antonino 43r tel: 055 288 383
Simple and spartan, but cheap and well-cooked basic dishes attract large lunchtime crowds.

Sabatini (£££)
Via Panzani 9a tel: 055 282 802
Formerly one of Florence's top restaurants, serving Italian-International cuisine. Still superstylish, but now only occasionally superlative. Excellent service and cellar, but very expensive. *Closed* Mon.

West

Al Lume di Candela (££–£££)
Via delle Terme 23r
  tel: 055 294 566 or 055 283 815)
'By Candlelight' has a reputation for romantic dining *à deux*, but the smoochy setting and cooking are international rather than Florentine in flavour. *Closed* Sun, lunch on Mon and Aug.
Belle Donne (£)
Via delle Belle Donne 16r tel: 055 238 2609
Tiny and wonderfully decorated place. Shared wooden tables with paper tablecloths; daily menus written on a blackboard and accomplished Tuscan cooking. *Closed* weekends and August.
Cantinetta Antinori (££)
Palazzo Antinori, Piazza Antinori 3r
tel: 055 292 234 or 055 235 9827
Definitely a place for a treat – but be sure to dress up. Owned by one of Tuscany's oldest and most famous wine families, the restaurant's exquisite panelled salons form part of a 15th-century *palazzo* and are always filled with immaculately groomed Florentines. *Closed* weekends and August.
Cocco Lezzone (£££)
Via Parioncino 26r tel: 055 287 178
A famous, rather chic restaurant whose white-tiled dining room dates from the building's past use as a dairy. High prices and top-class Tuscan cooking, but tables are communal and you are expected to move on quickly. *Closed* Sun, four weeks in July and August
Il Contadino (£)
Via Palazzuolo 71r tel: 055 238 2673
A students' and backpackers' haven: no concessions to decorative niceties, but some of the cheapest food in the city. *Closed* Sun.
Il Latini (£)
Via Palchetti 6r tel: 055 210 916
An always full Florentine institution, but not to all tastes: communal tables, rowdy atmosphere, and cheap Tuscan classics. *Closed* Mon, Tue lunch, and August.
Oliviero (££–£££)
Via delle Terme 51r tel: 055 287 643
Currently one of the city's best restaurants. Cooking is Tuscan, but with an innovative twist, and fish dishes, which are relatively unusual in Florence, are also sometimes available. *Closed* Mon, August and lunch daily.
Rose's (£)
Via del Parione 26r tel: 055 287 090
A bar-restaurant whose bright, modern appearance makes an interesting change from the predominantly medieval interior of most Florentine restaurants. Good for drinks, snacks, light lunches and evening drinks. *Closed* Sun.

East

Acquacotta (£)
Via dei Pilastri 51r tel: 055 242 907
Inexpensive, three-roomed eating place with
reliable Tuscan dishes. *Closed* Tue evening,
Wed, and three weeks over July and August.

Alle Murate (££–£££)
Via Ghibellina 52r tel: 055 240 618
One of the city's rising stars. An excellent
choice for innovative and very good cooking, as
well as for its noted cellar. Reasonable prices
(at present), with good set-price menus. *Open*
evenings only. *Closed* Mon and August.

Baldovino (£–££)
Via San Giuseppe 22r tel: 055 241 773
An informal and pleasantly modern-looking
restaurant run that appeals to Florentines and
foreigners alike. Excellent pizzas or full Tuscan
meals. *Closed* Mon.

Buca dell'Orafo (££)
Volta dei Girolami 28r tel: 055 213 619
Fair prices and a simple, friendly *trattoria* feel
ensure this place is always packed. *Closed*
Sun, Mon, and August.

Caffè Italiano (£–££)
Via Isola delle Stinche 11–13r
tel: 055 289 368
A choice of three fine eating places under one
roof, all with airy wood-beamed rooms and
terra-cotta floors: an inexpensive wine bar with
snacks, a more formal retaurant, and a smaller
trattoria that is perfect for lunch. *Closed* Mon.

Cantina Barbagianni (££)
Via Sant'Egidio 12 tel: 055 248 0508
A cellar bar restaurant with interesting Tuscan
food and courteous service. *Closed* Sat and
Sun (Sun and Mon lunch in winter plus two
weeks in February).

Cibrèo (££)
Via dei Macci 118r tel: 055 234 1100
This well-known place off the Sant'Ambrogio
market has spawned a similarly well-executed
café, delicatessen and cheaper *bistro* in the
same area (entered from Piazza Ghiberti 35r).
Closed Sun and Mon and August.

Da Ganino (££)
Piazza dei Cimatori 4r tel: 055 214 125
Small, old-fashioned interior, safe cooking, and
a few tables on the tiny piazza outside for outdoor eating. *Closed* Sun.

Da Pennello (£)
Via Dante Alighieri 4r tel: 055 294 848
Cheap and cheerful spot now so well known it
is often hard to find a table. Book ahead to
enjoy the famous *antipasti* or the summer terrace. *Closed* Sun evening and Mon and August.

Enoteca Pinchiorri (£££)
Via Ghibellina 87 tel: 055 242 777
Often described as Italy's best restaurant and
wine cellar (reputedly 80,000 bottles of Italian
and French vintages). Lovely 15th-century
setting and award-winning cooking. *Closed*
Sun, and Mon and Wed lunch, plus August.

La Baraonda (££)
Via Ghibellina 67r tel: 055 234 1171
Currently one of the city's most popular restau-
rants. *Closed* Sun, Mon lunch and August.

Paoli (£–££)
Via dei Tavolini 12r tel: 055 216 215
The food here is nothing special, but the
vaulted and frescoed medieval dining room is
one of the city's most atmospheric. Book to
avoid disappointment. *Closed* Tue.

Oltrarno

Borgo Antico (££)
Piazza Santo Spirito 6r
tel: 055 210 437 or 214 175
A pleasant restaurant with outside tables in
one of Florence's most charming squares.
Book in summer. *Closed* Mon.

Camillo (££–£££)
Borgo San Jacopo 57r tel: 055 212 427
Lively, family-run place of long-standing appeal
to foreign (especially US) visitors. The cooking
is consistently good. *Closed* Wed and Thu.

Da Omero (£)
Via Pian dei Giullari 11r tel: 055 220 053
A long way to come, usually full of foreigners,
and food is only of middling quality, but worth it
for outdoor eating in summer with a lovely view
across the city. *Closed* Tue.

Il Barone di Porta Romana (£–££)
Via Romana 123 tel: 055 220 585
Elegant but relaxed ambience, sensible prices,
and a large garden for summer *al fresco* eating. *Closed* Sun.

Osteria del Cinghiale Bianco (£–££)
Borgo San Jacopo 43r tel: 055 215 706
Popular with visitors for the robust food and
the setting – a 14th-century tower near the
Ponte Vecchio. *Closed* Tue and Wed.

Quattro Leoni (£–££)
Via dei Vellutini 1r tel: 055 218 562
Three informal rustic dining rooms with vast
wooden beams, rough-hewn stone walls and
big modern paintings. Outdoor tables in summer. *Closed* August and Wed in winter.

Ruggero (£)
Via Senese 89, beyond Porta Romana
tel: 055 220 542
Traditional *trattoria* with reliable and occasionally exceptional food. *Closed* Tue and Wed.

CAFÉS AND BARS

FLORENCE

Caffè Cibrèo
Via del Verrocchio 5r
Cosy wood-panelled café with a handful of
tables. Top-notch *cornetti* and pastries.

Caffelatte
Via degli Alfani 39r
A former dairy that still sells milk, butter, and
cheese. Excellent for breakfast or lunch.

Donnini
Piazza della Repubblica 15
The most modest of this piazza's 'Big Four'
cafés (see pages 22–3).

Festival del Gelato
Via del Corso 75r
More than 100 flavours of ice-cream.

279

Hotels and Restaurants

Frilli
Via San Niccolò 57
Among the city's best ice-cream parlours.

Giacosa
Via de' Tornabuoni 83r
Favoured meeting place of those in the know. The birthplace of the *negroni* cocktail.

Gilli
Piazza della Repubblica 39r
Florence's oldest café, with belle-epoque interior. Renowned cocktails and *marrons glacés*.

Giubbe Rosse
Piazza della Repubblica 13–14r
Once full of literary types, now popular with eldery Florentines who come for the music.

Il Rifrullo
Via San Niccolò
Popular with young, well-groomed Florentines. *Open* until late. Garden open in the summer.

Il Triangolo delle Bermude
Via Nazionale 61r
Handy for the station. 'New wave' ice-cream in madly exotic flavours.

La Dolce Vita
Piazza del Carmine 5r
Chic postmodernist bar on one of Oltrarno's biggest squares. Quiet by day but packed with the young set late at night (Thurs from 11pm).

La Loggia
Piazzale Michelangelo 1
Big and busy and away from the centre, but famous for its classic view over the city.

Manaresi
Via de' Lamberti 16r
Considered by many to pour the best cup of coffee in the city. A large selection of delicious roast and ground coffee can be bought here.

Paszkowski
Piazza della Repubblica 6r
Grand café with piano music and the occasional chamber orchestra playing light melodies to elderly Florentines.

Perchè No?
Via dei Tavolini 19r (just off Via dei Calzaiuoli)
Centrally situated ice-cream parlour, excellent for *semi-freddi* and countless types of cone.

Procacci
Via de' Tornabuoni 64r
No tea or coffee here, only cold drinks and wine, but the draw is the famous truffle sandwiches (ask for *un panino tartufato*).

Rex Caffè
Via Fiesolana 23r
Young, hip, modern bar favoured as a rendezvous before and after a big night out.

Rivoire
Piazza della Signoria 5r
The city's best-known café. Expensive, but worth it at least once for its outdoor tables and the views onto Piazza della Signoria.

Uffizi
Galleria degli Uffizi
The Uffizi gallery's café offers grand views over the Piazza della Signoria.

Vivoli
Via Isola delle Stinche 7r (off Via Ghibellina between the Bargello and Santa Croce
Florence's most famous ice-cream parlour.

280

RESTAURANTS

TUSCANY

Arezzo

Antica Osteria L'Agania (£–££)
Via Mazzini 10 tel: 0575/25 381
An informal, attractive restaurant at the heart of the old town. Reliable, traditional cooking and generous portions. *Closed* Mon and June.

Buca di San Francesco (£)
Via San Francesco 1 tel: 0575/23 271
Average food in a popular medieval setting. *Closed* Mon evening and Tue.

Da Cecco (£)
Corso Italia 215 tel: 0575/356 730
Old-fashioned, long-established family restaurant with peasant dishes, including famed *ravioli*, from Arezzo's past. *Closed* Mon.

Chianti

Albergaccio di Castellina (££–£££)
Via Fiorentina 35, Castellina in Chianti tel: 0577/741 042
A small restaurant with pretty medieval dining room just outside the town. Fine regional cooking that uses excellent local ingredients.

Badia a Coltibuono (£)
Badia a Coltibuono, near Gaiole in Chianti tel: 0577/749 424
Famous restaurant in the grounds of an 11th-century convent that uses ingredients from its adjoining estate. Tours and cookery courses are available. *Closed* Mon.

Castello di Spaltenna (££)
Via Spaltenna, Gaiole in Chianti tel: 0577/749 483
Flower-filled medieval restaurant on the outskirts of Gaiole. *Closed* Mon and Tue lunch.

Pietrafitta (££)
Pietrafitta 10, Località Pietrafitta, near Castellina in Chianti tel: 0577/741 123
Run by American-Australian proprietors, cooking mixes Italian and international to fine effect. Good wine list with plenty of New World choices. *Closed* November to Easter.

Trattoria il Gabbiano (£)
Via Chiantigiana 4, Ponte a Gabbiano (north of Greve on the SS222 Florence –Siena road tel: 0558/21 127
Rustic Tuscan food and surroundings. Very good value. *Closed* Fri.

Vignale (££)
Via XX Settembre 2; Radda in Chianti tel: 0577/738 094
Delicious, traditional food served in comfortable, wine-cellar-like space. *Closed* Thu and from November to March.

Cortona

La Loggetta (£)
Piazza Pescheria 3 tel: 0575/630 575
This lovely medieval restaurant looks down onto Piazza della Repubblica. Cool, calm interior and traditional cooking. *Closed* Mon.

Osteria del Teatro (£–££)
Via Maffei 5 tel: 0575/630 556
A family-run restaurant with regional cooking.
Closed Wed and two weeks in November.
Tonino (££)
Piazza Garibaldi 1 tel: 0575/630 500
A serious place with serious prices, long menu,
and good cellar. *Closed* Tue plus Mon lunch.

Lucca

Buca di Sant' Antonio (£)
Via della Cervia 3 tel: 0583/55 881
Local specialities. *Closed* Mon, Sun evening
and three weeks in July and August.
Giulio in Pelleria (£)
Via delle Croce 47 tel: 0583/55 948
Bright, busy neighbourhood restaurant – be
sure to book ahead. *Closed* Sun and Mon.
La Mora (££–£££)
*Via Sesto di Moriano, Ponte a Moriano
tel: 0583/406 402*
The best restaurant in the area, with Lucchese
cooking. *Closed* Wed and 10 days in June.

Montepulciano

Cantuccio (£)
Via delle Cantine 1 tel: 0578/757 870
A good, choice for a simple meal in unpreten-
tious surroundings. *Closed* Mon.
Diva (£)
Via di Gracciano nel Corso tel: 0578/716 951
The best place to eat in a town with few top-
class restaurants. *Closed* Tue.

Pienza

Falco (£–££)
Piazza Dante 3 tel: 0578/748 551
Bustling, simple, family-run restaurant with
medieval ambience. *Closed* Fri.
Latte di Luna
Via San Carlo 2 tel: 0578/748 606
Amiable and easygoing *trattoria* with small out-
side terrace for *al fresco* eating.

Pisa

Ai Ristori dei Vecchi Macelli (££)
Via Volturno 49 tel: 050/20 424
Pleasant atmosphere, light Tuscan cooking.
Closed Wed plus Sun lunch and August.
Osteria dei Cavalieri (£)
Via San Frediano 16 tel: 050 580 858
Simple, local dishes in a pleasant central
location. *Closed* Sun plus Sat lunch.

Pistoia

La Casa degli Amici (£–££)
Via Bonellina 111 tel: 0573/380 305
A family-run restaurant with fine home cooking.
Closed Mon evening, Tue and August.
Manzoni (££)
Corso Gramsci 112 tel: 0573/28 101
A stylish restaurant devoted solely to fish and
seafood. *Closed* Sat lunch, Sun and Aug.

Prato

Osvaldo Baroncelli (££)
Via Fra Bartolomeo 13 tel: 0574/23 810
More than 40 years under one owner have
ensured high standards. *Closed* Sun plus Sat
lunch and Aug.
Il Pirana (£££)
Via Valentini 110 tel: 0574/25 746
A modern interior and a semi-industrial subur-
ban setting barely detract from one of the most
highly regarded fish restaurants in the region.
Closed Sun plus Sat lunch and August.

San Gimignano

Dorandò (££)
Vicolo dell'Oro 2 tel: 0577/941 862
Recreated dishes form Tuscany's medieval and
Etruscan past. Booking essential. *Closed* Mon
and January.
Le Terrazze (£)
*Albergo La Cisterna, Piazza della Cisterna 24
tel: 0577/940 328*
A terrace with views, a medieval dining room
and regional cooking. *Closed* Tue and Wed.
Osteria delle Cateme (£–££)
Via Mainardi 18 tel: 0588/88 537
This good, simple trattoria has managed to
avoid the excesses that often result from mass
tourism. *Closed* Wed.

Siena

Ai Marsili (££)
Via del Castoro tel: 0577/47 154
Occasionally erratic cooking, but a central
location (just south of the Duomo), reasonable
prices, and an attractive old dining room make
this place the equal of Le Logge, its Sienese
rival. *Closed* Monday.
La Torre (££)
Via Salicotto 7–9 tel: 0577/287 548
This once unknown, old-fashioned *trattoria* just
off the Campo has been discovered. Arrive
early to secure one of the handful of tables.
Closed Thu.
Osteria Le Logge (££)
Via del Porrione 33 tel: 0577/48 013
Siena's prettiest restaurant, but expensive and
often fully booked. *Closed* Sun.

Viareggio

Romano (£££)
Via Mazzini 120 tel: 0584/31 382
Perhaps Tuscany's best fish restaurant. *Closed*
Mon and three weeks in January.

Volterra

Etruria (££)
Piazza dei Priori 6b tel: 0588/86 064
Volterra's best trattoria. *Closed* Thu.
Il Sacco Fiorentino (£–££)
Piazza XX Settembre 18 tel: 0588/86 537
An inexpensive trattoria close to the Etruscan
Museum. *Closed* Fri.

Index

Index

Index

287

Acknowledgements

Picture credits

The Automobile Association wishes to thank the following photographers and libraries for their assistance in the preparation of this book:

J ALLAN CASH PHOTOLIBRARY spine Fountain of Neptune. **THE BRIDGEMAN ART LIBRARY, LONDON** 28a black figure vase, Bucchero ware, Etruscan, 6th-century BC, Museo Archeologico, Chiusi/K & B News Foto, Florence; 39 Adoration of the Magi by Sandro Botticelli (1444/5–1510) Galleria degli Uffizi, Florence; 40b Portrait of Savonarola by Fra Bartolommeo (c1472–c1517) Museo di San Marco, Florence; 88 Adoration of the Christ Child with the Young St. John the Baptist by Pseudo Pier Francesco Fiorentino (fl.1475–1500) Museo Bardini, Florence; 101 The Annunciation by Fra Angelico, (c1387–1455) Museo di San Marco, Florence; 116 The Parting of Venus from Adonis, 1707–1708 (fresco) by Sebastiano Ricci (1658–1734) Palazzo Pitti, Florence; 118 Portrait of an Unknown Man (detail) by Titian (Tiziano Vecellio) (c1485–1576) Palazzo Pitti, Florence; 124b Portrait of Machiavelli by Santi di Tito (1536–1603) Palazzo Vecchio, Florence; 145 Adam and Eve Banished from Paradise by Tommaso Masaccio (1401–1428) Brancacci Chapel, Santa Maria del Carmine, Florence; 146–147 St. Peter Visited in Jail by St. Paul, c1480 by Filippino Lippi (c1457/8–1504) Brancacci Chapel, Santa Maria del Carmine, Florence; 161 The Madonna di Ognissanti, c1310 (post-restoration) by Ambrogio Bondone Giotto (c1266–1337) Galleria degli Uffizi, Florence; 246a Etruscan vase showing boxers fighting c500BC, British Museum, London. **MARY EVANS PICTURE LIBRARY** 45b Napoleon I; 74 Pope Sixtus IV; 222a Shelley; 222b Robert Browning. **KIT HOARE** 45a Tuscan landscape. **HULTON DEUTSCH COLLECTION LTD** 47 floods, books needing rebinding; 130a floods 1966–1967; 130b floods; 131 flood damage. **IMAGES COLOUR LIBRARY** front cover (b). **TIM JEPSON** 57 courtyard, Bargello; 108 Wax figure, La Specola, 149 Trinità by Masaccio. **THE MANSELL COLLECTION LTD** 36a Frederick Barbarossa's Court; 36b Frederick Barbarossa; 41 Savonarola; 42b Pope Giovanni de' Medici; 68 Giuliano de' Medici; 75a Giuliano; 75b Lorenzo; 104 instrument, Galileo; 106a Galileo; 106b Galileo; 223a Tobias Smollett; 223b Huxley. **PICTURES COLOUR LIBRARY** front cover (c). **ROYAL GEOGRAPHICAL SOCIETY** 43 map. **SPECTRUM COLOUR LIBRARY** 67 Madonna and Child by Michelangelo. **TONY STONE IMAGES** front cover (a. **DAVID WALSH** 102–103 Fra Angelico; **ZEFA PICTURE LIBRARY (UK) LTD** 17 Siena, Palio race; 28b figure (Etruscan); 52 interior of Accademia Gallery; 53 David by Michelangelo; 240b Siena, Palio race; 241 drummers.

The remaining photographs, including the spine and back cover photographs are held in the Automobile Association's own photo library (AA PHOTO LIBRARY) and were taken by Clive Sawyer, with the exception of the following pages: 7, 16b, 20–21, 20, 24–25, 27, 37, 38a, 48–49, 70a, 77, 80b, 92, 111, 154, 166–167, 182b, 187, 194, 238a, 241, 252, 256a, 258–259, 260a, 263, 271a (Jerry Edmanson); 210b (Eric Meacher); pages 4a, 4b, 9, 12b, 19, 26, 30–31, 31b, 56, 66, 80a, 81, 82, 84–85, 148, 151, 152b, 156, 168, 183, 189, 190a, 191, 196–197, 196b, 198, 203, 210a, 212a, 212b, 225, 227a, 228, 229, 230, 231, 232a, 232b, 233, 234, 242, 245, 246b, 248, 251, 262, 267 (Ken Paterson); 73 (James Robertson-Taylor); 7, 49, 151, 162, 175a, 253, 255, 273 (Barrie Smith); 211 (Antony Souter); 18–19, 181 (Wyn Voysey).

Contributors

Original copy editor: Julia Brittain

Revision Editor: Grapevine Publishing Services   Revision verifier: Tim Jepson